LINCOLN CHRISTIAN COLLEGE AND

P9-BZW-549

Salt and Light

Christian College Coalition Study Guides

Edited by John A. Bernbaum

Salt and Light

**Evangelical Political Thought
in Modern America**

Augustus Cerillo, Jr.

Murray W. Dempster

Baker Book House
Grand Rapids, Michigan 49516

Christian College Coalition
Washington, D.C. 20036

Copyright 1989 by
Baker Book House Company

Library-of-Congress Cataloging-in-Publication Data

Cerillo, Augustus.
  Salt and light.

  Bibliography: p.
    1. Christianity and politics—History—20th century.
  2. Evangelicalism—United States—History—20th century.
  3. Fundamentalism. I. Dempster, Murray W. II. Title.
  BR115.P7C366 1989   261.7'0973'0904   89-6581
  ISBN 0-8010-2536-2

The Christian College Coalition, an association of more than seventy colleges, was founded in 1976. With main offices located in Washington, D.C., the coalition services a vital sector of American private higher education—regionally accredited liberal arts colleges committed both to being excellent educational institutions and to keeping the Christian faith central to every facet of campus life. All member colleges seek faculty and administrators who are academically qualified, personally committed to the Christian faith, and determined to integrate that faith into their academic disciplines and daily lives.

The coalition brings member colleges into a cooperative relationship that strengthens them by enabling them to achieve common goals. It has steadily grown in membership and expanded the breadth of activities it offers to member colleges. These schools, affiliated with nearly thirty denominations, find enrichment in the diversity of religious traditions within the coalition, a diversity that draws upon a core of common concern for biblical values and truths. For further information write to:

Christian College Coalition
14 Fourth Street, NE
Washington, DC 20002

Contents

Series Editor's Preface

Evangelical political thought has not received much serious scholarly attention nor is it well understood by the general American public. In the popular media, "born-again politics" is viewed as a singular movement of conservative Protestants with a right-wing "moral agenda." Despite the fact that Reverend Jerry Falwell clearly describes himself as a "fundamentalist" and is sharply critical of "evangelicals," the media usually lumps fundamentalists and evangelicals together when they discuss "born-again voters."

This book by Augustus Cerillo, Jr., and Murray W. Dempster will fill a gap in the literature on evangelical political thought and is an important contribution for several reasons. First, it documents the diversity of political thought within evangelicalism and between evangelicalism and fundamentalism. By identifying four different political perspectives, the reader is introduced to significant differences that characterize theologically conservative Protestants in North America. Second, it establishes the historical context out of which the different evangelical and fundamentalist political perspectives were shaped and formed. Brief part introductions enable the reader to more fully understand the content of the selected readings included in the book. Third, the selected readings are important documents in the development of modern evangelicalism and are hereby preserved for readers who would otherwise not have access to them. Finally, the authors challenge advocates of each political perspective to recognize and respect the views of others from a similar theological tradition who have a different understanding of the nature of Christian involvement in politics. They challenge all of us to hold our ideological commitments tentatively, even as we all work together for public justice in the political order, and to hold fast to our common beliefs that Jesus Christ is Lord and that Scripture is authoritative for righteous living, including our political behavior.

The Christian College Coalition is pleased to include this book in its Study Guide series. It will encourage readers to wrestle authentically with the challenge of integrating Christian faith and political life. To build a more just political order in which all people are treated as image-bearers of God should be a goal of Christian political activity. This book will assist Christians in pursuing that goal.

Dr. John A. Bernbaum
Study Guide Series Editor
Vice President,
Christian College Coalition

Preface

Evangelical Christians have become a potent force in recent American politics. Most journalists and scholars examining this phenomenon concentrate on the fundamentalist new right and ignore evangelicals with different political views. This text is designed to meet a perceived need for a relatively short collection of essays that will introduce readers to the mosaic of contemporary evangelical political thought. We have identified four political perspectives within evangelicalism. At the left and right ends of the political spectrum we have placed, respectively, the evangelical radical left and the fundamentalist new right. In between we have identified two moderate political positions: the one to the right of center we have labeled "conservative"; the one to the left of center we have labeled "liberal."

The criteria we use to differentiate these four political stances are both political and theological. On the political side we note that evangelicals differ in their understanding of the nature of society, their philosophy of the proper role of government and the use of power in society, their view of a just economic system, and their appraisal of U.S. domestic and foreign policies. On the theological side we note that evangelicals divide over the proper role of the Bible in constructing a social ethic, a theology of social change, and the role of the church in politics. In *Salt and Light* we have reprinted readings in which the major voices of each political perspective engage in lively debate with each other over these controversial issues.

The essays are presented within a three-part chronological context. Each part begins with a narrative introduction that describes the historical intersection of national political trends and evangelical political thought. In part 1, we sketch the moderately conservative politics and cold war diplomacy of the 1950s, a decade in which evangelical political conservatives, led by theologian Carl F. H. Henry and *Christianity Today*, dominated evangelicalism. We then describe the resurgence of political liberalism under Presidents John F. Kennedy and Lyndon B. Johnson, years which also witnessed the rise of a politically liberal group of evangelicals. Theologian Lewis B. Smedes, sociologist David O. Moberg, and historian Richard V. Pierard, among others, espoused an evangelical liberal political philosophy and openly challenged the monopoly of political conservatives in formulating an evangelical social ethic.

Part 2 brackets off the politically tumultuous and socially divisive period from Vietnam through Watergate in order to explain the rise of a radical left political movement within evangelicalism. Critical of all evangelicals to the right and turned off by the nation's traditional conservative and liberal politics, radicals Jim Wallis, Sharon Gallagher, and John Alexander shaped a new evangelical radical political ethic and thus became a third major political voice within an increasingly fragmented evangelicalism.

Part 3 discusses the nation's turn toward traditional values and conservative policies during the Carter and Reagan presidencies, and the bursting onto the national scene of the fundamentalist new right. Led by Baptist pastor Jerry Falwell and his Moral Majority, politicized fundamentalist leaders brought into politics for the first time millions of ordinary evangelical churchgoers, pushed the issue of Christian political involvement into the national and secular arena, and articulated still a fourth political philosophy within evangelicalism.

At the conclusion of each part, study questions are provided to guide the reader through the essays. A general introduction provides the historical background necessary to understand the resurgence of evangelical social concern in post–World War II America. An afterword identifies the current status of evangelical political engagement in contemporary America. Selected books for further study are listed at the end of the volume. Also included are five original documents that illustrate the themes of this book.

Introduction
The Resurgence of Evangelical Social Concern in Modern America

The "Great Reversal" of Evangelical Social Action in a Modernizing America (1877–1942)

The evangelical Protestant character of nineteenth-century America was undermined by the nation's shift toward modernity around the turn of the century. This shift toward modernity has been described by historian Robert Wiebe as a transition "from a decentralized, agrarian-minded, nineteenth-century America to an increasingly integrated, urban-oriented, twentieth-century society."[1] Generally speaking, on the nineteenth-century side of the divide we find a nation of villages, farms, and small family-owned businesses; on the twentieth-century side of the divide we find a nation of factories, industrial cities, and huge impersonal corporations. Nineteenth-century America still was largely Anglo-Protestant or evangelical in its religious orientation and dominated by a northern European cultural identity. Twentieth-century America was more religiously and culturally diverse due to the influx of millions of Jewish and Roman Catholic immigrants from eastern and southern Europe. This new America—more urban, industrial, economically integrated, religiously and culturally pluralistic—was less hospitable to a narrow conservative Protestant cultural and ideological hegemony. Intense and at times bitter conflict between older Protestant traditionalists and the newer groups over

1. Robert Wiebe, "The Progressive Years, 1900–1917," in *The Reinterpretation of American History and Culture*, edited by William H. Cartwright and Richard L. Watson, Jr. (Washington D.C.: National Council for the Social Studies, 1973), p. 425.

issues such as prohibition, immigration restriction, and parochial schools lent an especially acrimonious tone to the nation's cultural politics.

The status of evangelical Protestants in American life was further weakened by scientific, intellectual, and cultural currents—Darwinism, evolutionary social science, historicism, higher biblical criticism, the comparative study of religion, a new morality, changing roles for women, and a growing materialism—that seemed to undermine the conservative Protestant view of God, man, the Scriptures, and a properly ordered society. Such cultural and intellectual developments, characteristic of a modernizing society, divided Protestantism into a liberal wing that sought to synthesize the newer ideas with biblical interpretation and a conservative wing that defended Protestant orthodoxy and resisted modernity. Sociologist James Hunter suggests that as the nation modernized, evangelical Protestantism "moved from a position of cultural dominance to a position of cognitive marginality and political impotence."[2] By the 1920s respectable evangelicals, in historian George Marsden's words, "had become a laughing stock, ideological strangers in their own land."[3]

This "collective uprooting" of conservative Protestants, as Marsden describes their plight, had at least three important consequences for the shape of evangelicalism during the first three decades of the twentieth century. First, by the late 1920s, if not before, evangelicals, a large number of whom were now known as fundamentalists, were viewed by the nation's cultural and social elites as antimodern defenders of older cultural values and were effectively shut out of the centers of national life. Second, evangelicals in what historians and other social scientists have termed the "Great Reversal" dramatically curtailed their political and social activities. Busy defending doctrinal orthodoxy against theological liberalism and the social gospel, and heavily influenced by a premillennial eschatology that reinforced a separatistic and anticultural stance, they only selectively engaged in political action. Evangelicals supported prohibition and fought its repeal, opposed the teaching of evolution and what they perceived as other secularizing tendencies in the nation's schools, and deplored the breakdown of traditional moral standards. Fearful of growing Roman Catholic political power, they opposed Catholic Al Smith for the presidency in 1928. By the 1930s and early 1940s they had added communism and the Soviet Union, Franklin Roosevelt's New Deal, and

2. James D. Hunter, *American Evangelicalism: Conservative Religion and the Quandary of Modernity* (New Brunswick, N.J.: Rutgers University Press, 1983), p. 37.

3. George M. Marsden, *Fundamentalism and American Culture: The Shaping of Twentieth-Century Evangelicalism, 1870–1925* (New York: Oxford University Press, 1980), p. 8.

other liberal and leftist activities to their list of causes to oppose. Some were even attracted to right-wing prophets such as Gerald B. Winrod, Gerald L. K. Smith, and the Roman Catholic "radio priest," Father Charles Coughlin.

Evangelicals believed they were not just confronting specific ills in society but were engaged in a battle to save American civilization from Armageddon, an event that paradoxically their eschatology told them was inevitable and in the not-too-distant future. In terms of political thought, American evangelicalism on the eve of World War II was characterized by a political and economic conservatism that supported individualism, laissez-faire capitalism, limited government, states' rights, and the Republican party. Some on the fringe of the evangelical camp, according to George H. Williams and Rodney L. Petersen, "seemed to become politically reactionary and even cryptofascist and sometimes anti-Semitic in an attempt to defend the Christian faith and American way of life."[4]

A third consequence of the displacement and alienation of evangelicals from the American mainstream was a turn toward evangelism and religious institution building. During the interwar years of national prosperity and then economic depression evangelicalism, in contrast to liberal Protestantism, grew in numbers and again was well on its way to becoming a popular religious movement. This growing collection of conservative religious groups on the margins of American cultural and political life included fundamentalists, Holiness and Pentecostal churches, the Southern Baptists, ethnic denominations such as the Christian Reformed Church, the Missouri Synod Lutheran and Evangelical Free Churches, as well as a host of smaller religious bodies.

Within their enclaves of difference, conservative Christians not only preserved biblically informed values and behavioral standards, but positively engaged in community building and reached out to others through the preaching of the gospel. Usually ignored by the shapers of the nation's politics and culture, these conservative evangelicals built large church congregations, Bible schools, seminaries, colleges, and missions societies; they created new denominations and established radio ministries, publishing houses, and magazines; they organized Bible conferences and youth camps. Moreover, they increasingly looked to old-fashioned revivalism as the way to expand their influence and to save America from the judgment of God. On the eve of Pearl Harbor, then, these religious

4. George H. Williams and Rodney L. Peterson, "Evangelicals: Society, the State, the Nation (1925–1975)," in *Evangelicals: What They Believe, Who They Are, Where They Are Changing*, edited by David F. Wells and John D. Woodbridge (Nashville: Abingdon Press, 1975), p. 220.

groups and ministries had created the institutional base necessary to become a formidable religious interest group in postwar American society.

The Renewal of an Evangelical Social Conscience in Postwar America (1942–1952)

A changing national mood in the postwar years aided the rapid re-emergence of evangelicalism as a respectable and significant force in American society. During the presidency of Harry S. Truman, cold war tensions and then a limited war in Korea combined with domestic economic and political crises to rob the American people of a sense of peace and well-being after their costly victory over the Axis powers in World War II. National unrest was further exacerbated by Truman's conflict with a Congress unwilling to enact most of his Fair Deal reform program, and by reports of alleged corruption and communism in high places of government. Evangelical leaders sensed that the beleaguered Truman administration and the American public might be receptive to pleas for personal and national spiritual renewal as an antidote to the political unrest.

Confident of their ability to regain public influence, a new breed of evangelical leadership took the evangelistic, political, and intellectual offensive during what proved to be watershed years in the history of evangelicalism in modern America. Highly successful evangelistic efforts by Youth for Christ, Billy Graham, numerous radio preachers, and a host of other similar outreach ministries greatly expanded evangelicalism's popular base. Evangelicals also sought to regain societal influence through coalition building. In the fall of 1941 separatistic-minded fundamentalists joined forces with Bible Presbyterian Carl McIntire in his staunchly anti-liberal and anticommunist American Council of Christian Churches. A larger, more inclusive group of evangelicals who sought "to retrieve Christianity from a mere eddy of the mainstream into the full current of modern life," created the National Association of Evangelicals (NAE) in 1942.[5]

In addition to sponsoring various religious and educational activities, the leaders of NAE intended to use the new organization as a vehicle for ongoing political commentary and activity. Harold John Ockenga, pastor of Boston's Park Street Church and a founder and first president of NAE, stressed that the new evangelical movement would make Christianity the "mainspring in many of the reforms of the societal order." Not surprisingly,

5. Harold J. Ockenga, "Resurgent Evangelical Leadership," *Christianity Today* 5 (October 10, 1960): 14.

two years after its creation NAE opened an Office of Public Affairs in Washington, D.C., to serve as an informal political lobby for evangelical Christians.[6] Among evangelicals, therefore, NAE "shaped an enlarging interest in government affairs."[7] In addition to the political offensive led by NAE, Norwegian immigrant Abram Vereide brought his prayer breakfast movement from Seattle to the nation's capital. Moreover, at about the same time, several congressmen—Republicans Frank Carlson of Kansas and Dr. Walter Judd of Minnesota and Democrat Brooks Hays of Arkansas—openly identified themselves as evangelical Christians.

As important as the resurgence of evangelistic and political activities for the future of evangelical political engagement was a renewed commitment to an intellectually sound evangelical Christianity. At the forefront of this intellectual renewal was a promising group of young scholars—Carl F. H. Henry, Edward J. Carnell, Bernard Ramm, and T. B. Maston, among others—educated at some of the nation's most prestigious universities and seminaries. Their teaching, editing, and writing significantly elevated the scholarly level and cultural tone of evangelical engagement with modern thought. Among this group Carl F. H. Henry was the individual who church historian Martin Marty claims, "made more than most of the intellectual formulation" of the modern evangelical movement.[8]

Henry was appalled that biblical Christian values and thought patterns no longer shaped modern cultural, intellectual, and political values and activities, and were largely absent from other spheres of life such as marriage, the home, the workplace, and education. Further energized by his belief that the generation of the 1930s and 1940s was witnessing the midnight of modern culture, Henry sought nothing less than for evangelicals to remake the modern mind by again thrusting biblical values into the mainstream of American life, including the political and cultural arenas.

Prodded by William B. Eerdmans, Sr., Henry, then professor of theology at the newly formed Fuller Theological Seminary, published *The Uneasy Conscience of Modern Fundamentalism* (1947), a landmark polemic that helped mobilize the resurgent political consciousness of evangelicals. In this series of essays, Henry dramatically spelled out an apologetic for the evangelicals' break with the earlier fundamentalist cultural and political isolationism. He severely condemned fundamentalist indifference to the

6. Ibid.

7. Carl F. H. Henry, *Aspects of Christian Social Ethics* (Grand Rapids: William B. Eerdmans Publishing Co., 1964), p. 128.

8. Carl F. H. Henry, "Tensions within Contemporary Evangelicalism: A Critical Appraisal," in *Evangelicals*, edited by Wells and Woodbridge, p. 176.

social implications of the gospel and called on fundamentalists and evangelicals to "link the evangelical message effectively to contemporary world conditions."[9] The following year in a lengthy essay, "The Vigor of the New Evangelicalism," published in *Christian Life and Times* magazine, he kept up the attack against a narrow and socially uninfluential fundamentalism, again stressing the social relevance of the gospel. He also criticized theological liberalism and nonbiblical philosophical systems.[10] A few years after these publications, Henry spearheaded the creation of NAE's Commission on Evangelical Social Action, which sponsored forums on social and political issues ranging from race problems to labor-management relations at NAE's annual conventions.

Henry and other NAE leaders who shared his vision of a politically engaged evangelicalism were elated with the strides they had made by 1952. They had placed social concerns regularly on the agendas of NAE's national conventions, had a permanent Commission on Social Action, had found outlets for their views not only in NAE's *United Evangelical Action* but also in other evangelical periodicals such as the *Watchman Examiner, Calvin Forum*, and *Moody Monthly*. They continuously sought to shape the evangelical conscience on political and social problems they perceived as threats to the American way of life during the presidency of Democrat Harry S. Truman: communism at home and abroad; the influence of secularism, especially in the public schools; domestic governmental corruption; growing Roman Catholic political power; the erosion of church-state separation; big government and welfare statism; and the breakdown of the American family.

Encouraged by conservative Protestant numerical and institutional growth, the new evangelical establishment confidently expected to have an increasing impact on the American people over the new few years. Since they had legitimated social and political concern once again among church leaders and informed laity, the evangelical leadership planned to construct a biblical political philosophy. Never reluctant to mask their dislike of Truman and his liberal politics, evangelicals awaited the presidential election of 1952, when, they hoped, a president who was more congenial to their conservative political tastes and receptive to their vision of a morally reconstructed America would occupy the White House. When the Republicans chose the popular World War II general Dwight David Eisenhower to head their presidential ticket, evangelical hopes skyrocketed.

9. Carl F. H. Henry, *The Uneasy Conscience of Modern Fundamentalism* (Grand Rapids: William B. Eerdmans Publishing Co., 1947), p. 33.

10. Martin E. Marty, "The Vigor of the New Evangelicalism," *Christian Life and Times* 3 (January 1948): 30–32; (March 1948): 35–38, 85; (April 1948): 32–35, 65–69.

Part 1

From Modern Republicanism to the Great Society

(1952–1968)

Evangelical Political Conservatives and Liberals Search for an Evangelical Social Ethic   1

Evangelical Political Conservative Triumphalism in the "Age of Ike"

When Dwight Eisenhower trounced his Democratic opponent Adlai E. Stevenson in the presidential election of 1952, evangelicals were elated. They resonated with the new president's attack on welfare statism and his tough talk about rolling back atheistic communism in Asia and Eastern Europe. They saw in Eisenhower's public display of religious commitment and support of patriotism, individualism, free enterprise, and states' rights an opportunity to remake the modern American mind and political system in the image of long-held evangelical values.

Evangelicals benefited from the paradoxical nature of postwar domestic and diplomatic trends. Domestically, the Eisenhower 1950s were characterized by limited federal legislative initiatives; they were a time of unparalleled economic prosperity, mass consumerism, and suburban expansion. Diplomatically, the president's secret threat to use nuclear weapons finally ended the stalemated Korean War in 1953. Eisenhower's generally cautious use of American military power kept the nation at peace during his eight years in office.

The 1950s had a darker side as well. Millions of Americans did not share in the decade's affluence and comprised an invisible poor. Black Americans, continuing their trek from the South to the central cores of the nation's metropolises, still largely were shut out of the American mainstream. Decaying inner cities stood in stark contrast to new suburbs. Television, rock music, Elvis Presley, and the emergence of the beatniks symbolized to countless worried parents a new sexual license and a break with traditional values of self-control, discipline, and personal achievement. The Soviet launching of Sputnik in 1957, Castro's triumph in Cuba two years later, and the unexpected downing of the American U-2 spy plane over the Soviet Union in 1960 shook the nation's self-confidence and contributed to the feeling that the United States might be losing its struggle against global communism.

On the one hand, then, the 1950s were years of prosperity, stability, and peace; on the other hand, they were years of insecurity, anxiety, and stress. Americans by the millions turned to religion to resolve the ambiguities of their personal and social lives. All religious faiths, including evangelicalism, registered quantitative gains, whether measured by the collection plate, people in the pew and on membership rolls, building construction, or local parish programs. Evangelicals successfully continued to build their church and parachurch infrastructure. Established groups such as NAE, the Billy Graham Association, Fuller Theological Seminary, the Evangelical Theological Society, and an assortment of scholars and prominent ministers provided a measure of national cohesion for the movement and contributed to the growing intellectual and political sophistication of evangelicals.

Without doubt the single most politically significant development within evangelicalism during the 1950s was the launching of *Christianity Today* in 1956 under the editorial leadership of Carl F. H. Henry. In the magazine's maiden editorial, Henry explained that one of the new journal's purposes was to "apply the biblical revelation to the contemporary social crisis, by presenting the implications of the total Gospel message for every area of life." More specifically with respect to social ethics, Henry wrote that the church and individual believers have "a vital responsibility to be both *salt* and *light* in a decaying and darkening world."[1] The editors and publishers concluded one of the other editorials in the initial issue with a statement that both symbolized the postwar political and cultural coming of age of evangelicalism and expressed the magazine's founders' hopes and aspirations for the future of evangelicalism in America. The editors informed their readers that the magazine's headquarters were in the Washington Building where they could "daily look down Pennsylvania Avenue and glimpse the White House,

---

1. Editorial, "Why Christianity Today?" *Christianity Today* 1 (October 15, 1956): 20–21. For the full text of this editorial, see appendix 1.

Blair House, and other strategic centers of national life." "Thus *Christianity Today*," they suggested, "is a symbol of the place of the evangelical witness in the life of a republic."[2]

Evangelical Political Conservatives Resist the Great Society

The congenial setting for evangelical growth and reentry into national life provided by the conservative Eisenhower administration changed radically after the presidential election of 1960 when first John F. Kennedy and then Lyndon B. Johnson, both liberal Democrats, occupied the White House. At home Kennedy and Johnson restored political liberalism to the center of national life. Their agenda included the stimulation of economic growth through tax cuts, defense, and space spending; civil rights laws that sought to eradicate racial discrimination in voting, housing, jobs, and education; the revitalization of the cities through slum clearance, housing, and urban development programs; the cleaning up of the nation's water and air; a war on poverty to bring the poor into the economic mainstream; health insurance for the elderly; and federal aid to elementary and secondary school children. These New Frontier and Great Society programs constituted a quantitative legislative record and expansion of the welfare state and federal bureaucracy comparable to the earlier New Deal.

Abroad both Presidents Kennedy and Johnson were intensely committed to winning the global cold war against the Soviet Union. Upon taking office Kennedy immediately moved to build up the nation's defense capabilities to contain communism. He reiterated America's commitment to defend West Berlin, risked nuclear war to force the removal of Soviet missiles from Cuba, and negotiated the Test Ban Treaty of 1963 ushering in a period of improved U.S.-Soviet relations. Inheriting from Presidents Truman and Eisenhower a commitment of military and economic aid to South Vietnam, Kennedy perceived the Vietnam struggle as a test case of America's resolve and willingness to stop communist aggression in a third world nation. Thus, at the time of his assassination, Kennedy bequeathed to President Lyndon Johnson a significantly expanded U.S. military role in Vietnam. Johnson, who likewise saw Vietnam as part of the nation's conflict with Soviet-inspired global

2. Editorial, "The Evangelical Witness in a Modern Medium," *Christianity Today* 1 (October 15, 1956): 21.

communism, in turn escalated America's involvement into a major war in Southeast Asia. Vietnam increasingly dominated Johnson's administration and led both to the abandonment of the Great Society and to the erosion of the president's political credibility and public support, forcing him to withdraw from the presidential race in 1968.

Evangelical political conservatives were put on the defensive by this resurgence of liberalism during the early 1960s. Their reliance on evangelism to transform people for the better, their political commitment to individualism and voluntarism as the preferred method of social change, their philosophical support of a free enterprise economy, and their opposition to the use of coercive government to reform society put evangelical conservatives ideologically at odds with many of the New Frontier–Great Society domestic programs. It was no surprise, therefore, that the majority of evangelical political conservatives supported Republican presidential candidates Barry Goldwater in 1964 and Richard Nixon in 1968 in the hope of reversing the liberal trend.

Evangelical Political Liberals
Challenge the Conservative Monopoly

A younger group of mainstream evangelicals, liberal in their politics, emerged by the mid-1960s to challenge the monopoly within evangelicalism of those whom they considered "doctrinaire political conservatives."[3] Many of these evangelical political liberals were scholars trained in the social sciences, others were politicians, and all were politically active citizens, both Republican and Democrat. Sociologist David Moberg, for example, was one of the earlier evangelical liberal spokesmen. In a landmark book, *Inasmuch: Christian Social Responsibility in Twentieth Century America* (1965), he sought to combine the social sciences with biblical teaching in formulating an apologetic for an evangelical liberal social program.

Moberg's liberal approach to social reform was echoed by fellow evangelical Vernon Grounds in *Evangelicalism and Social Responsibility* (1967): "Some problems today in our technological, urbanized, more and more depersonalized society are so complicated, so far-reaching, so deeprooted, so massive that they baffle the resources of individual action

3. Robert G. Clouse, Robert D. Linder, and Richard V. Pierard, eds., *Protest and Politics: Christianity and Contemporary Affairs* (Greenwood, S.C.: Attic Press, 1968), p. 2.

and private charity." "They require," Grounds argued, "governmental intervention on a mammoth scale; and this means the use of legislative and administrative apparatus."[4] The liberal political perspective of Moberg and Grounds gained a broader base of support in 1968 with the publication of *Protest and Politics*, a book edited by historians Robert G. Clouse, Robert D. Linder, and Richard V. Pierard. Protesting the assumed connection between evangelical theology and political conservatism, the eleven contributors to the volume provided a series of creative essays on Christianity and selected contemporary problems from a politically liberal evangelical perspective.

The ranks of these mainstream politically liberal evangelicals were enlarged by the addition of a rising young intellectual vanguard within the Reformed tradition. These new breed "Calvinistic evangelicals" sought to develop an evangelical social ethic for America and to speak out on specific social issues from a Calvinistically informed and yet politically liberal perspective. They also became some of the sharpest critics of establishment evangelical conservatives. Lewis B. Smedes, along with Nicholas Wolterstorff, James Daane, Henry Stob, Isaac C. Rottenberg, Marlin VanElderen, and George DeVries, among others, offered their politically liberal commentary in the *Reformed Journal* and occasionally in other evangelical publications.

These theologically conservative but politically liberal mainstream and Reformed evangelicals comprised a liberal camp within the larger evangelical political resurgence. Given their ideological support of a structurally pluralistic society, interventionist federal government, the rights of labor, and the welfare state, they found common cause in their support of many of the Great Society programs; and some liberals increasingly criticized the nation's cold war foreign policies. Thus by the end of the Johnson administration evangelicals were ideologically divided into politically conservative and politically liberal camps.

4. Vernon Grounds, *Evangelicalism and Social Responsibility* (Scottsdale, Pa.: Herald Press, 1969), p. 29.

Evangelical Political Conservatives and Liberals in Dialogue

The ideological differences between the evangelical political conservatives and political liberals are perhaps nowhere so clearly and acutely revealed than in the mid-1960s debate between theologians Carl F. H. Henry and Lewis B. Smedes. In "Evangelicals in the Social Struggle," an editorial Henry wrote for *Christianity Today* in 1965, he outlined the principles of an evangelical conservative political philosophy. Smedes, then at Calvin College, used the pages of the *Reformed Journal* to offer a liberal critique of Henry's political thought and to point the way toward a liberal political philosophy. Rejoinders by both men round out the first dialogue between these leading spokesmen for evangelical political conservativism and political liberalism.

Evangelicals in the Social Struggle

Carl F. H. Henry

Evangelical Christianity today confronts a "new theology," a "new evangelism," and a "new morality," each notably lacking in biblical content. A "new social ethics" has also emerged, and some ecumenical leaders mainly interested in politicoeconomic issues speak hopefully of a "new breed of evangelical" in this realm of activity. The red carpet rolls

Carl F. H. Henry, "Evangelicals in the Social Struggle," *Christianity Today* 10 (October 8, 1965):3–11. Reprinted by permission.

out when even a few evangelicals march at Selma, when they unite in organized picket protests and public demonstrations, when they join ecclesiastical pressure blocs on Capitol Hill or at the White House, or when they engineer resolutions on legislative matters through annual church meetings.

Since most evangelical churchmen traditionally have not mobilized their social concern in this way, nonevangelical sociologists are delighted over any and every such sign of apparent enlightenment. Moreover, they propagandize such church techniques as authentically Christian, and misrepresent evangelical nonparticipation as proof of social indifference and lack of compassion in conservative Christian circles. This favorite device of propagandists is effective among some evangelicals who desire to protect their genuine devotion to social concern from public misinterpretation. The claim that evangelicals as a whole are socially impotent, moreover, diverts attention from the long-range goals of social extremists by concentrating attention on existential involvement on an emergency basis.

That Christians are citizens of two worlds, that a divine mandate enjoins both their preaching of the gospel and their promotion of social justice, that the Lordship of Christ over all of life involves sociocultural obligations, that Christians bear a political responsibility, are historic evangelical emphases. Evangelicals regard government and jurisprudence as strategic realms of vocational service to humanity. They stress that government exists for the sake of all citizens, not simply for certain favored groups, and that a just or good society preserves for all citizens equal rights before the law. This emphasis has equally critical implications for a society that seeks special privilege for one race above another and for any church that seeks partisan and sectarian benefits from government. . . .

[E]vangelical Christians . . . were undeniably concerned with personal behavior in public social life, and with responsible community involvement in keeping with the standards and vocations of believers. To their further credit they realized that not an ethic of grace but rather an ethic of justice should govern social structures (including international relations, national government, and legal institutions generally). But evangelical Christians elaborated no Bible-based ethic impinging on the basis, method, and function of social structures and groups such as the state, labor movements and business corporations, minorities, and so on.

If excuses for neglect are in order, this may be the right place to note them. Evangelicals could plead, of course, that the social gospel's neglect of God's good news of salvation for sinners imposed upon conservative Christianity the burden of biblical evangelism and missions throughout a perishing world—a staggering task indeed. Evangelical capability was decimated by liberal control of denominations, schools, and other ecclesiastical resources. But evangelical withdrawal from the arena of public life came mainly in reaction to Protestant liberal attempts to achieve the kingdom of God on earth through political and economic changes. The modernists so excluded supernatural redemptive facets of the Christian faith and so modified the proper content of the Christian ethic that, as evangelicals saw it, they had altered the very nature and mission of the church. Evangelical Christianity reacted against the liberal Protestant concentration of effort in this area of concern by noninvolvement, and this withdrawal yielded the field to the speculative theories of liberal churchmen and largely deprived evangelicals of an ethical witness in the mainstream of public life.

Fallacies of Liberal Ethics

Precisely what is objectionable in liberal social ethics from the evangelical viewpoint? This is no small matter, for criticism extends to presuppositions, methods, and goals.

The theological presuppositions of liberal social ethics are hostile to biblical theology. A generation ago social gospel theologians deleted the wrath of God and dissolved his righteousness into benevolence or love; today the revolt has been extended. Dialectical and existential moralists surrender the objective being of God, while secular theologians disown his transcendence and, for that matter, his relevance as well. What passes for Christian social ethics in such circles dispenses with the supernatural essence of the Christian religion as foreign to problems of social justice and public righteousness. Evangelicals who insist on obedience to divinely revealed precepts, and who hold that redeemed men alone can truly fulfill the will of God and that only men of good will can enlarge the boundaries of God's kingdom, are caricatured as "rationalists," despite the fact that Scripture specifically associates Jesus' mission with an era of good will on earth. Yet while existentialists reject the absolutes of a transcendent morality for an absolute of their own decision, thereby making each person his own church, and reject an ethics based on principles because they consider it impossible to achieve moral obedience by decree, they nonetheless agitate for laws to compel others to act in a predictable, principled way.

It may seem pedantic, if not picayune, in a secular society so perilously near doom, to surround the moral demand for *agapē* with a complex of theological distinctions. After all, is not *agapē* itself the central Christian moral motif? But the reply is simple: *agapē* stripped of supernatural elements is no longer biblical *agapē*. For biblical *agapē* is first and foremost the love of God. Biblical *agapē* is nowhere simply a matter of humanistic charity toward one's neighbors. "You shall love the Lord your God with all your heart, and with all your soul, and with all your mind, and your neighbor as yourself"—love them, as a well-phrased prayer reiterates, "with a pure heart, fervently." Although just laws are desirable and imperative, law has the power only of outward restraint; it lacks power to ensure outward obedience and inner conformity to its command. In the absence of moral men—of men willing to do the good—no body of law, however just, can ensure a good society. Authentic Christian ethics concerns what is done through a desire to do God's will, in obedience to his command; this is made possible only by spiritual regeneration. No other motivation can counter the selfish drives that haunt the noblest of unredeemed men and correct the faulty vision of an unredeemed society. The current existential appeal for everyman's "identification with others" naively presupposes that the "identifiers" are morally equipped with motivations unthwarted by selfishness. But universal love, even in diluted forms, is a requirement that far exceeds the capacity of unregenerate men; for a Jew to have loved Hitler must have posed a problem not unlike that involved in a Selma marcher's love for the governor of Alabama, or a Birmingham demonstrator's affection for the local sheriff. The modern devotion to mankind *in place of* God, on the premise of "the infinite worth of the individual," indicates the inability of some Western intellectuals to assimilate the basic lessons of recent history. They blandly overlook the power of evil in human nature and man's limitations in coping with it—witness not only the patent egoism of individuals and social collectivities and the barbarism of the dictators, but also the tragic fact of two world wars at the pinnacle of Western scientific development and the unresolved threat of imminent universal destruction. As George F. Thomas says, "man is neither infinite nor perfect, and his ideal ends are worthy of devotion only insofar as they are subordinated to the purpose of One who is both."[1]

The evangelical Christian mobilizes for social action in the spiritual context of transcendent justice, supernatural law, revealed principles, concern for God's will in human affairs, and love of God and man.

1. George F. Thomas, *Religious Philosophies of the West* (New York: Charles Scribner's Sons, 1965), p. 351.

Against ecclesiastical young Turks who propagandize the notion that social concerns cannot be expressed within the inherited theology, the evangelical contends that insofar as social concerns are authentically biblical, they can be adequately expressed and fulfilled only within scriptural theology. What the evangelical does in the social order, as in every other realm of life, he does as a matter of principled spiritual obedience to the Lord of life.

Differences in Goals

It is, moreover, a gross underestimation of differences in social action between evangelicals and nonevangelicals to imply that, beyond motivation, they agree wholly on goals and differ only in method. The liberal Protestant identification of Christian love with pacifism, then with socialism, and even with communism by some modernists in the recent past, is too fresh a memory to allow one to blunder into the notion that the Bible sanctions whatever social goals the liberal moralists endorse. Even the communist hostility toward supernatural religion as an unscientific myth has moderated into tactical tolerance of religion as useful for promoting a social consciousness agreeable to the Soviet politicoeconomic ideology. Repudiation of private property, of the profit motive, of inequality of wealth, and other Marxist ideals have been arbitrarily promoted by liberal social reformers in supposed devotion to the biblical vision of the kingdom of God. Even their emphasis on equal rights has cheaply surrendered property rights as a fundamental human right, and also man's right to work apart from compulsory union membership.

Whenever the church advances a political ideology or promotes partisan legislation, its ecclesiastical leaders are soon forced into the position of impugning the integrity of influential Christians who sincerely dissent from the official views. It should surprise nobody, therefore, that as the National Council of Churches comes under increasing fire, its spokesmen tend to demean critics of its political commitments as reactionary advocates of arrogant nationalism and of social, economic, and racial privilege.

Not a few goals approved by modern social theorists are wholly desirable, and evangelical differences in such cases concern the means of achieving these ends. Elimination of poverty, opportunity for employment, racial equality, and many other goals that stand at the heart of contemporary social agitation are not only acceptable but highly desirable. Evangelicals are not indifferent to the desirability of such objectives even if liberal social ethics mistakenly conceives of the kingdom of God as basically a politicoeconomic phenomenon and tends to dilute redemptive spiritual forces into sociological ingredients. In fact, as evangelicals see it, such features of social life are essential to a just and good society.

30

Evangelicals no less than liberals recognize social justice as an authentic Christian concern, despite serious differences over definition and content. If evangelicals came to stress evangelism above social concern, it was because of liberalism's skepticism over supernatural redemptive dynamisms and its pursuit of the kingdom of God by sociological techniques only. Hence a sharp and costly disjunction arose, whereby many evangelicals made the mistake of relying on evangelism alone to preserve world order and many liberals made the mistake of relying wholly on sociopolitical action to solve world problems.

Conflict over Method

It would be naive to argue from this, however, that liberals and evangelicals need each other for complementary emphases. Over and above differences of motivation and of goals stand the differences between evangelical and liberal ethics in respect to methodology. Most evangelicals reject outright the liberal methodology of social reform, in which more and more liberals call for a "new evangelism" that substitutes sociological for spiritual concerns. Just as in his theological view of God the liberal dissolves righteousness into love, so in the political order he dilutes social justice into compassion. This kind of merger not only destroys the biblical view of God on the one hand but also produces the welfare state on the other. This confounding of justice and love confuses what God expects of government with what he expects of the church, and makes the state an instrument for legislating partisan and sectarian ideals upon society. Ideally the purpose of the state is to preserve justice, not to implement benevolence; ideally, the purpose of the church is to preach the gospel and to manifest unmerited, compassionate love.

Many sociologists and political scientists dislike this way of stating the case. But it is noteworthy that these particular disciplines are especially barren of evangelical perspectives; they tend to be theologically illiterate in respect both to eschatology and to a basic theology of justice. Current proposals to detach the gospel from "right-wing" social reaction and current pleas for "political compassion" are rooted in leftist political ideology more often than in an authentic spiritual view of the role of government.

But in the present explosive era of history the problem of acting on an acceptable methodology is an urgent one for evangelicals. It is one thing to deplore ministerial marches and picket lines and well-publicized public pressures; but if evangelical conscience is to be a remedial and transforming social force, then evangelical convictions require articulate mobilization on their own account.

Evangelicals and Social Concern

Despite the present confusion caused by ecclesiastical intervention in political affairs, evangelicals have something socially relevant to say to both the secular man and the church man. The Christian has social duties not simply as a Christian but as a man, and his sanctification therein does not come about automatically without pulpit instruction in sound scriptural principles. Evangelicals as a people consider themselves bound to the Word of God; for this reason they consider themselves a spiritual people with a divine message for themselves and for others in regard to social action. Evangelicals acknowledge a divine call to identify themselves with others—not with social customs or social vices or social discontents, but rather with persons in their survival needs: physical and moral and spiritual. These survival needs include material help in destitution, social justice, and the redemption that is in Christ Jesus.

Surely evangelical Christianity has more to offer mankind than its unique message of salvation, even if that is its highest and holiest mission. While it rightly chides the liberal for regarding the world as a unity (rather than divided into unregenerate and regenerate), it also has a message for all men as members of one society. The Christian is not, by his church identification, isolated from humanity, or from involvement in the political and economic orders. Not only is he called to identify himself with society: he *is* identified, by the very fact of his humanity, and as a Christian he bears a double responsibility in relation to the social needs and goals of mankind. Social justice is a need of the individual, whose dignity as a person is at stake, and of society and culture, which would soon collapse without it. The evangelical knows that spiritual regeneration restores men to moral earnestness; but he also knows the moral presuppositions of a virile society, and he is obligated to proclaim the "whole counsel" of God. He may have no message for society that insures unrepentant mankind against final doom—nor even against catastrophic destruction in our own time, while its leaders insist upon arbitrary human authority at the expense of the lordship of Jesus Christ. But he can and ought to use every platform of social involvement to promulgate the revealed moral principles that sustain a healthy society and that indict an unhealthy one. More than this, the evangelical Christian should be represented, in his personal convictions, on the frontiers of government and in the corporate processes of society. Convinced that the cooperation of godly men in the social and collective order can be decisively influential, he should be concerned about relations between nations and about minority rights. There is no reason at all why evangelical Christians should not engage energetically in projecting social structures that promote the interests of justice in every public realm; in fact, they have every legitimate sanction for social involvement.

Of course the church is to be ruled distinctively by an ethic of grace. But the church is also in a world that is to be ruled by justice, an ethic of justice that does not per se require regenerate social structures. In this context, a positive ethic and corrective principles enunciated on the broad world scene by regenerate believers who are engaged in the social struggle can have decisive influence. Such an ethic will include (1) the church's faithful exposition of divinely revealed standards of human justice as the only basis for a stable society and as the criteria by which the world will be finally judged; and (2) the Christian's energetic promotion and support of just laws as the formal hallmark of a good society. When Christian believers become thus involved in the struggle for justice, the world may recognize in a new way the presence of regenerate realities; noting the community of twice-born men that sees the restoration of sinners to fellowship with God and to holiness as the aim of the gospel, the world may even recognize the validity of regenerate structures through their moral impact.

Any Christian engaged in the pursuit of social justice is painfully aware that, in a tragic world of fallen men, government decisions often involve a choice between greater and lesser evils rather than between absolutes of good and evil, and that only the church of Christ can witness to a manifestation of absolute good in history. He will, however, avoid both the liberal error of "absolutizing relatives," as if these were identical with the will of God, and also the fundamentalist temptation to consider any gain short of the absolute ideal in history as worthless or unworthy.

Law and Gospel

But evangelicals must not perpetuate the liberal Protestant failure to distinguish between the social concerns of law and the social concerns of gospel. In law and justice—that is, the province of government—all men are obliged to support man's God-given rights as universally due to human beings whatever their race, color, or creed. The evangelical knows that no improvement can be made on a government that assures every man his rights and that limits the freedom of citizens where and when it intrudes upon the rights of others. Evangelicals do not view government as an instrument of benevolence or compassion, since love is preferential and shows favor or partiality. Constantly pressing the question, "Don't you care?" liberals enlist support for legislating programs of benevolence. Such an appeal to "compassion" in support of legislative programs commits a twofold error, however: it diverts government from an ideal preservation of equal human rights before the law, and it shifts to the state a responsibility for compassion or benevolence that belongs properly to the church. By concentrating on government to achieve the goals of both state and church in a "benevolent partnership," liberalism reflects a reliance on political techniques in society to the neglect of the redemptive dynamisms inherent in Christianity. This reliance on political techniques to achieve ecclesiastical objectives means the loss of a genuine supernatural grounding of ethical concerns, the loss of the church as church in society, the loss of the redemptive evangel in deference to secular solvents of social malformity, and the loss of evangelical loyalties in the congregation.

What distinguishes evangelical Christianity is its refusal to impose sectarian obligations upon government, which then employs compulsion to enforce a program of benevolence that individual citizens might or might not approve. Even if they did approve, they might consider the provision of such benevolences moral only if performed voluntarily; or they might consider it immoral to use taxation to compel others to do what they do not think to be right. While liberals justify their breaking of laws that appear unjust on the grounds of sensitivity to conscience, they nonetheless promote other laws that some persons regard as preferential and unjust.

To the evangelical Christian, the best alternative to the "welfare" state is the just state, and the best alternative to political demonstrations is civil obedience. The evangelical champions and strives for just legislation, obedience to law, and respect for judicial process rather than for directly coerced action. The evangelical sponsors a principled ethic whose course is determined by divinely revealed moral principles. Much of contemporary liberal social action is not a matter of obeying laws; rather, it is a case of everyone's being on his existential own. Dialectical-existential ethics cannot indicate in advance what the moral agent ought to do, and looks upon any structured objective ethics as mere rationalism.

The evangelical holds that all persons are divinely obligated by the Scriptures to love their neighbors. While progress has been slow in the area of race tensions, nonetheless there has been progress. Yet even evangelical believers fall short of their highest moral aspirations, and laws are necessary to hold just social standards before Christians and non-Christians alike. All citizens should strive to replace discriminatory laws by nondiscriminatory laws. The evangelical recognizes, however, that without public enthusiasm only moral earnestness vouchsafed by spiritual conviction and renewal assures the necessary devotion to right that guarantees social fulfillment. While the glory of ancient Rome was its genius for universal law, through its lack of heart for righteousness the Roman Empire sank into oblivion. The problem of racial discrimination can be permanently met only by Christian behavior that faces up to the ugliness of bias, the evils of immorality and delinquency, and the whole complex of problems that surrounds race feeling. The predilection for public issues over personal holiness in liberal social ethics is all the more disconcerting in view of this fact. Although liberal churchmen will throw their energies behind a public health program, they tend to remain silent about many of the personal vices; such concerns are left to the "purity nuts."

The history of Christian mission in the world makes it clear that evangelicals were interested in education, hospitals, care for the aged, and many current social concerns long before modern secular theory was ever born. Evangelicals were active in social work not only in the slums of America but also on distant mission fields a full century before the rise of modern welfare programs. To this day, rescue missions all across the land reflect a long-standing inner-city missionary concern for people in material and spiritual poverty. Evangelicals have not been as active as they need to be in the social arena; on the other hand, they have been far more active than they are sometimes said to have been.

The weakness of public demonstrations as the approved means of Christian social action is their limitation and externalization of Christian concern. It is arbitrary to imply that only those who demonstrate at a given point manifest authentic social concern. Moreover, since local demonstrations gain national significance through radio and television, the implications of massive civil disobedience are all the more distressing. Ecclesiastical demonstrators who never persuade observers to become disciples of Jesus Christ ought to ask how effectively Christian such amorphous "witness by demonstration" is. The motivations for demonstrating are internal, and apart from verbal interpretation might equally well be sub-Christian, non-Christian, or anti-Christian. As a matter of fact, Jews and humanists resent a Christian interpretation of their demonstrating. If authentic social concern demanded the ecumenical chartering of planes to officially designated out-of-town points, it would require a large expense account to enable everybody to travel to somebody else's hometown "to identify." If every supporter of an item of disputed legislation had to march to Capitol Hill, if every Christian citizen had to put in a personal appearance to let legislators know what laws he thought God specially wanted, what would tourist-jammed Washington be like then? If the representative role of congressmen were superseded by the group pressures of ministers, the whole machinery of American government would soon collapse. The question remains: Whose conscience answers for whom? These clergy are received by congressmen, not on the premise that they speak only for themselves, but as voices for their churches. No one disputes a clergyman's right as an individual to picket or demonstrate anywhere he wishes (the right of conscience is a Protestant principle). It is unlikely, however, that pastors can wholly detach themselves from responsibilities to their congregations. When prominent churchmen parade as Reverend Church, moreover, they are simply encouraging future counterdemonstrations at 475 Riverside Drive or the Witherspoon Building.

What many socially sensitive ministers especially deplore is the implication left by the well-publicized minority of marchers that non-marchers are lacking or inferior in social concern. "I don't mind another minister's marching if he must relieve his conscience that way," said one Washington minister, "but I don't see why my social concern—never before questioned—should now be in doubt because I didn't engage in this form of exhibitionism." In Copenhagen, when evangelist Billy Graham opened his crusade, a heckler interrupted him with the cry: "Why didn't you march in Selma?" But Graham had been integrating meetings in the South long before some of the marchers had become existentialized and, moreover, had done so in the context of biblical Christianity. It is a neat propaganda device to imply that evangelical social concern is immobile because it does not conform to liberal methods—it merely proves that political propagandism is a technique in which liberal ecclesiastical leaders have become adept. In some ecclesiastical circles, the defense of this one controversial method of action has apparently justified the repudiation of all theological grounds of social concern.

Evangelical Distinctives

When evangelicals manifest social concern, they do so first by proclaiming the supernatural revelation of God and the historical resurrection of Jesus Christ. Thus they emphasize the transcendent basis of justice and the divine basis of the gospel. They declare both the standards by which almighty God will judge the human race and the redemption from sin unto holiness that is to be found in Jesus Christ. They affirm God's institution of civil government to preserve justice and order, and the church as a spiritual fellowship of redeemed men who esteem their neighbors in holy love and dedicate themselves to social righteousness.

The evangelical Christian's social concern is first directed toward the family as the basic unit of society. He finds a hollow ring in the social passion for "one world" that simultaneously lacks indignation over divorce, infidelity, and vagrancy in the home. Because liberalism fails to see society as a macrocosm of the family, it is bankrupt to build a new society. Liberalism changes ideological loyalties and social perspectives every generation; evangelical Christianity treasures the family bound to the changeless will of God and to the apostolic faith. Hence evangelical Christianity regards the Sunday school, the prayer meeting, and the family in the church as a cohesive social unit that reflects in miniature the ideal social order. No new era of brotherliness and peace is likely to emerge in the absence of a new race of men. Evangelicals consider alliances of nations uncommitted to transcendent justice to be as futile a foundation for future mutuality as premarital promiscuity. As evangelical Christians see it, the vision of One World, or of United Nations, that is built on geographical representation rather than on principial agreement is as socially unpromising as is a lawless home that neglects the commandments of God. Walter Lippmann has somewhere said: "We ourselves were so sure that at long last a generation had arisen, keen and eager to put this disorderly earth to right . . . and fit to do it. . . . We meant so well, we tried so hard, and look what we have made of it. We can only muddle into muddle. What is required is a new kind of man."

Evangelical Christianity finds the most natural avenue for social witness beyond the family circle in the world of work when it is viewed as a divine calling. How sadly liberal Christianity, during its past-generation domination of ecclesiastical life, has failed in the organized church's social witness is nowhere more apparent than here. Almost all political leaders of the race-torn states are church members; Alabama's Governor Wallace belongs to the Methodist Church, which is in the forefront of liberal social action programs. Almost all congressmen are church members. Either the religious social activists have failed miserably in inspiring churchmen in political life to view their vocations as avenues for the advancement of social justice, or an elite ecclesiastical cadre is pressuring leaders to conform their political judgments to the partisan preferences of a special bloc of churchmen—or perhaps both are true. Since everyone lives in a world of labor and economics, evangelical Christianity emphasizes that man's work is a divinely appointed realm in which man is to glorify God and invest his talents for the good of his fellows; it is not only a means of livelihood but also an avenue of service.

This concept of divine vocation, of work as a calling, has all but vanished from the work-a-day world at the very time in modern history when liberal social action commissions have conspired with the labor unions in their skyrocketing material benefits. Meanwhile evangelical Protestants have organized a Christian Medical Society, Christian Business Men's Committee, Christian Professional Women's Club, Christian Law Society, Christian Teachers Association, Officers Christian Union in the Armed Forces—even a Christian Labor Union—in order to emphasize the spiritual responsibilities of vocation. It must be conceded that many of these Christian organizations serve mainly an evangelistic role, or one of vocational fellowship; only a beginning has been made in the equally urgent task of shaping an ethic of the social structures in which these groups operate. Beyond fulfilling person-to-person Christian opportunities, such agencies have an opportunity to supply guidance to both Christian and non-Christian on what is implied in a specified social order in the way of justice.

Evangelical Christians consider this recognition of the priestly nature of daily work to be more basic to social renewal than a reshuffling of economic features that locates the fundamental flaws of society in man's environment rather than in man himself and his works. The importance of just laws is not in dispute, since civil government is divinely designed as a coercive force to restrain evil, preserve order, and promote justice in a fallen and sinful society. Because there is no assurance that all men will repent and seek the will of God, and because even Christian believers must contend with the remnants of sin, just laws are indispensable in human history, and God's common grace in the lives of men everywhere matches conscience with law in the interest of social preservation. But evangelical Christianity is not so infatuated with the external power of coercion as to exaggerate its potentialities, nor so skeptical of the spiritual powers of regeneration as to minimize its possibilities. Precisely because law does not contain the power to compel obedience, evangelical Christianity recognizes that a good society turns upon the presence of good men—of regenerate sinners whose minds and hearts are effectively bound to the revealed will of God—and upon their ability under God to influence humanity to aspire to enduring values.

Although society at large has seldom been overwhelmed by the church's proclaiming the gospel from the pulpit, the obedient fulfillment of the Great Commission has called new disciples one by one into the circle of regenerate humanity. The voice of the church in society has been conspicuously weaker whenever the pulpit of proclamation has been forsaken for mass pressures upon the public through the adoption of resolutions, the promotion of legislation, and the organization of demonstrations. Whenever the institutional church seeks public influence by mounting a sociopolitical platform, she raises more fundamental doubts about the authenticity and uniqueness of the church than about the social aberrations against which she protests.

To evangelical Christianity, history at its best is the lengthened shadow of influential men, not the compulsive grip of impersonal environmental forces. A change of environmental forces will not transform bad men into good men—let alone into a good society. But transformed men will rise above a bad environment and will not long be lacking in a determination to alter it.

At the present time, involvement in the race problem is the crucial test of devotion to social justice. Of the evangelical Christian's love for men of all races the long-standing missionary effort leaves no doubt; from Adoniram Judson and David Livingstone to Hudson Taylor and Paul Carlson, the story is one of evangelical sacrifice of creature comforts, even of life itself, that men of every land and color might share the blessings of redemption. In mid-twentieth-century America, humanism and liberalism and evangelicalism alike were slow to protest political discrimination against blacks, although evangelical missionaries have deplored the incongruities of segregation. Regrettably, the blacks' plight became for some liberal reformers an opportunity for promoting social revolution, and for some conservative reactionaries an occasion for perpetuating segregation and discrimination. Evangelical Christianity has a burden for social renewal but no penchant for revolution or reaction. Because it champions the redemptive realities inherent in the Christian religion, evangelical Christianity will in the long run vindicate the judgment that the black man is not only politically an equal but also spiritually a brother.

Some Governing Principles

A new breed of evangelical? Yes, indeed! But not because evangelicals are switching from proclamation of the good tidings to pronouncements, picketing, and politicking as sacred means of legislating Christian sentiment on earth. Rather, evangelicals are a new breed because redemptive religion seeks first and foremost a new race of men, new creatures in Christ. Whenever Christians lose that motivation, they surrender more than their New Testament distinctiveness; they forfeit the New Testament evangel as well.

In summary, evangelicals face the social predicament today with four controlling convictions:

1. The Christian church's distinctive dynamic for social transformation is personal regeneration by the Holy Spirit, and the proclamation of this divine offer of redemption is the church's prime task. In the twentieth century the ecumenical movement has failed most conspicuously in its mission to the world by relying on political and sociological forces, and by neglecting spiritual dynamisms.
2. While the corporate or institutional church has no divine mandate, jurisdiction, or special competence for approving legislative proposals or political parties and persons, the pulpit is responsible for proclaiming divinely revealed principles of social justice as a part of the whole counsel of God.
3. The most natural transition from private to social action occurs in the world of daily work, in view of the Christian's need to consecrate his labor to the glory of God and to the service of mankind.
4. As citizens of two worlds, individual church members have the sacred duty to extend God's purpose of redemption through the church, and also to extend God's purpose of justice and order through civil government. Christians are to distinguish themselves by civil obedience except where this conflicts with the commandments of God, and are to use every political opportunity to support and promote just laws, to protest social injustice, and to serve their fellow men.

The Evangelicals and the Social Question

Lewis B. Smedes

Evangelicals *are* involved in the social question. One way or another, they have to be. Anyone trying to make the Christian gospel heard and practiced has got to tangle at some point with social and political affairs. The gospel cuts too wide a slice into life to let anyone who seeks to live by it enjoy the luxury of noninvolvement. We have known this.

Lewis B. Smedes, "The Evangelicals and the Social Question," *Reformed Journal* 16 (February 1966): 9–13. Reprinted by permission.

Carl McIntire knows it, and we know how *he* thinks we ought to be involved. The evangelicals know it, too. When Dr. Carl Henry, editor of *Christianity Today*, insists that evangelicals are and always have been socially concerned, we agree.

No single person has done more to awaken the fundamentalist conscience on the score of social ethics than has Carl Henry. Thanks in large measure to his educated conscience pricking, evangelicals today are struggling toward a conscious viewpoint on social questions. Others before him—notably neoorthodox people like the Niebuhrs—had chided fundamentalists for their apocalyptic neglect of social questions. Others—notably Calvinists like us—looked down their noses at fundamentalism for its myopic view of the gospel and its bearing on life. But Carl Henry spoke to fundamentalism from within.

He spoke with considerable historical learning and theological awareness. And he hit fundamentalism where it hurt—its stubborn insensitivity to the social struggle. He knew that fundamentalism was contributing to the social question if only by way of its quietism and irresponsibility. What he achieved is a *conscious* commitment to the social relevance of the gospel. This new-found commitment—or recommitment—is one of the earmarks of the evangelicalism for which Dr. Henry is a leading spokesman.

Lately, Dr. Henry has felt pressed to defend the record and argue the genuineness of evangelical concern. The civil rights struggle has forced everyone, including evangelicals, to examine their position, and sometimes to defend it. More specifically, the *Christian Century*—the liberal counterpart to *Christianity Today*—ran a testy editorial about evangelical involvement in the social struggle. The *Century* hit the evangelicals (and Dr. Henry in particular) hard—not for absenteeism in the social question, but for being involved on the wrong side. Soon afterward, in what may or may not have been meant as an answer, Dr. Henry wrote an impressive statement on social ethics in *Christianity Today*. He called it "Evangelicals in the Social Struggle." Coming when it did, it bore the marks of an evangelical manifesto.

Dr. Henry's piece deserves study and comment. We offer ours with the understanding that, in many respects, we are in the same boat with him. We do not have all the answers either. Like Dr. Henry, we are only working toward a viable and meaningful social ethic for today's world. We venture this public look at our colleague's statement as just another word in an ongoing dialogue between friends. When we raise questions here and there, we do not mean, of course, that Dr. Henry should have answered them all in his article. But we do mean them as questions that have to be answered.

The job Carl Henry set out to do in his essay was monumental. He was eager to defend the evangelical record. He was also trying to spell out the differences between the liberal and the evangelical approaches to the social question. And more important, he wanted to articulate the evangelical point of view. Our concern is with this last objective. We know that evangelicals are socially concerned. The question is: Where does Carl Henry want to lead them in social ethics?

We can divide his thoughts along the lines he suggests: the strategy, the goals, and the tactics.

The Strategy

The evangelical strategy for improving society is based upon the cleavage between regenerate and unregenerate men in society, and upon the moral influence of the regenerate segment on the unregenerate. This is the key to effective social action. "Evangelical Christianity recognizes that a good society turns upon the presence of good men—of regenerate sinners whose minds and hearts are effectively bound to the revealed will of God—and upon their ability to influence humanity to aspire to enduring values." The strategy, then, is for the preaching of the gospel to call men to the new life in Christ. Those who respond will be the morally regenerate core of society, the basis and hope for any genuine improvement in the social situation.

Men made good by the power of the gospel will inspire others who, though unregenerate, are able to appreciate the moral values exemplified by the regenerate. Good men, rather than good laws, are the key to social ethics. Dr. Henry is skeptical about the usefulness of laws. Laws, he says, are ineffective without good people. Laws can only change social structures: they cannot change people. Changes in environment promise little, because "a change of environment forces will not transform bad men into good men—let alone into a good society." But let a person be transformed morally, and he will soon rise above a bad environment. And, having risen above it himself, he will soon set about to change a bad environment into a good one.

The regenerate man, living by evangelical principles, works for social welfare according to transcendent rules. The liberal, in the name of love, tends to be existential. That is, says Henry, the liberal is sure that if one jumps feet-first into the present situation, ready to fight, he will intuit the right side to fight for and the right way to fight. The liberal, claims Henry, tends to ignore principle and to rely on love. But his actions are

42

therefore unpredictable and in the long run unconstructive. The evangelical, on the other hand, "mobilizes for social action in the spiritual context of transcendent justice, supernatural law, revealed principles, concern for God's will in human affairs, and love of God and man." Based on principle—and the rest of the list—the evangelical's actions presumably are predictable and constructive.

Social ethics is basically very simple, then. The gospel makes men good. Good men make good societies. The one element still needed is the will of good men to get into society and do something. Dr. Henry urges them into the struggle to use their supernatural potential for good. The fields of opportunity are wide open. The evangelical, he writes, "can and ought to use every platform of social involvement to promulgate the revealed moral principles that sustain a healthy society and that indict a healthy one."

So much then for the overall strategy. We have the presence of good men in possession of revealed moral principles, and ready to go anywhere to preach them. This is not a strategy for a direct approach to a change in environment. It is not a strategy for an immediate change in social structures by law. It is one that calls for evangelical preaching—from the pulpit and by individuals across the bench from one another, preaching with conversion as its goal and, that failing, with an appeal to "enduring values."

There is much to be said for this approach. A society of immoral men living under an ideal legal structure is hardly by that token a good society. The leaven of good men of good will is, without any question, an inexpendable ingredient of a good society. But does this help us along toward a *social* ethic? Dr. Henry knows as well as anyone does that Christian history is shamefacedly strewn with sad stories of regenerate men pressing with ugly manners toward absolutely wrongheaded goals. He knows that regenerate men have done and are doing some stupid and harmful things with full assurance that they have "revealed moral principles" behind them. There has got to be some hint as to where the regenerate ought to lead the rest of society. As a moralist, Dr. Henry knows this, and he has some answers. So, until we hear him tell the evangelical what he ought to be for, what he ought to be against, and how he ought to work for the right goals, we have not gotten to the gist of his social ethics.

But, even on this point we have some questions.

First, Dr. Henry pins his hopes on the ability of regenerate men to "influence humanity to aspire to enduring values." How earnest are his hopes? We note that he faults the liberals for their optimism about human nature. "They blandly overlook the power and evil in human nature and man's limitations in coping with it," he says. The evangelical does not overlook it. Yet he hopes that the unregenerate will see the regenerate's works and catch hold of his "enduring values." How much hope does Dr. Henry have? This is not a cute trick to catch someone in a contradiction. If you are skeptical about laws and changes in environment, if you rely instead on the personal influence of good men to get others to elevate their own values, you have got to assume considerable moral readiness in the unregenerate, or you had better forget about social ethics and stick to evangelism in the narrowest sense.

Second, Dr. Henry says there is little point in changing environment. For when a man emerges transformed from a bad environment, he will not be long in setting out to change the environment. But why should he? Why should not he, too, stick to evangelism? Why should Dr. Henry encourage the second generation of regenerate men to alter environment when by the terms of his own ethics changing the environment is of dubious worth?

Third, does Dr. Henry take into full account the fact that a bad social situation often prevents even the best-willed Christian person from fulfilling his Christian obligation? Could a regenerate white man effectively love a black man while his society kept him from sitting next to his brother in church, on a bus, or at a hot-dog stand? While we all know that a change in environment does not automatically turn bad men into good men, we know that a bad environment can keep a good man from doing the good as he ought. And by the same token, a good environment can inhibit a bad man from *doing* evil. And is this not what *social* ethics is all about?

Fourth, where does Dr. Henry get his confidence that regenerate men can be depended upon to overcome their own prejudices, shortsightedness, pride, and inertia? Dr. Henry will probably answer that he gets his confidence from faith in the Holy Spirit. But is this something you can presume upon? The Spirit offers a challenge as well as a promise. And the fact is that Christian people have been and are among the blind, the stupid, and the prejudiced. Maybe the Heidelberg Catechism is more realistic when it talks about the "small beginning" of sanctification in Christian life. Granted a cleavage at the roots of life between the regenerate man and unregenerate society, there is still plenty of the unregenerate life in every "saved soul." To base a social ethic on the personal powers of the regenerate to spread the overflow of his own values into society is to make of social ethics a risky adventure.

Finally, just what is the regenerate man informed by "revealed principles" to do about large hard-core areas of social deprivation? What does he do about the dislocations and hardships brought on people by shifts in the national economic and social patterns? Is he to "promulgate revealed principles" there, in the hopes that people victimized by these things will "aspire to enduring values"?

Dr. Henry knows, I am sure, that the strategy of regeneration—important as regeneration as such is—does not touch on specific and concrete questions of social ethics. So, let us go on to the question of goals and tactics.

The Goals

The matter of goals can be dealt with summarily here, for Dr. Henry says little about them. When he does, he speaks in terms of goals for individuals. He speaks of meeting the "survival needs" of people, for instance (as is done by rescue missions?). At any rate, Dr. Henry—as we are—is against Marxist goals. He does not want to eliminate private property. He does not want to do away with the profit motive. He sees no injustice in unequal distribution of wealth. We have no argument here, of course.

He goes on to concede that the goals of an evangelical ethic will coincide at some points with those of "modern social theorists." Henry says, for example: "Elimination of poverty, opportunity for employment, racial equality, and many other goals that stand at the heart of contemporary social agitation are not only acceptable, but highly desirable." A few lines later, he amends "desirable" to read "essential." With these concessions, he warns that evangelicals do differ with liberals as to goals.

No doubt Dr. Henry did not intend to spell out the evangelical social goals. Nor do we blame him. The question of goals, concretely stated, is a knotty one. But so far, we must also admit that nothing at all has been said that would provide a hint as to distinctly evangelical social goals. The ones that are mentioned will be acceptable to everyone from Pope Paul to Carl McIntire.

While he insists that the evangelical differs all down the line from the liberal on social ethics, Dr. Henry recognizes throughout that the most friction comes on the question of tactics.

The Tactics

The question of tactics is the question of who does what when. And the rub comes when we ask what government ought to do and what the church may do.

Dr. Henry is eager to keep the areas of responsibility very clear. The role of the government is to maintain justice. The role of the church is to practice love. Law is the province of government. Compassion or benevolence is the province of the church. These are the ground rules of evangelical consideration of tactics in social action.

The reasons for keeping compassion out of government are curious. One of them is that benevolence is bound to be partial and discriminatory. Compassion is a form of love, and "love is preferential and shows favor or partiality." Government, in justice, must be impartial. I am at a loss to know where Dr. Henry comes by the notion that love is always partial. Our Father, we are told, sets the pattern for human benevolence precisely in his compassionate impartiality. He lets the sun shine and the rain fall on the just and unjust alike. It is not the *essence* of compassion to show no favor and to be impartial?

The other reason for keeping compassion out of government is that compassion tends to push the government toward the welfare state. The welfare state is Dr. Henry's bête noir. He does not tell us why it is evil; he assumes, perhaps, that every literate evangelical will know why.

What is the best alternative to the welfare state? Why, the just state, of course. Now, Dr. Henry must know that this gets us nowhere. If, when ill, I am told that the only alternative I have to surgery is sound health, I know my doctor is kidding. When Dr. Henry tells us that the best alternative to a welfare state is a just state, I am sure that he is not kidding; I am equally sure that he has not shed any light.

What *is* the role of government in Dr. Henry's social ethics? The clearest hint we get is this: "The evangelical knows that no improvement can be made on a government that assures every man his rights, and that limits the freedom of citizens where and when it intrudes on the rights of others." This is another way of saying that the government's function is to see to justice in the land. But it tells us little unless we begin defining some of these rights that must be assured and protected.

Dr. Henry does mention something about property rights being fundamental. I suppose he would add the right to vote, the right to travel, and the "right to work" (the latter meaning, not the right of every man to a job, but the wrong of any union to keep him away from his job). But does every man have the right to provide decently for his family? Does every man have the right to live where he can afford a house? Does every man have the right of access to public accommodation? Does every aged and poor man have the right to adequate medical care? Are these rights—or are they matters of benevolence? If they are rights, then, by Dr. Henry's own definition, the government has an obligation to at least try to assure every man of them. And this would not be an exercise in compassion, but in law and justice.

Dr. Henry has a penchant for absolute, but abstract distinctions. One wishes he would land on some specific points and call his shots. Is he against the war on poverty (not against some administrative errors, but against the concept of the government engaging in such a war)? Is he against Social Security and Medicare? Is he against the Job Corps? Is he against civil rights legislation (again, not civil rights, which he is for, but government legislation)? Again, if the government is to stay out of compassion, must it stop giving grain to starving people in India? Dr. Henry is not specific. But does it do any good to say that governments must stick with justice (and stay clear of compassion) unless we know what the just claims of man on governments are?

A moment of promise appears when Dr. Henry chides the liberal for his blindness to society as a macrocosm of the family. But the promise hangs in the air. The society of men, Henry insists, is the family writ large. But he refuses to take his own thought seriously. Calvin took it seriously. This is why he saw government as analogous to the father of a family. And this is one reason why he was ready to give government a good deal more positive work to do in society than Dr. Henry appears willing to give it. The father has to do more than keep the kids out of each other's hair. He has the task of providing for the welfare of each child—and not as a matter of charity, but of right. Is Dr. Henry willing to follow the full implications of his own insight?

There is more than a touch of the all or nothing at all syndrome in Dr. Henry's essay. He turns his back on the fundamentalistic attitude that says if we cannot have the kingdom of God, we will not bother with anything else. But he does not make quite a full turn. For instance, he says: "As evangelical Christians see it, the vision of One World, or of United Nations, that is built on geographic representation rather than on principial agreement is as socially unpromising as is a lawless home that neglects the commandments of God." What does this mean?

If the United Nations is "socially unpromising" must we drop it? Is this, after all, the Carl McIntire line put more politely? Does evangelical ethics suppose that nations who do not agree principially ought not talk together as a better alternative to destroying each other? Or is this only to say that evangelical Christians ought not expect the U.N. to lead us into the new earth? If the latter is meant, the statement is innocuous. If the former, it is dangerous. But Dr. Henry does not like to be specific.

All in all, we are left with an "uneasy conscience" about evangelical social ethics. We are just not sure where Dr. Henry wants us to go. The *Christian Century* thinks it knows the answer. The editor of the *Century* never leaves the reader in doubt as to where he stands, and he thinks he knows which cards Dr. Henry is holding. The evangelical social involvement, he maintains, follows "a consistent and recognizable pattern." It is the conservative, reactionary, individualistic course. It is a call to keep the church out of social questions. It is a social ethic that leaves the social needs of man primarily in the hands of benevolent individuals.

We have no taste for taking sides with the *Century* against our evangelical friends of *Christianity Today*. The *Century* editorial shows little appreciation of the progress that has been made within evangelical circles on the score of social concern. And it betrays—we think—the cocky side of hubris in the face of its own problems and convictions. And when the *Century* hints darkly that evangelical leaders temper their tune to meet the approval of rich men who back evangelical projects, we had best take no notice. But this much must be granted. When the *Century* comes out of its corner, it comes out fighting. And whether it is right or wrong, it lets us know where it stands before the dust has settled. Whatever the justification for its criticism of evangelical social ethics, the *Century* puts *Christianity Today* on notice that if individual ethics are to be helpful, they must also be specific.

The net impression of Dr. Henry's essay is that evangelicals do not yet have a social ethic. They have a personal ethic for regenerate individuals. They do not have an ethic that prescribes a way of action and form for human society. We do not blame evangelicals for this. As we said earlier, we are in much the same boat—but with a difference. We insist that there has to be a social ethic derived from Christian principles, an ethic which prescribes a manner of life for society, the organic form of corporate human existence. We insist that environmental forms are terribly important to any social ethics. And we insist that government has a positive calling to see that the various segments of the organic society share properly in the social and economic privileges and responsibilities of the commonwealth. The call of the gospel to conversion and regeneration is not compromised, we believe, by saying that evangelism is not a substitute for social ethics. For, apart from the salvation of individuals, there is a God-willed structure for society which we must seek to know and apply. And only as we look to this will we be involved in Christian social ethics. As I said, we do not blame evangelicals for not having achieved a social ethic. What we are eager to know is whether they really want one.

One part of Dr. Henry's essay that we have not gotten into here is the role of the church in the social question. We have some questions on this aspect of evangelical social action too. But, for that, another time.

What Social Structures?

Carl F. H. Henry

In his essay "The Evangelicals and the Social Question"[2] Professor Smedes does me the honor of a constructive critique of facets of my view of Christian social ethics, and probably pays more tribute than is my due for the stimulation of fundamentalist social awareness. I rather think he has rightly judged the situation in his verdict that fundamentalism is now consciously committed to the social relevance of the gospel. In fact, the widening social involvement of evangelical Protestants is a hopeful sign in this hour when conservative Christianity is depicted by its foes as antihumanitarian, while they advance their own partisan objectives (of reformation, reconstruction or revolution, as the case may be) as a matter of Christian compassion. Along with Dr. Smedes I am convinced that the deepest springs of compassion flow from the Christian heritage, not from channels of secular humanism—although from time to time the ad hoc emergency programs of the latter and the lethargic response of the former create a contrary impression. In fact, even in their longing for social justice, the secular reformers are greatly indebted to the biblical heritage at a distance, even if in the specifics of their proposals they frequently promote quite alien alternatives.

To zoom in on Dr. Smedes' assessment of my essay "Evangelicals in the Social Struggle,"[3] I should perhaps comment first that it is not to be viewed, as he thinks, as an "evangelical manifesto," since it does not stand alone as an expression of my position. In *Aspects of Christian Social Ethics*[4] I have given a fuller statement. In either event, there is no basis for the judgment that I am "skeptical about the usefulness of laws"; in *Aspects* I devote most of a chapter to the importance and role of law. I do, however, hold the position that law cannot transform people while the gospel can; and also (what Dr. Smedes omits to add) that even

Carl F. H. Henry, "What Social Structures?" *Reformed Journal* 16 (May–June 1966): 6–7. Reprinted by permission.

2. Lewis B. Smedes, "The Evangelicals and the Social Question," *Reformed Journal* 16 (February 1966): 9–13.

3. Carl F. H. Henry, "Evangelicals in the Social Struggle," *Christianity Today* 10 (October 8, 1965): 3–11.

4. Carl F. H. Henry, *Aspects of Christian Social Ethics* (Grand Rapids: William B. Eerdmans Publishing Co., 1964).

regenerate persons require law because they too remain imperfect members of a sinful society. I cannot recall having anywhere said—as Professor Smedes quotes me—that "there is little point in changing environment," although I have doubtless said that *persons* ought to be the main objects of Christian concern, and that if in order to obey the mandate to evangelize we need first to wait for the achievement of social justice we may as well return to our nets. The evangelical mission in the world must be comprehended totally within Christ's commission and mandate. While the increase of Christians will not automatically assure social justice, the depletion of them will hardly set ahead the cause either of evangelical Christianity or of social righteousness. I do not mean that public righteousness is due only from believers; it is due from and owing to all men on the basis of their humanity. But it is not the church's task to conceal the relevance of the gospel in the social crisis.

When Professor Smedes contrasts a good and bad environment by stating that a bad environment can *keep* a good man from doing good, while a good environment can *inhibit* a bad man from doing evil, I have the impression that the contrast overplays the powers of social structure and underplays the redemptive dynamisms. While I do not contend that regenerate men will achieve total sanctification, I do hold that the *spiritual* environment in which they have their new life in Christ has greater potency to command the will than has the social environment in which they have their natural existence, and that the church should not neglect these constraints by shifting social concern one-sidedly to the latter.

When all else is said and done, Professor Smedes is impatient because I chart no specifics in terms of what, in the way of changing the social structures, the evangelical ought to approve and what he ought to disapprove—particularly in respect to large hard-core areas of social deprivation. Suppose Dr. Smedes were to grant my stated positions (which I shall not assume), just what specific changes of social structure are to be advocated as Christian imperatives? Dr. Smedes complains that I "do not like to be specific"—and so I shall invite him to specificity in respect to his own proposals regarding the role of the institutional church in changing social structures.

To me it seems ironic that the church—precisely at the time when she is lusting for novel forms and structures of her own, and is becoming increasingly unsure of what elements of fixity characterize her own community—should suddenly have become endowed with a divine afflatus for revising the social structures of the world. I do not imply that the Christian Reformed Church is reexamining its own structures (self-examination in view of biblical imperatives would be wholesome in all denominations), but there is little doubt that we now find an energetic espousal of new patterns of social involvement on the American scene. If changing social structures is the decisive test of the church's real engagement in social ethics, it is remarkable that the Christian Reformed Church—with its standing interest in social relevance (even in the now defunct *Calvin Forum*)—has so recently gained this insight, and that we seem here to have an instance of the church learning from the world (if not from the post-Marxist world) what her main social duty is.

While I insist that individual Christians ought to be politically active to the limit of their *competence*, and that they are obliged to join in the struggle for the just state and to seek the improvement of civil law, I would hold that whatever pertains to the world is provisional except as it has a basis in the revealed will of God for the social order. As I see it, the purpose of civil government is preservative, not regenerative; that is, it is to protect human rights and sustain peace by the promotion of justice and order. It is ridiculous, therefore, to imply that although I am for civil rights I am not necessarily for civil rights *legislation*. Law and liberty, insofar as we deal with legitimate rights, belong together. (I wish that Professor Smedes would himself not so swiftly exempt the right-to-work debate from this context.) I thought President Johnson's civil rights message to Congress was his high hour, and wrote him so—although I thought it was no business of the institutional church to endorse any specific legislative proposal in the name of the church, and still have personal reservations about some aspects of civil rights legislation.

Dr. Smedes' main interest, however, seems to veer from civil rights legislation to welfare legislation, and it will be well that its implications be widely debated. It is no longer, of course, a matter of the church "leading the way" to the welfare state; that type of state is already largely here, and not because of the lively sympathy of most churchgoers (who deplore the socialistic temper of clergymen presuming to speak for the whole church) but because of the secular drift. It is now mainly a question of the church approving a civil marriage, and hoping to influence the children.

Professor Smedes does not like my emphasis that except in dire emergency the responsibility of the state is in the realm of rights (which are nonpreferential) and not of compassion or benevolence (which is preferential). (I have formulated the argument in *Aspects of Christian Social Ethics*.) He thinks that benevolence should not be left to benevolent individuals but is a proper role of government, not simply on an emergency basis but ideally and normatively. He thinks, it appears, that "the essence of compassion" is "to show no favor and to be impartial."[5] Hence

5. Smedes, "Evangelicals and the Social Question," p. 12.

we are left with the overall impression that, as Professor Smedes sees it, the welfare state is neither evil nor partial, but preferential and ideal. He insists that "there has to be a social ethic derived from Christian principles, an ethic which prescribes the manner of life for *society*—the organic form of corporate human existence."[6]

It is this "God-willed structure for society," as Professor Smedes calls it, that I now call on him to formulate precisely, and in the context of the teaching and example of Jesus and the apostles.

I myself am convinced that the church has much to say and do in the world. But I am not inclined to applaud either the direction that Dr. Smedes seems to be pointing, or his identification of the main concern.

The church has the social task first of ordering its own life as a community of the faithful in distinction from the world of unbelief, and it does this under God for the sake of all mankind. In this ordering of the life of the redemptive community it ought to mirror what is implied in a good society—not simply as stipulated by law and grudgingly appropriated, but as impressively achieved on the basis of *agapē*. Not that ecclesiastical norms ought in turn to be implemented by governments in the world. The state has its own specific mission and limits and, while the good state will require nothing contrary to the social commandments of the Decalogue (Rom. 13), its province is not the compulsion of benevolence but the preservation of justice and order. Only as the church powerfully reflects the direct authority of Jesus Christ can she effectively witness to the world of the perils of ignoring the lordship of the invisible King whose claims the world spurns.

Where Do We Differ?

Lewis B. Smedes

D r. Henry has responded with magnanimity to my rather dogged questioning of his social ethics. I raised several questions last February that Dr. Henry's statements on the subject left unanswered. I am pleased that he has honored them by his present essay. Whether he has now carried us forward to a better understanding of one another's point of

6. Ibid., p. 13.

Lewis B. Smedes, "Where Do We Differ?" *Reformed Journal* 16 (May–June 1966): 8–10. Reprinted by permission.

view, to say nothing of agreement, remains to be seen. For the most part, Dr. Henry seems to say: "I prefer not to enter into a discussion of the questions you raise, sir, but I should like you to spell out the questionable implications of your own questions."

Perhaps Dr. Henry will deal with some of the other issues on another occasion. At least I hope so. For if we are ever going to find a common ground on social ethics, we are going to have to resolve precisely the kind of questions that I raised last February. Maybe what we need is a two- or three-day conference on social ethics.

I must admit to some frustration in reading Dr. Henry's present essay. I am sure that from his point of view he has a steady bead on the subject at hand. From my own, however, the subject keeps slipping away from him. I thought the subject was social ethics. He seems to be asking whether social ethics is as important as preaching the gospel. I was not aware that we had any problem on this score. Let the matter of social ethics be thirteenth on the ladder of evangelical priorities, we must still get at it as soundly as we can.

Dr. Henry also wants to talk about the role of the institutional church in Christian social action. This is, to be sure, a very urgent question. The trouble is that it does not happen to be the subject raised in the piece to which Dr. Henry is responding. In this regard, I am left with only a guess as to what his obscure references to the Christian Reformed Church signify. It is quite understandable that, in his position of crucial evangelical leadership, he is so nettled by persistent clamor for direct church involvement in social action that whenever people press him on social ethics he is inclined to think in terms of getting the church into the lobbies of Congress. We should not be able to speak long about social ethics before the problem of church involvement would have to be raised. But it was not this that bothered me first of all about Dr. Henry's views on social ethics. And, if he will permit me, I don't think my views on this subject are of interest here either.

There are, among others, three points Dr. Henry makes which touch on my own address to his position. Let me make a brief remark about each.

First, Dr. Henry reiterates that "law cannot transform people while the gospel can." This is the limit of the usefulness of laws in our striving toward a just society. With this understood, Dr. Henry insists that he in no way depreciates the usefulness of laws. I think his earnestness on this point is demonstrated by his approval of civil rights legislation. So far, so good.

Now, I do not know of any Christian moralist who supposes that laws can transform people. I certainly do not. But I do think that reliance on the gospel of personal regeneration as the evangelical strategy in social ethics is inadequate. It is for this reason, undoubtedly, that I set greater store by law in achieving a good society than does Dr. Henry. I gather that he thinks of the usefulness of law primarily—though probably not exclusively—as deterrent, inhibitive, protective, and not as potentially creative of a better social structure. Still, his endorsement of the Civil Rights Act keeps the door open for a more positive view.

Second, to Dr. Henry the purpose of government lies in the realm of preservation. "As I see it, government is preservative, not regenerative; that is, it is to protect human rights and sustain peace by the promotion of justice and order." If I have to make a choice between "preservative" and "regenerative," I will side with Dr. Henry. But what kind of choice is this? Does any Christian suppose that the government's task is to regenerate? The alternatives are so unreal that I am obliged to suppose that Dr. Henry means something pretty flexible by his term *preservative*.

What is the government supposed to preserve? The answer: human rights and peace. The means: "by the promotion of justice and order." To this, I say Amen! And when I note Dr. Henry's insistence on his approval of civil rights legislation (does this include the Civil Rights Act of 1964?), I get the feeling that we are not far apart. But was this a merely preservative act. It certainly was also a creative act. It was a decision by government to provide (by law and enforcement) a new social status for one group within the population, a status that had been denied them by a social structure imposed and sustained by another group. If Dr. Henry espouses this kind of governmental "preservation," I am happy to settle for the term—as long as it can be given this sort of content.

But Dr. Henry is wary of my readiness to carry this kind of governmental involvement over into the economic sphere of life. Why? Do people have no economic rights besides the right to keep what they already have? Why may and ought the government to legislate in the area of civil rights and not in the area of economic rights?

Third, the responsibility of the state lies "in the realm of rights (which are nonpreferential) and not of compassion or benevolence (which is preferential)." I questioned Dr. Henry about the *reasons* for this distinction; I wondered where he got the notion that compassion is per se preferential. It seems to me so clear that compassion is per se nondiscriminatory, that I am persuaded that Dr. Henry means something different by compassion than I do. I identify compassion—the Christian kind—with the *agapē* of the New Testament. Be that as it may, Dr. Henry concludes that I not only question his reason for making the distinction, but that I reject the distinction altogether.

In fact, I do not reject the distinction completely. I accept it for reasons other than his. But I do not find it possible to make the distinction as hard and rigid as he does. I am not eager to insist on a compassionless government. A government that is just but compassionless is likely to espouse a rigid, inflexible, and impersonal execution of justice. Nonetheless, I agree with Dr. Henry that the normal responsibility of government is the achievement and guardianship of justice. Government rests on law, not on love. It responds to the rights of men, not their human needs for mercy and affection.

What I find lacking about this distinction, however, is that it will not further our development of a Christian social ethic until we talk concretely about what the claims of justice are. It was at this point that I had hoped Dr. Henry would clarify his public position by stating his view on a few specific questions. Instead, he seizes on what he considers my own Achilles' heel and asks *me* to be specific.

"Smedes," he says, "thinks that benevolence should not be left to benevolent individuals, but is a proper role of government . . . ideally and normatively." This is a big conclusion to reach from the sparse data available. What I *do* think is that the philanthropy of benevolent individuals, as praiseworthy and helpful as it has often been, is not a solution to the problems involved in social ethics of our time. The more benevolent individuals there are, the better. The more the government works at justice, the better. Government cannot be based on benevolence, nor governmental action on compassion—not "ideally and normatively."

Where, then, do we differ? Apart from the hard and fast use Dr. Henry tends to make of extreme alternatives—alternatives so abstract that they are not real ones in our concrete situation—I think our difference lies in the concept we have of human rights. I do not think the difference lies so much in our concept of government. He applauds government for stepping into a societal structure and altering it in order to achieve human rights (in the case of civil rights legislation). This leads me to suppose that he is not really against a creative function for government, at least not absolutely. The difference must exist in our respective ideas of what is embraced among the inalienable rights of men.

The difference, that is, must lie in those areas in which he was disinclined to enter at this point. The right to vote and to eat in public places he recognizes. Therefore, justice demands the government act in this instance. But do men have no economic rights? Yes, they have a right to keep what they have earned, Dr. Henry says (property rights). But do they have no *right* to a share in the common goods? Do children have no right to be part of a family living in an environment where family life is truly possible? Do the elderly poor have no right to adequate medical care? Do fathers of families have no right to provide for their families? And does government not have a summons from justice to see that these rights, too, are honored as far as possible?

That Dr. Henry did not wish to go into such questions is his privilege. But unless we evangelicals do come to terms with these and similar questions about the nature of men's rights, we are not going to advance into a relevant social ethic for our time.

Dr. Henry does, however, ask *me* to be specific. I am glad to oblige as best I can.

I believe that the geographic and political segment of human society that we call the state is made of several basic and living social components. These are the essential membranes of human society. To mention some, there is the family, labor, industry and commerce, science and education, the church. There may be more; the number is not important. Each of these components of society is distinguishable from the other by the special functions it performs for society as a whole and by the basic structure of its life. No society is healthy or just unless each of these is free and able to develop its peculiar life in its own way and according to its own laws. And none of them can do so unless it has certain rudimentary materials with which to work.

For instance, the family cannot live and develop without a private and wholesome place to live. Nor can it function fruitfully in society if the elders do not have the means to feed and clothe their children properly, to say nothing of training and educating them. The elemental requirements of health are necessary to the family. All these involve the basic right to work and earnings for the father. The family has certain inalienable rights.

Where these rights are withheld because of regional disaster, economic breakdown, widespread dislocation of industry, natural calamity, or because of any reason not willed by the family itself, the government has a normal duty to act on behalf of society to rescue the family.

The rights of family are not ends in themselves. Rights are based on duty. The family has a function to fulfill in the society of men. And this function is imperative for a healthy society. This is basically why the government must recognize the just rights of the family—not out of compassion to provide free comforts for the indigent, but to maintain a just, whole, well-ordered society.

One could extend this type of reasoning into all spheres of society. In each one the individual takes his place, fulfills his life as a serving member, and is invested with certain basic rights in order that he may fulfill his responsibility to the various spheres of social life in which he lives and by which his life is horizontally defined. In all of them, he has a just claim on government for the maintenance of his rights when they are withheld and cannot be regained by himself.

Having said this, I am in a spot to answer the questions that I asked Dr. Henry to answer. I am for the war on poverty—not on the basis of compassion, but on the basis of justice. I am for the right to work. (By the way, I am not willing to exempt this matter from discussion. On another occasion I have used these pages to reject the union shop wherever it forces a man to violate his conscience in order to have the right to work.) I am for Social Security. I am for Medicare. I am for the Job Corps. I am for a massive governmental attack on the intolerable slums of our great cities; I am for this because the family cannot possibly live and grow normally and fruitfully under these circumstances and because it has been demonstrated that nothing less than a massive onslaught will do the job. And it is just because social justice requires the doing of these things that their being done badly is regrettable and intolerable.

I have a notion that what separates Dr. Henry's thinking and mine is not so much a question of big or small government as such. I am sure, too, that the distinctions he makes are not the point of division. (I cannot find myself unqualifiedly on either side of any of his too absolutistic distinctions.) I think that where we differ, and where evangelicals ought to talk things out at length, is in the area of the doctrine of man and his community. I think we do not agree on the subject of justice and rights among men because we have a significant shading of difference in our theology concerning man. (This, incidentally, is why many evangelicals shudder at the mention of "social structures" and the duty of reshaping them when justice requires it, and why Calvinistic evangelicals find this vocabulary native to their thinking.)

Dr. Henry, I am inclined to suppose, tends to think of the individual as the basic component of society. He thinks of government and the individual as the two polar existences in society. And this helps explain why many evangelicals are apprehensive of governmental action in the sphere of economics and welfare. On the other hand, Calvinistic evangelicals (and neo-Calvinists of Abraham Kuyper's sort) tend to see the individual—his rights and duties—in terms of his social nature. Not the individual as such, but the various social spheres are basic to society and the state. The difference in point of view at this level accounts for the difference in perspective on social ethics.

H. Richard Niebuhr said of an earlier evangelicalism: "It could not emancipate itself from the conviction—more true in its own time than in ours—that the human unit is the individual. It is unable therefore to deal with social crisis, with national disease, and the misery of human groups."[7] It is my hope that the evangelical of today, awakened as he is to revitalized social concern, will give new thought to the question of the nature of man. And if this discussion, modestly begun on these pages, could ripen to a full-scale discussion on another level, the question of individualism will have to be prominent on the agenda. The net impression left on me still is that expressed in my other essay: Evangelicals "have a personal ethic for regenerate individuals. They do not have an ethic that prescribes a way of action and form for human society." I think the Calvinist tradition provides the most promising base on which to develop one.

Study Questions

1. Evangelicals realize, Henry writes, "that not an ethic of grace but rather an ethic of justice should govern social structures." Explain Henry's distinction between an ethic of grace and an ethic of justice. Do you find such a distinction meaningful? What does Henry cite as examples of "social structures"?

2. Henry writes: "in the absence of moral men—of men willing to do the good—no body of law, however just, can ensure a good society." Do you agree with this sentiment? Why or why not? What are the implications of such a view for public policy decisions? How crucial is "spiritual regeneration" in Henry's theology of social change?

3. What is the purpose of government in Henry's view? Why is the welfare state a violation of the proper function of government in Henry's view?

4. In Henry's opinion, what is the role of the church in the area of Christian social responsibility?

5. What place does the Bible have in Henry's formulation of an evangelical political philosophy? Can you identify any of Henry's "divinely revealed principles"? Do you think the Bible alone is sufficient as a source of information for developing a personal evangelical perspective on political issues?

7. H. Richard Niebuhr, *The Kingdom of God in America* (New York: Harper, 1937), p. 162.

6. What avenues of service for the practical implementation of an evangelical social witness are identified by Henry? Can you cite others?

7. Does Smedes believe that Christians living responsibly by "revealed moral principles" can create a good society? Compare his view with Henry's.

8. List the "rights" Smedes believes government must establish and protect in order to promote a just state. How does his list differ from Henry's?

9. Can you detect in Smedes' views of civil rights, justice, and the welfare state an evangelical version of the liberal Great Society? What are the specifically Christian or biblical sources of Smedes' liberal politics?

10. In Henry's rejoinder ("What Social Structures?") to Smedes, what does Henry mean when he says, "The purpose of civil government is preservative, not regenerative"? In Smedes' final rejoinder, where does he claim that he and Henry fundamentally differ?

11. Assess Henry's and Smedes' views in light of your own understanding of Scripture and political philosophy.

Part **2**

America Coming Apart

(1965–1976)

The Evangelical Radical Left Expands
the Political Options   3

Evangelical Political Conservatives
and Liberals Experience an Unraveling America

The bright hopes for the future of America, so apparent in the early 1960s, dimmed dramatically in the period from Vietnam to Watergate as the nation experienced profound political and social upheaval. The Great Society proved elusive and the Vietnam War became a military and political nightmare. Radical movements emerged to test the nation's time-honored commitments to pluralism and to tear at the cohesive fabric of the nation.

The Vietnam War divided the American people like no other event during the presidencies of Lyndon Johnson and Richard Nixon. It shattered the bipartisan consensus behind the policy of containment and politicized many young Americans who—viewing the war as a symbol of U.S. imperialism—called for military withdrawal from Vietnam. Militant black leaders, rejecting the integrationist goals of the civil rights movement, polarized society further by preaching black separatism and supporting violent confrontations with the nation's white power structure. Black activism triggered other racial and ethnic groups to demand national recognition of their distinctive ethnic histories and a more equitable share in the American dream. Women organized feminist coalitions and also entered the battle for socioeconomic equality and personal liberation. Some more radical factions even attacked traditional marriage and the nuclear family.

An assortment of young student radicals and university intellectuals, collectively labeled "the new left," added to the domestic ferment. They sharply criticized the nation's political and economic institutions as inherently racist, oppressive, sexist, and elitist, and militantly called for the radical reconstruction of America. University students also spearheaded a countercultural rebellion that undermined established American beliefs, values, and behaviors. Hippies, as they were popularly known, rejected bureaucratic structures, middle-class values, consumerism, and militarism; ridiculed what they viewed as vestiges of Victorian sexual morality; and scorned the notion of upward economic mobility. No event of the decade better brought together all of the elements of the counterculture than the Woodstock music festival, a three-day orgy of sex, drugs, and rock music in August 1969. These countercultural rebels, then, like new left radicals, black nationalists, ethnic activists, and feminists, further expanded the nation's stock of accepted values. In doing so, however, they exacerbated the growing ideological polarization of American society along political, racial, ethnic, class, generation, and gender lines. Such social fragmentation peeled off the veneer of the melting pot so celebrated during the consensual 1950s.

Evangelical political conservatives and liberals were uneasy over the political turmoil, cultural relativism, and moral permissiveness pervading the nation's public life. Common concern, however, did not translate into a common response. Evangelical political conservatives rallied around Richard Nixon who, in his successful campaign for the presidency in 1968, spearheaded a conservative counterattack against the excesses of Great Society liberalism, cultural and social radicalism, and "unpatriotic" student antiwar protests. They liked Nixon's "law and order" rhetoric, his call for an "honorable" end to the Vietnam War, and his appeal to traditional values as a solution to the country's social unrest. Although not all evangelicals were mesmerized by Nixon's outward show of religious piety, close friendship with Billy Graham, and calculated courting of the evangelical vote, the majority of evangelical political conservatives nevertheless stood by Nixon until Watergate forced his resignation.

Long before Watergate, evangelical political liberals criticized Nixon's strategy to end the Vietnam War through massive bombing and hardline negotiations, and considered his administration's "hardball" confrontation with antiwar activists as counterproductive and contributing to the cycle of national violence. Liberals viewed the president's political exploitation of the white backlash against black civil rights and economic gains as crassly opportunistic and symptomatic of the administration's insensitivity to the poor and issues of social justice. Not surprisingly in 1972 some evangelical political liberals organized a campaign to promote the presidential candidacy of liberal Democratic Senator George McGovern. They argued that "the platform of Senator McGovern moves at many crucial points in the direction indicated by biblical principles." Through their support of McGovern they sought to "end the outdated stereotype that evangelical theology automatically means a politics unconcerned about the poor, minorities, and unnecessary military expenditures."[1]

President Nixon was reelected by the biggest landslide in history, winning 520 out of 538 electoral votes. Evangelical political conservatives were pleased and expected to have even greater public influence. Those evangelicals who supported McGovern were disappointed with his poor showing, but later felt vindicated by the Watergate revelations. In fact by 1974 mainstream evangelicals from both liberal and conservative camps were united in their disavowal of the disgraced president.

The Evangelical Radical Left Proposes a Biblical Agenda for a "Post-American" Society

Evangelical political conservatives and liberals were aggressively challenged during the early 1970s by a younger group of self-styled evangelical radicals who felt alienated both from mainstream evangelicalism and American society. Coming of intellectual age in the years from Kennedy to Nixon, the evangelical radicals' political and cultural views were influenced by the secular radical movements of the 1960s. Coming from fundamentalist and evangelical homes and churches they inevitably clashed with their more conservative elders. The ideological passion and rhetorical flavor of these young radicals is illustrated in the following brief manifesto originally published in 1971 in the first issue of the *Post-American*, edited by Jim Wallis:

> We fault political liberalism for its hollow rhetoric, sellout and implication in racism, poverty, the Vietnam War, imperialist foreign policy and a materialist, technocratic value system. We dedicate ourselves to no ideology, government, or system, but to active obedience to our Lord and His kingdom, and to sacrificial service to the people for whom He died.
>
> We wish to serve the people by proclaiming a gospel of liberation in the saving work of Christ, by articulation of the ethical implications of that gospel, by working for peace, justice and freedom. . . . we are a grassroots

1. For the full text of this letter, see appendix 2.

coalition calling for people committed to the revolutionary Christian message that is distinctively Post-American, that changes men's lives and generates a radical commitment to social justice which serves as the basis for social liberation. Serve the Lord. Serve the People.[2]

Wallis, along with John Alexander, editor of *The Other Side*, and Sharon Gallagher, editor of *Right On*, helped formulate the biblical and political agenda for the evangelical radical left. Their respective magazines provided a forum for radicals to discover each other, to critique American society and the evangelical church, and to hammer out their distinctive evangelical political philosophy. In a short time these leaders and their publications transformed a collection of dispersed political dissenters into a loosely knit national evangelical radical movement.

Combining the biblical motif of the demonic influences of "the principalities and powers" with the secular new left's analysis of the systemic nature of social evil and the corrupting dominance of corporate-military power, evangelical radicals viewed the hierarchical ordering of society and centralized, bureaucratic government as inherently evil. Linking their suspicion of power with their commitment to Jesus' teachings concerning the kingdom of God and the communal nature of discipleship, evangelical radicals envisioned the church as a counter-community, an instrument of political and social transformation. Representing a third alternative within an increasingly politically diversified evangelicalism, these Christian radicals took pride in their anti- or "post-American" political stance, in their defense of the have-nots—"the other side"—in American life, and in the fact that unlike evangelical reformers to the right who retained their faith in the basic soundness of the American political and economic system, they were "sojourners" in a fallen nation.

Evangelicals for Social Action Try for Consensus

Although divided into conservative, liberal, and radical camps, all politically concerned evangelicals shared a common commitment to develop an evangelical social ethic, to use biblical principles in the resolution of societal problems, to politicize the larger evangelical community, and to stimulate an evangelical engagement with American society.

2. Jim Wallis, "What is the People's Christian Coalition?" *Post-American* 1 (Fall 1971): 5. Also see appendix 3 for the lead editorial in the first issue of *Post-American*.

The attempt to build an evangelical political consensus on these common concerns reached a highwater mark in the fall of 1973. Called together by theologian Ronald J. Sider, a group of about fifty evangelical leaders, men and women, representing conservative, liberal, and radical positions, met over Thanksgiving weekend at Chicago's downtown YMCA and adopted "A Declaration of Evangelical Social Concern." The declaration identified love, justice, and mercy as constructive principles in a biblical social ethic. Although claiming to endorse "no political ideology or party," the declaration nevertheless seemed slanted toward radical concerns and rhetoric in the way it lashed out at the specific ills of racism, sexism, militarism, materialism, and the maldistribution of the nation's wealth and services.[3]

To implement the principles of the Chicago declaration, a second Evangelicals for Social Action workshop was held in 1974. After much heated debate, the participants adopted nonbinding proposals supporting a socially relevant evangelism, Christian feminism, community economic development among the poor, less materialistic Christian lifestyles, nonviolent direct political action, and a study center for biblical social concern. Beneath the apparent agreements, however, lay deep and profound ideological cleavages among the workshop's participants that would surface in subsequent gatherings. At a third ESA-sponsored meeting in 1975 and a fourth in 1976 the evangelical search for consensus disintegrated rapidly. Evangelical political conservatives were conspicuous by their absence. Blacks accused whites of racism, women complained about sexist language, activist whites belittled academic theorists, and evangelical political radicals vigorously debated political liberals over strategies of social change. The unraveling of the evangelical coalition for social action mirrored the more general sociopolitical unraveling of the nation.

3. For the full text of the declaration, see appendix 4.

The Evangelical Radical Left Debates
with Evangelical Political Conservatives

The radical-conservative dialogue opens with an excerpt from Richard Quebedeaux's *Young Evangelicals*. Quebedeaux provides a brief sketch of radical (his young evangelicals) political and theological attitudes. The publication of the book was the occasion of a review essay, "Revolt on Evangelical Frontiers," by Carl F. H. Henry. Henry's critique illuminates conservatives' differences with radical thought and cultural style. Jim Wallis's sharp response to Henry and his defense of the radical persuasion clarifies radical-conservative ideological differences.

The Young Evangelicals:
Revolution in Orthodoxy

Richard Quebedeaux

If the new evangelicalism is a very important stance within orthodoxy in its own right, it is even more notable for its influence on an emerging generation of college and university students, recent seminary

Richard Quebedeaux, *The Young Evangelicals: Revolution in Orthodoxy* (New York: Harper and Row, 1974), pp. 39–41, 99, 131–35. Reprinted by permission.

graduates, "street people," intellectuals, activists, pastors, evangelists, politicians, and concerned laypersons in general, all of whom we shall call the young evangelicals. Although the views held by these individuals are often indistinguishable from those espoused by new evangelical thinkers like Clarence Bass, Vernon Grounds, George Ladd, David Moberg, J. Rodman Williams, and the immortal Edward John Carnell, the young evangelical stance might be described more appropriately as a "spirit" rather than a well-defined theology. Furthermore, it would be improper to imply that all the young evangelicals are physically youthful. Indeed, some are not. But whether young or old, they are *all* characterized by (1) a fresh spirit of openness to all who seek to follow Jesus Christ and (2) a profound desire to apply the gospel to *every* dimension of life. Most of the young evangelicals are aware of the fundamentalist-modernist controversy only from their studies; they display none of the theological and cultural prejudices so vividly manifested in that debate and its aftermath. They have no axe to grind. And their older compatriots who share the same spirit also have firmly and completely rejected the separatist impulse, the bad manners as well as the social unconcern rightly associated with the fundamentalist position.

Rooted in biblical orthodoxy and its most dynamic contemporary expressions, the young evangelicals have been motivated on the one hand by the concerns of the new evangelicalism, and on the other hand by the conscience-rending social and political unrest of the 1960s—the civil rights struggle, the tragedy of Indochina, the student rights movement, the ecology movement, the increasingly visible generation gap, the decline of the historic denominations, the hypocrisy of the evangelical churches, and the worldwide cry for liberation. Carl Henry has astutely discerned a number of things the young evangelicals expect from their churches:

1. An interest in human beings not simply as souls to be saved but as whole persons
2. More active involvement by evangelical Christians in sociopolitical affairs
3. An honest look at many churches' idolatry of nationalism
4. Adoption of new forms of worship
5. An end to judging spiritual commitment by such externals as dress, hairstyle, and other participation in cultural trends, including rock music
6. A new spirit with regard to ecumenical or nonecumenical attitudes

7. Bold and, if need be, costly involvement in the revolutionary struggles of our day
8. A reappraisal of life values.[1]

The young evangelicals are coming to see that the standard conservative assault on the social gospel is often merely a convenient excuse to avoid the imperatives of practical Christian service. At the same time, they are also discovering that Christian faith cannot rightly be identified with any single religious style or with a particular political or economic philosophy, be it laissez-faire or Marxist. The young evangelicals fault establishment evangelicalism for too often exhibiting the fundamentalist sentiments it says it disdains, for its de facto separatism, and for its failure to implement its avowed (or supposed) social concern into concrete sacrificial action. . . .

It would be unfair to say that contemporary fundamentalists or establishment evangelicals have not felt at least some obligation to come to the aid of the downtrodden and helpless in society. But the young evangelicals believe that their churches' admirable attempt to relieve the short-term suffering of individuals—through food and clothing collections, rescue missions, and the like—is merely treating the symptoms rather than *curing* the disease itself. In order to treat social ills in even a *relatively* democratic society, the proper use of political power and economic pressure by persons and groups is a virtual necessity. Modern orthodoxy, however, has generally maintained that social action—especially when the issues involved are political in nature—is a matter for individual Christians, not churches or demonstrations corporately. Thus, establishment evangelical and fundamentalist churches feel they are abiding by the principle of separation of church and state. Reacting against this hypocritical stance, the young evangelicals point out that orthodox denominations and churches which criticize liberal religious bodies for their political activities are themselves often quite willing to act in the same way when the preservation of the status quo is at stake. These young men and women would also suggest that the doctrine of separation of church and state has, in fact, been misinterpreted, that it really pertains to the prohibition of government interference in church affairs and does not forbid the churches to speak and act prophetically when the state fosters political or social unrighteousness.

We have already seen that the young evangelicals are manifesting new

1. Carl F. H. Henry, "Winds of Promise," *Christianity Today* 14 (June 5, 1970): 29–30.

priorities based upon the conviction that positive social concern and action are as much a part of the gospel as personal salvation—they are reverse sides of the same coin. Furthermore, these young men and women also reject their churches' adherence to a personal and social ethic which they claim is rooted in Scripture but is, in fact, grounded much more in (1) antiquated social mores and the cultural baggage of revivalism, (2) civil religion and the American way of life, and (3) a harsh legalism contrary to the spirit of the New Testament. . . .

It should now be manifestly apparent what the young evangelicals hope for the institutional church as it seeks to fulfill its mission in the world. First, these young men and women feel that the church must always derive its authority for faith and action from the Bible—rightly understood as the Word of God written. Second, they recognize the absolute necessity of personal commitment to Jesus Christ as Savior and Lord, the results of which are complete life transformation and a new beginning for the convert. Third, the young evangelicals believe in the mandate for evangelism—the proclamation and demonstration of the whole gospel, relevant to every dimension of human life. Fourth, these young men and women sincerely hope that the institutional church will take the call to discipleship seriously by encouraging and teaching its members to bear the cross, and by motivating each disciple of Christ to discover his or her Christian vocation following the principles outlined by Paul in Romans 12 and 1 Corinthians 12. They trust that the membership of the institutional church—in uncovering the deep meaning of discipleship—will join them, individually and corporately, in their fresh priorities which include (as we have seen) sexual love as a joyful experience, meaningful interpersonal and social relationships and the dignity of women, racial justice, peace and conscientious political involvement, the fight against poverty, a healthy natural environment, and a positive and happy participation in contemporary culture. Finally, the young evangelicals realize that renewal of the church of Jesus Christ demands not only costly discipleship, but reconciliation and Christian unity as well.

We have already ascertained that some of these young men and women (e.g., CWLF and the People's Christian Coalition) have found it expedient to forsake the institutional church—for the time being, anyway—in order to exercise their prophetic function without undue hindrance or restriction. They wish to influence the community of faith from outside institutional walls. Because we live in an era of seemingly healthy religious movements per se, there is no reason why the young evangelicals operating outside the institutional church cannot achieve some measure of success in attaining their goals. For, we must admit the contemporary viability of the persistence of a movement without coherent internal structure, hierarchy, or real membership—the existence in modern society of a looser affiliation, carried by the mass media, without the explicit need to bring people together for formal (as distinct from "expressive") purposes.

At the same time, as we have said, it is also true that numerous young evangelicals are trying hard to pursue renewal by remaining *within* the institutional church, both in the characteristically evangelical structures and in the mainstream ecumenical liberal denominations (not to mention the Roman Catholic Church). Those who find themselves within the liberal ecclesiastical institutions will advocate that their churches again take seriously the need for personal conversion to Christ and the desirability of a solid biblical-theological foundation for social action. On the other hand, those who stay within the evangelical churches will probably be working to help translate biblical faith into Christian unity and concrete social involvement—conversion into discipleship. Thus, the young evangelicals can effectively promote renewal within the evangelical structures no less than the mainstream ecumenical liberal denominations, and even outside the institutional church altogether.

Nevertheless, we should not neglect the fact that now (as perhaps never before) the opportunity for meaningful reconciliation between Christians of seemingly contrary ideologies is a distinct possibility. Reconciling the cleavage between liberals and evangelicals, therefore, ought to become a priority for both camps engaged in the present theological warfare. And it is also clear that the young evangelicals can play a significant role in this search for healing and real Christian unity. So we shall now seek to discover just how and through whom reconciliation might be effected and in what manner wholeness can be restored to the body of Christ in America today.

Revolt on Evangelical Frontiers

Carl F. H. Henry

Despite the outward vigor of establishment evangelicalism—in contrast to declining liberal fortunes—attested by church growth, bur-

Carl F. H. Henry, "Revolt on Evangelical Frontiers," *Christianity Today* 18 (April 16, 1974): 5–8. Reprinted by permission.

geoning seminary enrollments, expanding publishing houses, vigorous student movements, and eager funding of evangelistic and missionary causes, the young evangelicals are less than gratified. They contend that although the evangelical churches offer ultimate and authoritative answers to the search for meaning and purpose and proffer an inner spiritual reality that liberal churches neglect, they fall woefully short of full Christianity. . . .

A deep criticism young evangelicals make of establishment evangelicals is that they proclaim that "new persons will build a new society" while ignoring man's social side, or life in corporate society and its structures. Billy Graham is said to have been for a time commendably ahead of his evangelical constituency in his social concerns, especially in his refusal to address segregated crusades. Compared with the views of his brother-in-law Leighton Ford, however, those concerns are now considered a disappointing compromise with "the American way." Quebedeaux notes that when Graham did take a stand, liberal ecumenists either kept silent or chided him for not doing enough; he thinks young evangelicals should support Graham's evangelistic crusades but criticize his social and political views. Ford's "revolutionary evangelism" is commended for correlating evangelism and social action and repudiating "the 'Second-Coming cop-out.'"[2]

Although the young evangelicals disdain cheap grace, some of their criticisms seem like cheap judgment—judgment that costs them little of the practical involvement and hard decision making facing evangelical elder-statesmen. They at times assume a fixed stance on certain issues that other ethically sensitive evangelicals consider debatable. The young evangelicals call for a firm rejection of "the hypocrisy of American society and its ecclesiastical institutions."[3] Along with InterVarsity and Leighton Ford, the Christian World Liberation Front is commended for supporting "the new kind of evangelism" espoused by the young evangelicals—a tag line that seems brand-restrictive to the correlation of evangelism with criticism of American policy in domestic and foreign affairs.

It should now be clear that the young evangelicals for whom Quebedeaux presumes to speak have three distinguishing marks: (1) a reconstruction of the traditional evangelical view of the inspiration and authority of Scripture; (2) a special interest in Scripture "as a basis for action in the world,"[4] that is, for evangelism relevant to the whole man;

2. Richard Quebedeaux, *The Young Evangelicals: Revolution in Orthodoxy* (New York: Harper and Row, 1974). p. 90.
3. Ibid., p. 94.
4. Ibid., p. 98.

and (3) over against the fundamentalist code, a restatement of moral values involved in discipleship. I will not argue the last point, nor the second properly expounded; I have made similar pleas across a quarter of a century, although without so abruptly identifying contemporary cultural indulgences as evangelical morality. The alcohol traffic and the sorry state of the cinema and theater call for something more creative than nonlegalistic acceptance. And one no less interested in meaningful personal relationships may be forgiven a smile over the commendation of sensitivity training, transactional analysis, and group encounter at a time when even competent secular scholars express doubts about the adequacy of such techniques. And what is one to do with sweeping generalizations such as that fundamentalism and evangelicalism "have actually been a *cause* of the contemporary ecological crisis,"[5] or that orthodoxy does not emphasize God's revelation in nature?[6]

On the issue of evangelical social involvement I share the disenchantment of the young evangelicals with establishment evangelicalism, but without sharing certain excesses or approving certain specifics. "The proper use of political power and economic pressure"[7] is something evangelicals must learn; it could, indeed, speak to the tobacco, alcohol, cinema, and other interests—including racially and economically discriminatory enterprises. Establishment evangelicals are criticized, however, for "merely treating the symptoms of social injustice rather than *curing* the disease itself,"[8] and orthodoxy is declared to be "no less heretical than liberalism for . . . neglecting the social dimension of the gospel."[9]

Marxists have long derogated Christianity's social concern as merely a dispensing of aspirin whereas the overcoming of alienation (i.e., the class struggle) requires major surgery (socialist revolution) to remove objectionable social structures (capitalism). Such an estimate caricatures the tidal wave of human compassion unleashed upon the world by Christianity, oversimplifies the problem of alienation, confuses capitalism with the devil, divinizes socialism, and suffers from utopian enthusiasm. But it does have the merit of attempting that serious social criticism which is readily and tragically neglected by those resigned to the status quo, and it emphasizes the significance of social structures for human justice and injustice. Establishment evangelicals have given Marxists an undeserved advantage by confusing secular capitalism with the kingdom of God (or at least defending it as if it could do no wrong and were

5. Ibid., p. 127.
6. Ibid., p. 128.
7. Ibid., pp. 98f.
8. Ibid., p. 98.
9. Ibid., p. 121.

not under the judgmental scrutiny of God as much as any other cultural manifestation) and by not articulating a courageous social ethic that deals with the practices and structures that perpetrate injustice.

The young evangelicals call for "a truly evangelical social gospel"[10] that reflects the priorities of racial justice, the politics of conscience, the fight against poverty, and the provision of a healthful natural environment. Surely these objectives are not alien to a healthy evangelical conscience; indeed, proper understanding of the eighteenth-century evangelical awakening in England reveals that later fundamentalist and evangelical attitudes have shriveled a proper concern for social change.

But to say that the fight against poverty in America requires above all else "more equitable distribution of wealth, which means . . . higher taxes—especially for the rich" and on the world level "that the wealthy, developed nations give generously to the poorer, developing countries"[11] reflects, in its heavy reliance on socialist proposals, a disappointing lack of evangelical imagination. If one thinks of perpetuating the structure of poverty, the best way to do so would be to minimize the importance of jobs, education, and literacy. Higher taxes may indeed be indispensable where voluntary solutions fail, and the sick, elderly, and destitute must in any case get immediate assistance. But socialist nations implementing Marxist economic solutions with totalitarian vengeance have hardly achieved utopian results, and in trying to overcome the insensitivities of a capitalist economy it will be well not to idealize utopian proposals that extend human disenchantment. The lack of incentive among the poor is not, as Quebedeaux would have it, "inevitable,"[12] nor is poverty likely to be "cured" by corporate political action.[13]

The call for "meaningful reconciliation between Christians of seemingly contrary ideologies"[14] has its place, and to insist on proportionate representation for evangelicals in the power structures of mainstream denominations as the price of meaningful reconciliation has merit. The young evangelicals would not only take active part in local ministerial councils and councils of churches, as is already the case, but would do so on the premise of a similarity of commitment.

> If the values and priorities of the young evangelicals and mainstream ecumenical liberals *really* are similar, continued separation serves no concrete purpose. . . . These young men of evangelical persuasion might become an instrument of healing by accepting their ecumenical

10. Ibid., p. 101.
11. Ibid., p. 124.
12. Ibid., p. 125.
13. Ibid., p. 126.
14. Ibid., p. 135.

counterparts, by saying words to the effect that "We accept you as brothers and sisters in Christ. Let's pool the gifts our Lord has given us for a more effective witness."[15]

Liberal pastors are encouraged to add evangelicals as staff members,[16] a proposal that recalls the situation in Germany, where ecumenical churches not infrequently have both a liberal and a conservative pastor to satisfy divided constituencies. We are told that ecumenical liberalism "will have to repudiate the notion . . . that the only heresy is orthodoxy,"[17] a verdict that curiously falls short of even Barth's denunciation of modernism as heresy. Evangelicals are criticized for insisting on "*doctrinal* unity in truth" rather than on "experiential unity in the Truth—Jesus Christ himself,"[18] an essentially neoorthodox and nonevangelical contrast that sheds light on the author's theological concessions and his notion that charismatic renewal is a hopeful avenue to unity.[19]

Some of these proposals are so theologically naive that they do more to extend the cleavage between young evangelicals and their evangelical contemporaries than they do to achieve true unity with nonevangelicals. That evangelicals and nonevangelicals may indeed cooperate for many limited objectives is not at all in question, but that they share the same priorities and similarly understand the body of Christ turns on a semantic illusion.

I share many of the young evangelicals' discontents: the failure of evangelicals to exhibit publicly the oneness that presupposes doctrinal unity; the failure of the Evangelical Theological Society to develop its insistence on an inerrant Bible into a bold initiative for evangelical theological positions; the failure of evangelical evangelism to speak effectively to the national conscience on public issues; the failure of evangelical periodicals to rise above editorial generalities about social injustice and to chart alternatives to unjust structures for which evangelicals should strive in stipulated ways. To these disenchantments one could add others, especially the failure of evangelicals to capture the opportunity to establish a great academic center or university of national renown. One can understand also why precipitous youth tends to overreact out of a sense of regret for opportunities lost, for energy consumed in secondary controversy, for neglect of legitimate priorities while many evangelicals major in minors.

15. Ibid., p. 141.
16. Ibid., pp. 145ff.
17. Ibid., p. 146.
18. Ibid., p. 147.
19. Ibid., p. 149.

The young evangelicals seem eager for ecumenical acceptance, and this is in part due to a hard line by evangelical contemporaries devoted to the status quo. Quebedeaux thinks the greater attendance of evangelical seminarians at nonevangelical seminaries might result in a token number of evangelical faculty members and a token reward of evangelical clergy by denomination decision-making offices. If elemental justice has any meaning, however, tokenism ought to be unacceptable to an evangelical majority. The proposal, moreover, that young evangelicals become "subversives" for Christ in their home churches is hardly the best way to inspire confidence or to illumine differences within the local churches. When we are told that "the church, like any other institution, is political" and that it "requires competent and dedicated politicians to bring about needed change,"[20] we need clarification, for a "more fully united and renewed church" is as unlikely to be achieved by evangelical as by nonevangelical politicians and bureaucrats, however important official leadership and decison making may be in the Christian community. The same confusing of the church with religious political structures seems to lurk in the notion that giving proportionate representation to evangelicals "may be the only way to save those ecclesiastical institutions from a slow and painful decline and death."[21] This is a strange notion, indeed, of the salvation Christianity bears. . . .

In conclusion, I think that Quebedeaux's representation of Jesus as a true radical crucified for his revolutionary activity[22] does less than justice to his mission as Redeemer. Moreover, the confidence in "righteous social change that only political action can bring about"[23] may imply too simplistic a view of fallen history, as does also the overriding implication that a radical Christian response to war and injustice requires pacifism and socialism. What is sound in Quebedeaux is the recognition that Christian faith demands a radical commitment to social justice, a commitment that subordinates confidence in any ideology, government, or system to obedience to the Lord Jesus and conforms to what the kingdom of God requires of us at this stage in fallen history. But to say with the *Post-American* magazine that "our faith must be distinctively Post-American"[24]—rather than supra-American—is to venture a final judgment upon the nation that God has not yet uttered. Much as one may recognize the indispensability of new national priorities and goals,

20. Ibid., p. 143.
21. Ibid., p. 146.
22. Ibid., p. 117.
23. Ibid., p. 119.
24. Ibid., p. 120.

the young evangelicals seem excessively judgmental in speaking without qualification about "the continued pervasiveness of militarism in our national life" and about "the manifest hypocrisy of civil religion"; after all, mistakes in Vietnam aside, U.S. power repelled Japanese aggression, toppled Hitler, checked Stalin, and frustrated Khrushchev. Civil religion, moreover, is rather inescapable and can be what we make it.

Establishment evangelicals should consider the challenge posed by the young evangelicals as a summons to reinforce what is good, to debate what is controversial, and to give a biblical reason for disowning the remainder, so that the present opportunity for evangelical awakening may not be lost upon any of us.

Revolt on Evangelical Frontiers:
A Response

Jim Wallis

It was with a deep sense of disappointment that I read Carl F. H. Henry's review essay of Richard Quebedeaux's *Young Evangelicals.* "Revolt on Evangelical Frontiers" was especially disappointing because of the sympathetic stance toward many of us "young evangelicals" previously taken by Carl Henry. My basic argument with the article is that it contains some fundamental distortions and inaccurate caricatures in relation to the young evangelical consciousness that certainly is emerging. After reading Quebedeaux's book, I also am left with the feeling that Henry misrepresented much of its basic thrust; but my primary purpose here is not to defend a book but to clarify some points that could foster division and misunderstanding among evangelicals.

First, Henry implies throughout his essay that the young evangelicals are characterized by a deteriorating view of Scripture. On the contrary, the new evangelical consciousness is most characterized by a return to biblical Christianity and the desire to apply fresh biblical insights to the need for new forms of sociopolitical engagement. Young evangelicals, *just like* "establishment evangelicalism," have differing views as to the meaning and extent of inerrancy and infallibility, but clearly accept the orthodox belief in the authority and inspiration of Scripture. In fact, I would contend that much of this new evangelical consciousness takes

Jim Wallis, "Revolt on Evangelical Frontiers," *Christianity Today* 18 (June 21, 1974): 20–21. Reprinted by permission.

Scripture more seriously than many evangelicals who accept the authority of Scripture doctrinally but balk at some of the more exacting biblical demands in relation to social justice and to their style of life. Quebedeaux states that most young evangelicals affirm "the principle of historical criticism," which is hardly the "acceptance of higher criticism" that Henry charges. The principle of historical criticism in the context of full biblical authority is held by biblical scholars at evangelical seminaries and in the Evangelical Theological Society. The editorial stance of the *Post-American*, one forum for the young evangelical consciousness, has clearly demonstrated (as Henry should know) strong commitment to biblical authority. In the wider contacts made possible by the growing ministries and witness of the young evangelicals, they are clearly upholding and articulating a strong biblical faith. Other evangelicals should feel good about that as it is genuinely an evangelical cause.

Second, Henry's article leaves the reader with the impression that theological blurring and even compromising is implicit in the suggestions Quebedeaux makes for more cooperation between evangelicals and liberals. He quotes Quebedeaux as saying, "If the values and priorities of the young evangelicals and ecumenical liberals are really similar, continued separation serves no purpose . . ." and as suggesting that the young evangelicals could become "an instrument of healing by accepting their ecumenical counterparts" and pooling their resources for more effective witness. Whether Quebedeaux's suggestions are helpful or not, he is clearly speaking of a similarity in social concern and not in theology. Henry omits Quebedeaux's very next sentence which makes the author's primary point: "The young evangelicals thus might find a welcome in ecumenical circles they never dreamed possible, for liberals themselves cannot help being attracted to the dedication and strong biblical-theological foundation for action manifested by these young men and women." Our own ministry has demonstrated this possibility to us. Throughout his book, Quebedeaux expresses the critique of religious liberalism made by young evangelicals: its lack of biblical rootage; its disregard for evangelism; its inability to offer spiritual life and resources in resolution of human problems; its clear lack of Christian foundations and distinctiveness. However, meaningful encounter between evangelicals and liberals is possible through young evangelicals who can shed the cultic and cultural baggage of fundamentalist history, the ethically crippling heresies of dispensationalism, and the unbiblical lack of prophetic social conscience so long characteristic of establishment evangelicalism. The proclamation and demonstration of a more holistic gospel which is addressed to all that binds and oppresses people, spiritually and economically, personally and politically, could well spark renewal and reconciliation among both evangelicals and liberals.

Third, a fundamental difference between the "young evangelicals" and "establishment evangelicalism" running through Henry's article is, I think, a real difference and should be discussed. Primarily, it is a difference in how we view the world and U.S. power in particular. Henry and others are quick to attribute Marxist leanings to young evangelical activists. His bias toward the general acceptability of the present U.S. economic and political system is betrayed along with a rather paranoid and unbalanced view of socialism. Unfortunately, he neglects the fact that many young evangelicals are far more sophisticated in their Christian critique of a thoroughgoing Marxism: in its epistemology and eschatology; in its ethical failures over the question of ends and means; in its inadequate view of the human condition. A fair reading of the views of the young evangelicals reveals their insistence that a Christian's basic allegiance be to the kingdom of God and that all ideologies, systems, and governments stand under the judgment of Jesus Christ and his kingdom.

It is characteristic of establishment evangelicalism to view the structure and exercise of U.S. power in a generally positive way. (This is readily apparent from the last paragraphs of Henry's article.) Most young evangelicals do not feel it is possible to do that and still be faithful to the biblical mandate to seek justice for the poor and oppressed, who experience the consequences of U.S. wealth and power in basically negative ways. While Henry is willing to set "Vietnamese mistakes aside," young evangelicals regard the U.S. role in Indochina as a moral obscenity matched only by official evangelical silence and support for U.S. war policy. While many evangelicals minimize the possibilities for meaningful social change while enjoying the prosperity of the present system, young evangelicals insist that the call to discipleship demands fundamental breaks with the dominant values and life-style of the majority culture and provides the Christian with a different agenda than that of our political economy. Henry's suggestion that civil religion "is rather inescapable and can be what we make it" strikes many young evangelicals as suggesting that we make the best of idolatry. The less than critical identification with the nation by many evangelicals is just not biblically responsible and could only be felt by those who are benefiting from the system instead of being victims of it. Young evangelicals are seeking to recover the meaning of being aliens and exiles who "sing the Lord's song in a strange land."

A biblical protest is being mounted against the brutalities of war and global dominance, a materialistic profit culture, institutionally structured racism and injustice, and government by deceit and manipulation. New movements toward costly discipleship and social justice have been occurring among evangelicals which directly challenge the credibility of those who would still serve as chaplain to the status quo. With the decline of movements for social change present in the 1960s (due to internal inconsistencies, co-optation, and lack of an adequate basis), it is highly probable that the strongest thrusts for prophetic witness and social justice may come from those whose faith is Christ-centered and who hold an unapologetic biblical faith. This can be accomplished if evangelicals of all ages (to put aside Quebedeaux's categories of "young" and "establishment" evangelicals) begin to demonstrate the power of their sound doctrine by the style of life and action it creates in them.

Study Questions

1. After reading Henry's critique of Quebedeaux's *Young Evangelicals*, list and explain Henry's objections to radical thought. From what you have read of Henry's conservative philosophy here and in chapter 2, identify the grounds of Henry's criticism.
2. How does Wallis's response to Henry reveal differences between radical and conservative perspectives with respect to the role of Scripture in social ethics and the moral character of American culture and global responsibilities?

The Evangelical Radical Left Debates
with Evangelical Political Liberals 5

The second dialogue includes essays by radical *Sojourners'* (formerly *Post-American*) editor Jim Wallis and political liberals Isaac Rottenberg, an official with the Reformed Church in America, and Nicholas Wolterstorff, professor of philosophy at Calvin College. A selection from Wallis's *Agenda for Biblical People* begins the debate by summarizing some of the major radical themes. Rottenberg, in "The Shape of the Church's Social-Economic Witness," not only uses a literary scalpel to dissect Wallis's radical philosophy from a politically liberal perspective, but in the process adds some additional planks to the liberal platform. Wallis provides a spirited rejoinder, and Wolterstorff concludes the debate with an attempt to sum up the differences between political radicals and liberals and suggests grounds for future dialogue.

Agenda for Biblical People:
Gospel of a New Order

Jim Wallis

Breaking the Cycle

With us therefore worldly standards have ceased to count in our estimate of any man; . . . When anyone is united to Christ, there is a whole new world; the old order has gone, and a new order has already begun.

Jim Wallis, *Agenda for Biblical People: Gospel of a New Order* (New York: Harper and Row, 1976), pp. 13–18, 103–4. Reprinted by permission.

> From first to last this has been a work of God. He has reconciled us men to himself through Christ, and he has enlisted us in this service of reconciliation. What I mean is, that God was in Christ reconciling the world to himself, no longer holding men's misdeeds against them, and that he has entrusted us with the message of reconciliation. We come therefore as Christ's ambassadors. It is as if God were appealing to you through us: in Christ's name, we implore you, be reconciled to God! (2 Cor. 5:16–21, NEB).

As I was growing up in Middle America, certain things about the nature and structure of the world I knew began to make a deep impression. Becoming involved in the radical student movement, the antiwar struggle, and the movements of the black and poor served to deepen my impressions. During those years, the most powerful fact of reality that continued to confront me was something I would now call the cycle of the world. Beyond the visible devils of racism, poverty, and war, there seemed to be a cycle operating in the world which was inherent in the very structure of things. The world appeared to be dominated by a whole cycle of injustice and violence, of exploitation and manipulation, of profit and power, of self-interest and competition, of hate and fear, of loneliness and brokenness, a cycle whose final meaning seemed to be death itself. This moral cycle of death appeared to be pervasive and seemed to be at the root of the condition of the world.

Like many others, I became involved in social and political movements which were fighting against that cycle of oppression, human suffering, and moral death. However, we were never really able to break that cycle. Mostly, we were only able to protest its existence. In fact, our very lives and, I think, the life of most of our movements came to reflect that cycle and, ultimately, was co-opted by it. Certainly, the major social movements of recent U.S. history have been without adequate foundations to sustain themselves.

The thing that struck me so powerfully about the claim and meaning of the gospel was that, in Jesus Christ, the cycle of death in the world had been broken. The gospel presented in the New Testament is a scandal to the values and standards of the world whose condition is dominated by the cycle of death. While assimilation, complicity, and compromise best describe the modern church's relationship to the world, the gospel is in direct collision with the world system. Talk of realism, respectability, and reasonableness dominates the conversations of contemporary religion, but the New Testament speaks of the abandonment, insecurity, persecution, and exile that come from seeking *first* the kingdom. A church of comfort, property, privilege, and position stands in sharp contrast with the biblical description of the people of God as aliens, exiles, sojourners, strangers, and pilgrims. "If the world hates you, it hated me first, as you know well. If you belonged to the world, the world would love its own; but because you do not belong to the world, because I have chosen you out of the world, for that reason the world hates you" (John 15:18,19, NEB).

The claim of the New Testament writers is that the power of the cycle of the world that holds men, women, and institutions so captive has been decisively broken by the cross and resurrection of Jesus Christ. The absolute authority and dominion of the destructive forces and structures of the world has been ended by the inauguration of a whole new order in human affairs called the kingdom of God, according to the New Testament evangelists. The gospel calls for radical allegiance to a kingdom that is at fundamental variance with the "principalities and powers" which rule the world system. The standards and values of the world undergo a transvaluation, a reversal, an inversion in Jesus Christ. A commitment to Christ entails a radical change in our relationship to money and possessions, violence and war, power, status, success, leadership, ideology, and the state. Our relationship to Christ gives us a new relationship to persons and especially to the poor, the weak, the broken, the outcasts, the "enemies," and the victims of the various systems of the world. In his Nazareth inaugural, Jesus speaks of those who are so central to the meaning of his coming:

> The Spirit of the Lord is upon me,
> Because he anointed me to preach the gospel to the poor.
> He has sent me to proclaim release to the captives,
> And recovery of sight to the blind,
> To set free those who are downtrodden,
> To proclaim the favorable year of the Lord.
> (Luke 4:18–19, NASB)

In this kingdom, whoever would save his life will lose it; the last are first and the first are last; and whoever would be great must become the servant of all, which is the principal sign of the kingdom.

The proclamation of the New Testament is the gospel of the kingdom, a gospel of a "new order," a "new creation," a "new world," a "new age," as it is variously referred to by the biblical writers. Jesus proclaims that a new age has come and calls us to be free of former allegiances, attachments, securities, and assumptions in the present age, to break from our bondage to the standards of the world that are passing away. Clearly, the New Testament evangel is something much more than a gospel of individual salvation and personal fulfillment. The evangel is something much more than a gospel of social action. It is even more than an attempted synthesis which combines a personal gospel with social reform. In fact, the meaning of the gospel that dominates the New Testament is not usually the same as the meaning of the various gospels that dominate the evangelism and preaching of our churches. The gospel of the kingdom is the central message of the New Testament. The inauguration of a whole new order in Jesus Christ and the establishing of a new peoplehood whose common life bears witness to that new order in history is what the New Testament message seems to be all about. The proclamation is not a personal gospel, not a social gospel, not even a gospel of "both," but rather the gospel of a new order and a new people. The evangel is not merely a set of principles, ethics, and moral teachings. It is about a Person and the meaning of his coming. . . .

The New Testament sees the Christian community as the place where, first of all in its own shared common life, the cycle of the world begins to be broken. By rendering impotent the power of those things which oppress and divide people, the facts of race, class, and sex, the Christian community demonstrates the victory of Christ who has "broken down the walls" and "put to death the enmity" between people (Eph. 2). "There is neither Jew nor Greek, there is neither slave nor freeman, there is neither male nor female; for you are all one in Christ Jesus" (Gal. 3:28, NASB). By showing the irrelevance of the oppressive and divisive factors of the world, the Christian community begins to be witness to the breaking of the cycle of death. By the quality of their new style of life, by their active presence in the world, the Christian community can show that the cycle of death in the world need no longer have dominion over us, that new possibilities of human life and society emerge as we give our lives over to Christ and his kingdom.

The possibility of breaking the cycle of death in the world and ending its dominion in people's lives is something I did not see in the other ideological and philosophical options in my experience. However, the victory of Christ must be concretely demonstrated by the Christian community in history. A church that is merely perpetuating the cycle of death in the world and is a mere reflection of it has lost its identity. A church that is living in support of the cycle of the world system is disobedient and fails to comprehend the meaning of the death and resurrection of Christ. When the church takes its values and standards from its culture and society, when it takes its authority from Caesar and the various powers of the world, the victory of Christ is blasphemed because the life of the church has become conformed to the very things for which Christ was crucified. A church whose life is lived in complicity and conformity to the world and its cycle of death again nails Jesus Christ to the cross.

Our most persistent problem is that we try to make the claims of Christ negotiable with the claims and demands of the world. The New Testament seems to say rather clearly that, for those who would be disciples, the claims of Christ are nonnegotiable. The principal way the world system seeks to overcome the church is by trying to squeeze the church into its own mold, to reduce the church to conformity. Therefore, the church must resist the constant temptation to reduce the claims of Christ, soften the demands of the gospel, ease the tension between the church and the world, and allow the ever-radical message to be squeezed into more comfortable and congenial forms and styles. If we truly believe that Jesus Christ has broken the authority and dominion of the corporate and personal powers of death in the world, then the life of the church in the world must demonstrate some signs and indications of that victory. The community of believers must expect to find themselves at variance with the social consensus, the political conformity, and the popular wisdom of their society, for they are witnesses to a whole new order. . . .

The making of community is essentially a revolutionary act. It is revolutionary because it proposes to detach men and women from their dependence upon the dominant institutions, powers, and idolatries of the world system and creates an alternative corporate reality based upon deviant social values, which challenges the hold of the world system over the lives of people. The most politically responsible undertaking for men and women of faith is to rebuild the church which, when biblically understood, is a spiritual task that creates a revolutionary situation. Repentance and redirection are possible for people only when they are presented with an alternative. It is crucial that we not merely speak of alternatives but, rather, begin to live and be those alternatives. Most importantly, the church is to be a sign of Christ's presence in the world rather than an ecclesiastical reproduction of the twisted values of a technocratic society. The church's life must show practical and demonstrative manifestations of the meaning of Christ that a broken world cannot fail to recognize.

Our time is one of large-scale and concentrated power, of giant corporate institutions whose influence is nearly all persuasive. We have grown to depend upon large corporations and state bureaucracies for our basic needs and, to a frightening extent, have allowed these institutions to decide for us how we will live. In many ways, their values have become our own. Large institutions of concentrated power and influence consciously seek to bring people's lives into conformity with their will and purposes. Large-scale technology, huge amounts of private capital, and a growing economic and political centralization place tremendous power in the hands of a few people. Most of our decisions are made for us by the institutions to whose presence and authority we have all become so accustomed. Power elites, whether they be directors of corporate capitalism or of central state bureaucracies, act to control and dominate, removing the decision-making process from the people who are affected by the decisions. The predominance of these giant institutions is unprecedented and is supreme in production, distribution, and control of the economic process, in the political arena of both domestic and foreign public policy, in information, advertising, and the mass media, in education and cultural activities, in labor and the various professions, in the legal and judicial process, in religion. The population has forfeited decision making to the all-powerful institutions in exchange for a "prepackaged" life of comfort, security, convenience. The public has become consumed with "needs" created by the controlling institutions and then fulfilled in ways to make the population into a dependent, servile, and docile mass society.

These economic and political structures that dominate the world suppress masses of humanity while they keep the rest in mindless conformity. They hurt and destroy more people than the worst of wars and do it all in the name of business as usual, through the natural, regular, and legal operations of the systems of the world. These structures have one primary aim: their own self-interest and perpetuation. Human costs and considerations have little or no place in the decisions made by the ruling principalities and powers.

These dominant institutions control not only socioeconomic and political systems but also shape cultural patterns and engineer the very personal values of the population. This is because the vast majority of the people depends upon them for their very livelihood and security and cannot afford to fall out of favor with them. These institutions have developed sophisticated and intimidating methods of reward, punishment, and threat that can easily be enforced. In such a situation, the values and priorities of the institutions become the values and priorities of the people. . . .

The task of the Christian revolution is not only to change and reform the economic and political facts and form of the world, but to seek fundamental change in the very framework and structure of a world system that needs to be continually examined and tested by the judgment of the Word of God. Such an undertaking will often result in profound political and economic changes but is essentially a more pervasive and perpetual mission .than the effecting of a series of social changes. All of these social changes will be temporary and limited in scope and, while they are important, are never to be thought to satisfy the more absolute demands of the kingdom. The Christian community can never be satisfied with social achievements and progress and must continue to assert the claim of God upon the world and the ultimate will of God that righteousness, peace, and justice prevail in human affairs. In a world that always tends toward injustice and disorder, the Christian community will be an unceasing agent of change, a continual center of questioning, dissent, and opposition to the idolatries of the established order, a perpetual advocate of human life in the midst of a world still dominated by death. In so doing, the Christian community becomes an inexhaustible revolutionary force in the life of the world, never content to conform to history, prepared only to give its ultimate allegiance to the kingdom of God which is coming and is made a present reality by the faithfulness and obedience of the people of God.

The Shape of the Church's Social-Economic Witness

Isaac C. Rottenberg

In seeking to formulate my own position on Christian witness in the social-economic sphere, I have not found the capitalism-versus-socialism framework very fruitful. To begin with, those using it often fail to define their terms and blur distinctions in what they say and write. Economic orders are described, not as the constantly evolving realities they actually are, but as systems once delivered to the saints. While simplistic schemes are convenient for either/or approaches to complex problems, the results they yield tend to bear greater resemblance to propaganda than to prophetic witness. . . .

For many of us who have been looking for a "third way" in Christian

Isaac C. Rottenberg, "The Shape of the Church's Social-Economic Witness," *Reformed Journal* 27 (May 1977): 16–19. Reprinted by permission.

social witness, the emergence of the radical-evangelical movement on the American scene meant that a fresh new voice had entered the rather stale debate between "conservatives" and "liberals." I still believe that this is so. In recent months, however, the writings of people associated with *Sojourners* have given me the increasing impression that they find their common commitment in a biblical radicalism that has a close affinity with the historical position of the Radical Reformation. As a result, rather than providing a "home" for a broad spectrum of biblical radicals, they tend to revive some of the major disputes of the Reformation era.

The Chicago Declaration of Evangelical Social Concern, significant as its publication undoubtedly was, must still be considered a lowest-common-denominator document in which evangelicals of different stripes affirmed that matters of justice are indeed gospel concerns and confessed past failures to be true to that dimension of the Christian faith.

A very different sound is being heard in radical evangelical papers like *Sojourners*. These writers are not content with merely calling attention to injustice; they call it by its manifold names, attack it in the name of the gospel of the kingdom, and advocate alternative approaches to social-economic issues. In the following paragraphs, I shall be mainly concerned with what I see as a major thrust in *Sojourners*, particularly as it relates to the question of the relationship between the church and the world.

For most of the evangelicals to whom I am referring, a choice between capitalism and socialism is like a choice between two sets of idols. They oppose what they see as an ideological captivity in both the left and the right, believing that "establishment Christianity," that great sanctifier of the status quo, is the real enemy. To these evangelicals, the distinctions between the "conservative" and "liberal" factions in most denominations are far less important than their common tendency to accommodate themselves to the various agendas of the predominant culture.

These evangelicals take their starting-point in the shape of the church. The renewal, yes, the rebuilding of the church is the great priority item on their agenda. The church is called to be the manifestation of the very presence of the kingdom, a demonstration of the new creation in the midst of the present world order. In the development of this vision of the church, very strong emphasis is placed on Christian community and commitment. The building of Christian community among those who have consciously adopted a new life-style is seen as a genuinely revolutionary act. The rebuilding of the church is portrayed as the most politically responsible act men and women of faith can undertake.

But, does not this strong preoccupation with the shape of the church imply a withdrawal from the pressing social-political and economic issues that confront the world? Radical evangelicals do not see it that way. Rather, they see themselves deeply involved in the world, but *in the form of being a countersign* to the cultural values of the day.

Christian community, they say, will be an alternative form of corporate power in a world where corporate power so often assumes demonic dimensions. In the context of this community new forms of interpersonal relationships are to be expressed and nurtured, constituting by their very nature a challenge to the manipulative arrangements that commonly prevail in our society. The practice of a "Pentecostal economics" (a term referring to the account in Acts 2, where the sharing of all possessions among the early Christians in Jerusalem is described) is seen as a powerful witness in the social-economic sphere. Thus, the church as a countersign will be the visible manifestation of a new order challenging the values and assumptions of American society. As such it will be able to serve the world as an agent of change.

Jim Wallis has given a comprehensive account of this position in his recent book, *Agenda for Biblical People*. There is much in this book that I accept as a true reflection of the biblical vision and as relevant to our present cultural situation. Take, for example, the emphasis on new forms of community. In an era like ours, when a massive process of bureaucratization both in the corporate capitalism of so-called free economies and the state capitalism of socialist societies has an erosive effect on human relationships, the development of genuinely Christian community is, I agree, a radical act with potentially profound social-political implications.

However, when the theme of the church as countersign is developed in such a way that the relationship of the new order of the kingdom to the existing social order is seen almost exclusively in terms of "over-againstness," dissent, resistance, and scandal, my Reformed heritage causes me to hesitate and to ask some critical questions. To me, the gospel of the kingdom calls for more than a counterculture movement; it also proclaims the possibility of social transformation.

The radical evangelical stance of "over-againstness" becomes particularly pronounced in their attitude toward the state, which in Wallis's book is described as "the great seducer, the great captor and destroyer of life"[1]. The Beast of Revelation 13 emerges as the dominant image; the

---

1. Jim Wallis, *Agenda for Biblical People* (New York: Harper and Row, 1976), p. 72.

"servant of God" of Romans 13 becomes an almost illusory notion that is not to be taken very seriously in the present dispensation.

William Stringfellow wrote in the September 1976 issue of *Sojourners* that

> the exemplification of redeemed humanity in the lordship of Jesus Christ in this age means a resilient and tireless witness to confound, rebuke and undo every regime, and every potential regime, until the moment when humankind is accounted over the nations, ideologies and other principalities in the last judgment of the Word of God.[2]

I can understand how people who were deeply involved in the anti-Vietnam War protest movement could reach such a position, but in the end, it seems to me, it is another example of a truncated gospel.

While the radical evangelicals have been expressing serious reservations about "the Calvinists," some of us who consider ourselves part of a broad Reformed tradition and who have welcomed the new evangelical witness as a liberating voice, have begun to wonder as well. Will a movement which consciously adopts such a narrow base develop into a new kind of fundamentalism? Will a narrow view of orthopraxis replace the rigid orthodoxy of a past era? To use H. Richard Niebuhr's typology of Christian social vision, we are dealing here in essence with a "Christ against culture" position, which Niebuhr has called "necessary but inadequate" vis-à-vis the "conversionist" view, which confesses Christ as the transformer of culture.

John Calvin is probably most widely known for his theocratic ideas, although the implications of his basic perspective on the relationship of the church and state are rarely understood in their various nuances. It is less well known that Calvin has frequently been referred to as "the theologian of the Holy Spirit." To many people today—who have been taught to think of the Spirit in almost exclusively personalistic terms, or at most as the source of Christian community—these two designations will seem to be contradictory. Calvin, however, thought of the Spirit in historical terms.

In Calvin's theology, Christ the risen Lord rules *spirituali modo*, in the manner and the power of the Holy Spirit. In Jim Wallis's *Agenda for Biblical People*, the focus is almost exclusively on the implications of the cross for historical existence. Hence the strong emphasis on conflict, revolt, and alienation. Little is said about the implications of the lordship of the risen Christ, not only for the Christian community of the

2. William Stringfellow, "The Bible and Ideology," *Sojourners* 5 (September 1976): 7.

committed, but for culture as well. This omission reflects a profound skepticism about the possibility of signs of the kingdom in the social-political and economic realms.

Radical evangelicals warn repeatedly against underestimating the principalities and powers of this world. The Reformed tradition has shown little inclination to hold romantic illusions about human nature. It has, however, affirmed great confidence in the power of the Word and the Spirit. When the Word of God is truly proclaimed, something happens *spirituali modo*, not only in individual hearts and not only in believing communities, but in the world. Somehow signs of the kingdom are established in the social-political order, which represents a very relative, a very fragmentary, but nevertheless a very real and very important sanctification of public life. A new law, providing a little more justice for the oppressed, is as essential a part of the gospel of the kingdom as a reborn heart. Both are a sign and a foretaste of the promised re-creation of all things.

In the proclamation of the gospel of the kingdom, the church goes public, and that is an event of world-historical significance. It prays for "kings and all those in authority" (1 Tim. 2:2), realizing that their task is superhuman. It also addresses the message of revelation to all authorities, all principalities and powers, realizing that in the final analysis a government cannot live by its natural revelations alone. Just when we think that we have the state nicely humanized, it is bound to reveal itself in its demonic nature as the apotheosis of naked power.

The heart of the political apostolate in the Reformed tradition lies not in the "rule of the saints," a practice that is all too easily accorded idolatrous sanctity, but in the proclamation of the Word to the governing authorities. A world constantly threatened by political idolatries is desperately in need of such a ministry.

We do not underestimate the rebelliousness of the powers. Proclaiming the Word is risky business, whether it be to an individual, a people, or a state. There never is a guarantee of receptiveness or glorious results. But the gospel of the kingdom, more than anything else, can undemonize the state with its totalitarian pretensions and demythologize its claims to autonomy. It can also undemonize the so-called "economic realities" and demythologize the "laws" of economic life.

When we in the Christian community become preoccupied with spiritual realities that are so deep, so inward, so intense, and so intimate, we are inclined to smile a bit sadly at what I earlier called a very relative and fragmentary sanctification of public life. It all seems so superficial.

But have we still not learned from the horrors of recent European history what happens when the forces just below the surface break through with all their nihilistic power? It is simply not true that the gospel of the kingdom is interested only in the depth of things.

When we talk about the signs of the kingdom in the midst of the world, we talk about "firstfruits," not the harvest. Rather, these signs are a foretaste of the future which increases our hunger and thirst for the promised new order. A greater measure of justice in a political and economic order does not mean that the kingdom of God has been established. But it does mean that the power of the kingdom is being manifested. And for those who look at history from the perspective of the biblical prophetic vision, it is precisely such signs that give the faith, hope, and love to speak out, and to address all the principalities and powers in the world with the Word.

What Does Washington Have to Say to Grand Rapids?

Jim Wallis

A rather persistent pattern of criticism has emerged against *Sojourners* from a group of people suggesting that our commitment to the building of community signals a withdrawal from the world, that we are more concerned with an "alternative life-style" than with social justice, and that we are apolitical, or not political enough, or at least not political in the right ways. The explanation which is being offered for these manifold errors is that the Sojourners have become Anabaptists, and of course everyone knows how wrong the Anabaptists were.

The bulk of such criticism has come from a group of Reformed theologians and academics, most of whom are contributors to the *Reformed Journal* of Grand Rapids, Michigan. The *Journal* has regularly warned of the growing influence of the Anabaptist tradition among younger evangelicals, and has especially gone on the offensive against the work of John Howard Yoder, whose *Politics of Jesus* has gained a wide and sympathetic hearing.

Jim Wallis, "What Does Washington Have to Say to Grand Rapids?" *Sojourners* 6 (July 1977): 3–4. Reprinted by permission.

It is not my task here to evaluate or defend either the contributions of my friend John Yoder or the Anabaptist tradition more generally. It is enough to say that the witness and courage of the Radical Reformation of the sixteenth century is one of the traditions of the church in which we at *Sojourners* have found clarity, nurture, and inspiration. The Anabaptist story shows us a radical faithfulness to the point of suffering and a community whose obedience to the gospel of the kingdom turned them into a servant people willing to accept a minority status in the world. Theirs is a story (much more than a theological system) that, like many other similar stories in other theological traditions, stands in stark contrast to the realities of congregational life in most of our churches today, including, unfortunately, most of those churches who are the heirs of Anabaptists.

My concern, however, is not to discuss the strengths and weaknesses of the Anabaptist tradition. Rather, it is to raise some serious questions about the criticism that is coming from Grand Rapids these days.

In recent issues of the *Reformed Journal*, John Howard Yoder, Mark Hatfield, *Sojourners*, and myself have all been taken to task. In several articles as well as in the editorial pages, a rather clear message seems to be coming through. Those who are singled out for criticism are guilty of not being politically responsible, which is extended to mean not being really political, or at least not being political in the way Christians ought to be.

For example, in Isaac Rottenberg's recent article in the May 1977 issue entitled "The Shape of the Churches' Social-Economic Witness," he accused *Sojourners* of a communal withdrawal from the world, preoccupation with personal life-style over political action, and a lack of concern or engagement with questions of public policy because of an overly negative view of the state. Rottenberg charges that the biblical vision is "removed from the scene of political realities . . . when we limit the impact of the gospel to a small community of committed people who practice the disciplines of 'Pentecostal Economics.'" I have continually wondered, often in bewilderment, why such things are said. The whole thrust of such arguments is full of caricature and charges that are simply untrue.

Can anyone read the pages of *Sojourners* magazine and say that we have removed the biblical vision from the scene of social, political, and economic realities? Can anyone seriously examine our editorial coverage and find a lack of concern over matters of public policy? Copies of *Sojourners* are finding their way into congressional offices, the State Department, and even into the White House. Increasingly, *Sojourners'* treatment of public policy issues is picked up by the national press. Last week, the president of the South Korean embassy's information office, in a personal meeting, tried to convince me to change our editorial criticism of U.S. support for his dictatorial regime. Such responses would hardly indicate that *Sojourners* is committed to a communal existence withdrawn from the world.

This year alone, Sojourners fellowship has engaged in or initiated over forty public actions around such issues as torture and the denial of human rights in U.S.-supported dictatorships, the proliferation of nuclear armaments and power, and the District of Columbia government's repressive housing policies which displace the poor in Washington's inner city. In all these campaigns and actions a number of methods have been employed, including public education, political organizing, petition, personal dialogue and relationship with officials, support for legislative initiatives in Congress, and civil disobedience.

The location of our community in the inner city and the ministries and services that have grown up out of just being where we are have a very clear political meaning. So do the ways we are being changed and stretched because of our growing relationship with the poor in the city. The essential political character of following Jesus and of living together as the body of Christ in the world has been basic to our self-understanding since the beginning of our community.[3]

Why is it then that *Sojourners* is accused of being apolitical when it seems evident that we are and have always been deeply political, as John Howard Yoder and Mark Hatfield are, each in their own way? It seems to me the problem is not that we are not political, but that we are not political in the same way that our Reformed critics are—and the way they think Christians ought to be.

Their own stance, as I read it, is one of moderate to liberal reform of existing structures, using a "realistic" approach which accepts the fundamental values and the basic framework of the American system of economics and politics. Thus, beneath all the doctrinal assertions, what one finds is a theological version of traditional Western liberalism. That perspective is neither new nor unique, nor more biblical than other alternatives. In other words, a central part of the disagreement is that *Sojourners* and Grand Rapids have a different theological understanding of what biblical politics ought to be as well as a very different analysis of present historical problems and what needs to be done about them.

3. The political character of discipleship in community is well described by Juan Mateos in this issue, in his article "The Message of Jesus."

A persistent theme in the many criticisms of radical Christians is that we have "an overly negative view of the state." Isaac Rottenberg joins others in objecting to Christian witness "in the form of being a counter-sign to the cultural values of the day." That, he feels, inevitably leads one to a stance of "over-againstness, dissent, resistance, and scandal," in relationship to the existing social order. He confesses that his Reformed heritage makes him uncomfortable with that stance.

But again, one could respond that most Reformed critics have an overly positive view of the state, one that is far too uncritical on both theological and historical grounds. It certainly has been my observation that there seems to be a basic conservatism and accommodation to the state in the present thinking and practice of the Reformed theoreticians which seems also to be historically characteristic of Calvinist political theory.

A recent editorial in the *Reformed Journal*, for example, criticized *Sojourners* for urging Christians to consider resisting the payment of taxes used for an escalating arms race, and took issue with Senator Mark Hatfield's proposal for the World Peace Tax Fund in the Congress. This proposal would give Christians and others the right to object to the use of their taxes for war purposes, diverting them instead to more peaceful pursuits in much the same way that persons now have the right to conscientiously object to participation in the military. The editorial objected to these approaches on the grounds that they reflect a basically negative view of the state as an institution and would produce socially undesirable consequences like "fiscal chaos." This is not the first time that the Reformed position has defended the state against the expression of conscience by other Christians.

It could easily be said that it is the Calvinist position that is politically irresponsible—in failing to accept the political example and style of Jesus.

However, would it not be better to cease accusing one another of not being really political or really responsible? Would it not be better to recognize that all Christians are very political, consciously or not? Would it not be better to honestly identify the real differences of opinion among us and begin a more open and fruitful dialogue that might aid us all in discerning the shape of biblical politics?

We were never accused by anyone of political withdrawal *until* we began to speak of the crucial need for the rebuilding of the church, for finding a deeper experience in worship, for committing ourselves to the creation of a pastoral life which can undergird a genuinely prophetic presence and action in the world. It is our belief, more deeply than ever before, that authentic political existence requires an authentic personal and communal existence.

Unless our sense of peoplehood is strong, unless the life we share as the body of Christ is rich and flowing, unless the gifts and presence of God's Holy Spirit are visibly evident among us—unless all of these things are true in our experience and not only in our theology, we can never hope to understand the meaning of biblical politics. This is why the building of community is a revolutionary task at the same time that it is a pastoral task. That is why we say that the rebuilding of the church is the single most politically responsible act men and women of faith can undertake.

This is why the question like the one Issac Rottenberg asked in his article is so important: "Does not this strong preoccupation with the shape of the church imply withdrawal from the pressing social, political, and economic issues that confront the world?" The answer must always be no! What is so disconcerting about the present state of theology and the life of the church is that such a question even needs to be asked. It is the very preoccupation with the shape of the common life of the people of God that most enables us to answer the daily questions we must confront of how the Word of God might be proclaimed and incarnated in the midst of the politics of our own age.

How Does Grand Rapids Reply to Washington?

Nicholas P. Wolterstorff

The July 1977 issue of *Sojourners* contained a pained editorial addressed, in effect, to the *Reformed Journal*. As one of the editors of the *Journal*—though not as an official spokesman on behalf of the *Journal*—I should like to respond, and to do so in such a way that bonds of Christian fellowship are restored or strengthened and the possibility of open discussion is advanced. . . .

The immediate occasion for much of the grievance of Jim Wallis, who wrote the *Sojourners* editorial, was an article by Isaac Rottenberg, "The

Nicholas P. Wolterstorff, "How Does Grand Rapids Reply to Washington?" *Reformed Journal* 27 (October 1977): 10–14. Reprinted by permission.

Shape of the Church's Social-Economic Witness"[4]. In this case I think the grievance is misplaced. For I do not think it at all accurate to say, as does Wallis, that Rottenberg "accused *Sojourners* of a communal withdrawal from the world, preoccupation with personal life-style over political actions, and a lack of concern or engagement with questions of public policy because of an overly negative view of the state." In fact it seemed to me that Rottenberg cautiously refrained from any such sweeping accusations while at the same time expressing certain of his own misgivings. But Rottenberg can no doubt defend himself better than I can; and he is of course welcome to do so in these pages.

It has in fact sometimes been said, whether in these pages or elsewhere, that *Sojourners* is apolitical. In my judgment that charge is false. I have never felt confident that I understand what those who make this charge have in mind. Perhaps they mean that *Sojourners* ignores the American state—but that is patently false. Perhaps they mean that *Sojourners* is content to act prophetically toward the American state, pronouncing a word of judgment on it and showing in its own community a better way, of which they hope the state will take some notice. Certainly that is not consistently true of *Sojourners*. Or perhaps what is meant is that *Sojourners* is against anyone's entering the legislative/administrative/judicial process of the American state. That, too, is false. So there seems to be no substance whatever in the charge that *Sojourners* is apolitical.

Equally it is false to suggest that concern with the building of Christian community signals withdrawal from the world, though the two have sometimes gone together. My deep conviction is that God's people must not just wait for the new life in Christ until we "get to heaven" but that here already we must *give evidence* of that new life, not only promised but also brought about by Christ's resurrection. And part of that new life is a new community, though of course there are differing understandings of the form that community should take. The church is irresponsible when it is unconcerned over the building of community. But at the same time that it gives evidence of the new life, the church must *bear witness* before the world to God's action in history and his call for repentance; and it must *be an agent* in the world on behalf of God in his work of renewing human existence. The formation of an evidentiary community does not conflict with but supports these works of bearing witness and being an agent.

4. Isaac Rottenberg, "The Shape of the Church's Social-Economic Witness," *Reformed Journal* 27 (May 1977): 16–21.

So on all the issues cited by Wallis I am on the side of *Sojourners.* Yet on quite a few occasions I find myself disagreeing with what I take them to be saying. I confess that I find these disagreements strangely troubling, for I do not understand their roots. I do not understand why our emphases often, and our views sometimes, turn out so different. Sometimes I think I have gotten hold of the essence of our differences, and then everything just slips away.

I think it is in general important to be aware that classical lines of Christian thought continue on into the twentieth century—Lutheran, Reformed, Anglican, Anabaptist, Orthodox, and so forth. For often illumination is gained by placing contemporary Christian thinkers within the classical lines which have most influenced them. Now it seems to me indisputable that the *Journal* is more in the Reformed tradition than is *Sojourners*, and that *Sojourners* is more in the Anabaptist tradition than is the *Journal.* Yet caricature will result if we think of *Sojourners* as just a contemporary version of sixteenth-century Anabaptism or the *Journal* as just a contemporary version of sixteenth-century Calvinism.

In one way we have all become Anabaptist, more or less. The sixteenth-century Anabaptists urged the abolition of a *sacral* society, society in which the state gave legal preference to one particular religion or to one particular denomination within a particular religion. That heritage of Anabaptism is the policy we all today embrace, and which on many occasions I have defended. Indeed, I have repeatedly argued for a more consistent application than is usual of this repudiation of the sacral society. For example, the monopoly of the American public school system is a powerful vestige of the sacral society. I think that this monopoly must be broken, and the oppression that it produces relieved. I find it strange that *Sojourners* is so silent on this particular form of massive oppression in American society. My main point can be put the other way round: None of us today is a Constantinian. None of us today thinks that the state should be a Christian commonwealth which is an earthly reflection of the heavenly commonwealth, with the chief magistrate engaging in the divine rituals of statecraft.

In other ways, though, *Sojourners* is not at all Anabaptist in the manner of the sixteenth century, and neither am I. I do not hear them saying that the state is merely God's gift to the unbeliever, nor do I hear them urging Mark Hatfield to get out of operative politics forthwith.

In short, even if the Reformed and Anabaptist traditions on the relation of the Christian citizen to the state had the consistency we'd like to think they had, we cannot simply identify our disagreements as those of

Anabaptist and Reformed. That may help as an initial placement. But from then on we must just listen closely and patiently to each other.

Incidentally, Wallis says that "the witness and courage of the Radical Reformation of the sixteenth century is one of the traditions of the church in which we at *Sojourners* have found clarity, nurture, and inspiration." I too find the history of the Anabaptists a moving example of fidelity under terrible suffering, wreaked on them by their fellow Christians. But may I ask: Are those at *Sojourners* similarly inspired by Calvin's attempt at Geneva to establish a society of economic and political equity?

So what accounts for our disagreements?

First, perhaps we have different views of the place of the state in God's order. I read Paul in the opening eight verses of Romans 13 as saying that civil authority is instituted in human affairs by God. What I take that to mean is something like this: To have authority over someone in some domain is to have the right to ask obedience of that person in that domain, and for that person then to be obliged to render that obedience. Consequently, to say that civil authority is instituted or ordained by God is to say that the magistrate can legitimately ask obedience and that in his legitimately asking obedience, *God* is asking obedience. Conversely, to obey the magistrate is to obey God. In verse 5, for example, Paul says that "one must be subject, not only to avoid God's wrath, but also for the sake of conscience." Thus obedience is not just a matter of ultimate prudence, but of *right*. And so it is that Paul speaks of civil authority in verse 4 as "God's deacon," and in verse 6 as "God's liturgete."

This is of course an awesome view of civil authority that Paul teaches. But in fact I think it is the biblical view of authority in general: human beings genuinely have authority over other people with respect to specific domains of action; and to obey them when they legitimately request obedience is to obey God. That is as true for parents and teachers and pastors as it is for civil authorities.

At the same time, it must be said at once and emphatically that it does not follow from this that every parent must always be obeyed, nor every preacher, nor every teacher, nor every magistrate. There are times when disobedience is not only allowed but demanded. But just because a given pastor may become a wolf in sheep's clothing we must not be led to water down our understanding of the authority in the position (not the person) of the pastor.

Could it be that our disagreements are located in the fact that those at *Sojourners* do not accept what Paul says here, or interpret it differently?

Second, it could be that different views of the church are at stake. My impression is that those at *Sojourners* would say, without qualification, that the church is the community of the explicitly committed ones. If so, they are in this respect faithful to the Anabaptist tradition. No one alert to and sympathetic with the nuances of the Reformed tradition would ever be content with this. There, two concepts of the church are equally at work—the church as the community of the explicitly committed ones, and the church as the community of the baptized ones. How those two concepts are to be fitted together into a unified doctrine of the church has always been a difficult and complicated matter, involving large issues such as the nature of baptism, and even more generally, the nature of God's action in history and the relation of that action to natural groupings such as the family. Obviously one's view as to the nature of the community which we should be working to create will be influenced by one's views on the nature of the church.

Third, maybe our disagreements are rooted in the differing roles we assign to the doctrine of creation. This doctrine enters massively into the thought of the Reformed tradition; it seems scarcely at all to enter into the thought of those at *Sojourners*. Theirs seems to me to be almost exclusively a christological pattern of thought and within that context to concentrate on the incarnation and the crucifixion and scarcely at all on the significance of Christ's resurrection. (This last is a point made by Rottenberg, who favors taking the significance of the resurrection with more seriousness. The debate between him and *Sojourners* looks for all the world like an intra-Barthian dispute!)

That is why the *imitatio Christi* becomes so centrally important for *Sojourners*. In his editorial, for example, Wallis says that "it could as easily be said that it is the Calvinist position that is politically irresponsible—in failing to accept the political example and style of Jesus." Now of course the imitation of Christ is a dominant theme in the New Testament epistles, and it should be that too in the life and thought of Christians. Yet I see no way of understanding the comprehensive significance of Jesus Christ except to see in him God working effectively for the renewal of his creation. Creation is the context for redemption; the renewal of creation the purpose of redemption. And then the fact that Jesus never ran for political office does not become an objection to running for political office, any more than the fact that he never heard a piano concerto becomes an objection to listening to piano concertos. Christ's body is truly and genuinely to *carry forward* his work, not to confine itself to literal imitation.

Fourth, our disagreements may be less theological. Perhaps we only disagree over the extent to which Christians should confine their political action to prophetic witness, as opposed to engaging in considerations of strategic effectiveness. In my view both are necessary. One must pronounce God's word of judgment on the rebelliousness and sordidness of political activity while, in the church, giving evidence of what the new life is like. But at the same time one must do what one can to alleviate the suffering, injustice, and oppression caused by political regimes. One must engage in ameliorative politics, and to do so one must calculate what would bring success. How can one seriously preach judgment to the oppressors and not do what one can to relieve the oppressed? The fact that the politics of earth is not the harmony of heaven renders neither irrelevant nor illegitimate our engagement in that politics.

Perhaps we disagree on this. Speaking of the *Journal,* Wallis says "their own stance . . . is one of moderate to liberal reform of existing structures, using a 'realistic' approach which accepts the fundamental values and the basic framework of the American system of economics and politics. Thus, beneath all the doctrinal assertions, what one finds is the theological version of traditional western liberalism." Apparently, then, Wallis is against a "realistic" approach, one concerned with questions of strategic effectiveness. But the argument that he alludes to seems to me to exhibit a crucial confusion. In doing what one can, within the structures of American politics and economics, to relieve the suffering and injustice which those structures cause, while at the same time doing what one can do to change components in the overall structure, one is emphatically not necessarily accepting that total structure and the values which created it. Short of revolution, there is nothing else to do than work within the structures at some point, while changing them at others. From the fact that the *Journal* consistently advocates that Christians be engaged in politics it does not follow at all that we accept the structure of American politics and economics as fundamentally right.

The *Sojourners* community, living as it does in Washington, D.C., likewise makes all its decisions within the basic framework of American society, using the American system of communications, the American system of food production and distribution, the American systems of transportation, and so forth. That does not entail that they *accept* all those structures, or regard them all as basically the way things should be, needing only a bit of tinkering here and there. Not at all. To work within a structure to alleviate the evils it causes and to change it wherever one can for the better is not to accept that structure as fundamentally good.

Thus *Sojourners*, too, if it does not advocate total revolution, is working along with the rest of us at ameliorative politics within the embracing structure of our society. Since the 1960s the phrase *radical politics* has carried a wondrous rhetorical wallop. But it obscures realities, and in my view is best discarded. Between so-called "radical" politics and other forms of nonrevolutionary politics there is not a chasm but a gradation.

Finally, maybe we differ over our assessment of that particular state which is the American state. Maybe *Sojourners* regards it as more curse than blessing in the world, and almost totally resistant to change besides. I, by contrast, see it as very much a mixture of blessing and curse, while at the same time neither despairing of its being changed for the better, nor regarding it as appropriate to "give up" even when change does not seem likely. . . .

Study Questions

1. What does Wallis mean by the claim in *Agenda for Biblical People* that the proclamation of the kingdom of God "is not a personal gospel, not a social gospel, not even a gospel of 'both,' but rather the gospel of a new order and a new people"? How does this view of the gospel shape Wallis's understanding of the church and his strategy of social change?
2. Based on your reading of the *Agenda*, where do you think Wallis locates the source of moral evil in society? How does Wallis's view differ from Henry's argument that social change requires the spiritual regeneration of individuals? (See Henry's essays in chapter 2.)
3. What fundamental differences do you see between Rottenberg's and Wallis's views of the church as an agent of change? Do both proclaim the possibility of social transformation? Is Rottenberg fair in characterizing Wallis's position as anticultural? What does Rottenberg mean by the characterization of his own Reformed position as "conversionist"?
4. In Wallis's rebuttal to Rottenberg, what do you learn about a radical view of the state and its exercise of power?
5. Wallis argues that Rottenberg's reformist stance "is a theological version of traditional Western liberalism." In your own opinion do you think that the social ethics of different evangelical groups are shaped primarily by theological principles, political ideology, or other socioeconomic factors?

6. Wolterstorff lists five areas of disagreement between the political liberalism of many in the Reformed tradition and the political radicalism of the Sojourners community. Identify these five areas and explain the issues of debate between the two camps. Based on your reading of the evangelical political conservative position, can you construct a conservative response to these five areas of concern?

7. What connections, if any, do you see between the unraveling of America and the proliferation of evangelical political thought?

3

"Born-Again" America

(1976–1988)

The Fundamentalist New Right
Activates the Grass Roots   6

Evangelical Political Disarray under Carter

The year 1976 proved to be a significant one as the nation celebrated the two-hundredth anniversary of its birth. "The bicentennial observance," as Richard Pierard noted, "gave the nation an opportunity to relax and to recover from the twin traumas of Watergate and Vietnam."[1] Focusing on what was good about America, the year-long patriotic celebration restored some measure of cohesion among the American people.

The year was also designated by *Newsweek* as "the year of the evangelicals."[2] The bicentennial year ushered in an era of "born-again" politics that spanned from the beginning of Jimmy Carter's presidency in 1976 to the end of Ronald Reagan's administration in 1988. Democratic presidential candidate Jimmy Carter, in the election of 1976, unashamedly identified himself as a "born-again" Christian, and made the political significance of his evangelical faith a recurrent theme of his campaign. Carter's Republican opponent, President Gerald R. Ford, also claimed a "born-again" experience. Such "born-again" rhetoric sent the nation's secular establishment, especially the media elites, scurrying to decipher the language and thought forms of an evangelical subculture that most had assumed was a relic of the nation's religious past.

1. Richard Pierard, "Cacophony on Capitol Hill: Evangelical Voices in Politics," in *The Political Role of Religion in the United States*, edited by Stephen D. Johnson and Joseph B. Tamney (Boulder, Colo.: Westview, 1986), p. 88.
2. *Newsweek* (October 25, 1976): 69.

What can we learn about evangelical political involvement from the bicentennial election? First, "born-again" politics did not occur in a historical vacuum. Both Ford and Carter rode the crest of the evangelical political resurgence that began after World War II even as they contributed to accelerating its impact on American public life. Second, the election revealed that political partisanship and ideology took priority over religious loyalty in evangelical voting psychology. Although Carter's Southern Baptist style of religious piety clearly was closer to the religious identity of evangelicals than was Ford's high church tradition, evangelical voters, according to the best estimates, preferred Ford over Carter 60 to 40 percent. Third, evangelical voters for the first time in modern presidential politics received the media-imposed consecration as a special interest group to be watched in the future. Ironically, at the very time evangelicals were gaining national recognition, in reality, they were in political and theological disarray.

During the years Carter occupied the White House, evangelical political conservatives, liberals, and radicals continued to divide over social and political issues such as women's rights, the moral legitimacy of nuclear weapons, the achievement of social, economic, and racial justice through government programs, the politics of abortion, and the civil rights of homosexuals. Attempts to resolve these differences through working out the sociopolitical implications of commonly held theological convictions only seemed to deepen the disarray by playing into another set of evangelical battles over biblical inerrancy, the practical implementation of the kingdom of God, and the political nature and moral mission of the church. Differences over these and other issues, the inability to forge a comprehensive evangelical political philosophy, and a widening and bitter rift between black and white evangelicals caused the collapse of Evangelicals for Social Action (ESA) as a cohesive integrative structure to coordinate social action across the entire evangelical political spectrum. After 1976 the ESA, reconstituted as a membership organization with a national coordinating office and regional affiliations, increasingly pursued a more radical agenda.

This organizational and philosophical shift in ESA was accompanied by a proliferation of concrete experiments in evangelical social action ministries. John Perkins' Voice of Calvary stimulated black community development through economic cooperatives while the radical Sojourners' house-church combined simple living in the slums of Washington, D.C., with legal advocacy for the capital's urban poor. Radicals also organized Liberty to the Captives to fight torture and oppression and Dunamis to enlist a community of "pastor-prophets" to provide both prayerful support and a prophetic word to governmental leaders.

Long standing World Vision International supplemented its traditional social welfare ministry with programs of indigenous economic development and was joined by several newly created evangelical organizations to relieve world hunger. A significant number of evangelicals participated in Bread for the World, an ecumenical Christian citizens' movement seeking to influence U.S. govenment policies that directly affect the poor. The Association for Public Justice, another Christian citizens' organization, was formed to integrate practical social action and public policy analysis with a comprehensive, biblically based political philosophy. Evolving directly out of ESA, the Evangelical Women's Caucus championed the feminist cause for equal rights for women in church and society. Convicted Watergate felon Charles Colson's Prison Fellowship sought to evangelize prison inmates and worked for penal reform.

Such worthy social action projects rallied support from a variety of politically active evangelicals. But the very growth of these practical ministries further fragmented the evangelical political witness around special interest groups and prevented a renewed effort at political coalition making.

The Fundamentalist New Right Co-opts the Evangelical Political Resurgence During the Reagan Era

Evangelical political conservatives, liberals, and radicals, as most of the American public, were caught off guard during the late 1970s and early 1980s by the sudden public emergence and apparent political clout of the ultraconservative fundamentalist new right. Fundamentalists shared with other evangelicals a common doctrinal orthodoxy, but since the mid-1940s had remained militantly separatistic in their ecclesiastical development and in their relationship to modern culture. Comprised largely of independent Baptist and Presbyterian congregations, these fundamentalists stressed personal evangelism, Bible study, and withdrawal from political and cultural involvement. Nevertheless, during the conservative 1950s, some politicized fundamentalist leaders—Carl McIntire, Billy James Hargis, Stuart McBirnie, and others—articulated a theologically based attack on liberalism, communism, and Roman Catholicism. These "radical right" crusaders originally appealed to a large number of politically conservative evangelicals, but by the mid-1960s were already in decline.

The links between the fundamentalist new right of the 1970s and

109

1980s and the old religious right of the 1950s and 1960s are unclear. While the fundamentalist new right did share with the old radical right a religious and social history of cultural marginalization, a common constituency, and a good deal of political rhetoric and ideology, the two movements probably were not part of a continuous social process. The fundamentalist new right can best be viewed as a distinctive response to the social and political upheaval of the late 1960s and early 1970s.

Fundamentalists and their politically conservative evangelical allies responded to the forces of secularization sweeping the country during this period by formulating a conservative social agenda and by organizing a counterattack. They promoted American patriotism, the traditional family, prayer, and Bible reading in the public schools, capital punishment, and Israel's right to exist. They attacked the 1973 *Roe v. Wade* Supreme Court decision that legalized abortion, the feminist push for the Equal Rights Amendment, the public emergence of the gay rights movement, the pornography explosion, and the use of quotas to achieve racial justice. Fundamentalist leaders viewed this agenda as the only way to stop what they perceived as the new anti-Christian religion of "secular humanism" in American public life.[3] More so than their politically active brothers and sisters from the evangelical tradition, these politicized fundamentalists also participated directly in the electoral process. Through effective use of television and grass roots recruitment they mobilized millions of ordinary churchgoers behind their favorite candidates and issues. Recipients of massive secular media exposure, they forged alliances with other Christian, religious, and secular groups in support of conservative political causes.

The three most significant fundamentalist new right political organizations were created in 1979. Superchurch Baptist pastor and television preacher Jerry Falwell, at the urging of Richard Viguerie, Paul Weyrich, and other secular new right activists seeking to broaden the conservative movement in America, organized the Moral Majority to mobilize fundamentalists and evangelicals behind conservative issues and political candidates. Moral Majority was joined by Robert Grant's California-based Christian Voice, which gained notoriety by evaluating candidates according to a "biblical scoreboard," and Ed McAteer's Religious Roundtable, which sponsored workshops to teach pastors how to politicize their congregations. These three political action groups, along with influential television ministries led by Pat Robertson, James Robison, Charles Stanley, and other morally conservative Jewish, Catholic, and

3. For these and other emphases of the fundamentalist new right, see appendix 5.

Mormon organizations comprised what was called the new religious right, a loosely knit political coalition with a formidable grass roots base.

The power of this new religious right became evident in the election of 1980. Dissatisfied with Democratic President Jimmy Carter's foreign and domestic policies and feeling betrayed by the president's lack of enthusiasm for the conservative social agenda, the new religious right, together with its secular allies, rallied behind the presidential candidacy of Ronald Reagan, former movie actor and California Republican governor. Much to the chagrin of evangelical political radicals, liberals, and some conservatives, the new religious right was able to co-opt the long-standing evangelical political resurgence on behalf of its conservative social and political crusade by monopolizing the secular mass media's coverage of evangelical political involvement. Through its mass-mailing techniques, biblical scorecards, television programs, and grass roots politicking, the new religious right effectively shaped the public mind to equate their positions on political and social issues with the evangelical Christian view. Moreover, in contrast to the radical, liberal, and conservative voices of the evangelical political renaissance, the fundamentalist-led new religious right brought its message and organizing expertise down to the level of the pew in countless fundamentalist, evangelical, pentecostal, and other theologically conservative churches.

Although political analysts have downplayed the importance of the new religious right's contribution to Reagan's victory in 1980, the new religious right believed its organization of the evangelical and conservative religious vote for the president had been decisive in his election. Their postelection euphoria about morally reconstructing the Republic, however, in time gave way to a more sober and realistic recognition that their agenda would take longer to achieve than four years of Reagan rule. Undaunted by the president's inability or unwillingness to make the new religious right's agenda his top priority during his first term, fundamentalist new right leaders continued to build their organizational network, champion conservative causes, and educate their grass roots followers. Buttressed by the newly created American Coalition for Traditional Values under Tim La Haye's leadership, which conducted voter registration drives in local churches, and by Assemblies of God television evangelist Jimmy Swaggart's continuous, hard-hitting attacks against secular humanism, the new religious right mounted an all-out campaign on behalf of President Reagan's re-election bid in 1984. The president's landslide victory over Walter Mondale was hailed by the new religious right as a God-given opportunity to perpetuate the Reagan conservative counterrevolution and to reestablish Judeo-Christian moral values as the foundation of American national life.

The Fundamentalist New Right Blueprint for Reconstructing the Republic

Ronald Reagan's conservative philosophy meshed well with the fundamentalist new right's theological and political convictions. Firmly convinced that godly founding fathers had built America's institutions and culture upon biblical values, and that over the past several decades ungodly humanists had steered the nation away from its scriptural foundations, fundamentalist new rightists tended to see themselves as soldiers of the Lord girding up for a last great battle to save American Christian civilization. Combining their interpretation of America's Christian history with their conviction that the Bible contained a divine blueprint of political, economic, and social principles, fundamentalist leaders called on the general public to repent, experience a spiritual awakening, and establish biblical righteousness in the land.

Convinced that the Scriptures supported an individualistic view of society, fundamentalist new right leaders unreservedly advocated a free enterprise economy unhampered by federal bureaucratic regulations. To the delight of the Reagan administration, they also advocated the elimination of most welfare programs, believing that an expanding private economy created sufficient job opportunities for those willing to work. Again in step with the administration in Washington, fundamentalist new rightists viewed a militarily superior United States as the last and best hope for the defeat of communist aggression, the survival of Israel, and the triumph of democracy and capitalism in the world.

Evangelicals Confront Fundamentalist
New Right Politics   7

This final set of essays constructs an imaginary dialogue between politically conservative, liberal, and radical evangelicals and the fundamentalist new right. It begins appropriately with an essay by Jerry Falwell that briefly sketches the history of the Moral Majority, where it stands on the future of America and on major issues, its political strategy and tactics, and its challenge and appeal to the larger evangelical movement. For a politically conservative discussant, we come back to Carl Henry. In "The Evangel and Public Duty," from which only a brief section is printed, the evangelical elder statesman confronts head on the issue of moral justification in a pluralistic society raised by the new religious right. Henry's essay reveals some of the affinities and differences between evangelical political conservative and fundamentalist new right political thought.

Reformed historian George DeVries, Jr., critiques the new religious right from a politically liberal perspective. Although he sympathizes with the right's concerns about the secularization of American society, he nevertheless fears its overall impact on the nation's politics. In "A Wolf in Sheep's Clothing," evangelical radical Jim Wallis pointedly accuses the new religious right of preaching "an alien and false gospel." We conclude the dialogue with a recent assessment of the new religious right's future tasks by Ed Hindson, Liberty University faculty member and contributing editor to *Religious Broadcasting* magazine.

Future-Word:
An Agenda for the Eighties

Jerry Falwell

These are the greatest days of the twentieth century. We have the opportunity to formulate a new beginning for America in this decade. For the first time in my lifetime we have the opportunity to see spiritual revival and political renewal in the United States. We now have a platform to express the concerns of the majority of moral Americans who still love those things for which this country stands. We have the opportunity to rebuild America to the greatness it once had as a leader among leaders in the world.

The 1980s are certainly a decade of destiny for America. The rising tide of secularism threatens to obliterate the Judeo-Christian influence on American society. In the realm of religion, liberal clergy have seduced the average American away from the Bible and the kind of simple faith on which this country was built. We need to call America back to God, back to the Bible, and back to moral sanity.

Positive Christianity recognizes that reformation of the institutional structure of the church is futile without the spiritual revitalization of people's lives. It is the people whose lives have been dynamically changed by their personal relationship to Christ who are the real strength of the church. It is no "mere pietism" that will dynamically energize the evangelical church into social action. In our attempt to rally a diversity of morally conservative Americans together in Moral Majority, we were convinced that millions of people were fed up with the fruits of liberalism, both in politics and in religion. I am well aware that it is unpopular in some circles to equate the two. But I say that they must be viewed as cousins in the same family because both rest upon the same foundational presupposition of the inherent goodness of mankind. The ultimate product of theological liberalism is a vague kind of religious humanism that is devoid of any true gospel content.

In 1969 Dr. Harold O. J. Brown observed that there was still a "moral majority" left in America when he said:

Jerry Falwell, "Future-Word: An Agenda for the Eighties," in *The Fundamentalist Phenomenon: The Resurgence of Conservative Christianity*, edited by Jerry Falwell, Ed Dobson, and Ed Hindson (New York: Doubleday, 1981), pp. 186–95, 221–23. Reprinted by permission.

The United States may have a great deal of Christianity deep down. There is evidence of this. There is much to indicate that something basic in America is still healthy, both in a spiritual and in a moral sense. But wherever it is and whatever it is doing, it is not setting the tone, it is not giving direction to mid-twentieth-century America. It is not immune to disease. There is plenty of reason to think that America has a large reservoir of Christian faith, sound morality, and of idealism. But there is also a great deal of reason to fear that this reservoir is in danger of being polluted.[1]

Dr. Brown further observed that it was the influence of the liberal impulse in American theology that had produced a climate that spawned celebrated "theologians" who openly taught atheism and left the average person in search of God as a "prisoner of the total culture."[2] During the 1960s and 1970s, people felt confused and began to turn away from the liberalized institutional church that was not meeting their real spiritual needs. As attendance drastically declined in the mainline denominations, it dramatically increased in conservative denominations. Liberalism is obviously losing its influence on America. The time has come for the fundamentalists and evangelicals to return our nation to its spiritual and moral roots.

As a pastor, I kept waiting for someone to come to the forefront of the American religious scene to lead the way out of the wilderness. Like thousands of other preachers, I kept waiting, but no real leader appeared. Finally I realized that we had to act ourselves. Something had to be done now. The government was encroaching upon the sovereignty of both the church and the family. The Supreme Court had legalized abortion on demand. The Equal Rights Amendment, with its vague language, threatened to do further damage to the traditional family, as did the rising sentiment toward so-called homosexual rights. Most Americans were shocked, but kept hoping someone would do something about all this moral chaos.

Organizing the Moral Majority

Facing the desperate need in the impending crisis of the hour, several

1. Harold O. J. Brown, *The Protest of a Troubled Protestant* (New Rochelle, N.Y.: Arlington House, 1969), p. 72. See also the excellent study on the relationship of true revival to social action by R. F. Lovelace, *Dynamics of Spiritual Life: An Evangelical Theology of Renewal* (Downers Grove, Ill.: Inter-Varsity Press, 1979); and his more recent article, "Completing an Awakening," *Christian Century* (March 18, 1981): 296–300.
2. Brown, *Protest*, p. 205.

concerned pastors began to urge me to put together a political organization that could provide a vehicle to address these crucial issues. Men like James Kennedy (Fort Lauderdale, Florida), Charles Stanley (Atlanta, Georgia), Tim La Haye (San Diego, California), and Greg Dixon (Indianapolis, Indiana) began to share with me a common concern. They urged that we form a nonpartisan political organization to promote morality in public life and to combat legislation that favored the legalization of immorality. Together we formed the Moral Majority, Inc. Today Moral Majority, Inc., is made up of millions of Americans, including 72,000 ministers, priests, and rabbis, who are deeply concerned about the moral decline of our nation, the traditional family, and the moral values on which our nation was built. We are Catholics, Jews, Protestants, Mormons, fundamentalists—blacks and whites, farmers, housewives, businessmen and businesswomen. We are Americans from all walks of life united by one central concern: to serve as a special interest group providing a voice for a return to moral sanity in these United States of America. Moral Majority is a political organization and is not based on theological considerations. We are Americans who share similar moral convictions. We are opposed to abortion, pornography, the drug epidemic, the breakdown of the traditional family, the establishment of homosexuality as an accepted alternate life-style, and other moral cancers that are causing our society to rot from within. Moral Majority strongly supports a pluralistic America. While we believe that this nation was founded upon the Judeo-Christian ethic by men and women who were strongly influenced by biblical moral principles, we are committed to the separation of church and state.

Here is how Moral Majority stands on today's vital issues:

1. *We believe in the separation of church and state.* Moral Majority, Inc., is a political organization providing a platform for religious and nonreligious Americans who share moral values to address their concerns in these areas. Members of Moral Majority, Inc., have no common theological premise. We are Americans who are proud to be conservative in our approach to moral, social, and political concerns.
2. *We are pro-life.* We believe that life begins at fertilization. We strongly oppose the massive "biological holocaust" that is resulting in the abortion of one and a half million babies each year in America. We believe that unborn babies have the right to life as much as babies who have been born. We are providing a voice and a defense for the human and civil rights of millions of unborn babies.

116

3. *We are pro-traditional family.* We believe that the only acceptable family begins with a legal marriage of a man and woman. We feel that homosexual marriages and common-law marriages should not be accepted as traditional families. We oppose legislation that favors these kinds of "diverse family forms," thereby penalizing the traditional family. We do not oppose civil rights for homosexuals. We do oppose "special rights" for homosexuals who have chosen a perverted life-style rather than a traditional life-style.

4. *We oppose the illegal drug traffic in America.* The youth in America are presently in the midst of a drug epidemic. Through education, legislation, and other means we want to do our part to save our young people from death on the installment plan through illegal drug addiction.

5. *We oppose pornography.* While we do not advocate censorship, we do believe that education and legislation can help stem the tide of pornography and obscenity that is poisoning the American spirit today. Economic boycotts are a proper way in America's free-enterprise system to help persuade the media to move back to a sensible and reasonable moral stand. We most certainly believe in the First Amendment for everyone. We are not willing to sit back, however, while many television programs create cesspools of obscenity and vulgarity in our nation's living rooms.

6. *We support the state of Israel and Jewish people everywhere.* It is impossible to separate the state of Israel from the Jewish family internationally. Many Moral Majority members, because of their theological convictions, are committed to the Jewish people. Others stand upon the human and civil rights of all persons as a premise for support of the state of Israel. Support of Israel is one of the essential commitments of Moral Majority. No anti-Semitic influence is allowed in Moral Majority, Inc.

7. *We believe that a strong national defense is the best deterrent to war.* We believe that liberty is the basic moral issue of all moral issues. The only way America can remain free is to remain strong. Therefore we support the efforts of our present administration to regain our position of military preparedness—with a sincere hope that we will never need to use any of our weapons against any people anywhere.

8. *We support equal rights for women.* We agree with President Reagan's commitment to help every governor and every state legislature to move quickly to ensure that during the 1980s every American woman will earn as much money and enjoy the same opportunities for advancement as her male counterpart in the

same vocation.

9. *We believe ERA is the wrong vehicle to obtain equal rights for women.* We feel that the ambiguous and simplistic language of the amendment could lead to court interpretations that might put women in combat, sanction homosexual marriages, and financially penalize widows and deserted wives.

10. *We encourage our Moral Majority state organizations to be autonomous and indigenous.* Moral Majority state organizations may, from time to time, hold positions that are not held by the Moral Majority, Inc., national organization.

Facing the Opposition

We have been labeled by our critics as arrogant, irresponsible, and simplistic. They accuse us of violating the separation of church and state. However, the National Council of Churches (NCC) has been heavily involved in politics for years, and virtually no one has complained. Since many moral problems, such as abortion, require solutions that are both legal and political, it is necessary for religious leaders to speak on these matters in order to be heard.

What Moral Majority Is Not

1. *We are not a political party.* We are committed to work within the multiple-party system in this nation. We are not a political party and do not intend to become one.

2. *We do not endorse political candidates.* Moral Majority informs American citizens regarding the vital moral issues facing our nation. We have no "hit lists." While we fully support the constitutional rights of any special interest group to target candidates with whom they disagree, Moral Majority, Inc., has chosen not to take this course. We are committed to principles and issues, not candidates and parties.

3. *We are not attempting to elect "born-again" candidates.* We are committed to pluralism. The membership of Moral Majority, Inc., is so totally pluralistic that the acceptability of any candidate could never be based upon one's religious affiliation. Our support of candidates is based upon two criteria: (a) the commitment of the candidate to the principles that we espouse; (b) the competency of the candidate to fill that office.

4. *Moral Majority, Inc., is not a religious organization attempting to control the government.* Moral Majority is a special interest group of millions of Americans who share the same moral values. We

simply desire to influence government—not control government. This, of course, is the right of every American, and Moral Majority, Inc., would vigorously oppose any Ayatollah type of person's rising to power in this country.

5. *We are not a censorship organization.* We believe in freedom of speech, freedom of the press, and freedom of religion. Therefore while we do not agree that the Equal Rights Amendment would ultimately benefit the cause of women in America, we do agree with the right of its supporters to boycott those states that have not ratified the amendment. Likewise, we feel that all Americans have the right to refuse to purchase products from manufacturers whose advertising dollars support publications and television programming that violate their own moral code.

6. *Moral Majority, Inc., is not an organization committed to depriving homosexuals of their civil rights as Americans.* While we believe that homosexuality is a moral perversion, we are committed to guaranteeing the civil rights of homosexuals. We do oppose the efforts of homosexuals to obtain special privileges as a bona fide minority. And we oppose any efforts by homosexuals to flaunt their perversion as an acceptable life-style. We view heterosexual promiscuity with the same distaste which we express toward homosexuality.

7. *We do not believe that individuals or organizations that disagree with Moral Majority, Inc., belong to an immoral minority.* However, we do feel that our position represents a consensus of the majority of Americans. This belief in no way reflects on the morality of those who disagree with us or who are not involved in our organizational structures. We are committed to the total freedom of all Americans regardless of race, creed, or color.

Out of the Pew and into the Precinct

Many Christians are raising the question of whether they should be involved in politics at all. Some raise the question of the separation of church and state; others feel that politics is the devil's arena and Christians should stay out; and others say politics requires compromising and Christians should not compromise. Many liberal church people are also claiming that evangelicals are violating the separation of church and state. Recently Richard Dingman said: "As one who has held local public office for 10 years and worked in Congress for 11 years, it is my opinion that it is not only proper for Christians to become involved, but it is absolutely biblical and absolutely necessary."[3]

3. R. Dingman, in *Moral Majority Report* (June 6, 1980): 4

The recent emergence of fundamentalists and evangelicals into politics in no way violates the historical principles of this nation. The incorporation of Christian principles into both the structure and the basic documents of our nation is a matter of historical fact. The doctrine of the separation of church and state simply means that the state shall not control religion and religion shall not control the state. It does not mean that the two may never work together.

Moral Majority, Inc., contributes in the following ways to bringing America back to moral sanity:

1. *By educating millions of Americans concerning the vital moral issues of our day.* This is accomplished through such avenues as our newspaper, the *Moral Majority Report,* a radio commentary by the same name, seminars, and other training programs conducted daily throughout the nation.

2. *By mobilizing millions of previously "inactive" Americans.* We have registered millions of voters and reactivated more millions of frustrated citizens into a special interest group who are effectively making themselves heard in the halls of Congress, in the White House, and in every state legislature.

3. *By lobbying intensively in Congress to defeat any legislation that would further erode our constitutionally guaranteed freedom* and by introducing and/or supporting legislation that promotes traditional family and moral values, followed by the passage of a Human Life Amendment, which is a top priority of the Moral Majority agenda. We support the return of voluntary prayer to public schools while opposing mandated or written prayers. We are concerned to promote acceptance and adoption of legislation that keeps America morally balanced.

4. *By informing all Americans about the voting records of their representatives so that every American, with full information available, can vote intelligently following his or her own convictions.* We are nonpartisan. We are not committed to politicians or political parties; we are committed to principles and issues that we believe are essential to America's survival at this crucial hour. It is our desire to represent these concerns to the American public and allow it to make its own decisions on these matters.

5. *By organizing and training millions of Americans to become moral activists.* This heretofore silent majority in America can help develop a responsive government which is truly "of the people, by the people, for the people" instead of "in spite of the people," which we have had for too many years now.

6. *By encouraging and promoting nonpublic schools in their attempt to excel in academics while simultaneously teaching traditional family and moral values.* There are thousands of nonpublic schools in America that accept no tax moneys. Some of these schools are Catholic, fundamentalist, Jewish, Adventist, or of other faiths. Some are not religious. But Moral Majority, Inc., supports the right of these schools to teach young people not only how to make a living, but how to live.

Moral Majority, Inc., does not advocate the abolition of public schools. Public schools will always be needed in our pluralistic society. We are committed to helping public schools regain excellence. That is why we support the return of voluntary prayer to public schools and strongly oppose the teaching of the "religion" of secular humanism in the public classroom.

The First Amendment says: "Congress shall make no law respecting an establishment of religion, or prohibiting the free exercise thereof." This does not rule out church influence in government. Presbyterian theologian John Gerstner has said: "Establishment of religion is not the same thing as no influence of religion. I think Moral Majority is right in stating that the church should seek to have influence in political matters."[4]

California pastor Dr. Tim La Haye believes that the pulpit must be active in resisting encroaching federal bureaucracy that threatens both the church and the traditional family. He has stated: "God founded the government to protect the home against external enemies. The prophet of God is derelict if he does not, in God's name, rebuke government when it fails to protect the family."[5]

Catholic theologian and journalist Father Robert Burns, C.S.P., stated in the national Catholic weekly the *Wanderer:* "If our great nation collapses, it will not be because of the efforts of some foreign power, Soviet or otherwise, but rather for the same reason that ancient Rome collapsed because it was morally rotten to the core." He further comments: "The members of Moral Majority believe in fighting for the basic moral values on which this nation was built and upon which its strength rests. They are determined to prevent materialists, secular-humanists, and

4. J. Gerstner, quoted in an article in the *Birmingham News* (September 26, 1980).
5. T. La Haye, in *Moral Majority Report* (June 6, 1980). See also his incisive study on the influence of secular humanism in *The Battle for the Mind* (Old Tappan, N.J.: Revell, 1980). For a more technical study, see R. J. Rushdoony, *The Messianic Character of American Education* (Nutley, N.J.: Craig Press, 1979).

non-believers from destroying these values by replacing them with a valueless, amoral society."[6]

Christians are now realizing that governmental actions directly affect their lives. They are questioning the government's right to carry out such programs. They are beginning to realize that the only way to change the actions of government is to change those elected to govern. We are now beginning to do just that. We must continue to exert a strong moral influence upon America if our children and grandchildren are to enjoy the same freedoms that we have known.

The evangelical movement has been a vital part of this country for two centuries. Evangelical pastors have provided mature and stable leadership for the churches of America. They have demonstrated the love of Christ to their congregations and have been expositors and defenders of the Christian faith. Where others have been extreme, they have remained balanced. They have attempted to apply the truth of the gospel to the needs of society. In general, the evangelical movement has been faithful to the fundamental doctrines of the Christian faith.

In reality, there is little difference theologically between fundamentalists and evangelicals. We both hold to a strong belief in the inspiration and inerrancy of the Bible. We hold to the deity of Christ and to the necessity of personal salvation. Though evangelicalism tends to be tolerant of varying viewpoints, the vast majority of evangelical pastors tell me that they are concerned about the drift of so-called young evangelicals to the left. They do not like the current trend within the movement, which is getting dangerously close to moderate liberalism.

The lines are not clearly drawn today among evangelicals. The movement is so broad that it at times takes in everything from Bible churches to charismatic Catholics. Theologically it extends from Josh McDowell to Helmut Thielicke. Philosophically, it includes strong defenders of inerrancy such as Norman Geisler and John W. Montgomery. It has provided the conservative movement in general with such able social critics as Harold O. J. Brown. But at the same time it unfortunately includes some who are ready to deny their fundamentalist heritage and exchange their theological birthright for a mess of socioacademic pottage!

We appeal to our evangelical brethren to stand with us for the truth of the gospel in this hour when America needs us most. Stop looking down your theological and ecclesiastical noses at your fundamentalist brethren. As the English theologian James Barr has already pointed out, nonevangelicals view evangelicals and fundamentalists alike anyhow.

6. R. Burns, *Wanderer* (October 2, 1980).

We have so much in common. Only the radicals among us (to the left and to the right) divide us. I say it is time we denied the "lunatic fringe" of our movements and worked for a great conservative crusade to turn America back to God. We do not need an organic unity. Such is not necessary in order to achieve a mutual appreciation and respect.

We appeal to you to reacknowledge your fundamentalist roots. Stop being intimidated by what others think. Stop worrying about academic credibility and social acceptability. If evangelicals have one glaring weakness, it is that they are too concerned what the world thinks about them. They are hesitant to speak up on vital issues for fear of what the intellectual elite may think. Let them think what they wish. They have been wrong before, and they will be wrong again! . . .

Evangelicals need to reaffirm the foundation. Come back to the fundamentals of the Christian faith and stand firm on that which is essential. Throw down the anchor of truth and stop drifting with every new wave of religious fad that comes along. Stop trying to accommodate the gospel to the pitiful philosophies of unregenerate humankind. You have the truth, and the truth shall set you free.

You talk much of love, but often you have only words of bitter contempt for those of us who call ourselves fundamentalists. Do not be embarrassed because we believe the same things you do. Acknowledge us. Accept us as Bible-believing brethren who love the same Christ you love. Let us work to reach the world for Christ.

We conservative fundamentalists and evangelicals can be used of God to bring about a great revival of true Christianity in America and the world in our lifetime.

The Evangel and Public Duty

Carl F. H. Henry

Nothing is more conspicuous on the American religious scene than the reentry of evangelical Christians into public affairs and their renewed interest in long-neglected cultural concerns. A long-smoldering uneasy conscience over sociopolitical detachment during the last gener-

Carl F. H. Henry, "The Evangel and Public Duty," in *The Christian Mindset in a Secular Society: Promoting Evangelical Renewal and National Righteousness* (Portland, Oreg.: Multnomah Press, 1984), pp. 97, 114–15, 119–20, 127. Reprinted by permission.

ation has gradually escalated into aggressive political engagement accelerated by the last election campaign and extended by the electronic church, particularly through the activities of Moral Majority, Religious Roundtable, and related movements on the religious right. . . .

Moral Justification in a Pluralistic Society

The religious right evoked a storm of secular reaction when some of its leaders emphasized that America is a Christian country where most citizens still believe in Christian values and urged that the nation's Christian foundations be restored by political renewal. A good government, it was said, will uphold the moral principles stipulated by the Bible. Christian standards, rather than the permissive alternatives preferred by a secular society, should therefore be championed as legislative ideals. Christians consider the social imperatives of Scripture—protection of monogamous marriage and property rights, respect for the dignity of human life, capital punishment for murder, and so on—important for national well-being and survival. Either explicitly or implicitly the Bible declares what the truly just state will legislate as right and good in public life.

A number of ecumenical critics hurriedly lampooned the Moral Majority for thrusting a biblically based religious ethic upon a pluralistic democracy. Spokespersons on the political left raised the specter of a religious establishment that might dominate the state, although lobbyists for the National Council of Churches had themselves earlier and often advocated specific legislative positions on the ground of their supposed religioethical superiority, even if the biblical basis for such ecumenically affirmed positions was often obscure. Moreover, the federal government's possible encroachment on religious conscience in respect to positions on abortion and homosexuality, for example, had now also become an issue.

To say that the Bible stipulates what government ideally legislates inevitably evokes political debate among rival religious and philosophical traditions, a conflict that is properly no concern of government. Only a totalitarian society, whether theocratic or atheistic, imposes metaphysical beliefs upon its citizens. The Bible nowhere stipulates statute laws that pluralistic governments are to impose in the name of a divine-command morality. No nation today stands in a theocratic covenantal relationship with the God of all nations. The Bible nowhere adduces statute law to be theocratically imposed upon the pluralistic powers of the world on the ground of God's specially revealed Word and command. The metaphysical grounds on which citizens affirm the content of justice is of high theological, philosophical, and apologetic importance but it is not a matter of political interest. The state can take sides in matters of religious or metaphysical disputation only by disregarding religious freedom. To be sure, unless a methodology for validating transcendent values exists, moral alternatives have no persuasive epistemological basis. But adjudicating between religions and philosophies is not the task of civil government; such concerns fall outside the scope of political authority.

Metaphysical assumptions underlie not only Christian but also non-Christian ethical positions. The humanist is selfconsciously committed to naturalism, and process philosophy's emphasis on ecological concerns is not unrelated to its undergirding conviction that nature is streaked with divinity. But the religious or metaphysical foundations of values are not of governmental relevance. It is wrong for the Christian or the humanist or for anyone else to try to impose a theological or metaphysical morality as such upon a pluralistic society. Religious freedom is an indispensable treasure that must not be jeopardized in the public debate over values. Moral justification in the public order must be civil rather than theological, even though the civil is privately informed by the theological. Civil government defines what is unlawful, not what is sinful.

Moral Majority's tardy insistence that their movement is not a religious effort based on theological considerations is propitious, even if they have drawn fire for appealing to "pluralistic" rather than to "Christian" supports for their public positions. The use of political means to enforce sectarian principles in a pluralistic society has no biblical legitimacy and is incompatible with church–state separation. . . .

Is the appeal to a moral majority therefore antidemocratic? No more so, it would seem, and doubtless far less so, than if the positions of antimajority influences were to prevail. If a nondemocratic elite determines the laws of the land the pattern leads readily to the Soviet misconception of "democracy" in which people really have no voice in articulating the content of legislation.

The role of any majority is plain enough: While minorities can block legislation, majorities are in a better position to pass it. An ethically sensitive majority will, of course, be sensitive to minority rights. Yet minorities, Christian or non-Christian, will always face certain problems of conformity or nonconformity to majority consensus. Law is not coercive in that it allows noncompliance if one affirms the primacy of religious freedom; Christians know full well what it is to suffer penalties for noncompliance.

The weakness of the view that the majority will determine the content of legislation is that while it suspends on a majority vote the validity of the Christian or any other view of what is right, it provides no criterion for judging and assessing that consensus. A majority—even a majority of Americans—can be wrong. Majority rule is preferable to minority rule in that it provides a shelter against tyrants, but it does not of itself guarantee the rule of justice. . . .

A clear conflict exists in the Christian community—even among evangelicals, including leaders of activist groups—on a number of important political issues. According to Professor Robert Webber of Wheaton College, nine out of ten professors of social ethics in evangelical colleges and seminaries hold views, as he does, akin to those of *Sojourners* magazine. Is that a fair reading of evangelical leadership in sociopolitical affairs? Moral Majority and Religious Roundtable contend, on the other hand, that the vast majority of evangelical Christians are firmly on the political right. What do these conflicting claims forbode for the future of the evangelical thrust in American national life? Jerry Falwell, who has emerged as the most prominent spokesperson for the fundamentalist right, has called for a coalition of conservatives on common objectives. Can evangelicals and fundamentalists forge a coalition of common political concerns instead of expending their energies mostly in internal conflict?

The "New" Old Right

George DeVries, Jr.

The genesis of this piece was my reading of a review in *Fides et Historia* (June 1986) entitled "Reconsecrating the Public Square." The writer, Professor Stanley J. Grenz of the North American Baptist Seminary in Sioux Falls, South Dakota, reviewed six books: John Eidsmoe's *God and Caesar*, George Goldberg's *Reconsecrating America*, Paul Marshall's *Thine Is the Kingdom*, Richard John Neuhaus's *Naked Public Square*, Francis Schaeffer's *Great Evangelical Disaster*, and William W. Van Alstyne's *Interpretations of the First Amendment*. Suffice it to say that Professor Grenz faced a formidable task, one that he performed admirably. It is not my purpose here to recite Grenz's review, but simply to note

George DeVries, Jr., "The 'New' Old Right," *Reformed Journal* 36 (October 1986): 8–10. Reprinted by permission.

that it focuses on books that deal largely with the phenomenon known as the new religious right and its place in the current American political scene. Reading this review reminded me of the recent foray of evangelist Pat Robertson onto the political turf of the Michigan primary, as well as the renewed political activity of other Christian fundamentalists (Christian Voice, for example) aimed particularly at election year 1988, when the new right means to select the Republican nominee for president and write the platform. It should be noted that they have already handpicked Reagan's judicial nominees and launched the Supreme Court in what they hope will be a more positive future direction. It goes without saying that all this is terribly significant for the contemporary American political scene, with implications far beyond that limited arena.

What follows, then, are some ruminations of my own on the new right and its directions. At the outset, let me say that I remain committed to what my friend and former colleague Ed Ericson has labeled the "old new radicalism"[7]; and I would suggest that if this ideology currently lacks wide appeal and popularity, as Ericson suggests, its reception has very little to do with its validity. I wonder also whether its abandonment by those who have seen the true light of conservatism may not be more typical of secular thinkers (i.e., the Colliers and Horowitzes whom Ericson mentions) than of Christians. Indeed, it seems to me that in the wider realm of Christendom, there is a growing sensitivity and concern for the glaring social, economic, and political problems and injustices of this world. As one evidence of the latter I cite the various studies and statements of the American Catholic bishops, who are speaking out on such matters as land and farm policy and the American economy.

It is true, of course, that the prevailing political winds blow strongly in favor of "new old conservatism" that basically idolizes and enshrines the individual, seeking to limit that "evil" which is government (whatever happened to the Reformed view that government is ordained by God for society's positive good?) and allowing the individual greater political, and especially economic, freedom. This, for the individual at least, leads to more freedom or liberty, the latter word one that could well be categorized as a buzzword for the conservative. For the conservative, freedom or liberty is always measured in individual terms; what is often forgotten is that we gain greater freedom in a collectivized society by placing restrictions upon the individual. Complete freedom, of course, leads to anarchy, with its loss of all freedom. More important,

7. Edward E. Ericson, Jr., "Hello Again to All That," *Reformed Journal* 35 (August 1985): 2–4.

what is often forgotten by the Christian conservative is that the biblical concept of freedom that we have in Jesus Christ is quite different from the concept we inherited as part of our Anglo-Saxon baggage. In the latter heritage, property and political rights take on meanings quite different from their biblical ones. And even our secular heritage suggests that freedom needs limits. As we prepare to celebrate the two-hundredth anniversary of our Constitution, we should remember that the framers of the Constitution struggled with the balance between freedom and authority even then, and concluded that freedom must give way to a central authority for the common good.

No one, of course, opposes freedom. It is rather a question of freedom for whom, to what extent or degree, and to what end or purpose. For Christians, whatever freedom we have must be in subservience to the King and Lord of creation, Jesus Christ. So it may be that the individual as a consumer or producer is free in the private marketplace to exploit goods, services, and resources for his or her own purposes; but when it is clear that such behavior frequently hurts others, then the Christian must cease and desist from such. Our own luxurious standard of living serves as another example. We draw heavily upon the resources of the world, and especially the poor world, which, through internationally determined marketing systems largely designed by the West for the West, receives very inadequate returns for its contributions.

Such freedom to consume and produce is obviously in the interest of the individual; it is in our interest, other considerations aside. But how can we square such behavior with God's demand (through Micah) that we "be fair and just and merciful and walk humbly with our God"? God requires us to manage his creation with justice and stewardship. I would submit that in a highly complex, structured, interrelated society, there are strict limits on what we can do individually because we are part of structures, systems, institutions, and complexes that mold us and hold us. This is not to deny the responsibility or place of individual action, but simply to point out that it is insufficient for those evils and problems that are structural and institutional.

Think for a moment about how much of what we take for granted is the result of a collective involvement or undertaking, whether it be the gas that is piped into our houses or the institutions we work for or are a part of. This is as true of the goods and services we use as of how we live and where and how we work, play, and even worship. Our society is a highly collectivized one.

It is interesting how the right, new or old, opposes collectivism in government (all government is collective action), especially when action is taken to aid those groups that are economically underprivileged and politically powerless. Aid to the rich and powerful is one thing; aid to the poor is socialism. In that connection it is interesting to observe that the American business corporation was really a collective undertaking designed to limit competition; thus it was, in a very real sense, the first true departure from laissez-faire enterprise in this country. Not only did it substitute collective for individual action, but it eventually separated the ownership of property from the responsibility of managing it and made huge industrial and financial empires possible. Furthermore, within the corporation, a corporate bureaucracy, headed by a highly structured "team" complete with fabulous salaries, bonuses, stock options, corporate perks, and other benefits, is really a miniature welfare state, complete with medical care and retirement benefits. At the same time, those who really "own" the corporate property are like the absentee landlords of old, receiving returns without any direct involvement in their property. Ironically, these "giants" (a far cry from Adam Smith's economic man) speak the loudest for free enterprise! Such behemoths of property and industry and finance are the main sources of finances for conservatives for the simple reason that they are the chief beneficiaries of conservative government. Themselves giant collective undertakings, they speak with a powerful political voice for benefits that they would deny others, benefits that are as truly paid by society generally as any other governmental benefits. I mention business enterprises as only one example, albeit a very important one, of how our society has become structured, organized, and collectivized. We are light-years away from the society where individual enterprise (that of one person or relatively few people) dominated our economy.

The ideology of the right is for most of us a comfortable one. It blesses who we are, and where we have come from historically, and it approves our continuing our course as is. It proclaims "laissez faire" in the political, economic, and social spheres; and this for most translates into "freedom" and "liberty." There are limits, of course. We would not wish to extend complete laissez-faire to the air lanes, for example, although in the last years we have moved a considerable distance toward that end, doubtless at the sacrifice of air safety. We still want some collective supervision of such matters as aircraft licensing, safety standards, airport procedures, controls on flight paths and directions, and so on. Even conservatives recognize that freedom has its limits.

Basically, the chief difference between the left and the right is the degree to which one is willing to use political power to ameliorate the ills of society, and especially those ills that are economic by nature and are indeed largely born in the economic structures and institutions. At issue, really, are one's goals for society and its place in the world, for out of these arise one's political orientation.

I share Richard Pierard's concern[8] about a conservatism that has effectively militarized our society; that has "monarchized" the presidency; that has polarized the country between the haves and the have-nots; that underfunds or eliminates vital societal programs; that determines foreign policy actions by military concerns and substitutes military action for more constructive methods in promoting American interests; that has promoted an "atmosphere of hostility" in U.S.-Soviet relations; that ignores our growing and menacing budgetary and trade deficits (all to be taken care of by a freer market and "less" government); that applauds an administration that has emasculated the Bill of Rights and restricts the authority of the Supreme Court; that endorses an uneven justice (leaders of the "Right to Sanctuary Movement" are given long jail terms, whereas perpetrators of fraudulent defense contracts involving huge sums get no jail senetences); that supports economic policies which take a heavy toll on those least able to bear it; that supports foreign governments, no matter how autocratic, as long as they somehow manage to appear anticommunist; and that threatens to impose its ideology on society through its control of the government and through pressure on the media.

We are confronted with an ideology that supports the lavishing of our great wealth on the comparative few; that favors the reckless use of resources without concern for the future or the environment; that ignores the unemployed, the underemployed, and the farmers; that has no real concern for problems of development in the poor world; that ignores the plight of the homeless and hopeless at home and abroad but is willing to waste billions and billions in its efforts at military security; that defines all problems in terms of a cold war stance; and that takes pride in our military power and prestige. Such an ideology, popular as it may be, is not one that a Christian, committed to principles God laid down for the governance of this world, can really be comfortable with. For is not the essence of the biblical message love, that which embodies selflessness, humility, compassion, mercy, patience, and long-suffering, all of which constitute a denial of self and self-interest? And we must never forget that the overarching rule of God for the cultural order is justice, for God himself is justice incarnate.

The religious right has a valid concern—the secularization of American life and politics—and it has some valid goals. Still, I fear its overall

8. Richard Pierard, letter to the editor, *Reformed Journal* (August 1986): 7–8.

impact. I am fearful when I read that a Los Angeles fundamentalist preacher asks his congregation to pray for the death of Supreme Court Justice William J. Brennan because he voted for the 1973 Supreme Court decision legalizing abortion. I am fearful when I read that a young fundamentalist in Seattle killed a reputable lawyer, his wife, and two sons because he believed (wrongly) that the lawyer was a communist leader. I am fearful when I read of fundamentalists bombing abortion clinics. But most of all I am fearful because these fundamentalists, shepherded by such radio and television performers as Jerry Falwell and Pat Robertson, support the kind of conservative ideology that I have already outlined. That ideology has already reached high places and has a strong attraction for many of us.

I am concerned because many Christians believe with Pat Robertson that *this is the way.* (He told a political rally that "it's no coincidence" that Reagan's 1980 election came after half a million Christians prayed "to please heal our land.") I am even more concerned when astute and learned academics like Ericson suggest that we of the "left" are obsolescent, and that we are "morally selective" in our concerns. We are perhaps guilty of the latter, a matter that can be attributed to our finiteness—of time, capacity, knowledge, and interest.

I note, for example, that Ericson aches, and rightly so, for the suffering and dying in Ethiopia, Afghanistan, Nicaragua, and Russia[9] and for the Cambodians.[10] Just today, however, my *Seed* magazine reports that forty thousand children will die today from hunger-related causes (multiply that by 365 for a horrendous figure; and, of course, these children are only the tip of the iceberg). This is not a new problem, and it is not one that Ericson saw fit to address. His omission of this concern does not mean that he is insensitive to it; it simply means that he, like the rest of us, picks those concerns on which he wishes to focus. I would point out for the record, relative to one of Ericson's concerns, that I wrote a piece entitled "Another Holocaust,"[11] in which I sought to call attention to the monstrous Cambodian tragedy. So much, then, for moral insensitivity.

It may be, then, that there are those of us who remain unreconstructed "old new radicals," but I submit this is so because we have reached that position by (I hope) the growing knowledge and maturity and vision of our Christian faith, with its convictions about our place and calling in the world. Admittedly, we see "but darkly through a glass," but it is the best view we have.

9. Ericson, "Hello Again," p. 3.
10. Edward E. Ericson, Jr., "Cry for Cambodia," *Reformed Journal* 36 (February 1986): 2–3.
11. George DeVries, Jr., "Another Holocaust," *Banner* 113 (November 3, 1978): 15.

A Wolf in Sheep's Clothing:
The Political Right Invades the Evangelical Fold

Jim Wallis

I remember so many things about my home church. Dunning Park Chapel is a Plymouth Brethren "assembly" of hard-working people in the motor city of Detroit.

Originally from England, the Plymouth Brethren left after breaking away from the state church and suffering years of religious persecution. They came to the United States seeking the freedom to worship and practice their faith as they saw fit. In sharp contrast to high-church Anglicanism, Plymouth Brethren congregations were characterized by simplicity, lay leadership, personal piety, and a great devotion to the Bible. Ritual, liturgy, and hierarchy were shunned in favor of plain services with wide participation.

There was a strong emphasis on the separation of church and state, and, as my mother once told me, there were no American flags in Plymouth Brethren congregations before World War II. In their earliest days, they were even pacifists. The Plymouth Brethren communities were genuinely countercultural, consciously rejecting many of the values of their surrounding culture on the basis of their steadfast biblical faith.

Much of that was still true as I was growing up in the 1950s and 1960s. These were people for whom faith was at the center of life. Indeed, most of our family activity revolved around the church which my parents had helped to found. My father was always an elder in the church, and my mother would have been if women had been allowed to publicly exercise their gifts of leadership. Really, they were both lay pastors, he out front and she behind the scenes.

Many other families were also deeply involved, and that was the strength of the church. Personal faith and commitment were the highest priority and, despite the lack of professional ministry and a certain disdain for intellectual scholarship, the level of Bible knowledge was remarkably high. The people I grew up with in the church were mostly working class to middle class. They were drafters for Ford Motor Company or line workers for Detroit Edison or secretaries or housekeepers

Jim Wallis, "A Wolf in Sheep's Clothing: The Political Right Invades the Evangelical Fold," *Sojourners* 15 (May 1986): 20–23. Reprinted by permission.

with a smattering of teachers and business people. They were all white, midwestern, and very middle American.

While there are unique qualities about the Plymouth Brethren, these people are more or less typical of the forty million conservative white evangelicals of "born-again" status so often mentioned in the religious and secular media. They are not right-wing extremists and, in fact, are not particularly political at all. Rather, they are just ordinary working people who believe the Bible and are worried when their values are threatened or ignored.

There are a number of core values I received from my growing-up years in the church, values that we perceived to be at the heart of our Christian faith, values that are still with me. Jesus was at the absolute center of everything. He was our Savior and our Lord, and I remember countless sermons and conversations about what "the Lord" would have us be and do.

The Bible was the primary source of authority among us; Bible study and scripture memorization were highly prized. The walls of my father's basement study were lined with biblical commentaries and he, like many others, arose early in the morning to study the Bible before going off to work. The Bible taught us the Word of God, and we were hungry for that Word.

Out of our devotion to Jesus and the authority of the Bible in our lives came many commitments. For example, I remember a very definite resistance to materialism. I often heard how money would never make you happy but easily got in the way of "serving the Lord." The rich were never admired but rather were a little suspect spiritually.

Instead, the real heroes who were exalted in my church were the missionaries who gave up material comforts and financial success and even risked their lives to preach the gospel on foreign shores, or the itinerant preachers who traveled the circuit of our little churches to teach us the Bible and had no earthly rewards to show for it. These Bible teachers and preachers often stayed in our home and made a deep impression on me as a small boy. I've often thought that they would have been utterly repulsed by the materialism that later swept through the evangelical churches.

There was a very deep conviction in my church that we were to be different from the world because of our Christian faith. A great vigilance was maintained lest we become "too worldly." We were pilgrims and aliens, not the leading citizens and successful wielders of power. We loved our country but didn't think we had, or should have, much to do with running it. Power was as suspect as wealth.

The old hymn said it well, "This world is not my home, I'm just a-passing through." Our countercultural identity often expressed itself in unfortunate and ill-conceived legalisms (I got into trouble because I loved movies and dancing), but at the core of it, there was a central biblical truth.

While there was never anything so self-conscious as "social action," the church was always very supportive of the downtown mission for the "down and out." And any family in trouble because of unemployment or alcoholism or marital problems could find help and support from the church in which there was a genuine compassion for hurting people.

The early Plymouth Brethren pacifism had long since been displaced, and we prayed often for our young men in the service. But though we often got God and country all mixed up together, there was a sense that war was a horrible rather than a glamorous thing and that the nations of the world had let their own sin drive them into violence. After all, the Bible said the causes of war were covetousness and pride.

The family was foundational among us, marriage commitments were sacred, sexual morality was essential, and children were precious gifts from God. The declining morality of the culture was viewed as a serious threat.

To this day, I treasure many of the values I was raised with in my little church. But we, like other kinds of churches, were tremendously affected by the values and assumptions of our surrounding culture. My church chose many of the wrong places to take its stand, and the result was spiritual compromise with the culture at fundamental points, while hanging on to vestiges of separation that had less and less meaning.

My own conflicts with the church came not over the centrality of Jesus or the authority of the Bible but over racism and war, during the days of the civil rights movement and the Vietnam War. Over those questions, I believed we were acting like typical white Americans, not biblical Christians. In other words, we had become "worldly." The cold war anticommunism of the postwar period that became such all-purveying propaganda in the 1950s took a heavy toll on the people of my church. Like most other Americans, we accepted the growing militarism that was overtaking the country.

The rising prosperity of the period also began to have a profound impact on attitudes in the church. The distinctive differences our faith made gradually eroded as we identified more and more with the postwar values of the American empire and the upward mobility of our middle-class neighbors.

But during the 1960s and the 1970s, a number of young people from the evangelical churches, including the Plymouth Brethren, began to challenge that cultural conformity and call for a more biblical faith. These "young evangelicals" began to recover the biblical foundations of social justice, compassion for the poor, warnings against militarism, and dangers of civil religion. And an alternative to the evangelical endorsement of the status quo began to emerge.

However, the evangelical fold was about to be invaded by a wolf in sheep's clothing. The forces of the political far right, which were gathering with renewed energy in response to the social crisis of the 1960s and early 1970s, decided to target the evangelical constituency. In the mid-1970s, Richard Viguerie openly announced plans to aim his computers at the evangelical community, which he and other new right operatives hoped would be fertile soil for their political ambitions. The first right-wing political move to recruit evangelicals in large numbers came during the 1976 election campaign.[12] That first effort did not prove particularly successful, but it laid the ideological and financial groundwork for a much bigger push toward 1980.

The first step was for the veteran political activists from the new right to make the crucial political alliance with a group of rising fundamentalist media stars—the television preachers. The television preachers and the new right activists found the relationship mutually advantageous, very lucrative, and extremely beneficial to the powerful ambitions of both groups.

From the beginning an appeal was made to conservative evangelical values, the fears and failures of liberalism were carefully exploited, and a new gospel was created—one that would provide religious sanction and support for an extreme right-wing political agenda.

For example, to the richest country in the history of the world, a new gospel of prosperity was proclaimed that saw wealth as a sign of God's favor and poverty as evidence of spiritual failure. Traditional evangelical frugality was replaced by the extravagant life-styles of television preachers who claimed that God's children should have the best of everything and who ended up with far more than the people who supported them with their hard-earned dollars.

Similarly, to the most heavily armed nation in world history, a new gospel of strength was preached, extolling military might, proclaiming our nation's cause and even our nuclear weapons as righteous, while condemning all our adversaries as evil empires, communists, and terrorists. The Soviet threat became more important in evangelical sermons than the words of Jesus.

12. See "The Plan to Save America," *Sojourners* (April 1976).

Legitimate evangelical concern for the family, for sexual integrity, and for the lives of unborn children were all exploited and twisted to gain support for restoring patriarchy, rolling back the progress women had made, and launching vicious attacks on homosexuals. Absurd linkages were made between the "moral issues" like abortion and family and the economic and military goals that form the heart of the real conservative political agenda. Somehow, support for the family got translated into support for the MX missile and cutting social programs for poor people.

Claiming to be the true inheritors of the evangelical tradition, the religious right has imposed an alien and false gospel on the evangelical community. In doing so the preachers and practitioners of the religious right are providing an invaluable service to the powers that be. The biblical gospel is a threat to the wealth, power, and violence of the American establishment, so it was replaced with an American gospel that sanctions the values of the system as it aggressively reasserts its power.

By making inroads into conservative evangelical churches like the one I grew up in, the new right political activities found fresh recruits for their cause. By tying their religious message to a very specific political agenda, television preachers have gained access to power and a media prominence only dreamed of before. The longtime political professionals of the far right seemed increasingly religious and deeply concerned about the real "moral issues" at stake.

Television preachers also showed their great adaptability in working the back rooms of political power and influence. The fundamentalists' longtime religious exclusiveness and aversion to working with nonfundamentalists was suddenly transformed into a new ecumenism. The litmus test of fellowship was no longer biblical doctrine but rather adherence to the essentials of a right-wing political doctrine.

For example, Christian Voice is a new right group which publishes an annual scorecard rating of every member of Congress on how they vote on "Christian" issues. According to the Christian Voice rating, the "correct" Christian positions have included support for the highest levels of military spending, including Star Wars, the MX missile, and chemical weapons; opposition to social programs for the poor; aid to the El Salvadoran military, the now-deposed Marcos government in the Philippines, and the contras seeking to overthrow the government of Nicaragua; support for anti-abortion legislation, tuition tax credits, and school prayer; opposition to economic sanctions against South Africa's apartheid regime; and opposition to the nuclear freeze and the Equal Rights Amendment.

Among those who have received 100 percent ratings from Christian

136

Voice are former Representative Richard Kelly (R-Fla.), who was convicted of taking a bribe in the Abscam scandal, and Representative Dan Crane (R-Ill.), who was censured by the House for sleeping with a teenage congressional page. Among those who received zero ratings were Representative Bill Gray and Representative Bob Edgar—both clergy and Democrats from Pennsylvania. Fundamentalist and chief tobacco spokesperson Senator Jesse Helms (R-N.C.) got 100 percent ratings, while evangelical Senator Mark Hatfield (R-Ore.) got ratings of 20 to 30 percent.

Under the new leadership of the religious right, the body of Christ, a minority community of pilgrims and aliens, gives way to a "moral majority," a political force committed to turning the country back to the values of American capitalism, materialism, imperialism, and military superiority. In the name *conservative evangelical*, the label *conservative* suddenly became much more important than *evangelical*. It was easy to see that the message being preached was much more new right than Christian. The television preachers wanted us all to believe there was really no difference between the two.

The television preachers not only became the promoters of a new American gospel, they also began to play increasingly specific roles for the new conservative government in Washington. Their annual National Religious Broadcasters Convention has virtually become the National *Republican* Broadcasters Convention, with the heads of state and party serving as keynote speakers and leading attractions.

A number of television preachers perform crucial roles as point men and storm troopers for the Reagan administration on key issues. At a key point in the nuclear debate, Jerry Falwell went on the stump against the nuclear freeze. Before his nationwide speaking tour and series of debates, he was briefed at the White House by the National Security Agency and by the president himself. When challenged on a national television show about such access, Falwell replied, "Anyone can talk to the president."

Falwell's trips to South Africa and the Philippines played a similar role. In both cases he returned to the United States taking positions the administration held but was afraid to publicly assert for fear of the political fallout. The Reagan government could not afford to say that in South Africa and the Philippines the real issue was communism rather than apartheid or Marcos. But Falwell could and would say it and, in so doing, could test the waters by putting out the extreme conservative line to see how it would float. It sank, and along with it, Falwell's contribution income and political capital.

Pat Robertson is playing a similar role around U.S. support for the contras in Nicaragua. And now, with his possible presidential bid,

Robertson becomes a very attractive religious stalking horse for the far right forces of the Republican party.

The television preachers are ideally suited for their political role. First, they give a religious and moral credibility to the right-wing political position. In so doing they have helped to narrow the range of discussion and dissent on key questions. Through effective religious oratory, extreme right-wing political views can be made to sound like the things that made this country great and the good old-fashioned values that most Americans believe.

Second, the television preachers bring with them a built-in constituency, a genuinely grass roots network that the political right has always lacked. The people I grew up with are now constantly subjected to the best state-of-the-art technology and techniques of persuasion through television, computers, and direct mail, as the political far-right attempts to secure their support, money, and votes. In the name of evangelical values, my people are being sold on and recruited to a nationalist, exclusivist, materialist, militarist, and repressive world view that is decidedly unevangelical.

The projection of power requires ideologists and apologists, culturally, politically, and, of course, religiously. In a calculated bargain, many television preachers have made themselves available for that purpose.

An independent biblical vision is what the present U.S. government and its religious apologists are most afraid of. The job of the religious right is to try to discredit genuine religious dissent by always screaming "left-wing" or "communist." They do their job well as the highly rewarded chaplains of the American system.

The gospel of the political right is not good news to the poor, to the marginalized and disenfranchised, to racial minorities and women, to the starving millions who suffer from the way the world is presently arranged. In other words, it is not the gospel of Jesus Christ. It is the gospel of American wealth and power, which is only good news to those on top.

The Bible warns against a close association with the powers that be and against those false prophets who make such alliances with earthly rulers. It is suspicious of any and all concentrations of power because of human sinfulness, and it is especially sensitive to the victims of the power systems.

But there is good news on the home front. Despite evangelical susceptibility to the gospel of the television preachers, they have yet to win the day. Many evangelicals are not so sure that their opposition to abortion should also include support for nuclear weapons. Or that Christians should strive for riches while so many are poor. Some are suspicious about getting so involved with political power and remember when the separation of church and state seemed more important.

Perhaps most importantly, some of the children of the evangelical churches have grown up and now work with the poor in the inner city, are trying to stop the arms race, are seeking to make peace in Central America, and are doing it all because of strong Christian faith. Some of their elders do not agree with them, but everyone knows their church's children are not communists.

The evangelical community is an equally natural constituency for a consistent political morality that stands up for truth and defends life wherever it is threatened. That kind of evangelical social conscience is a prophetic challenge to the selective and inconsistent moralities of both the right and the left and is especially sensitive to the poor and the oppressed who are so close to the heart of God. It rejects narrow nationalism in favor of the kind of international perspective that grows so naturally from our identity as the worldwide body of Christ. And an evangelical social conscience resists the dangerous impulses toward violence and war precisely because of the ministry of reconciliation we have been given as followers of the Prince of Peace.

The plans and purposes of the religious right are personal issues with me. There is a battle going on for the hearts and minds of the evangelical community. These are the people with whom I grew up, from whom I learned faith, and with whom I still identify. They are under attack by the most powerful political forces in the world. They are in danger of being literally devoured by wolves in sheep's clothing.

But I'm going to trust the faith that reared me. I'm going to believe that a simple and vibrant evangelical faith can resist the corruption of right-wing political power. I'm going to hope that, faced with the ultimate choice, evangelicals will choose to be biblical rather than to consort with worldly power.

Religion and Politics:
Do They Mix?

Ed Hindson

The recent resurgence of conservative Christian involvement in the social and political life of America is indeed the religious phenomenon of our time. It has become the most heatedly debated religious

Ed Hindson, "Religion and Politics: Do They Mix?" *Religious Broadcasting* 20 (January 1988): 34–35. Reprinted by permission.

issue of the 1980s. With the founding of the Moral Majority in 1979, fundamentalists/evangelicals ventured into the political process in force. They were not welcomed with open arms by the political or religious establishments. Rather, they kicked down the door and marched in with such force that they sent panic and paranoia through most sectors of American society.

The media was shocked! Where did all these fundamentalists/evangelicals come from? Who were they and what did they want? Since the general public has assumed that fundamentalists disappeared after the Scopes trial in 1925, they were at a loss to explain their sudden public resurgence. A kind of "fundomania" set in and some began to assert that hordes of bigoted Bible-bangers had formed a conspiracy to take over America and set up a theocratic dictatorship. Since then, responsible analysis has shown "fundomania" to be a myth provoked mainly by media exaggeration.

Today most of the rhetoric has subsided, but there is still an underlying uneasiness about fundamentalist involvement in the political process. With Pat Robertson's bid for the presidency, the issue of religion and politics will not go away. The candidacy of a preacher brings Christian political involvement to a precarious moment in history. If the balance between religion and politics can be further advanced, then such candidacy will prove beneficial to the American democratic process. However, if the issue polarizes American society, the course of religious involvement in politics may well be lost.

This leads to the need to establish a clearly defined philosophy of Christian political involvement which would include several key factors.

Theological and Philosophical Basis

If we are going to seriously influence American political and social life, we must understand what it is we are trying to accomplish. We are not merely advocating the election of certain officials as an end in itself. Francis Schaeffer clearly understood this when he argued that Christ must be Lord in all of life. He wrote, "He is our Lord not just in religious things and not just in cultural things . . . but in our intellectual lives, and in business, and in our relation to society, and in our attitude toward the moral breakdown of our culture."[13] Acknowledging his lordship involves placing ourselves under the authority of Scripture and thinking and acting as citizens of his kingdom as well as citizens of earth.

13. Francis A. Schaeffer, *The Great Evangelical Disaster* (Westchester, Ill.: Crossway, 1984), p. 39.

140

It is in this regard that the Christian understands that the wrongs of society are not merely social ills but spiritual ills. As such, they require spiritual help, not merely political readjustment. Ultimately, there are no permanent political solutions to the problems of society. But that does not mean that we should all retreat to a monastery and advocate social anarchy for the rest of the world.

Because the Christian is a citizen of two kingdoms, one earthly, the other heavenly, he has an obligation to both. He cannot divorce himself from either or both. He is under divine mandate to both. Nevertheless, he realizes that the one is temporal and the other eternal. But that in no way prohibits his involvement in the temporal; in fact, it enhances it. The Christian cannot merely sit by and passively watch society self-destruct. Something within him, namely the Spirit of God, cries out for truth and justice. Wherever that cry has been articulated into action, truth and justice have prevailed.

Long-Range Strategy

There are no instant solutions to complex problems. The New Right has often been criticized for offering simple answers to complex questions. However, this need not be the case. We do have valuable answers to the really important issues of the day and those answers need to be articulated clearly and thoughtfully. This is not the time for arrogance or overstatement of our case. Neither is this the time for capitulation. No one ever said this process would be easy. Those who naively thought Ronald Reagan would solve all the ills of American society by himself have been gravely disappointed. On the other hand, conditions have improved in which religious conservatives have been able to make their voices heard in a way that was not possible prior to 1980.

One of our greatest needs today is for a long-range strategy to enact our goals and objectives. We cannot rest on the laurels of the past or the future will catch us totally off guard. Serious questions need to be addressed now. Where do we go after Reagan? What if the next president is more hostile to our agenda? Do we give up or do we dig in deeper?

Power and Influence

People expect politicians to talk about politics, but when preachers start talking about politics they begin using the power of their position to legitimatize political issues. Preachers are perceived as spiritual leaders and religious authorities by the general public. When they defend political or social issues they are perceived as somehow speaking for

God; and it is very difficult for the average layman to distinguish between the two, whether he is listening to a Catholic bishop or a Pentecostal evangelist.

The particular power of televangelists is that they are the only preachers some people listen to since they rarely attend a local church. Many of these people lack the spiritual discernment to properly evaluate what they are hearing. Therefore, we must be very cautious in the statements we make regarding religion and politics.

At times the greater issues of human justice transcend political boundaries. The real issue today is not whether one is a Democrat or a Republican but whether he is committed to justice for people. This means that we must defend the rights of those with whom we disagree. Suppressing their freedoms in the name of religion is just as wrong as their suppressing ours. We are only asking for the opportunity to be heard in the debate on public policy. Now that we have everyone's attention, we need to think carefully about what we are going to say.

Study Questions

1. In *Agenda for the Eighties,* Jerry Falwell writes: "We have the opportunity to see spiritual revival and political renewal in the United States." What connections does he make between the spiritual and the political? What view of America's Christian past undergirds Falwell's agenda?
2. What does Falwell suggest were the reasons for the founding of the Moral Majority? List the moral/political issues of chief concern to the Moral Majority and describe its position on each. How might a list of political/moral issues drawn up by politically liberal evangelicals and politically radical evangelicals differ from the Moral Majority's?
3. Is the new religious right, as exemplified by the Moral Majority, an aberration in American public life? A threat to American democracy? A threat to a pluralistic society?
4. Assume you are preparing an essay for publication in a magazine on the topic "What I Like and Do Not Like about the New Religious Right." List and explain your reasons for the observations you place on each side of the ledger.
5. Contrast Jerry Falwell's view of the nature and functions of government in society with that of an evangelical conservative, liberal, and radical.

6. Carl Henry claims that "it is wrong for the Christian or the humanist or for anyone else to try to impose a theological or metaphysical morality as such upon a pluralistic society." In your view, do the Moral Majority and the other new religious right groups do this?

7. In what ways does George DeVries's politically liberal position differ from the new religious right's with respect to individualism, the nature of society, the purposes of government, and the uses of political power? Would DeVries's criticism of new religious right political thought apply equally as well to evangelical political conservative thought?

8. What connections do you see between DeVries's political thinking and that of Lewis B. Smedes' (see chapter 2)? What concerns does DeVries express about the ideology and politics of the new religious right? Do you think his concerns are reasonable?

9. Jim Wallis writes: "The religious right has imposed an alien and false gospel on the evangelical community." What is the basis for Wallis's harsh judgment? In Wallis's mind, what distinguishes the "biblical gospel" from this "alien and false gospel"? Since both Wallis and Falwell claim to be Bible-believing Christians, how could they differ so drastically in their understanding of the meaning of the gospel and its political implications?

10. According to Wallis, what role did television preachers play in the rise and effectiveness of the new religious right?

11. After assessing new right gains during the Reagan years, Hindson suggests the need to identify three key factors in a philosophy of Christian political involvement: (1) theological and philosophical basis; (2) long-range strategy; and (3) power and influence. On the basis of all the readings in this book, how would representatives of the four political perspectives address these factors? Can you think of other issues that need to be addressed?

12. Of the four political perspectives identified in this book, which do you find most persuasive and why?

13. Compare and contrast the way the four political views interface the theological sphere with the political sphere.

Afterword

As the presidency of Ronald Reagan came to a close and the nation entered a new political era, evangelicals continued in political disarray. Most rank-and-file evangelical political conservatives ardently supported Reagan and much of the new religious right's agenda, and consequently were barely distinguishable from the fundamentalist new right. The NAE's Office of Public Affairs, however, did seek to keep alive the politically conservative option within mainline evangelicalism by educating pastors and denominational leaders on public policy issues through its newsletter and occasional Washington seminars. In 1986, it organized a national program of "Peace, Freedom and Security Studies" to shape evangelical thinking in the areas of defense and foreign policy.

Although evangelical political liberals maintained their ideological distinctiveness during the conservative Reagan years, they made few inroads among evangelical churchgoers. Mostly academics, liberals did increase their influence among evangelical college students and seminarians and produced a significant number of books and articles on evangelical politics. Much like the liberals, evangelical political radicals retained their ideological identity by attacking Reagan administration policies and the new religious right's theological and political platform. More than conservatives or liberals, evangelical radicals built their own grass roots constituency. Under the executive leadership of Ronald Sider, a revived Evangelicals for Social Action worked to bring evangelicals of all political stripes together around its "pro-life" agenda; in contrast those radicals connected with Jim Wallis and Sojourners made common cause with mainline Protestants and Roman Catholics around what they identified as peace and justice issues of Christian conscience.

In creating this ecumenical social action movement, the radicals' evangelical identity was challenged by more conservative evangelical groups.

The fundamentalist new right, along with the broader new religious right, unexpectedly declined as an organized political force during the election campaign of 1988. New right televangelist Pat Robertson's ill-fated run for the White House fizzled in part because many fundamentalists and evangelical conservatives preferred other candidates, thus diluting the evangelical rights' electoral impact. Jerry Falwell even publically endorsed Robertson's Republican rival, George Bush, for the presidency. Moreover, Falwell's resignation from the Liberty Federation, successor organization to the Moral Majority, caused a leadership vacuum in the new religious right. The fundamentalist new right's abrasive political tactics and "Armageddon" rhetoric also contributed to its growing negative public image. In addition, because politicized fundamentalists so closely identified their movement with the Reagan administration, they inevitably lost momentum as President Reagan's years in the Oval Office came to an end. Coincidently, the sex and money scandals that rocked the ministries of televangelists Jim Bakker and Jimmy Swaggart and the ensuing "holy wars," although hurting all evangelicals, especially tarnished the public reputation of the fundamentalist new right.

The public demise of the fundamentalist new right opens the way for all politically active evangelicals to remake the evangelical political image in the public mind. More than image building is needed, however. As they enter the decade of the 1990s, politically involved evangelicals should identify the principle of a biblical social ethic that they share in common. More importantly, evangelical political conservatives, liberals, and radicals, as well as fundamentalist new right leaders, must acknowledge that their different political philosophies can all be legitimated within a framework of biblical interpretation. Without such intramural civility, evangelical political leaders will only continue to talk past each other. Further, evangelicals should recognize that the diversity of their political thinking represents a strength in a pluralistic and ever politically changing modern America. While tolerating their own political pluralism, however, evangelicals need to be open to learn from each other and to work together for public justice within the framework of their common theological heritage.

Appendix 1: Why *Christianity Today?*

*C*hristianity Today has its origin in a deeply felt desire to express historical Christianity to the present generation. Neglected, slighted, misrepresented, evangelical Christianity needs a clear voice, to speak with conviction and love, and to state its true position and its relevance to the world crisis. A generation has grown up unaware of the basic truths of the Christian faith taught in the Scriptures and expressed in the creeds of the historic evangelical churches.

Theological liberalism has failed to meet the moral and spiritual needs of people. Neither the man on the street nor the intellectual is much attracted by its preaching and theology. All too frequently, it finds itself adrift in speculation that neither solves the problem of the individual nor of the society of which he is a part.

For the preacher, an unending source of wisdom and power lies in a return to truly biblical preaching. For the layman, this same Book will prove to be light on the pathway of life, the record of the one who alone meets our needs for now and for eternity.

Christianity Today is confident that the answer to the theological confusion existing in the world is found in Christ and the Scriptures. There is evidence that more and more people are rediscovering the Word of God as their source of authority and power. Many of these searchers for the truth are unaware of the existence of an increasing group of evangelical scholars throughout the world. Through the pages of *Christianity Today* these men will expound and defend the basic truths of the Christian faith in terms of reverent scholarship and of practical application to the needs of the present generation.

Editorial, "Why 'Christianity Today'?" *Christianity Today* 1 (October 15, 1956): 20–21. Reprinted by permission.

Those who direct the editorial policy of *Christianity Today* unreservedly accept the complete reliability and authority of the written Word of God. It is their conviction that the Scriptures teach the doctrine of plenary inspiration. This doctrine has been misrepresented and misunderstood. To state the biblical concept of inspiration will be one of the aims of this magazine.

The doctrinal content of historic Christianity will be presented and defended. Among the distinctive doctrines to be stressed are those of God, Christ, man, salvation, and the last things. The best modern scholarship recognizes the bearing of doctrine on moral and spiritual life. This emphasis will find encouragement in the pages of *Christianity Today*.

True ecumenicity will be fostered by setting forth the New Testament teaching of the unity of believers in Jesus Christ. External organic unity is not likely to succeed unless the unity engendered by the Holy Spirit prevails. A unity that endures must have as its spiritual basis a like faith, an authentic hope, and the renewing power of Christian love.

National stability and survival depend upon enduring spiritual and moral qualities. Revival as the answer to national problems may seem to be an oversimplified solution to a distressingly complex situation. Nevertheless statesmen as well as theologians realize that the basic solution to the world crisis is theological. *Christianity Today* will stress the impact of evangelism on life and will encourage it.

Christianity Today will apply the biblical revelation to the contemporary social crisis, by presenting the implications of the total gospel message for every area of life. This fundamentalism has often failed to do. Christian laypeople are becoming increasingly aware that the answer to the many problems of political, industrial, and social life is a theological one. They are looking to the Christian church for guidance, and they are looking for a demonstration of the fact that the gospel of Jesus Christ is a transforming and vital force. We have the conviction that consecrated and gifted evangelical scholarship can provide concrete proof and strategic answers.

Christianity Today takes cognizance of the dissolving effect of modern scientific theory upon religion. To counteract this tendency, it will set forth the unity of the divine revelation in nature and Scripture.

Three years in a theological seminary is not sufficient to prepare a student fully for the ministry. *Christianity Today* will seek to supplement seminary training with sermonic helps, pastoral advice, and book reviews, by leading ministers and scholars.

The interpretation of the news becomes more and more important in the present world situation. Correspondents conversant with local conditions have been enlisted in the United States and abroad. Through their reports *Christianity Today* will seek to provide its readers with a comprehensive and relevant view of religious movements and life throughout the world.

While affirming the great emphases of the historic creeds, this magazine will seek to avoid controversial denominational differences. It does not intend to concern itself with personalities or with purely internal problems and conflicts of the various denominations. If significant enough, these will be objectively reported.

Into an era of unparalleled problems and opportunities for the church comes *Christianity Today* with the firm conviction that the historic evangelical faith is vital for the life of the church and of the nations. We believe that the gospel is still the power of God unto salvation for all who believe; that the basic needs of the social order must meet their solution first in the redemption of the individual; that the church and the individual Christian *do* have a vital responsibility to be both *salt* and *light* in a decaying and darkening world.

Believing that a great host of true Christians, whose faith has been impaired, are today earnestly seeking for a faith to live by and a message to proclaim, *Christianity Today* dedicates itself to the presentation of the reasonableness and effectiveness of the Christian evangel. This we undertake with sincere Christian love for those who may differ with us, and with whom we may be compelled to differ, and with the assurance in our hearts that God's Holy Spirit alone can activate any vital witness for him.

Appendix 2: Evangelicals for McGovern

Walden Howard

Dear Friend,

We are in the middle of a crucial presidential election that will affect the future of America and the world for far more than four years. More than in 1968, the two candidates offer us a genuine alternative.

Clearly nobody has a direct word from God on how Christians should vote in November. Through the prophets and our Lord, however, God has revealed some fundamental principles about the nature of a just society. Social structures that favor the rich displease God. Policies, however camouflaged, that are designed to slow down or reverse racial progress grieve the one whose eternal son became incarnate in the Middle East. If Jesus is to be Lord of our entire life, then he must be Lord of our politics. And that means trying individually and as groups of believers to discern how fundamental principles of biblical revelation apply to each new political event.

Honest Christians will not always agree! When we do not, then we must respect each other.

In 1972, however, many evangelicals feel that the platform of Senator McGovern moves at many crucial points in the direction indicated by biblical principles. The richest 10 percent of Americans make more than the poorest 50 percent! That is true even after one takes the income tax (with all its loopholes) into account. If Amos is right in declaring that God disapproves when the rich live in luxury at the expense of the poor, then surely Christians should help McGovern close the loopholes and make the rich pay their fair share. McGovern dared to take a courageous stand for racial justice on the busing issue at a time when Nixon was doing his best to profit from a white backlash. If Vietnamese boys mean as much to God as American boys, then a "solution" that kills Vietnamese instead of us is not a just solution. The honesty of George McGovern's Wesleyan Methodist parents has helped produce a candid, decent man, who can restore credibility to the presidency and reorder our national priorities. Evangelicals for McGovern (some of us are Independents, some Republicans, some Democrats) believe that evangelicals across the country should consider McGovern's candidacy carefully.

Electing McGovern will not bring in the kingdom! Our Lord will do that when he returns. But electing McGovern does offer the hope of taking some significant steps toward greater justice in national and international society.

Would you be willing to call five friends about contributing to this cause? We will be glad either to send you several of these letters or mail the letters directly to people whose names and addresses you send us.

To date McGovern has raised only about $4 million for his campaign for the presidency. Yet one hour on national television costs $200,000. It is clear by now that the wealthy are not going to contribute to McGovern. So his financial support depends on the response of ordinary citizens who believe his desire to re-set priorities is correct. Ten dollars from each of ten thousand evangelicals or $100 from one thousand would mean $100,000.

All checks sent to us will be forwarded to Senator McGovern's national headquarters. Mail your checks here so that evangelicals as a group can be heard. By contributing a significant amount, we evangelicals can both gain a voice and also declare publicly that orthodox theology does not necessarily mean a politics unconcerned about poverty, minorities, and inflated military budgets.

A new federal law (H.R. 10947 passed last December) permits taxpayers an income tax deduction for political contributions to candidates, parties, and committees. You may either take a tax reduction—a $100 deduction on a joint return, $50 on an individual return—or you can take a tax credit (this is subtracted from actual taxes owed) of $1 for every $2 contributed—up to a total of $25 on a joint return or up to $12.50 on an individual return.

If your contribution is to affect the last three weeks of the campaign, please sit down, write your check now to *McGovern for President*, and mail it today.
Sincerely,
Walden Howard
Chairman
Evangelicals for McGovern

P.S. Let's end the outdated stereotype that evangelical theology automatically means a politics unconcerned about the poor, minorities, and unnecessary military expenditures.

Appendix 3: Post-American Christianity

Jim Wallis

We find ourselves in the midst of a radical awakening, among people who are raising basic and critical questions about the nature of our society and about the quality of life in the world we inherit. The questioning of a new generation has generated a new awareness and activism which pose a direct challenge to the American status quo. We are characterized by our protest and our frustrated search for counter-cultural alternatives more amenable to justice, peace, human values, and spiritual meaning.

We have become disillusioned, alienated, and angered by an American system that we regard as oppressive, a society whose values are corrupt and destructive. We have unmasked the myth of the American dream by exposing the reality of the American nightmare. Establishment speeches ring hollow in our ears in the face of a society cancerous with racism, exploitation, repression, and war. Our revolt is against the deception and hypocrisy that divides America's rhetoric from its actions; from Watts to Saigon, from Columbia to Chicago, from Wall Street to South Africa, from Mississippi to My Lai, from Kent State to Jackson State and Orangeburg, from the F.B.I. to the Pentagon papers. We have learned most about this country not from presidential press conferences but from the suffering faces and sad eyes of the oppressed, exploited, and hopeless, locked in dark ghettos of human misery, rat-

Jim Wallis, "Post-American Christianity," *Post-American* 1 (Fall 1971): 2–3. Reprinted by permission.

infested tenements, rural prisons of poverty, and concentration camps called reservations. We recoil from a perverted mentality that destroys Asian villages to "save them" and judges its success by inflated body counts of peasants and children whose country is being napalmed, burned, defoliated, and bombed out of existence to "protect it." Our moral sensitivity is wounded by student cries of human anguish and death which rise from the graves of a million Vietnamese, from fifty thousand American boys used as cannon fodder for generals, politicians, and corporate profiteers, from students beaten and shot for opposing the madness, and from the Black Panthers murdered in bed to "secure law and order."

Our ethical revolt against systematic injustice, militarism, and the imperialism of a "power elite" is accompanied by our protest of a technocratic society and a materialistic profit culture where human values are out of place. We see that suffering is not confined to the exploited classes, but exists throughout society as people experience the meaninglessness and oppression of their own lives. Obedience and conformity are the price of a "success" that is defined as nine to five corporate jobs and lives of quiet desperation in split-level suburbia. Money is a measure of status and worth in a society of created needs and garbage heaps of wasted abundance in the midst of want; a society in which things are valued more than people. The ulcerating drive for air-conditioned affluence has not given satisfaction or fulfillment, but has instead produced lives that are hollow, plastic, and superficial, characterized by economic surplus and spiritual starvation. Fundamentally, we protest a society that stresses "having" rather than "being." We see American society as rich and full of everything but justice, meaning, and spiritual consciousness. Recurrent themes of life without purpose and direction, alienation, lack of identity, meaninglessness, and existential despair, are clearly seen in our media and culture, in the confused lives of people around us, and in our own frustrated searching. The black man suffers, but the life of the white man is not as beautiful as the oppressed sometimes paint it. We are all prisoners, victims of our society and ourselves, struggling to find the manhood that has eluded us.

This radical awakening that we have experienced, this new awareness that pleads for change, requires a rethinking of basic assumptions about our society and about ourselves. Our protest must be more than negation and refusal; it must also include affirmation and radical alternatives.

Our affirmation must have an adequate basis for our values, vision, and goals which can provide the motivation, direction, and self-criticism necessary in seeking radical change; a vision that can keep us from the bitterness, despair, hatred and desperation that causes people to drop out, sell out, or turn their fight for justice and social change into a murderous crusade. We require radical transformation, a new understanding of society and ourselves. As the analysis of our dilemma must be radical so must our solutions, going to the heart, the root causes of our problems, being comprehensive enough to avoid simplistic pitfalls. Clearly our liberation must be personal as well as social. Marcuse has said, "Political radicalism thus implies moral radicalism: the emergence of a morality which might precondition man for freedom." Man must be changed as well as his social structures. It is man who built oppressive social structures, man who exploits and kills his brother. The brutality and stupidity of the twentieth century have painfully revealed man's inhumanity to man, and rudely shattered our naive illusions about ourselves. Man's oppressive ego, self-centeredness, hatred, greed, prejudice, and aggression have again surfaced as motivations of our individual and corporate lives. We must escape the illusions of every simplistic group that looks only beyond itself for the source of human misery. We must realize that the evil we oppose lies also within ourselves. Herman Hesse says it well:

> Now and again I have expressed the opinion that every nation and every person would do better, instead of rocking himself to sleep with political catchwords about war guilt, to ask himself how far his own faults and negligences and evil tendencies are guilty of the war and all the other wrongs of the world, and that there lies the only possible means of avoiding the next war.

All this is simply to say that our new vision must be a vehicle for personal transformation, the emergence of the new man, as well as providing the basis for social liberation. To challenge the system, we must be willing to have our own lives changed, and become radical ourselves. To repudiate the old is not enough. We must act on the basis of a new reality that we have experienced. We must not merely suggest radical alternatives, but rather, we must live and be those alternatives.

We contend that the new vision that is necessary is to be found in radical Christian faith that is grounded in commitment to Jesus Christ. "If any man be in Christ, he is a new creature; the old has passed, the new has come." We believe that the gospel of Jesus Christ is a liberating force which has radical consequences for human life and society. However, for the radical nature of the Christian faith to be realized, it must break the chains of American culture and be proclaimed to all peoples. The offense of established religion is the proclamation and practice of a caricature of Christianity so enculturated, domesticated, and lifeless that our generation easily and naturally rejects it as ethically insensitive, hypocritical, and irrelevant to the needs of our times.

We find that the American church is in captivity to the values and lifestyle of our culture. Institutional Christianity in America has allowed itself to become a conservative defender of the status quo, a church largely co-opted and conformed to the American system in direct disobedience to biblical teaching (Rom. 12:2). The American captivity of the church has resulted in the disastrous equation of the American way of life with the Christian way of life. This cultural captivity has caused the church to lose its prophetic voice by preaching and exporting a pro-American gospel and a materialistic faith which supports and sanctifies the values of American society, rather than calling them into question. By its implication in the American status quo, by participating in the anti-Christian mindset of our society (racism, materialism, nationalism), the church has lost its ethical authority and has become the chaplain of the American nation, preaching a harmless folk religion of comfort, convenience, and presidential prayer breakfasts.

We fault a narrow orthodoxy that speaks of salvation but is often disobedient to the teaching of the prophets, the apostles, and Christ himself, who clearly states that faith divorced from a radical commitment to social justice is a mockery. Salvation never occurs in isolation from one's brother. True spirituality manifests itself in active concern for the needs and rights of people. We fault also a naive and inadequate liberal theology which neglects man's need of personal transformation and liberation, perverts the historic content of the Christian faith, and reduces Jesus Christ to a Galilean boy scout. Our Christian messages are incomplete, hollow shells, manipulated by the forces of nationalism, wealth, and conformity into helpless captivity. Our church needs to be deorientated from American culture and reformed biblically. A faith rooted in biblical data must stress both personal liberation and dynamic commitment to social justice that contains the seeds of social liberation.

A new generation of radical Christians is coming together to decry the church's accommodation to non-Christian ways, to reach out to others who have become aware of the radical implications of the Christian faith, and to commit ourselves to discipleship to Jesus Christ and the proclamation of the total Christian message of personal and social liberation. To be Christian is to be radical—it is to know the central biblical expectation of the death of the old and the birth of the new. "Behold I make all things new." Christian radicalism provides the vehicle for people willing to change their own lives, to challenge the system, to take the problem of change seriously. Radicalism is revelational in its basis and revolutionary in its consciousness. The good news of the gospel is the entrance of Jesus Christ into history, the inbreaking of a new order, the proclamation of a message of reconciliation and new life to alienated men. The revelation of God in Jesus Christ and his kingdom provides our basis of value, hope, and a radicalism that cannot be crushed. Radical Christians seek to recover the earliest doctrines of Christianity, its historical basis, its radical ethical spirit, and its revolutionary consciousness. The radical Christian must resist those who would equate Christianity with the American way of life or baptize American foreign policy, or agree with those who compartmentalize religion and so emphasize the personal Savior as to mitigate his being Lord over all life. Radical Christians view the personal and social dimensions of salvation as integrally related in biblical definitions. The biblical concepts of rebirth, new life, and justice point to fundamental change from sin to grace, from selfishness to love, from captivity and oppression to freedom and liberation.

Christians must be active in rejecting the values of our corrupt society, radical in our resistance and activism against the injustice of a racist society, warfare state, and materialistic system. We must be people of God, "salt and light," those of a new order who live by the values and ethical priorities of Jesus Christ and his kingdom. We must be radical disciples applying the comprehensive Christian message to all areas of life, culture, and human need—committed to reconciliation, justice, peace, and faith which is distinctly post-American.

Appendix 4: A Declaration of Evangelical Social Concern

As evangelical Christians committed to the Lord Jesus Christ and the full authority of the Word of God, we affirm that God lays total claim upon the lives of his people. We cannot, therefore, separate our lives in Christ from the situation in which God has placed us in the United States and the world.

We confess that we have not acknowledged the complete claims of God on our lives.

We acknowledge that God requires love. But we have not demonstrated the love of God to those suffering social abuses.

We acknowledge that God requires justice. But we have not proclaimed or demonstrated his justice to an unjust American society. Although the Lord calls us to defend the social and economic rights of the poor and the oppressed, we have mostly remained silent. We deplore the historic involvement of the church in America with racism and the conspicuous responsibility of the evangelical community for perpetuating the personal attitudes and institutional structures that have divided the body of Christ along color lines. Further, we have failed to condemn the exploitation of racism at home and abroad by our economic system.

We affirm that God abounds in mercy and that he forgives all who repent and turn from their sins. So we call our fellow evangelical Christians to demonstrate repentance in a Christian discipleship that confronts the social and political injustice of our nation.

"A Declaration of Evangelical Social Concern," adopted November 25, 1973, Thanksgiving Workshop on Evangelicals and Social Concern, Chicago, Illinois. Reprinted by permission.

We must attack the materialism of our culture and the maldistribution of the nation's wealth and services. We recognize that as a nation we play a crucial role in the imbalance and injustice of international trade and development. Before God and a billion hungry neighbors, we must rethink our values regarding our present standard of living and promote more just acquisition and distribution of the world's resources.

We acknowledge our Christian responsibilities of citizenship. Therefore, we must challenge the misplaced trust of the nation in economic and military might—a proud trust that promotes a national pathology of war and violence which victimizes our neighbors at home and abroad. We must resist the temptation to make the nation and its institutions objects of near-religious loyalty.

We acknowledge that we have encouraged men to prideful domination and women to irresponsible passivity. So we call both men and women to mutual submission and active discipleship.

We proclaim no new gospel, but the gospel of our Lord Jesus Christ who, through the power of the Holy Spirit, frees people from sin so that they might praise God through works of righteousness.

By this declaration, we endorse no political ideology or party, but call our nation's leaders and people to that righteousness which exalts a nation.

We make this declaration in the biblical hope that Christ is coming to consummate the kingdom and we accept his claim on our total discipleship till he comes.

(Adopted November 25, 1973, Chicago, Illinois)

Original Signers

John F. Alexander	Daniel Ebersole
Joseph Bayly	Samuel Escobar
Ruth L. Bentley	Warren C. Falcon
William Bentley	Frank Gaebelein
Dale Brown	Sharon Gallagher
James C. Cross	Theodore Gannon
Donald Dayton	Art Gish
Roger Dewey	Vernon Grounds
James Dunn	Nancy Hardesty

Mark Hatfield

Carl F. H. Henry

Paul Henry

Clarence Hilliard

Walden Howard

Rufus Jones

Robert Tad Lehe

William Leslie

C. T. McIntire

Wes Michaelson

David C. Moberg

Stephen Mott

Richard Mouw

David Nelson

F. Burton Nelson

William Pannell

John Perkins

William Petersen

Richard Pierard

Ron Potter

Wyn Wright Potter

Bernard Ramm

Paul Rees

Boyd Reese

Joe Roos

James Robert Ross

Ronald J. Sider

Eunice Schatz

Donna Simons

Lewis Smedes

Foy Valentine

Marlin Van Elderen

Jim Wallis

Robert Webber

Merold Westphal

Appendix 5: Ninety-five Theses for the 1980s

Jerry Falwell

Concerning America

1. That the concept of government itself, like that of marriage, is an institution divinely ordained by God.
2. That America, unlike any other country in the world today, owes its origin to men of God who desired to build a nation for the glory of God.
3. That the American system of government, though imperfect, is nevertheless the best political concept in the history of the world.
4. That any needed change in its structure should be achieved through peaceful, legal processes.
5. That all Americans should love and honor their flag.
6. That all its citizens have the right to receive just and equal treatment under the law.
7. That all its citizens have a right to religious freedom.
8. That all its citizens have a right to peaceful assembly.
9. That all citizens of legal age have both the right and responsibility to register and vote in every election.

10. That this nation serves as the only barrier to worldwide communistic occupation.
11. That because of this, we are obligated to remain strong to assure our own liberty and to protect the very concept of freedom itself.
12. That any attempt to weaken our defense systems is both an act of treason and a crime against the remaining free nations in the world's community.
13. That all able-bodied U.S. male citizens are obligated to fight to the death, if necessary, to defend the flag.
14. That all others, including female citizens, are to aid in every possible way.
15. That all female citizens are to be exempt from any draft laws.
16. That the free enterprise system of profit be encouraged to grow, being unhampered by any socialistic laws or red tape.
17. That, to maintain human dignity and individual respect, each able-bodied male citizen perform useful and honest work to support himself and his dependents.
18. That all welfare aid be immediately and permanently withdrawn from any able-bodied man refusing to perform an honest day's work.
19. That all other unproductive governmental financial programs be terminated, harmful programs which in themselves perpetuate poverty and laziness.
20. That a balanced national budget be a yearly goal of both the president and Congress.
21. That all elected officials found guilty of sexual promiscuity, whether heterosexual or homosexual, and/or financial deceit, be removed from public office rather than receiving a mild rebuke from their peers.
22. That less authority be vested in federal government.
23. That more of this authority be given to state and city governments.
24. That this country cease from aiding those unfriendly nations (the Soviet Union, China, etc.) through massive low interest loans, the selling of wheat below market costs, and the like.
25. That this country help those friendly nations such as Israel, Taiwan, South Korea, South Africa, and so on.
26. That any and all efforts to bring about a central world government be unceasingly opposed.
27. That while we support all genuine efforts for world peace in the community of nations, we nevertheless express little confidence

in the United Nations to achieve this because of past failures and the anti-American philosophies displayed by that organization.

28. That we totally condemn the vicious aggression of the Soviet Union as seen by their ruthless land grabs of many eastern European countries and, of recent times, Afghanistan.
29. That through the process of a twentieth-century moral and spiritual awakening our nation once again take its rightful and historical place as leader and example to the other countries in the world's community.
30. That this renewal of the 1980s begin with the joining of hands of church and political leaders, both promising to help and support the other in accomplishing their God-appointed tasks.

Concerning the Family

31. That God himself has instituted marriage.
32. That ideal marriage consists of the joining of one man to one woman for one life-time.
33. That no other institution in human history has proven so successful or satisfactory.
34. That children are the normally expected fruit of this union.
35. That the husband is looked upon as the divinely appointed head of this institution.
36. That both husband and wife have the responsibility of raising their children without outside governmental interference.
37. That children belong to the parents and are not wards of the state.
38. That communal living is wrong because it is antifamily.
39. That abortion is wrong because it is antifamily.
40. That homosexuality is wrong because it is antifamily.
41. That polygamy is wrong because it is antifamily.
42. That child or wife abuse is wrong because it is antifamily.
43. That abusive use of alcohol and drugs is wrong because it is antifamily.
44. That premarital sex is wrong because it is antifamily.
45. That incest is wrong because it is antifamily.
46. That adultery is wrong because it is antifamily.
47. That pornography, in any form, is wrong because it is antifamily.
48. That no-fault divorce laws are wrong because these are antifamily.
49. That the Equal Rights Amendment (ERA) is wrong because it is antifamily.

50. That the ratification of the ERA would endorse and make lawful homosexual marriages.
51. That the ratification of ERA could cause the drafting of women for combat.
52. That the ERA ridicules the historical role of the woman as a faithful housewife and mother.
53. That certain IRS laws today, which permit unmarried couples living together to receive tax benefits unallowable to wedded couples, are wrong because they are antifamily.
54. That history has consistently taught that any nation which allows the family unit to deteriorate is automatically marked for destruction.

Concerning the Value of Life

55. That man was created in the image of God.
56. That human life is therefore sacred.
57. That human life begins at the moment of conception.
58. That abortion is wrong because it is the murder of human life.
59. That the crime of abortion not be financed by federal funding.
60. That the parents of unmarried and pregnant teenage girls be consulted prior to any medical action taken between their daughter and her doctor.
61. That abortion blunts the national conscience.
62. That abortion weakens the ethics of the medical profession.
63. That abortion creates maternal guilt.
64. That abortion destroys individual and personal responsibilities.
65. That infanticide is wrong because it is antilife.
66. That mercy killing is wrong because it is antilife.

Concerning the Separation of Church and State

67. That the U.S. Constitution explicitly declares the separation of church and state.
68. That churches and private religious schools be therefore free from state and federal harassment.
69. That no church or private religious school be subjected to taxation.

70. That no church or private religious school be underwritten by the government.
71. That the mission of the church is to create a moral climate influencing good government.
72. That when moral issues enter the political arena, it becomes both the right and the responsibility of the church to speak out concerning those issues.
73. That politicians running for office be expected to state their position concerning the moral issues of the day.
74. That the Fairness Doctrine not be used as an excuse to prohibit church leaders from using the media to speak out against immorality.

Concerning Law and Order

75. That the process of indulgent judges coddling hardened criminals be stopped, which actions often result in the offender being back on the streets even before his victim is out of the hospital.
76. That those convicted of premeditated murder be put to death as payment for their crimes.
77. That police officials be allowed to investigate and arrest law-breakers with a minimum of red tape and bureaucratic meddling.
78. That existing criminal laws be tightened to prevent those convicted of felonies from being acquitted on minor technicalities.
79. That new laws be introduced providing for the immediate deportation of trouble-making noncitizens in this country.

Concerning Education

80. That all tax-supported educational systems be pro-flag and pro-freedom in their philosophy.
81. That voluntary prayer be reinstated in all public schools.
82. That voluntary Bible reading be reinstated in all public schools.
83. That in the spirit of true education, both prevalent theories of origin be impartially taught in the public school system. These two models are special creation and evolution.
84. That Christmas observances be allowed to continue in public schools.
85. That Easter observances be allowed to continue in public schools.

86. That no antifamily advocate be employed in the public school system.
87. That no pornographic and amoral sex instruction be permitted in the public school system.
88. That public school teachers be protected against the threats of young hoodlum students.
89. That all private schools be controlled and supported by their own constituency without outside governmental interference.
90. That no law be introduced to force private schools to hire individuals solely to achieve minority group balance.

Concerning the Nation of Israel

91. That the nation of Israel has a right to exist in the world community today.
92. That this is based upon a theological, historical, human, and political right.
93. That the nation of Israel is America's foremost friend in the Middle East.
94. That America guarantee the continued existence of Israel as a nation.
95. That America oppose any U.N. action which would pressure Israel to return to the 1967 geographical boundaries in the Middle East.

Appendix 6: Member Institutions of the Christian College Coalition

Anderson College
Anderson, IN 46012

Asbury College
Wilmore, KY 40390

Azusa Pacific University
Azusa, CA 91702

Bartlesville Wesleyan College
Bartlesville, OK 74003

Belhaven College
Jackson, MS 39202

Bethany Nazarene College
Bethany, OK 73008

Bethel College
Mishawaka, IN 46545

Bethel College
North Newton, KS 67117

Bethel College
3900 Bethel Drive
St. Paul, MN 55112

Biola University
13800 Biola Avenue
La Mirada, CA 90639

Bryan College
Dayton, TN 37321

Calvin College
Grand Rapids, MI 49506

Campbell University
Buies Creek, NC 27506

Campbellsville College
Campbellsville, KY 42718

Central Wesleyan College
Central, SC 29630

Colorado Christian College
Lakewood, CO 80226

Covenant College
Lookout Mountain, TN 37350

Dallas Baptist
Dallas, TX 75211

Dordt College
Sioux Center, IA 51250

Eastern College
St. Davids, PA 19087

Eastern Mennonite College
Harrisonburg, VA 22801

Eastern Nazarene College
23 E. Elm Avenue
Quincy, MA 02170

Evangel College
Springfield, MO 65802

Fresno Pacific College
Fresno, CA 93702

Geneva College
Beaver Falls, PA 15010

George Fox College
Newberg, OR 97132

Gordon College
Wenham, MA 01984

Goshen College
Goshen, IN 46526

Grace College
200 Seminary Drive
Winona Lake, IN 46590

Grand Canyon College
P.O. Box 11097
Phoenix, AZ 85061

Greenville College
Greenville, IL 62246

Houghton College
Houghton, NY 14744

Huntington College
Huntington, IN 46750

John Brown University
Siloam Springs, AR 72761

Judson College
Elgin, IL 60120

King College
Bristol, TN 37620

The King's College
Briarcliff Manor, NY 10510

Lee College
Cleveland, TN 37311

LeTourneau College
Longview, TX 75607

Malone College
Canton, OH 44709

Marion College
Marion, IN 46952

The Master's College
Newhall, CA 91322

Messiah College
Grantham, PA 17027

Mid-America Nazarene College
Olathe, KS 66061

Milligan College
Milligan, TN 37682

Mississippi College
Clinton, MS 39058

Mount Vernon Nazarene College
Mt. Vernon, OH 43050

North Park College
5125 North Spaulding Ave.
Chicago, IL 60625

Northwest Christian College
11th and Alder
Eugene, OR 97401

Northwest Nazarene College
Nampa, ID 83651

Northwestern College
Orange City, IA 51041

Northwestern College
3003 Snelling N.
Roseville, MN 55113

Nyack College
Nyack, NY 10960

Olivet Nazarene College
Kankakee, IL 60901

Oral Roberts University
7777 South Lewis
Tulsa, OK 74171

Palm Beach Atlantic College
1101 South Olive Avenue
West Palm Beach, FL 33401

Point Loma Nazarene College
3900 Lomaland Drive
San Diego, CA 92106

Roberts Wesleyan College
2301 Westside Drive
Rochester, NY 14624

Seattle Pacific University
Seattle, WA 98119

Simpson College
San Francisco, CA 94134

Sioux Falls College
Sioux Falls, SD 57101

Southern California College
55 Fair Drive
Costa Mesa, CA 92626

Spring Arbor College
Spring Arbor, MI 49283

Sterling College
Sterling, KS 67579

Tabor College
Hillsboro, KS 67063

Taylor University
Upland, IN 46989

Trevecca Nazarene College
333 Murfreesboro Road
Nashville, TN 37210

Trinity College
2077 Half Day Road
Deerfield, IL 60015

Trinity Christian College
6601 West College Drive
Palos Heights, IL 60463

Warner Pacific College
2219 Southeast 68th Avenue
Portland, OR 97215

Warner Southern College
Lake Wales, FL 33853

Westmont College
955 La Paz Road
Santa Barbara, CA 93108

Wheaton College
Wheaton, IL 60187

Whitworth College
Spokane, WA 99251

Select Bibliography

Interpretative Studies of Evangelical Political Thought

Fowler, Robert. *A New Engagement: Evangelical Political Thought, 1966–1976.* Grand Rapids: William B. Eerdmans Publishing Co., 1982.

Hunter, James Davison. *American Evangelicalism: Conservative Religion and the Quandary of Modernity.* New Brunswick, N.J.: Rutgers University Press, 1983.

Johnston, Robert K. *Evangelicals at an Impasse: Biblical Authority in Practice.* Atlanta: John Knox Press, 1979.

Jorstad, Erling. *Evangelicals in the White House: The Cultural Maturation of Born-Again Christianity, 1960–1981.* New York and Toronto: Edwin Mellen Press, 1981.

Marsden, George. *Fundamentalism and American Culture: The Shaping of Twentieth-Century Evangelicalism, 1870–1925.* New York: Oxford University Press, 1980.

———, ed. *Evangelicalism and Modern America.* Grand Rapids: William B. Eerdmans Publishing Co., 1984.

Smith, Timothy L. *Revivalism and Social Reform: American Protestantism on the Eve of the Civil War.* Baltimore: Johns Hopkins University Press, 1980.

Sweet, Leonard I., ed. *The Evangelical Tradition in America.* Macon, Ga.: Mercer University Press, 1984.

Wells, David F., and John D. Woodbridge, eds. *Evangelicals: What They Believe, Who They Are, Where They Are Changing.* Nashville: Abingdon Press, 1975.

Evangelical Political Conservative Thought

Bajema, Clifford E. *Abortion and the Meaning of Personhood.* Grand Rapids: Baker Book House, 1974.

Brown, Harold O. J. *The Protest of a Troubled Protestant*. New Rochelle, N.Y.: Arlington House, 1969.

————. *The Reconstruction of the Republic: A Modern Theory of the State "Under God" and its Political, Social, and Economic Structures*. New Rochelle, N.Y.: Arlington House, 1970.

————. *Christianity and the Class Struggle*. Grand Rapids: Zondervan, 1971.

Christenson, Larry. *Social Action: Jesus Style*. Minneapolis: Bethany Fellowship, 1976.

Cotham, Perry C. *Politics, Americanism and Christianity*. Grand Rapids: Baker Book House, 1976.

Culver, Robert. *Toward a Biblical View of Civil Government*. Chicago: Moody Press, 1974.

Davis, John Jefferson. *Evangelical Ethics: Issues Facing the Church Today*. Phillipsburg, N.J.: Presbyterian and Reformed Publishing Co., 1985.

Elliot, Elisabeth. *The Liberty of Obedience*. Waco, Tex.: Word Books, 1973.

————. *Let Me Be A Woman*. Wheaton, Ill.: Tyndale House, 1976.

Furness, Charles Y. *The Christian and Social Action*. Old Tappan, N.J.: Revell, 1972.

Henry, Carl F. H. *Aspects of Christian Social Ethics*. Grand Rapids: William B. Eerdmans Publishing Co., 1964.

————. *Evangelicals at the Brink of Crisis*. Waco, Tex.: Word Books, 1967.

————. *A Plea for Evangelical Demonstration*. Grand Rapids: Baker Book House, 1971.

————. *God, Revelation and Authority*. 6 vols. Waco, Tex.: Word Books, 1976–1979.

————. *The Christian Mindset in a Secular Society: Promoting Evangelical Renewal and National Righteousness*. Portland, Oreg.: Multnomah Press, 1984.

Lindsell, Harold. *Free Enterprise: A Judeo-Christian Defense*. Wheaton, Ill.: Tyndale House, 1982.

Mooneyham, W. Stanley. *What Do You Say to a Hungry World?* Waco, Tex.: Word Books, 1975.

Nash, Ronald. *Freedom, Justice and the State*. Washington, D.C.: University Press of America, 1980.

————. *Social Justice and the Christian Church*. Milford, Mich.: Mott Media, 1983.

Rees, Paul S. *Don't Sleep Through the Revolution*. Waco, Tex.: Word Books, 1969.

Schaeffer, Francis A. *Pollution and the Death of Man: The Christian View of Ecology*. Wheaton, Ill.: Tyndale House, 1970.

Valentine, Foy. *Citizenship for Christians*. Nashville: Broadman, 1965.

————. *The Cross in the Marketplace*. Waco, Tex.: Word Books, 1966.

Wirt, Sherwood Eliot. *The Social Conscience of the Evangelical*. New York: Harper and Row, 1968.

Evangelical Political Liberal Thought

Amstutz, Mark R. *Christian Ethics and U.S. Foreign Policy*. Grand Rapids: William B. Eerdmans Publishing Co., 1983.

Anderson, John B. *Between Two Worlds: A Congressman's Choice*. Grand Rapids: Zondervan, 1970.

————. "American Protestantism and Political Ideology." In *Congress and Conscience*, edited by John B. Anderson, 155–82. Philadelphia: J. B. Lippincott, 1970.

Clouse, Robert G., Robert D. Linder, and Richard V. Pierard, eds. *Protest and Politics: Christianity and Contemporary Affairs*. Greenwood, S.C.: Attic Press, 1968.

————. *The Cross and the Flag*. Carol Stream, Ill.: Creation House, 1972.

Grounds, Vernon C. *Evangelicalism and Social Responsibility*. Scottsdale, Pa.: Herald Press, 1969.

————. *Revolution and the Christian Faith*. Philadelphia: J. B. Lippincott, 1971.

Hatfield, Mark O. *Not Quite So Simple*. New York: Harper and Row, 1968.

————. *Conflict and Conscience*. Waco, Tex.: Word Books, 1971.

————. *Between a Rock and a Hard Place*. Waco, Tex.: Word Books, 1976.

Henry, Paul B. *Politics for Evangelicals*. Valley Forge, Pa.: Judson Press, 1974.

————. "Christian Perspectives on Power Politics." In *Christian Social Ethics*, edited by Perry C. Cotham, 61–80. Grand Rapids: Baker Book House, 1979.

Linder, Robert D., and Richard V. Pierard. *Politics: A Case for Christian Action*. Downers Grove, Ill.: Inter-Varsity Press, 1973.

————. *Twilight of the Saints: Biblical Christianity and Civil Religion in America*. Downers Grove, Ill.: Inter-Varsity Press, 1978.

Moberg, David O. *Inasmuch: Christian Social Responsibility in the Twentieth Century*. Grand Rapids: William B. Eerdmans Publishing Co., 1965.

————. *The Great Reversal: Evangelism Versus Social Concern*. Philadelphia: J. B. Lippincott, 1972.

Monsma, Stephen V. *The Unraveling of America*. Downers Grove, Ill.: Inter-Varsity Press, 1974.

————. *Pursuing Justice in a Sinful World*. Grand Rapids: William B. Eerdmans Publishing Co., 1984.

Montgomery, John Warwick. "Evangelical Social Responsibility in Theological Perspective." In *Our Society in Turmoil*, edited by Gary R. Collins, 13–23. Carol Stream, Ill.: Creation House, 1970.

———. *Human Rights and Human Dignity*. Grand Rapids: Zondervan, 1986.

Mott, Stephen C. *Biblical Ethics and Social Change*. New York: Oxford University Press, 1982.

Mouw, Richard J. *Political Evangelism*. Grand Rapids: William B. Eerdmans Publishing Co., 1973.

———. *Politics and the Biblical Drama*. Grand Rapids: William B. Eerdmans Publishing Co., 1976.

———. *Called to Holy Worldliness*. Philadelphia: Fortress Press, 1980.

Pannell, William E. *My Friend, the Enemy*. Waco, Tex.: Word Books, 1968.

Pierard, Richard V. *The Unequal Yoke: Evangelical Christianity and Political Conservatism*. Philadelphia: J. B. Lippincott, 1970.

———. "One Nation Under God: Judgment or Jingoism?" In *Christian Social Ethics*, edited by Perry C. Cotham, 81–103. Grand Rapids: Baker Book House, 1979.

Pierard, Richard V., and Robert D. Linder. *Civil Religion and the Presidency*. Grand Rapids: Zondervan, 1988.

Skinner, Tom. *How Black is the Gospel?* Philadelphia: J. B. Lippincott, 1970.

———. *Words of Revolution*. Grand Rapids: Zondervan, 1970.

Smedes, Lewis B. *Mere Morality: What God Expects from Ordinary People*. Grand Rapids: William B. Eerdmans Publishing Co., 1983.

Wolterstorff, Nicholas. *Until Justice and Peace Embrace*. Grand Rapids: William B. Eerdmans Publishing Co., 1983.

Evangelical Political Radical Thought

Alexander, John A. *Your Money or Your Life: A New Look at Jesus' View of Wealth and Power*. San Francisco: Harper and Row, 1986.

Brown, Dale W. *The Christian Revolutionary*. Grand Rapids: William B. Eerdmans Publishing Co., 1971.

Dayton, Donald W. *Discovering an Evangelical Heritage*. New York: Harper and Row, 1976.

Eller, Vernard. *The Simple Life: The Christian Stance Toward Possessions*. Grand Rapids: William B. Eerdmans Publishing Co., 1973.

Gish, Arthur G. *The New Left and Christian Radicalism*. Grand Rapids: William B. Eerdmans Publishing Co., 1970.

————. *Beyond the Rat Race.* Scottsdale, Pa.: Herald Press, 1973.

Jackson, Dave and Neta. *Living Together in a World Falling Apart.* Carol Stream, Ill.: Creation House, 1974.

Kraybill, Donald B. *The Upside Down Kingdom.* Scottsdale, Pa.: Herald Press, 1978.

Mollenkott, Virginia R. *Women, Men and the Bible.* Nashville: Abingdon Press, 1972.

Perkins, John. *Let Justice Roll Down.* Glendale, Calif.: Regal Books, 1976.

————. *A Quiet Revolution.* Waco, Tex.: Word Books, 1977.

————. *With Justice for All.* Ventura, Calif.: Regal Books, 1982.

Quebedeaux, Richard. *The Young Evangelicals: Revolution in Orthodoxy.* New York: Harper and Row, 1974.

Salley, Columbus, and Ronald Behm. *Your God Is Too White.* Downers Grove, Ill.: Inter-Varsity Press, 1970.

Scanzoni, Letha, and Nancy Hardesty. *All We're Meant to Be—A Biblical Approach to Women's Liberation.* Waco, Tex.: Word Books, 1974.

Scanzoni, Letha, and Virginia R. Mollenkott. *Is the Homosexual My Neighbor? Another Christian View.* San Francisco: Harper and Row, 1978.

Sider, Ronald J. *Christ and Violence.* Scottsdale, Pa.: Herald Press, 1979.

————, ed. *Cry Justice: The Bible Speaks on Hunger and Poverty.* Downers Grove, Ill.: Inter-Varsity Press; New York: Paulist Press, 1980.

————. *Rich Christians in an Age of Hunger.* 2d ed. Downers Grove, Ill.: Inter-Varsity Press, 1984.

Sider, Ronald J., and Richard K. Taylor. *Nuclear Holocaust and Christian Hope.* Downers Grove, Ill.: Inter-Varsity Press, 1982.

Sine, Tom. *The Mustard Seed Conspiracy.* Waco, Tex.: Word Books, 1981.

Stringfellow, William. *An Ethic for Christians and Other Aliens in a Strange Land.* Waco, Tex.: Word Books, 1973.

Wallis, Jim. *Agenda for Biblical People.* New York: Harper and Row, 1976.

————. *The Call to Conversion: Recovering the Gospel for These Times.* San Francisco: Harper and Row, 1981.

————. *Revive Us Again: A Sojourner's Story.* Nashville: Abingdon Press, 1983.

————, ed. *The Rise of Christian Conscience.* San Francisco: Harper and Row, 1987.

Yoder, John Howard. *Nevertheless: A Meditation on the Varieties and Shortcomings of Religious Pacifism.* Scottsdale, Pa.: Herald Press, 1971.

————. *The Politics of Jesus.* Grand Rapids: William B. Eerdmans Publishing Co., 1972.

———. *The Priestly Kingdom: Social Ethics as Gospel.* Notre Dame, Ind.: University of Notre Dame Press, 1986.

Fundamentalist New Right Thought

Buzzard, Lynn. *Schools: They Haven't Got a Prayer.* Elgin, Ill.: David C. Cook, 1982.

Conn, Harry. *Four Trojan Horses of Humanism.* Milford, Mich.: Mott Media, 1982.

Duncan, Homer. *Secular Humanism: The Most Dangerous Religion in America.* Lubbock, Tex.: Missionary Crusader, 1979.

Falwell, Jerry. *Listen, America!* New York: Bantam Books, 1981.

———. *Strength for the Journey: An Autobiography.* New York: Simon and Schuster, 1987.

Falwell, Jerry, Ed Dobson, and Ed Hindson. *The Fundamentalist Phenomenon: The Resurgence of Conservative Christianity.* Garden City, N.Y.: Doubleday, 1980.

Foster, Marshall, and Mary-Elaine Swanson. *The American Covenant: The Untold Story.* Thousand Oaks, Calif.: Foundation for Christian Self-Government, 1981.

LaHaye, Tim. *What Everyone Should Know about Homosexuality.* Wheaton, Ill.: Tyndale House, 1978.

———. *The Battle for the Mind.* Old Tappan, N.J.: Revell, 1980.

———. *The Battle for the Family.* Old Tappan, N.J.: Revell, 1981.

———. *The Coming Peace in the Middle East.* Grand Rapids: Zondervan, 1984.

Robertson, Pat. *The Secret Kingdom: A Promise of Hope and Freedom in a World of Turmoil.* With Bob Slosser. Nashville: Thomas Nelson Publishers, 1982.

———. *America's Date with Destiny.* Nashville: Thomas Nelson Publishers, 1986.

Robison, James. *Pornography: The Polluting of America.* Wheaton, Ill.: Tyndale House, 1982.

Schaeffer, Franky. *A Time for Anger: The Myth of Neutrality.* Westchester, Ill.: Crossway Books, 1981.

———, ed. *Is Capitalism Christian? Toward a Christian Perspective on Economics.* Westchester, Ill.: Crossway Books, 1985.

Swaggart, Jimmy. *Rape of a Nation.* Baton Rouge, La.: Jimmy Swaggart Ministries, 1985.

Thomas, Cal. *Book Burning.* Westchester, Ill.: Crossway Books, 1983.

————. *Liberals for Lunch: An Epicurean Collection of Columns and Cartoons.* Westchester, Ill.: Crossway Books, 1985.

Whitehead, John W. *The Separation Illusion: A Lawyer Examines the First Amendment.* Milford, Mich.: Mott Media, 1977.

————. *The Second American Revolution.* Elgin, Ill.: David C. Cook, 1982.

————. *The Stealing of America.* Westchester, Ill.: Crossway Books, 1983.

————. *Parents' Rights.* Westchester, Ill.: Crossway Books, 1985.

————. *An American Dream.* Westchester, Ill.: Crossway Books, 1987.

Whitehead, John W., and Jon Barton. *Schools on Fire.* Wheaton, Ill.: Tyndale House, 1980.

261.7
C415

79718

LINCOLN CHRISTIAN COLLEGE AND SEMINARY

DATE DUE

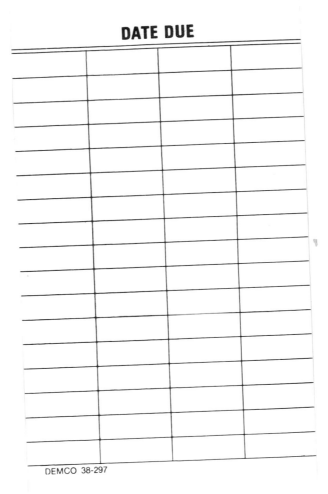

DEMCO 38-297

P9-BZB-389

About the Author

Gina Misiroglu began noting dozens of questions and answers for the second edition of *The Handy Answer Book for Children (and Parents)* while fielding life's questions from her two children, who are now 6 and 16. When she's not busy parenting, she spends her time writing books, specializing in the authorship and editing of pop culture, biography, American history, and general interest titles. Misiroglu has developed dozens of titles for publishers as varied as Warner Bros. Worldwide Publishing, Price Stern Sloan, New World Library, Macmillan Reference USA, and Sharpe Reference. She is the editor of *American Countercultures: An Encyclopedia of Nonconformists, Alternative Lifestyles, and Radical Ideas in U.S. History* (2008); *Girls Like Us: 40 Extraordinary Women Celebrate Girlhood in Story, Poetry, and Song* (2000)—winner of the New York Public Library's "Best Book for Teens" Award—and *Imagine: The Spirit of Twentieth-Century American Heroes* (2001). Her books for Visible Ink Press include *The Handy Politics Answer Book* (2002), *The Superhero Book: The Encyclopedia of Comic-Book Icons and Hollywood Heroes* (2004), and *The Handy Presidents Answer Book* (2005). She lives in Los Angeles.

Also from Visible Ink Press

The Handy Anatomy Answer Book
by James Bobick and Naomi Balaban
ISBN: 978-1-57859-190-9

The Handy Astronomy Answer Book
by Charles Liu
ISBN: 978-1-57859-193-0

The Handy Biology Answer Book
by James Bobick, Naomi Balaban,
Sandra Bobick, and Laurel Roberts
ISBN: 978-1-57859-150-3

The Handy Dinosaur Answer Book
2nd edition
by Patricia Barnes-Svarney
and Thomas E Svarney
ISBN: 978-1-57859-218-0

The Handy Geography Answer Book
2nd edition
by Paul A. Tucci
and Matthew T. Rosenberg
ISBN: 978-1-57859-215-9

The Handy Geology Answer Book
by Patricia Barnes-Svarney
and Thomas E Svarney
ISBN: 978-1-57859-156-5

The Handy History Answer Book
2nd Edition
by Rebecca Nelson Ferguson
ISBN: 978-1-57859-170-1

The Handy Math Answer Book
by Patricia Barnes-Svarney
and Thomas E Svarney
ISBN: 978-1-57859-171-8

The Handy Ocean Answer Book
by Patricia Barnes-Svarney
and Thomas E Svarney
ISBN: 978-1-57859-063-6

The Handy Philosophy Answer Book
by Naomi Zack
ISBN: 978-1-57859-226-5

The Handy Physics Answer Book
by P. Erik Gundersen
ISBN: 978-1-57859-058-2

The Handy Politics Answer Book
by Gina Misiroglu
ISBN: 978-1-57859-139-8

The Handy Religion Answer Book
by John Renard
ISBN: 978-1-57859-125-1

The Handy Science Answer Book™
Centennial Edition
by The Science and Technology Department, Carnegie Library of Pittsburgh
ISBN: 978-1-57859-140-4

The Handy Sports Answer Book
by Kevin Hillstrom, Laurie Hillstrom,
and Roger Matuz
ISBN: 978-1-57859-075-9

The Handy Supreme Court Answer Book
by David L Hudson, Jr.
ISBN: 978-1-57859-196-1

The Handy Weather Answer Book
by Kevin Hile
ISBN: 978-1-57859-221-0

Please visit us at visibleink.com.

THE
HANDY
ANSWER
BOOK *for*
KIDS
(and Parents)

THE
HANDY
ANSWER
BOOK *for*
KIDS
(and Parents)

SECOND EDITION

Gina Misiroglu

VISIBLE
INK
PRESS

Detroit

THE HANDY ANSWER BOOK *for* KIDS (and Parents)

Copyright © 2010 by Visible Ink Press®

This publication is a creative work fully protected by all applicable copyright laws, as well as by misappropriation, trade secret, unfair competition, and other applicable laws.

No part of this book may be reproduced in any form without permission in writing from the publisher, except by a reviewer who wishes to quote brief passages in connection with a review written for inclusion in a magazine, newspaper, or web site.

All rights to this publication will be vigorously defended.

Visible Ink Press®
43311 Joy Rd., #414
Canton, MI 48187-2075

Visible Ink Press is a registered trademark of Visible Ink Press LLC.

Most Visible Ink Press books are available at special quantity discounts when purchased in bulk by corporations, organizations, or groups. Customized printings, special imprints, messages, and excerpts can be produced to meet your needs. For more information, contact Special Markets Director, Visible Ink Press, www.visibleink.com, or 734-667-3211.

Managing Editor: Kevin S. Hile
Art Director: Mary Claire Krzewinski
Typesetting: Marco Di Vita
Indexing: Lawrence W. Baker
Proofreader: Sharon R. Gunton

ISBN 978-1-57859-219-7

Cover images: iStock.com.

Library of Congress Cataloging-in-Publication Data

Misiroglu, Gina Renée.
   The handy answer book for kids (and parents) / by Gina Misiroglu. — 2nd ed.
      p. cm.
   Includes bibliographical references and index.
   ISBN 978-1-57859-219-7
1. Children's questions and answers. I. Title.
   AG195.G25 2009
   031'.02—dc22

2009020191

Printed in Thailand by Imago.

10 9 8 7 6 5 4 3 2 1

Contents

Introduction

When Visible Ink's publisher, Roger Jänecke, approached me about updating the first edition of *The Handy Answer Book for Kids (and Parents),* I was a bit skeptical. Why, one might ask, update a great reference book that contains just about every question kids from ages 4 to 12? Well, the answer is simple: Because kids ask the darndest things … and they keep asking … and asking.…

Anyone who has ever been a kid, or had a kid, or hung out with a kid, knows that asking questions is what kids do. It happens to be a great way to find out about the world around you. Kids have an insatiable hunger for information and a curiosity that winds its way down every road. And it's an adult's job to satisfy that yearning for learning—by answering the questions you know, or by pointing kids in the direction of a good reference book when you don't.

Written with a child's imagination in mind, this revised edition of *The Handy Answer Book for Kids (and Parents)* is bursting with nearly 800 questions and answers on just about every topic in a kid's world. After collecting many new questions from moms and dads across the country, we were able supplement the book's already popular edition with intriguing information on dozens of different topics, helping parents provide answers that go beyond "because" and "it just is" and "I don't know." Consider *The Handy Answer Book* as a starting point—or for those who own the first edition, a punctuation mark—a launching pad that will send an inquisitive mind in many different directions. Or think of it as a fun way to spend a few hours, flipping from page to page and absorbing new nuggets of trivia to introduce to your friends.

The expanded second edition focuses on subjects that are front-and-center in a child's world, things that are part of kids' daily lives or spark their imaginations—from the stars twinkling overhead to earthworms burrowing into the earth. By the way, do you know why stars seem to twinkle? Or how big Earth is? Can you name our plants and pull a quick definition of a dwarf star out of your hat? Can you answer the ever-popular question, "Why is the sky blue?" The expanded "Outer Space" and "Planet Earth and Our Moon" chapters provide answers to these questions, explore the mysteries of the universe, and investigate weather-related phenomena ("What is a hurricane? An avalanche? Lightning? Thunder?") and various features of our planet, including rainforests, deserts, oceans, and volcanoes.

"People around the World" takes you on a journey around the globe, delivering answers to intriguing questions like which country is the smallest (Vatican City) and which country is the largest (Russia). This chapter also provides details about different cultures throughout the world, explaining why we have different religions, why people speak different languages, and which language is spoken by the most people in the world (Mandarin Chinese). You can also compare the starkly different lifestyles of those who live amid the bustle of a city and those who work the land. Speaking of farm life, do you know why so many barns are painted red? Or why horses sleep standing up? "Politics and Government " supplements this chapter with explanations about different types of government and the troubling question of why countries fight wars. Included here are also fascinating answers about state trivia. Is the District of Columbia a state? Which U.S. state was once its own kingdom? You'll find out in this section.

Perhaps the most interesting subject for kids (and adults, too) is the sometimes mysterious workings of their own bodies, particularly as they navigate their way through the minefield of burgeoning adolescence. "All about My Body" addresses the many changes a kid's body goes through and covers the body's basic functions, from how muscles work to why knuckles crack. And we don't shy away from the less appealing (or more appealing, depending upon your age and point of view) aspects of the human body, answering questions about sweat, pimples, warts, scabs, vomit, burps, and hiccups.

From a very young age, children become aware of and are fascinated by animals, and for many of us that fascination continues throughout our lives. "Creatures Big and Small" answers scores of questions about animals of all kinds, from the ancient dinosaurs to the tiniest insects and bee-sized bats to the slowest mammal (the sloth) and the biggest animal that has ever lived (the blue whale). Sometimes learning one small fact—like why each zebra has unique black-and-white stripes—can inspire us to look around and see things a bit differently.

In "Plant Life," curious minds will learn that plants are more than just attractive ways to decorate a yard; the Earth's unique ecosystem depends on plants, and their life systems are complex and amazing. Looking for a concise explanation of photosynthesis? Look no further. Do you wonder about the differences between the plants in your own backyard and those that survive in the Arctic tundra? Wonder no more. Have you always wanted to know if there's a flower big enough to float in? In the Amazon jungle, the Giant Water Platter grows leaves that reach six to eight feet across and can support the weight of small child.

All of us—young and not so old—use numerous high-tech tools and gadgets everyday. It's hard to imagine life without cellular phones and e-mail, not to mention elevators, airplanes, televisions, and light bulbs. But what miracles of technology make these items function? The chapter "How Things Work" explains it all. Did you know that a television relies on photo cells, electrical signals, and a microphone to function? And how do those things work together, anyway? Ever wonder how an X-ray takes pictures or how a submarine can submerge and rise in the water? What are barcodes, anyway? And why do stores—and consumers—rely on them? And what about numbers, counting, weights and measures, and telling time? The new chapter on "Math, Measurement, and Time" complements the "How Things Work" chapter and supports topics that kids encounter in school.

The chapter "Daily Life" addresses such critical questions as "How can I get a bigger allowance?" "Why do I need to get along with my brother and sister?" "Why do I have to go to school?" "Why do dogs wag their tails and bark?" "And why do I have to do homework, anyway (assuming the dog didn't eat it)?" This chapter also helps kids define the roles of various family members and explains the value of things like telling the truth, behaving politely, and being a good sport. It also anticipates some of the more difficult questions kids ask about divorce, growing old, and dying.

It's been said that children are like sponges, soaking up an amazing array and depth of information at a mind-spinning rate. Part of this rapid learning rate can be explained by physiological developments, but little knowledge would be possible without a sense of wonder and interest. And while those qualities can be found in abundance in most children, they are by no means the exclusive province of the young. If we're lucky, we continue to feel the excitement of learning new things and deepening our understanding our entire lives.

—Gina Misiroglu

For Oliver and Luke—
who always keep the questions coming!

OUTER SPACE

MYSTERIES OF
THE UNIVERSE

How did the **universe begin**?

Humankind has always puzzled over the origins of the universe. Scientists believe that the universe began with the Big Bang, a cosmic explosion that occurred between 10 and 20 billion years ago and threw matter in all directions. The universe began as a dense, hot fireball, a scrambling of space and time. Within the first second after the bang, gravity came into being. The universe expanded rapidly and became flooded with subatomic particles that slammed into one another, forming protons and neutrons. Three minutes later, when the temperature was 500 billion degrees Fahrenheit (280 billion degrees Celsius), protons and neutrons formed the simplest elements, including hydrogen, helium, and lithium.

According to the Big Bang theory, it took another 500,000 years for atoms to form and 300 million more years for stars and galaxies to begin to appear. Countless stars evolved and died before our own Sun and its planets came into being in our galaxy, called the Milky Way. And it was only 4.5 billion years ago that our solar system was formed from a cloud of dust and gas.

How **big** is the **universe**?

No one really knows just how big the universe is. The universe is everything that exists: the planets, moons, stars, and galaxies. There are over 100 billion galaxies—or massive star systems—in the visible universe. The number of stars in each galaxy varies, but each galaxy probably contains billions of stars. Now that's a big universe!

How does the **universe stay together**?

Gravity, the same force that keeps your two feet on the ground, holds the entire universe together. Gravity is the force of attraction that exists between any two particles of matter, or any two objects. It holds planets in their orbits around the Sun, and the Moon in its orbit around Earth. Gravity is also the force that holds any object to Earth—or to any other heavenly body—instead of allowing it to fly into space. The larger an object, the greater its gravitational pull.

What is a **light year**?

A light year is a way of measuring distance, and astronomers use light years to measure the distances between stars. It is the distance that light travels in one year, and is equal to almost 5.9 trillion miles (9.5 trillion kilometers). To think about how long a light year is, consider this: The Sun is about 93 million miles (149 million kilometers) from Earth, and a person would have to travel 31,620 *round trips* from Earth to the Sun to travel the distance of a light year. Scientists can see things in the universe more than 15 billion light years away.

Is the **universe expanding**?

In the 1990s, Australian and British astronomers compiled the largest map of the universe by plotting the positions of more than 30,000 galaxies. Most of these galaxies are moving away from us here on Earth. Most astronomers believe that the universe is expanding—that all points in the universe are getting farther apart all the time. It's not that stars and galaxies are getting bigger, but rather the space between all objects is expanding with time.

We never notice the expansion on planet Earth because it happens over such a large scale. In fact, it was only in 1929 that the expansion of the universe was discovered, when American astronomer Edwin Hubble brought together many scientists' work. He studied the sky and created "Hubble's diagram," which showed that the redness of a galaxy's light, and thus the speed with which the galaxy moved away from Earth, increased with its distance from Earth, and that the increase graphed into a straight line. The farther away a galaxy is, the faster it moves away from us.

Is it possible for the **universe to collapse** instead?

According to the Big Crunch theory, at some point all matter will reverse direction and crunch back into the single point from which it began. Another theory, called the Plateau theory, says that the expansion of the universe will slow to the point where it will nearly cease, at which time the universe will reach a plateau and remain essentially the same.

Is **Earth** at the **center of the universe**?

The Greek philosopher Aristotle proposed that the heavens were composed of 55 concentric, crystalline spheres to which the celestial objects were attached and

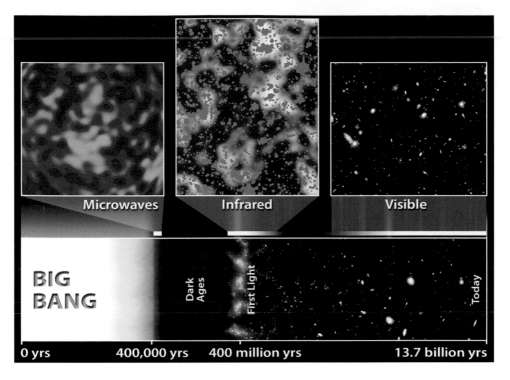

Microwaves	Infrared	Visible

BIG BANG

Dark Ages

First Light

Today

| 0 yrs | 400,000 yrs | 400 million yrs | 13.7 billion yrs |

Scientists figured out that the universe began with a Big Bang. Background microwave radiation and infrared light gives clues as to how the universe was formed and how it is still expanding today. (*NASA/JPL-Caltech/A. Kashlinsky*)

which rotated at different velocities, with the Earth at the center. People believed this for almost 2000 years, until Polish astronomer Nicolai Copernicus proposed that the Sun, not Earth, was the center of the solar system. His model, called a heliocentric system, said that Earth is just another planet (the third outward from the Sun), and the Moon is in orbit around Earth, not the Sun. While this might be true of our solar system, astronomers cannot see the whole universe through their telescopes, so no one knows where the true "center" of it lies.

What is **outer space**?

Outer space, sometimes simply called "space," are the areas between Earth and the Moon, between the planets of the solar system, and between the stars. Space is not completely empty. It does not contain any air, but it does contain a few specks of dust and atoms of gases.

Which **galaxy is closest** to ours?

The nearest big spiral galaxy to our galaxy, the Milky Way, is the Andromeda galaxy. Appearing as a smudge of light in the constellation Andromeda, this galaxy is about twice as big as the Milky Way. It is about 2.3 million light years away from us, although its vast size and luminosity make it visible to the naked eye. In fact, it is the most distant object that can been seen from Earth without a telescope.

3

Why is the Andromeda galaxy so special?

A ndromeda has a bright disk that scientists believe spans as much as 260,000 light years—almost twice the size of the bright disk seen in photographs. The outer disk emits nearly 10 percent of the galaxy's total light and may be made up of stars stripped from smaller galaxies that strayed too close. In 2007, a team of astronomers announced the discovery of low-metallic, red giant stars up to some 500,000 light years from Andromeda's core. This discovery suggests that the galaxy is much larger than scientists originally thought, and that Andromeda's glowing halo may actually overlap with that of the Milky Way.

PLANETS AND THE SOLAR SYSTEM

What is the **solar system**?

The solar system is made up of the Sun and all things orbiting around it, including the nine major planets, several dozen satellites like our Moon, and all the asteroids and comets. Each one moves in a unique path around the Sun, and the Sun's force of gravity holds all the celestial bodies together. Our solar system is part of the Milky Way galaxy, a group of some hundred billion stars that are arranged in a vast disk-like shape held together by gravitational forces. Our solar system is located about halfway between one edge of the Milky Way and its center, so all the stars that we can see from Earth belong to our galaxy. But with giant telescopes, scientists have been able to observe many other galaxies in our universe; they believe there are 100 billion other galaxies.

How **old** is the **solar system**?

Scientists believe that the solar system in about 4.6 billion years old. Earth and the rest of the solar system formed from a giant cloud of gas and dust. Gravity and rotational forces caused the cloud to flatten into a disc and much of the cloud's mass to drift into the center. This material became the Sun. The leftover parts of the cloud formed small bodies called planetesimals. These planetesimals collided with each other, gradually forming larger and larger bodies, some of which became the planets. This process took approximately 25 million years, according to scientific estimates.

What is an **orbit**?

An orbit is the circular or oval path that something follows as it moves through space. For example, the planets move in orbits around the Sun and the moons travel in orbits around the planets. To get into orbit around Earth, a spacecraft must fly out into space at a speed of at least 17,500 miles (28,163 kilometers) per hour. If a spacecraft does not reach this speed, it will fall back to Earth.

For many years, the solar system included Pluto, for a total of nine planets. Pluto is now considered a planetoid and not a true planet. This drawing shows the arrangement of the planets, as well as how far each planet tilts on its axis.

What is a **planet**?

The word "planet" comes from the Greek word for "wanderer." Ancient astronomers defined planets as objects that moved in the night sky against a background of fixed stars. Today, astronomers define a planet as an object in orbit around the Sun that is large enough (massive enough) to have its self-gravity pull itself into a round, or nearly round, shape. In addition, a planet orbits in a clear path around the Sun—there are no other bodies in its path that it must "sweep up" (or clear) as it moves around the Sun.

How many planets are there?

Scientists do not know how many planets there are in the universe. However, eight planets orbit the Sun. They are Mercury (which is closest to the Sun), Venus, Earth, Mars, Jupiter, Saturn, Uranus, and Neptune.

Which planets are the **rocky planets**?

Planets come in different sizes, compositions, and colors. Mercury, Venus, Earth, and Mars, the four planets closest to the Sun, are called "rocky" or "terrestrial" planets. Mars, Mercury, and Venus are similar to Earth in composition. Heat from the Sun evaporated lightweight elements like hydrogen and helium into interplanetary space. Mostly rock and metal were left in this zone and clumped together to form the inner rocky planets. These planets have no rings and only two of them—Earth and Mars—have moons.

5

Why isn't Pluto a planet anymore?

Pluto was once included in the list of planets, but is now considered a "dwarf" planet—an object in orbit around the Sun that is massive enough to have its own gravity to pull itself into a round (or nearly round) shape. Dwarf planets are generally smaller than Mercury. Pluto's composition is similar to that of comets, and its orbit is quite different from that of the other planets. Pluto also has one moon, Charon. It is located within a part of our solar system called the Kuiper Belt.

Scientists have discovered many objects in our solar system recently, but none of them have been classified as planets. Most are called either asteroids or minor planets, also called small solar system bodies. Some are called trans-Neptunian objects (TNO), because they are objects located past Neptune. One of the most recent discoveries of a TNO was in October 2000, when astronomers discovered a TNO and called it 2000 EB 173. It is between 186 and 435 miles (300 and 700 kilometers) in size and, as far as non-planets go in the solar system, it is second in size to the asteroid Ceres.

Which planets are called the **gas giants**?

The four outer planets—Jupiter, Saturn, Uranus, and Neptune—are called the gas giant planets. Much larger than the rocky planets, they all have rings and many moons. They are made up mostly of hydrogen, helium, frozen water, ammonia, methane, and carbon monoxide. Jupiter and Saturn contain the largest percentages of hydrogen and helium, while Uranus and Neptune contain the largest amounts of ices (frozen water, ammonia, methane, and carbon dioxide).

What is **Planet X**?

In the 1930s, when American mathematician and astronomer Percival Lowell decided to search for a planet beyond Neptune, he called the hypothetical planet "Planet X." This search led to the discovery of Pluto, but for many years some astronomers believed that another world larger than Pluto must exist undiscovered beyond Neptune. They thought this because Neptune's orbit seemed to be influenced by the gravity of an unseen planet. More recent studies indicate that a large Planet X most likely does not exist, but the term Planet X is still used in pop culture for an undiscovered planet in our solar system.

Who named our planets?

Except for the name Earth, our planets' names come from Roman and Greek mythology. The five planets easily visible to the naked eye—Mercury, Venus, Mars, Jupiter, and Saturn—were called different things by different cultures. The Romans named these planets, meaning "wanderers," according to their movements and appearance. For example, they named Jupiter after the king of the gods; they named Venus, the planet that appears the brightest, after the Roman goddess of beauty; they named the reddish Mars after the god of war. Saturn is named after the god of agriculture. These Roman names were adopted by European languages and culture and became standard in science.

Is a **day** the same on **all planets**?

No, it varies from planet to planet. A day is the period of time it takes for a planet to make one complete turn on its axis. Venus and Uranus display retrograde motion, which means they rotate in the opposite direction from other planets. There are 24 hours in a day on planet Earth and 10.5 hours on Saturn.

Which **planets** have **rings**?

Jupiter, Saturn, Uranus, and Neptune have rings—or thin belts of rocks—around them. Jupiter's

Saturn's rings are the most noticeable in the solar system, but other planets, including Jupiter, Uranus, and Neptune, have rings, too. (*NASA*)

ring is thin and dark, and cannot be seen from Earth. Saturn's rings are bright, wide, and colorful. Uranus has nine dark rings around it, and Neptune's rings are also dark, but contain a few bright arcs. At one time all of the planets, Earth included, had rings. These rings were unstable and the material was either lost in space or collected into the satellites of these planets.

Is there a **red planet**?

Yes. Mars, the fourth planet from the Sun, is called the Red Planet. It looks red because the rocks on the surface contain rusted iron. It has an atmosphere with clouds, winds, and dust storms—its red dust floats in the atmosphere and gives the planet a red sky. Mars, which has two moons, orbits the Sun every 687 days and rotates on its axis once every 24 hours and 37 minutes.

Which **planet** might **float on water**?

Saturn, the second largest planet in the solar system, is the least dense. Water has a density of 1.0 grams per centimeter cubed. Saturn, which is made mostly of gas

The greenhouse effect refers to the way in which gases in our planet's atmosphere can keep heat from escaping into space.

and liquid, has a density of 0.69 grams per centimeter cubed. This means that if you could somehow take a chunk of the planet and haul it back to Earth, it would float in your swimming pool.

Which **planet** could **melt metal**?

Most people think that Mercury is the hottest planet because it is nearest to the Sun. However, Venus, the second nearest planet, is the hottest because it has an atmosphere. Its atmosphere is primarily composed of carbon dioxide, which acts like a greenhouse. The solar heat enters Venus's atmosphere, but it cannot leave, heating the planet's surface to about 900 degrees Fahrenheit (482 degrees Celsius). This temperature is hot enough to melt several metals, including lead, tin, and zinc.

Where in **space** could you **ice skate**?

On Europa, one of Jupiter's moons, it is possible to ice skate, as long as you wore a space suit. A little smaller than Earth's moon, Europa is covered in smooth ice. Its gravity is only about one-eighth of planet Earth's, which makes for great leaps. However, Europa temperatures reach about –328 degrees Fahrenheit (–200 degrees Celsius), which means you would be frozen stiff in a nanosecond. The only colder object in the solar system is Neptune's moon, Triton, which has unique "ice volcanoes" and a surface temperature of –391 degrees Fahrenheit (–235 degrees Celsius).

Which is the **windiest planet**?

Although there are other windy planets (like Uranus), Neptune's winds are the fastest in the solar system, reaching 1,600 miles (2,575 kilometers) per hour. Neptune's large, sweeping wind storms could consume the entire planet Earth!

Could the greenhouse gas buildup ever make Earth as hot as Venus?

With a slow but steady increase in Earth's temperature, it could—far off in the future—become scorching hot like Venus. Earth's temperature increase has caused more water to evaporate from the oceans and some ice to melt in the Arctic, which increases the clouds in the atmosphere. The greater cloud covering blocks some solar heat from entering Earth's atmosphere, but it also worsens the greenhouse effect by trapping more of the heat that does make it down to the surface. Prolonged heating of the atmosphere could shut down Earth's tectonic plates—free-floating sections of crust—and cause the planet's crust to become locked in place, making it more like Venus's bone-dry surface.

Which **planets** experience the **greenhouse effect**?

The greenhouse effect describes a warming phenomenon. (In a greenhouse, closed glass windows cause heat to become trapped inside.) The greenhouse effect occurs when a planet's atmosphere allows heat from the Sun to enter, but refuses to let it leave. A good example of the greenhouse effect can be found on Venus. There, solar radiation penetrates the atmosphere, reaches the surface, and is reflected back into the atmosphere. The re-radiated heat is trapped by carbon dioxide, which is abundant in Venus's atmosphere. The result is that Venus has a scorching surface temperature of 900 degrees Fahrenheit (482 degrees Celsius). The greenhouse effect can also be found on Earth and in the upper atmospheres of the giant planets: Jupiter, Saturn, Uranus, and Neptune.

How does the **greenhouse effect** work on **Earth**?

On Earth, solar radiation passes through the atmosphere and strikes the surface. As it is reflected back up, some solar radiation is trapped by gases in the atmosphere, including carbon dioxide, methane, chlorofluorocarbons (CFCs), and water vapor, resulting in the gradual increase of Earth's temperature. The rest of the radiation escapes back into space.

Human activity is largely responsible for the buildup of greenhouse gases in Earth's atmosphere, and hence Earth's gradual warming. For instance, the burning of fossil fuels (such as coal, oil, and natural gas) and forest fires add carbon dioxide to the atmosphere. Methane buildup comes from the use of pesticides and fertilizers in agriculture. Large amounts of water vapor are released from various industries. And CFCs are released by some aerosol cans and coolants in refrigerators and air conditioners.

How is **Mars different** from Earth?

Mars is smaller, about half the size of Earth, with a radius of 2,108 miles (3,393 kilometers) compared to 3,963 miles (6,378 kilometers) for Earth. Because of its small size, Mars' interior cooled more quickly than Earth's, and thus it has less volcanic activity than Earth. The red planet also has no plate tectonics. Its crust is rigid, unlike the constantly moving crust of Earth. Therefore, Mars does not have extensive mountain chains, oceans, or lines of volcanoes, such as those found on Earth.

Is there **life on Mars**?

Earth is the only place that scientists know for certain supports life. The United States and other countries have been sending spacecraft to orbit or land on Mars since the 1960s, and each mission teaches scientists more about this fascinating planet. Although Mars is more similar to Earth than other planets in the solar system, it is still different from Earth in many ways. In 1976, NASA landed robotic spacecraft named *Viking 1* and *Viking 2* on Mars. *Viking 1* scooped up samples of Martian soil and tested it for signs of life, but none were found. In the future, NASA will be looking for live bacteria and searching for tiny fossils that might indicate life may have existed early in Mars's history but—unlike on Earth—did not survive and evolve into larger life forms. In 2008, NASA's *Phoenix* Mars Lander landed on the planet to search for complex organic molecules in the ice-rich soil of the arctic region.

Is there **life** on planets in **other solar systems**?

Because of great distances, it has been impossible for scientists to determine whether or not planets in other solar systems contain life. If we were able to gather data about the extrasolar planets, we might be able to tell if there is life on another planet. In particular, the presence of carbon dioxide could tell us that the planets have an atmosphere; a significant amount of water vapor—which is unique to Earth's atmosphere in our solar system—would tell us that a planet has an ocean; and ozone, the layer of gas that protects life on Earth from the ultraviolet radiation from the Sun, may tell us if a planet has life.

What is the **difference** between a **planet and a moon**?

There is a very basic difference between the two: A planet revolves around the Sun and a moon orbits a planet. Technically, the moon also orbits the Sun as it spins around its planet, but because it has its own suborbit of a planet scientists define it as a moon. All planets have moons, except for Mercury and Venus. Earth and Pluto have one moon, and Jupiter has 16. Saturn has the most known moons—more than 22.

OUR SUN AND THE STARS

What is the **difference** between a **planet and a star**?

A star is a huge ball of hot glowing gas, like the Sun, and a planet is a world, like Earth. Stars produce their own light; they undergo nuclear reactions that burn hydrogen in their cores. But planets are lit by light from the Sun. When you look

Why do stars twinkle?

On a clear, dark night in your backyard, you can see about 2,000 or so stars in the sky, a small fraction of the 100,000 or so stars that make up our galaxy. They seem to twinkle, or change their brightness. In reality, most of the stars are shining with a steady light. The movement of air (sometimes called turbulence) in the atmosphere of Earth causes the starlight to get slightly bent as it travels from the distant star through the atmosphere down to the ground. This means that some of the light reaches us directly and some gets bent slightly away. To the human eye, this makes the star seem to twinkle.

up into the night sky, it is hard to tell planets and stars apart. However, early astronomers were able to tell the difference because planets in our solar system appear to move in complicated paths across the sky, but stars don't. There are also other observational differences: planets almost never twinkle, but stars do.

What is the **Sun made out of**?

The Sun is a star, made up of hot gases that contain elements such as hydrogen, helium, calcium, sodium, magnesium, and iron. Its temperature is so high that it glows white, emitting both light and heat rays. It is also very large: if the Sun were the size of a basketball, Earth would only be the size of the head of a pin.

How **hot** is the **Sun**?

The Sun is extremely hot. The surface of the Sun (or its outer visible layer, called the photosphere) is about 10,000 degrees Fahrenheit (5,537 degrees Celsius)— about 50 times the temperature required to boil water. The core of the Sun, where solar energy is created, reaches 27 million degrees Fahrenheit (15 million degrees Celsius). It is so intense that nuclear reactions take place there.

What **would happen** if there **wasn't a Sun**?

Without the Sun, life on Earth would not exist. The planet would be a frozen dark ball, drifting in space. The Sun provides light, heat, and energy, which stirs up the atmosphere to create winds and rain. With it, plants grow, and animals and humans eat. However, the Sun's heat output changes over time, which affects our daily lives, the climate, and our satellite communications.

What happens during an **eclipse of the Sun**?

Once in a while the Moon passes directly in front of the Sun as it makes its way around Earth. It temporarily blocks out the Sun, casting a shadow on a portion of Earth that is experiencing day. When this total eclipse of the Sun—a solar eclipse—

11

When shown next to the Earth (the little dot on the right) you can really get a sense of how huge our Sun is! (*NASA/JPL-Caltech/R. Hurt*)

occurs, the part of Earth affected becomes dark and cold until the Moon passes by. Surrounding areas experience a partial eclipse, when just part of the Sun is temporarily covered by the Moon.

Where does the **Sun shine** the **most**?

In the United States, Yuma, Arizona has a yearly average of 90 percent of sunny days, or more than 4,000 sunny hours per year. St. Petersburg, Florida, is a close second; that city had 768 consecutive sunny days from February 9, 1967 to March 17, 1969. If you were to travel, you would find the eastern end of the Sahara Desert in North Africa the sunniest—the Sun shines there 97 percent of the time.

Is there a **place** on Earth where the **Sun does not rise**?

In the Arctic and Antarctic circles there is at least one day a year when the Sun does not rise and one day when the Sun does not set. This is because of their close location to Earth's poles. The Sun does not set on the summer solstice (June 21 in the north and December 21 in the south) and does not rise on the winter solstice (December 21 for the north and June 21 for the south). For this reason, the Arctic and Antarctic are called the "lands of midnight Sun" in the summer and "lands of noon darkness" in the winter.

What is a **supernova**?

A supernova is the explosion caused when a massive star, at least eight times the Sun's mass, exhausts its fuel (or dies) and then collapses. If the original star is less than 20 solar masses, the supernova will leave behind a neutron star, or remnant. Heavier stars will collapse into black holes. Supernova explosions are among the most energetic events in the universe, and are a rare sight. The last supernova seen in our galaxy, the Milky Way, was in 1604.

What is a **black hole**?

A black hole is an invisible region of space that is thought to have such intense gravity that not even light can escape. Scientists believe that a black hole is created when a giant star collapses in upon itself as it dies. A star lives as long as it can burn fuel. The burning of fuel acts as a counterforce against gravity; without that counterforce, a star's gravity would cause it to collapse in on itself. So when that fuel runs out, gravity takes over and crushes the star. If the star is large enough and has a strong enough force of gravity, it will become a black hole when it collapses. Scientists have discovered evidence of several black holes in our galaxy, and they believe there may be millions more that have not been identified.

What is a **quasar**?

In 1960, astronomers discovered some mysterious space objects and called them quasars because they were discovered to be a strong source of radio waves. In fact, the term "quasar" comes from the words "quasi-stellar radio source." Quasars are sources of light or radio waves, just like galaxies, that emit enormous amounts of energy. They are the most distant objects scientists have discovered. They are very bright (as bright as hundreds of galaxies, burning with the energy of 1 trillion Suns) and much smaller than most galaxies. Today, many astronomers refer to these objects as quasi-stellar objects, or QSOs.

What are the **patterns of stars** called?

Fixed groups of stars that seem to form a particular shape, such as that of a person, animal, or object, are called constellations. Astronomers have identified 88 constellations and many of them represent characters from Greek and Roman mythology. For example, the name Hydra, the largest constellation, comes from the water snake monster killed by Hercules in ancient mythology. Some of the constellation names are in Latin; for example, Cygnus means Swan and Scorpius means Scorpion.

COMETS, METEORS, AND ASTEROIDS

What are **comets**?

Comets are solar system bodies that orbit the Sun, just as planets do, except a comet usually has a very elongated orbit. Part of its orbit is very, very far from the Sun and

13

This is an image of Comet 73P, also called the Schwassman-Wachmann 3 comet. In 1995 it broke into pieces, two of which are seen here. This particular comet orbits our Sun every 5.5 years. (*NASA/JPL-Caltech/W. Reach*)

part is quite close to the Sun. They are sometimes nicknamed dirty "cosmic snow-balls," because they are small, irregularly shaped chunks of rock, various ices, and dust. As the comet gets closer to the Sun, some of the ice starts to melt and boil off, along with particles of dust. These particles and gases make a cloud around the nucleus, called a coma. The coma is lit by the Sun. The sunlight also pushes this material into the brightly lit "tail" of the comet.

What is an **asteroid**?

Asteroids are rocky objects that orbit around the Sun; most of them are located in a belt between Mars and Jupiter. Scientists believe there may be more than 50,000 asteroids in that belt, and perhaps millions more elsewhere in space. They range in size from nearly 20 feet (6 meters) in diameter to some as large as 600 miles (965 kilometers) across. (While 20 feet seems small compared to 600 miles, the smallest asteroids would still have a strong impact if they hit Earth.) Slight changes in aster-oids' orbits occasionally cause them to collide with each other, resulting in small fragments breaking off from the whole. Sometimes these small fragments leave their orbit and fall through Earth's atmosphere as meteors. Some scientists have suggested that it was a huge asteroid's collision with Earth 65 million years ago that caused the massive damage that led to the extinction of dinosaurs.

What is the difference between a **meteor** and a **shooting star**?

None, but the terms can sometimes be confusing. A *meteoroid* is a rock in space—it can be any size, from microscopic to many meters across. A *meteor* is the same rock falling through Earth's atmosphere, creating a streak of light, sometimes also called a "shooting star" after the white-hot glow produced by the heat of friction between the meteor and the air. Fragments of meteors that survive the trip through the atmosphere and land on Earth's surface are called *meteorites*. Some of Earth's craters were caused by meteorites, but eventually Earth's wind and rain erode the evidence of most craters. Because the Moon has no air to rub against, meteors do not burn up before hitting the Moon's surface, which is one reason why the Moon has lots of craters.

How many **meteorites reach Earth** in one year?

In any given year, approximately 26,000 meteorites, each weighing more than 3.5 ounces (99.2 grams) land on Earth. About 3,000 of these meteorites weigh more than 2.2 pounds (1 kilogram), according to the number of fireballs actually seen by scientists. Only a handful of these are witnessed or cause property damage; the majority of them fall into the oceans, which cover about 70 percent of Earth's surface.

EXPLORING SPACE

Who **invented** the **telescope**?

In 1608, Hans Lippershey, a Dutch eyeglass maker, invented the telescope, a device used by an astronomer to magnify images of distant objects. He noticed that objects appeared nearer when seen through two eyeglass lenses, so he mounted the lenses in a tube, making the first telescope. Crude telescopes and spyglasses may have been created much earlier, but Lippershey is believed to be the first to apply for a patent for his design (called the "Dutch perspective glass"), thus making it available for general use in 1608. A year later, the Italian astronomer Galileo Galilei built a telescope and was the first to use it to study the solar system systematically. He built about 30 telescopes but used only 10 to observe the sky. Through his careful observations, he found support for the Copernican, or Sun-centered, view of the solar system.

How **powerful** are astronomers' **telescopes**?

Before Lippershey and Galileo, magnification instruments had not been used to investigate objects beyond Earth. Since their time, far more powerful visible-light telescopes have been developed along with other types of telescopes capable of "seeing" invisible forms of radiation, such as infrared, ultraviolet, radio, X-ray, and gamma-ray. Today's optical telescopes (made from glass, lenses, or mirrors) are 100 million times more sensitive than Galileo's telescope. For example, Hawaii's twin Keck Tele-

The Hubble Space Telescope is seen here as it is being serviced by a space shuttle. (*NASA*)

15

scopes are the world's largest optical and infrared telescopes. Each stands eight stories tall and weighs 300 tons. The Hubble Space Telescope, named after astronomer Edwin Hubble and launched into space in 1990, orbits Earth at a speed of 5 miles (8 kilometers) per second, and beams images back to Earth. Because its position is above the atmosphere (which distorts and blocks the light that reaches Earth) it is able to view the universe more thoroughly and clearly than ground-based telescopes.

How does a rocket blast off?

Explosive chemical reactions are what send spacecraft into space. A rocket burns fuel to produce a jet of hot, expanding gas. What fuel is used varies, but whatever the mixture, it causes the explosive chemical reaction. Because a rocket needs thrust to escape Earth's gravity, the explosive chemical reaction takes place in a confined chamber and releases gases into a cone-shaped nozzle out the back end of the rocket. The cone shape accelerates the gases and they blast out of the engine at up to 9,941 miles (15,998 kilometers) per hour.

When did the first spacecraft go up into space?

The Soviet satellite *Sputnik 1,* which was launched into space on October 4, 1957, was the first spacecraft to go into orbit around Earth. It had no crew members or animals aboard, but instead contained machines that sent information back to Earth via radio. The former Soviet Union's (now Russia) launch of *Sputnik* prompted the United States to get its first satellite, *Explorer 1,* into orbit quickly, igniting the so-called space race. This was the two countries' rivalry over being the "first" in many areas of space exploration. *Explorer 1*'s test run in December 1957 burned on the ground, but the satellite was successfully launched into orbit around Earth on January 31, 1958.

What is a space shuttle?

NASA's space shuttle, also called the Space Transportation System (STS), takes off from Earth like a rocket but lands like an aircraft. It cannot fly to the Moon, but is used to orbit Earth, where the crew can do scientific work, place satellites in orbit, and visit orbiting space stations. Usually five to seven crew members ride the space shuttles, which have all been launched from Kennedy Space Center in Florida. Six shuttles have been built: the first orbiter, *Enterprise,* was built in 1974 for testing purposes. Five others have gone into space: *Columbia, Challenger, Discovery, Atlantis,* and *Endeavour.* The space shuttle *Challenger* disintegrated 73 seconds after launch in 1986, and *Endeavour* was built as a replacement. *Columbia* broke apart during re-entry in 2003. NASA announced that the space shuttle would no longer be used after 2010, and from 2014 on would be replaced by the *Orion,* a new space vehicle that is designed to take humans to the Moon and beyond.

What do the astronauts wear in space?

Crew members of the space shuttle are required to wear their space suits for launch and landing. Soviet cosmonauts are required to wear them during takeoff, landing,

What has the Hubble Space Telescope discovered?

According to the National Aeronautics and Space Administration (NASA), which is in charge of space exploration and scientific discovery for the United States, the Hubble transmits about 120 gigabytes of science data every week. That's equal to about 3,600 feet (1,097 meters) of books on a shelf. The growing collection of pictures and data is stored on magneto-optical disks. Among its many discoveries, Hubble has revealed the age of the universe to be about 13 to 14 billion years, which is a more accurate estimate than the Big Bang range of between 10 to 20 billion years. Hubble also played a key role in the discovery of dark energy, a mysterious force that causes the expansion of the universe to accelerate. Hubble has shown scientists galaxies in "toddler" stages of growth, helping them understand how galaxies form. It found protoplanetary disks, clumps of gas and dust around young stars that likely function as birthing grounds for new planets. It discovered that gamma-ray bursts—strange, incredibly powerful explosions of energy—occur in far-distant galaxies when massive stars collapse.

and docking—a big difference from when they originally used to fly in only their underwear.

Space suits come in different sizes, and the various body parts, such as the arms and legs, attach together for a customized fit. The inner suit is made of a layer of tubing, which is filled with a cool liquid; the outer suit is made of multiple layers of materials such as Dacron, nylon, and aluminum (Mylar). The boots come attached to the pants, and the middle part of the spacesuit, which covers the torso, is made of inflexible fiberglass. In all, the modern space suit is like a modern-day suit of arms, which is put over the head. Built-in backpacks hold life-support systems, a camera, and other useful items for space exploration.

What are space probes?

A space probe is an unmanned spacecraft that flies into outer space. It may land on the Moon or other planets, go into orbit around them, or fly past them. Its purpose is to conduct research: It contains cameras and other advanced equipment so that it can send pictures back to Earth by radio. The first successful space probe took place in 1959 with the Soviet *Luna 1,* which passed within 3,725 miles (5,995 kilometers) of the Moon's surface after 83 hours of flight. It then went into orbit around the Sun, between the orbits of Earth and Mars. In 1977, the United States launched *Voyager 1* and *Voyager 2* from rockets. These space probes explored all the giant planets of our outer solar system (Jupiter, Saturn, Uranus, and Neptune), 48 of their moons, and the unique system of rings and magnetic fields for each of those planets.

What does a **satellite** do?

A satellite is any body or object that moves around another; for example, the Moon is a satellite of Earth. But when most scientists use the word "satellite" they are referring to a man-made object that orbits Earth and collects and returns data. A single satellite may serve many purposes. Satellites can be used for weather forecasts by measuring clouds, winds, and the temperature of the atmosphere from space. They are also used in military contexts to track battle zones, watch for missile launches and nuclear testing, spy on countries, and track incoming objects like meteoroids. Satellites also send television programs and telephone calls from one continent to another. The first Global Positioning Satellite (GPS) was launched on November 22, 1978, and today GPS is the standard navigation tool used by the military, scientists, and industry. Space satellites are used for learning about the universe, including how the Sun and Earth interact and details about planets.

Who was the **first man in space**?

The Soviet cosmonaut Yuri Gagarin became the first man in space when he made a full orbit of Earth in *Vostok I* on April 12, 1961. Although he was in space less than two hours, he became an international hero. The United States launched the first American into orbit on February 20, 1962: Astronaut John Glenn completed three orbits of Earth in *Friendship 7*, traveling about 81,000 miles (130,329 kilometers).

Who was the **first woman in space**?

Valentina V. Tereshkova-Nikolaeva, a Soviet cosmonaut, was the first woman in space. She spent three days circling Earth, completing 48 orbits aboard *Vostok 6*, which launched on June 16, 1963. Although she had little cosmonaut training, she was an expert parachutist. The United States put a woman in space twenty years later, on June 18, 1983, when astronaut Sally K. Ride flew aboard the space shuttle *Challenger* mission STS-7.

Who was the **first African American in space**?

Guion S. Bluford Jr. became the first African American to fly in space during the space shuttle *Challenger* mission STS-8, which took place from August 30 to September 5, 1983. He returned to space again in 1985 aboard *Challenger* mission STA-61-A/Spacelab D1. Mae C. Jemison became the first African American woman in space on September 12, 1992, when she flew aboard the space shuttle *Endeavour* mission Spacelab-J.

The Soviet cosmonaut Yuri Gagarin was the first man in outer space. He rode aboard the *Vostok I* in 1961. (*NASA*)

Can astronauts drink soda in space?

Yes! U.S. astronauts aboard *Challenger*'s 1985 flight drank Coke and Pepsi from special cans. Other astronauts have enjoyed corned beef sandwiches, hot dogs, graham crackers, and Life Savers. At *Mir* station in 1988, French cosmonaut Jean-Loup Chrétien treated fellow cosmonauts to 23 gourmet foods from a French chef, including compote of pigeon with dates and dried raisins, duck with artichokes, oxtail fondue with tomatoes and pickles, and beef bourguignon. Now that's fine dining!

How **many U.S. astronauts** have **walked** on the **Moon**?

Twelve astronauts have walked on the Moon, all via *Apollo* lunar aircrafts. Each of the six *Apollo* flights, which took place between 1969 and 1972, had a crew of three. However, since one crew member remained in orbit in the command service module (CSM), the other two actually stepped onto the Moon. When Neil Armstrong became the first astronaut in history to walk on the Moon on July 20, 1969, he said, "That's one small step for a man, one giant leap for mankind."

When were **animals** sent up **in space**?

In 1957, the first animal, a small female dog named Laika, was launched aboard the Soviet *Sputnik 2*. Laika was placed in a pressurized compartment within a capsule that weighed 1,103 pounds (500 kilograms), and died after a few days in orbit. The United States send a squirrel monkey named Old Reliable into space aboard the December 12, 1958, *Jupiter* flight, but it drowned during recovery. The next year, on another *Jupiter* flight, NASA sent two female monkeys into space and both were recovered alive.

What is the space station *Skylab*?

A space station is an orbiting satellite that allows astronauts to live in space for weeks or months at a time. The first U.S. space station, called *Skylab,* was launched unmanned on May 14, 1973. In 1973 and 1974, three more manned missions followed with *Skylab,* during which astronauts observed Earth, solar flares, and the comet Kohoutek. *Skylab* included a solar observatory, a laboratory for studying the effects of microgravity, and a refrigerator that held prime rib, German potato salad, and ice cream. *Skylab* orbited Earth 2,476 times during the 171 days and 13 hours of its three manned missions.

What was the *Challenger* disaster?

Seven astronauts were aboard *Challenger* flight STS-51L when it exploded during liftoff on January 28, 1986. Christa McAuliffe was a Concord, New Hampshire, high school social studies teacher. She and the other six crew members were killed when

19

Astronauts Kathryn Sullivan (left) and Sally Ride use Velcro and bungee cords to keep from floating too much in the shuttle. Life in space can be difficult, but exciting! (*NASA*)

a solid-fuel booster rocket leak led to a massive fuel tank explosion during liftoff from its launch pad. NASA's next flight was *Discovery,* which was launched on September 28, 1988. After the *Challenger* disaster, NASA's three remaining shuttles—*Atlantis, Discovery,* and *Columbia*—were rebuilt, each with more than 250 modifications improving safety and performance.

Will people **live in space** one day?

Many films and science-fiction books have shown colonies of humans living on the Moon or Mars, but at this time it is still a distant possibility. Since the 1960s, NASA has been planning lunar bases to use for scientific study or for training astronauts to go to Mars. Space stations have been designed to keep astronauts as comfortable as possible, with a 70 degrees Fahrenheit (21 degrees Celsius) constant temperature and all of the freeze-dried food, exercise equipment, and other amenities necessary for short-term life in space. However, only some people can actually adapt to a life in space, which includes a weightless environment, living in close quarters, and using technology necessary for carrying out routine daily activities. While it is possible for a scientific community to be functioning in space by the year 2020, it is less likely that the average citizen will be able to permanently relocate there anytime soon.

PLANET EARTH AND OUR MOON

THE BLUE PLANET

How **old** is **Earth**?

Scientists estimate that Earth—born out of a swirling cloud of gas and dust—is about 4.6 billion years old. They have reached this conclusion by studying Moon rocks and meteorites (rocks that have fallen from space to Earth) that they believe were formed at the same time as our planet.

How **big** is **Earth**?

Earth, which is almost round in shape, measures 24,901 miles (39,842 kilometers) around at its widest part, the equator. (The equator is the imaginary line that crosses the planet midway between the North and South Poles.) A measurement through Earth at the equator—in other words, the planet's diameter—reveals that it is 7,926 miles (about 12,700 kilometers) across. Earth's weight, or mass (the amount of matter it is made of), is around 6 sextillion tons. That is 6 with 21 zeros after it! Because Earth cannot be put on an enormous scale to find its weight, scientists use the laws of gravity and mathematical equations to figure this out.

Is the **Earth round**?

The Earth is not round, but slightly squashed; it's diameter at the equator (the imaginary line on Earth's surface that divides Earth into a Northern and a Southern Hemisphere) is about 24 miles (38 kilometers) greater than its diameter at the poles. Why? Because the planet is constantly spinning, forcing material out toward the equator. The Earth's surface is both smooth and bumpy, with vast oceans, tall mountains, rolling plains, canyons, swamps, and deserts. The tallest mountain on our planet, Mount Everest in the Himalayas, stands at an altitude of 29,108 feet

How is Earth like an onion?

Scientists often compare Earth to an onion because the planet is made up of many layers of rocks of different densities. On the outside, there is a think crust of hard, cold rock, which is about 4 miles (7 kilometers) thick under the oceans and 22 miles (35 kilometers) thick under the continents. The crust—the layer we live on—surrounds a hard, rocky surface that marks the top of the mantle, called the lithosphere. Most of Earth is made of its mantle, which goes almost halfway down to Earth's center. At the very center is Earth's core, which has a center of solid iron and nickel about the size of the Moon (called the inner core) and a molten exterior (called the outer core). The temperature of Earth increases about 36 degrees Fahrenheit (2.2 degrees Celsius) for every 0.62 miles (1 kilometer) down you go, reaching temperatures as high as 11,000 degrees Fahrenheit (6,093 degrees Celsius) at its center.

(8,872 meters), while Africa's Sahara, the largest desert on Earth, spans over 2.1 million square miles (500,000 square kilometers) of land.

How **many continents** are there?

A continent is one of several major land masses on the Earth. Most people say that there are seven continents: Africa, Antarctica, Asia, Australia, Europe, North America, and South America. However, in Europe and other parts of the world, many students are taught there are six continents, because teachers consider North and South America to be one single continent: America. Many scientists also agree that there are six continents, but for different reasons: they combine Europe and Asia, since they're one solid geologic landmass. Thus, these six continents are Africa, Antarctica, Australia, Eurasia, North America, and South America.

Is there a place where **two continents almost touch**?

There are several places in the world where the continents almost touch. Asia and North America are only 56 miles (90 kilometers) apart at the Bering Straight between the Pacific and Arctic Oceans. Africa and Europe are only 8 miles (12.8 kilometers) apart at the Straight of Gibraltar, the strait that connects the Atlantic Ocean to the Mediterranean Sea and separates Spain from Morocco. Europe and Asia are separated by about half a mile (0.80 kilometers) at the Bosporus Straight in Turkey, where Istanbul's Bosporus Bridge joins the two continents. In May 2005 tennis star Venus Williams played a show game on the bridge, making it the only game of tennis to be played on two continents.

Did the **continents always look like** they do **now**?

No. About 200 million years ago, the continents started out as a single land mass, a gigantic supercontinent called Pangaea (meaning "all the land" in Greek). The land

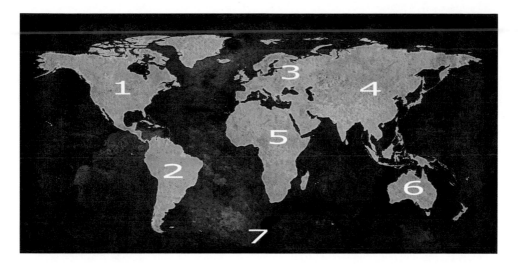

Our planet has seven continents: 1) North America, 2) South America, 3) Europe, 4) Asia, 5) Africa, 6) Australia, and 7) Antarctica (not shown).

tore apart from itself and formed two smaller supercontinents, called Laurasia and Gondwanaland, during the Jurassic period. By the end of the Cretaceous period, the continents were separating into landmasses that look like our modern-day continents. These continents split because hot areas in Earth's mantle below them caused the crust to get thin, and start moving away from the hot areas. (This phenomenon creates a new spreading ridge, and the continent becomes two smaller continents.) Because the continents are constantly moving, in a billion years they will look a lot different than they do today. For example, Australia is moving northward toward Asia at a rate of about 5 centimeters per year—which is about the same rate at which your fingernails grow!

Why does **Earth look blue** from outer space?

Earth looks blue from outer space because about two-thirds of the planet is covered with water. In fact, Earth is called the "Blue Planet" for this reason. (In reality, the oceans aren't blue; they only appear that way because the water reflects the color of the sky overhead—which also appears to us as blue, due to refraction of light.)

Is it true that **parts of Earth** are always **covered in ice**?

About one-tenth of Earth's surface is always under the cover of ice. And almost 90 percent of that ice is found in the continent of Antarctica. The remaining 10 percent is found on the mountains in the form of glaciers. The ice sheet that covers Antarctica is almost one-and-a-half times the size of the United States.

Why did **life develop on Earth** and not on the other planets?

Earth is the only planet on which water can exist in liquid form on the surface. Earth had the right temperature to allow water to circulate in all three states—

23

solids, liquid, and water vapor—conditions that helped produce life. Scientists believe that early life was primitive single-celled organisms that lived in the oceans. The reason is simple: life needed a filter to protect it from the incoming ultraviolet energy from the Sun, and the deep ocean waters gave life that protection.

Why do **deserts** have **special plants and animals**?

Deserts cover about one-fifth of Earth's surface and occur where rainfall is less than 10 inches (25 centimeters) per year. Most deserts—such as the Sahara of North Africa and the deserts of the southwestern U.S., Mexico, and Australia—occur at low latitudes. Another kind of desert, cold deserts, formed in the basin area of Utah and Nevada and in parts of western Asia. Most deserts grow a large amount of specialized vegetation. Soils are rich in nutrients because they need only water to become very productive and have little or no organic matter. Deserts often have the most "weird weather," such as occasional fires, cold weather, and sudden, intense rains that cause flooding. There are relatively few large mammals in deserts because most are not able to store sufficient water and withstand the heat, which often reaches 113 degrees Fahrenheit (45 degrees Celsius) in the summer months. Deserts provide little shelter from the Sun for large animals. Mammals are usually small, like the kangaroo rats of North American deserts. Other life that can be seen in the desert includes insects and spiders, such as stinkbugs, ticks, and tarantulas; reptiles such as snakes and lizards; and birds, such as hawks, owls, roadrunners, and woodpeckers, who make their homes in cactuses.

Where are the world's **rain forests**?

The name "rain forest" comes from the fact that these lush areas of land receive a lot of rain—between 160 and 400 inches per year. They are located near the equator, which means that their climate is warm. Rain forests cover only a small part of Earth's surface, about 6 percent, yet they are home to over half the species of plants and animals in the world. For example, the jungles and mangrove swamps of Central America contain many plants and animals found nowhere else, including many types of parrots. The Amazon jungle in South America is the world's largest tropical rain forest, and is home to one-fifth of the world's plants and animals. The forest covers the basin of the Amazon, the world's second longest river. Central Africa has the world's second largest rain forest. To the southeast, the large island of Madagascar is home to many unique animals. The rain forests of Asia stretch from India and Burma in the west to Malaysia and the islands of Java and Borneo in the east. Bangladesh has the largest area of mangrove forests in the world. Australia, too, has rain forests: undergrowth in this county's tropical forests is dense and lush.

What is the **Arctic tundra**?

Known for its cold, desert-like conditions, Arctic tundra is located in the Northern Hemisphere, encircling the North Pole. The stark landscape is frozen for most of the year, and water is unavailable. Temperatures during the arctic winter can dip to –60 Fahrenheit (–51 Celsius). In the summer the ground thaws for just a few weeks, and the region's plants and animals—which include geese, sea birds, polar bears, caribou, and shrews—fight for survival. Because the tundra is not usually exposed to human activity it is most susceptible to change and damage from human use or pollution. Oil spills damage the plants, land, and animals that live along the coast.

THE MOON

What is the **Moon**?

The planets of our solar system orbit the Sun, held in their paths by the Sun's gravitational force. Other heavenly bodies in our solar system—called natural satellites or moons—orbit the planets in a similar way. Some planets have many moons (Saturn has 18!), but Earth has just one. Our Moon is an almost-round natural satellite that consists of layers of different rock, similar in structure to Earth. It is believed that both were created at the same time, when our solar system was formed. (Some scientists think that the Moon broke off from Earth after our planet collided with another.) Unlike Earth, however, the Moon has no water or atmosphere, so nothing can live or grow on it. Without an atmosphere, nights (where the Moon is turned away from the Sun) are fiercely cold, and days (where the Moon receives the Sun's full rays) are very hot.

The Moon is located about 240,000 miles (386,400 kilometers) from Earth, close enough for astronauts to make a visit. The Moon's diameter is about 2,160 miles (3,478 kilometers), roughly one-quarter that of Earth, and Earth has about 80 times more mass, or weight. The Moon does not shine on its own: the moonlight that we see is simply sunlight reflected off its surface.

Is there a **Man in the Moon**?

There is no real Man in the Moon, but the expression comes from the dark patches on the Moon's surfaces (the lunar maria, or "seas"), which some people think look like two eyes and a big smile. In the early evening, when the Moon is nearly full, you can most easily see the face. Some cultures perceive different shapes, such as the silhouette of a woman, a moose, a buffalo, a hare, a frog, or a dragon in the full Moon.

What are **moonquakes**?

Moonquakes are quakes that happen on the Moon. Moonquakes are much less

Our Moon causes tides in our oceans and is the only place outside of Earth that humans have actually visited. (*NASA*)

How high could you jump on the Moon?

You could jump higher on the Moon than on Earth because your body would weigh less. The Moon's gravity is one-sixth of the gravity on Earth, but you probably could not jump six times as high as you could on Earth because you would be wearing a heavy, bulky spacesuit!

common and weaker than earthquakes, but certain types can register up to 5.5 on the Richter scale—which would damage buildings if they occurred on Earth. Vibration from shallow moonquakes usually continues for more than ten minutes compared to earthquakes which last around one or two minutes on Earth.

Does the **Moon** really have **volcanoes**?

Yes, the Moon has some volcanoes, but scientists classify them as "dead" volcanoes because they have not erupted for millions, perhaps billions, of years. In fact, studies based on rocks collected from the Moon's surface during the *Apollo* missions between 1969 and 1972 suggest that the bulk of the Moon's volcanic activity occurred around 3.9 billion years ago. Most of the deep craters on the Moon are from the surface being hit by asteroids and comets at that time.

How does the **Moon affect** the **ocean tides**?

Without the Moon, Earth would have no ocean tides, or periodic rises and falls in the level of the sea. Tides occur because the Moon exerts pull (or gravity) on the ocean water, causing it to rise and fall on a regular schedule. The gravitational pull of the Moon tugs on the surface of the ocean until its surface mounds up and outward in the direction of the Moon. When the mound of water has reached its highest point it is called high tide. On the side of the Earth opposite the Moon, the centrifugal force caused by Earth's rotation produces another mound of water and high tide on the opposite side of the globe. Somewhere in between these two high tides are two flat areas on the surface of the ocean, which are low tides.

Why does the **Moon follow us** when we're driving?

According to astronomers, the reason why the Moon seems to be following us is because it is so far away. The Moon is about 240,000 miles (386,400 kilometers) away from Earth. Because of this distance, the angle you view it from changes very little as you drive down the highway. So mile after mile, the Moon remains in roughly the same spot of sky. No matter how fast you drive, you just can't "pass" it. And just as you can't pass the Moon, neither can you dodge the presence of the Sun, planets, or stars.

Why is **Earth mostly crater-free** compared to the **pockmarked Moon**?

Earth is more active, in terms of both geology and weather, which makes it hard for craters to remain. Even those craters scientists can see on the surface—which may be millions of years old—have been overgrown by vegetation, weathered by wind and rain, and changed by earthquakes and landslides. The Moon, meanwhile, is geologically quiet and has almost no weather, so its hundreds of thousands of craters are easy to see. The craters are the result of both meteorites and volcanic activity. Interestingly, some of the oldest Earth rocks might be awaiting discovery on the Moon, having been blasted there billions of years ago by asteroid impacts that shook both worlds.

UP IN THE SKY

What is **air made of**?

Air is a mixture of gases that circle Earth, kept in place by gravity. Air makes up Earth's atmosphere. The air we breathe is 78 percent nitrogen gas, 21 percent oxygen, 0.9 percent argon, and 0.03 percent carbon dioxide, along with water vapor (floating molecules of water). Also present are traces of other gases and tiny bits of dust, pollen grains from plants, and other solid particles. As our atmosphere extends higher and higher above Earth, toward outer space, air becomes thinner and the combination of gases in the air changes.

Why is the **ozone layer important** to Earth?

Ozone, or three molecules of oxygen (O_3, compared with the O_2 that humans breathe) is a blanket in the atmosphere that covers Earth. The ozone layer is located between 9 and 25 miles (15 and 40 kilometers) up in the atmosphere, and it is produced by the interaction of the Sun's radiation with certain air molecules. While this blue-tinged gas benefits the atmosphere, ozone forms a layer of chemical smog at ground level. The smog is a secondary pollutant produced by the photochemical reactions of certain air pollutants, which usually come from cars and industrial activities.

The ozone layer is important to all life on planet Earth because it protects all living things from the effects of Sun's damaging ultraviolet radiation. Scientists believe that, about 2 billion years ago, oxygen was being produced by shallow-water marine animals. This outgoing oxygen helped produced the ozone layer. As the oxygen levels increased, ocean ani-

This image taken by satellite shows the hole in the ozone over Antarctica. The redder colors indicate low levels of ozone. (*National Oceanic and Atmospheric Administration*)

mals evolved. Once the protective layer was in place in the atmosphere, marine plants and animals were able to safely spread onto land. The loss of ozone means some sensitive organisms—necessary to Earth's food chain—may be killed by exposure to intense ultraviolet radiation from the Sun.

Is it true that at **one time** there was **no oxygen**?

Oxygen is necessary for all humans, animals, and plant life to survive. When Earth was first formed, its atmosphere had no oxygen—the colorless, odorless and tasteless gas that makes up about 20 percent of the air we breathe. It had only a deadly combination of hydrogen, methane, ammonia, and hydrogen cyanide. The hydrogen escaped into space and ultraviolet radiation from the Sun broke down the mixture, leaving only nitrogen and carbon dioxide. Only when life began and photosynthesis (the conversion of light energy into chemical energy by living organisms) occurred did oxygen first appear—about 3.4 billion years ago.

Why is the **sky blue**?

The white light of the Sun consists of many wavelengths. When seen separately, each wavelength corresponds with a different color. The air molecules and particles of matter that make up our atmosphere scatter some of the Sun's light as it travels to Earth, especially the shorter wavelengths that give us the color blue. Coming to us from all angles in the sky, these light waves make the sky appear blue.

How do we **see the wind**?

A big layer of air called the atmosphere surrounds Earth. The air within this layer moves from place to place when it warms up or cools down. This moving air is called wind. Winds move moisture and heat around the world and also produce much of our weather. You can see wind—which sometimes moves slowly and is barely noticeable—blowing through the trees. You can also sometimes feel wind as a gentle breeze in your face and in your hair. At other times, the air can move very quickly and become a hurricane, blowing down trees and damaging cars and buildings.

Where is the **windiest place on Earth**?

Antarctica is the coldest, highest, windiest, driest, and iciest continent on Earth. Winds can reach up to 200 miles (322 kilometers) per hour for five hours per day!

CLOUDS AND STORMS

What are **clouds made of**?

Clouds are formed from billions of minute water droplets and tiny ice crystals that float together in the air. Each of the droplets in a cloud is about 100 times smaller than a raindrop. In general, low-level clouds, or those that are lower than 6,000 feet

Can it rain cats and dogs?

Although there are no records of cats and dogs falling from the sky, rain can sometimes bring other things with it besides water, such as fish, snakes, snails, worms, and frogs. The strong updrafts that bring heavy rain, called waterspouts, suck up water along with creatures from ponds and lakes and whirl them up into the air. Sometimes the waterspout will move over dry land; when it starts to die out, the fish or amphibians fall to the ground. Some of the early instances include a 10-minute shower of toads in Jout-en-Jous, near Versailles, France, in June 1833, and a shower of jellyfish in Bath, England, in 1894.

(1,828 meters) above the ground, are mostly made of water droplets. However in cold weather, they can also contain small snow and ice crystals. Mid-level clouds, or those between 6,000 and 20,000 feet (1,828 and 6,096 meters), are composed of water droplets during the summer months but have a high concentration of ice crystals during winter. High-level clouds above 20,000 feet are largely made of ice crystals. In addition to carrying water and ice crystals, many clouds contain small quantities of solid particles such as smoke and dust.

How do **clouds float**?

Although the water and ice in clouds may typically weigh tons, the weight of a cloud is spread out over a very large area. The cloud's droplets are also very small—about one-hundred-thousandth of an inch across. A cloud's individual particles are so small, in fact, that warm air rising from Earth's surface is able to keep them floating in the air.

Why do **jet airplanes** leave white **trails in the sky**?

Jets leave white trails, called contrails, in their paths for the same reason you can sometimes see your breath on a cold winter morning. The hot, humid exhaust from jet engines mixes with the atmosphere, which at a high altitude is of much lower vapor pressure and temperature than the exhaust gas. The water vapor contained in the jet exhaust condenses and may freeze, and this mixing process forms a cloud. Depending how high the plane is flying, and the temperature and humidity of the atmosphere, contrails may be thick or thin, long or short. The different types of jet contrails can be used to predict the weather. For example, a thin, short-lived contrail indicates low-humidity air at high altitude, a sign of fair weather, whereas a thick, long-lasting contrail reveals humid air at high altitudes and can be an early indicator of a storm.

Why are **rain clouds gray**?

Rain clouds are generally dark gray because light cannot penetrate them due to the deep and densely packed water droplets and ice inside the cloud. Generally, the color of a cloud depends on the cloud's relationship to the sunlight: Clouds appear gray when they block sunlight. The thicker the cloud, the more light it blocks. When a cloud is about 3,000 feet (914 meters) thick, hardly any sunlight will make its way through the cloud.

What causes a **rainbow**?

A rainbow is an arc that shows all the colors, with their different wavelengths, that make up visible light. Seven colors make up a rainbow, and they always appear in the same order: red, with the longest wavelength, is on the top, followed by orange, yellow, green, blue, indigo (a deep reddish-blue that is often difficult to see), and violet, which has the shortest wavelength. A good way to remember the order of those colors is by taking the first letter of each to spell "ROYGBIV," pronounced "roy-jee-biv."

A rainbow occurs when sunlight passes through water droplets and is refracted or bent by their rounded shape into separate wavelengths. Rainbows can sometimes be spotted in the spray of lawn sprinklers, in the mist of water-falls, and—most spectacularly—in the sky during a rain shower when the Sun is still shining. A rainbow appears in the part of the sky opposite the Sun. Because the Sun must also be low in the sky, near the horizon, late afternoon is the best time to look for a rainbow if the day has been sunny with a few short rain showers or thunderstorms.

How **thick** is a **lighting bolt**?

In a large rain cloud, as water droplets bump into each other and increase in size, they become electrically charged. This activity causes electric charges on the ground, too. Sometimes the charges increase until they become so strong (up to 200 million volts!) that electricity runs through the air between the cloud and the ground in the form of a giant spark or lightning bolt. The diameter of a lightning bolt is about a 0.5 to 1 inch (1.3 to 2.5 centimeters) wide, but can be up to 5 inches (12.7 centimeters) wide. The average length of a lightning bolt from a cloud to the ground is 3 to 4 miles (4.8 to 6.4 kilometers) long. Lightning can occur not only in thunderstorms, but also in snowstorms, sand storms, and above erupting volcanoes.

How **far away** is **thunder and lightning**?

As lightning flashes in the sky, it causes a thunderclap. Light from the flash travels almost instantly to your eyes, but the sound of the thunder arrives a few seconds later. If you count the seconds between the flash and the thunder, you can estimate the distance of the flash of lightning: Every five seconds equals 1 mile (1.6 kilometers).

Where is the **wettest place** in the world?

Lloro, Colombia, in South America receives the most rain in any given year, about 523.6 inches (1,330 centimeters).

Lightning can be beautiful, but also dangerous! Thousands of lightning bolts shoot through our atmosphere every day.

Where is the **driest place** in the world?

The driest place on Earth is the 15-million-year-old Atacama Desert in Northern Chile. Made up of salt basins, sand, and lava flows, it is 50 times more arid than California's Death Valley. The average rainfall is just 1 millimeter per year!

Which **snowstorm** was the **worst in U.S. history**?

Called the "Storm of the Century," the worst snowstorm in U.S. history occurred in March 1993, when heavy snow blanketed most areas of the East Coast, with several states seeing record snow falls. Every airport on the East Coast closed at some point during the storm. At its height, the stormy blizzard stretched from Canada to Central America, but its main impact was on the eastern United States and Cuba. As much as 50 inches of snow fell in North Carolina and Tennessee, and $2 billion in damages were attributed to the storm, and over 300 people died as a result. The storm also spawned tornadoes, heavy wind gusts, and other severe weather. The Great Blizzard of 1899, which occurred in the northeastern United States in February of that year, is also considered among the worst. And the greatest snowfall in one day happened between April 14 and 15, 1921, at Silver Lake, Colorado, where more than 75 inches fell.

Why are **hurricanes** called **monster storms**?

A hurricane—from the Arawak Indian word *huracán*—is a massive storm in which a vast system of dark clouds, heavy rains, and strong winds circle around a calm

Is it true that no two snowflakes are the same?

Yes. Snowflakes fall from the sky in an infinite variety of shapes, but no two are exactly the same. Snowflakes are made of clusters of ice crystals and most are six-sided (hexagonal). Rarer varieties with needle-like crystals (formed at particularly low temperatures) and columns (formed at temperatures close to freezing) are also found, but you would need a microscope to tell the difference. More than 100 years ago, Wilson A. Bentley, an American farmer from the small town of Jericho, Vermont, photographed snowflakes through a microscope. By adapting a microscope to a bellows camera, he became the first person to photograph a single snowflake in 1885. In his lifetime he photographed more than 5,000 snowflakes, earning him the moniker "The Snowflake Man."

center. It originates in the warm waters of the tropics, then lumbers slowly across the world's oceans (such as the Atlantic, the Gulf of Mexico, the Caribbean, and the Western Pacific Ocean, where they are called typhoons), at speeds of 5 to 20 miles (8 to 32 kilometers) per hour, spinning around a core of low atmospheric pressure. Although the whole storm moves slowly, the circling winds in the storm blow at speeds ranging from 75 miles per hour up to nearly 150 miles (121 to 241 kilometers) per hour. During these "monster storms," houses fly apart, leaves and branches are ripped off of strong trees, plants are torn out of the ground, and flash floods carry away anything not firmly rooted to the ground, including houses, animals, and people. The central core of the storm—in some cases almost 15 miles (24 kilometers) in diameter—is called the eye of the hurricane. In the North Atlantic, hurricane season is from June 1 to November 3; in the East Pacific they are mostly just tropical storms. Today, space satellites track the course of hurricanes so that early warning can be given to those cities in the path of the storm.

Why are **tornadoes** so **dangerous**?

Tornadoes—violent, funnel-like storms of strong winds that usually form during thunderstorms—present danger to anyone nearby. These "twisters" can demolish anything in their path, including homes, people, cars, trees, animals, and even entire communities. Sometimes lightweight mobile homes are flipped over. A strong tornado that swept into Xenia, Ohio, on April 3, 1974, leveled a farmhouse and broke everything inside, leaving only three fragile items totally intact: a mirror, a case of eggs, and a box of Christmas ornaments! Occasionally, tornadoes do other strange things—like lifting a 386-ton railway train off its tracks and dropping it 16 feet (5 meters) away!

In the United States, an average of 1,000 tornadoes spin up beneath thunderstorms each year. A downward flow of cold air from clouds meets a rising flow of warm air from the ground; if atmospheric conditions are just right, a tornado starts. They occur mainly in a 10-state area known as Tornado Alley, stretching from Texas

The United States is hit with more tornadoes than any other country. They are particularly bad in the Central Plains states, such as Oklahoma and Kansas. (*NOAA Photo Library, NOAA Central Library; OAR/ERL/National Severe Storms Laboratory*)

to Nebraska that also includes Colorado, Iowa, Illinois, Indiana, Missouri, and Arkansas. Most weak tornadoes last less than 10 minutes and travel short distances. Powerful tornadoes have been known to last for hours and a few have traveled more than 100 miles (161 kilometers).

How far can a **tornado lift** and **carry items**?

The furthest distance a one-pound object can be carried is about 100 miles (161 kilometers). In the Great Bend, Kansas, tornado of November 10, 1915, debris from the town was carried 80 miles (128 kilometers). This included receipts, checks, photographs, money, clothing, shingles, and pages of books, which fell on almost every farm north and west of Glasco, 80 miles to the northeast. After passing through the town, the tornado went through Cheyenne Bottoms, and 45,000 migrating ducks fell from the sky 25 miles (40 kilometers) northeast of the end of the tornado path. And after the Worcester, Massachusetts tornado of 1953, chunks of soggy, frozen mattress fell into Boston Harbor, 50 miles (80 kilometers) to the east of where the mattress was picked up.

HOT AND COLD DAYS

When were the **hottest and coldest days** of the year?

In the United States, the hottest day that we know of was July 10, 1913. On that day, Death Valley, California, reached 134 degrees Fahrenheit (56 degrees Celsius). The

33

Was pond ice used as the first refrigerator?

In a way, yes. Before the invention of refrigeration machines in 1805, people cut ice from ponds in winter and stored it in an icehouse. These icehouses were pits dug into the ground and lined with wood or straw and packed with snow and ice. They were covered with an insulated roof. Because cold air sinks, the pit remained very cold, keeping foodstuffs cold and unspoiled until the early summer months.

highest temperature in the world was recorded on September 13, 1922 in Al Aziziyah, Libya, where it reached 136.4 degrees Fahrenheit (58 degrees Celsius). The coldest temperature ever measured was −129 Fahrenheit (−89 Celsius) at Vostok, Antarctica, on July 21, 1983. The world's most extreme temperatures take place in Verhoyansk, northeast Siberia, where temperatures fall as low as −90 degrees Fahrenheit (−68 degrees Celsius) in winter and rise as high as 98 degrees Fahrenheit (37 degrees Celsius) in summer.

What are "dog days"?

"Dog days" are the hot, humid days of summer that usually take place in the Northern Hemisphere in July and August—typically between July 3 and August 11. The days get their name from the dog star Sirius of the constellation Canis Major. At this time of year, Sirius, the brightest visible star, rises in the east at the same time as the Sun in the northern hemisphere. Ancient Egyptians believed that the heat of this brilliant star added to the Sun's heat to create this hot weather—and they blamed the star for everything from withering droughts to sickness.

If I don't have a thermometer handy, can I count cricket chirps to calculate the temperature outside?

Yes! The current temperature can be estimated by using a simple mathematical calculation involving counting the number of times a cricket chirps over a period of time. Male crickets chirp (usually at night when it's cooler) to attract female crickets and to scare other males away from their territory. The chirping sound is made by the male cricket rubbing together little teeth on its wings. The frequency of chirping varies according to temperature. When the temperature rises, so does the frequency of the cricket's chirp. To get a rough estimate of the temperature in degrees Fahrenheit, count the number of chirps in 15 seconds and then add 37. The number you get will be an approximation of the outside temperature.

Who were Gabriel Fahrenheit and Anders Celsius?

Today's thermometers are calibrated in standard temperature units of Fahrenheit or Celsius, both named for early researchers. In the early 1700s, the German scientist and engineer Gabriel Fahrenheit developed the alcohol and mercury thermometers and in 1724 invented the first temperature scale. The zero-degrees point was based on the lowest point to which the mercury fell during Germany's cold winters. The freezing point of water was 32 degrees Fahrenheit, the boiling point of water was 212 degrees Fahrenheit, and the human body temperature was defined as 96 degrees Fahrenheit. The Fahrenheit scale was widely used in the Europe, until Alders Celsius, a Swedish astronomer, developed the Celsius temperature scale in 1742. His thermometer labeled 0 degrees for the freezing point of water, and 100 degrees for water's boiling point. The Celsius temperature scale is also called the "centigrade" scale; centigrade means "consisting of or divided into 100 degrees."

How has the **world's climate changed** over the years?

Over the past few million years, Earth's climate has changed many times. In the last million years, there have been four ice ages, or glacials, which occurred about every 100,000 years and were interspersed with shorter, warmer interglacials. During the ice ages there was severe cold and large sections of ice spread across the land. The average temperature of Earth was six to eight degrees Fahrenheit below today's averages. As the ice moved, it made hollows in the land, pushing soil and rocks ahead of it. The sea level dropped and much of the water froze. After the ice ages, the interglacial period brought warmer weather. The ice melted and the huge hollows filled with water and became lakes. About 7,000 years ago the North American and Scandinavian ice sheets melted, and as sea levels rose the coastlines of the continents slowly took on their present shape. Scientists gather evidence about these past climates by studying sediment samples from the beds of the oceans or ice samples taken from Antarctica.

What was the **Little Ice Age**?

For about six hundred years, from 1250 to 1850, most parts of the world experienced colder and harsher climates than usual. The cooler temperatures were caused by a combination of less solar activity and large volcanic eruptions. Northern Europe's Little Ice Age took place between 1430 and 1850. When the climate became colder, crops died, and there was widespread famine and disease. Although it was not a true ice age because it did not get cold enough for long enough to cause ice sheets to grow larger, England experienced some of the coldest winters in its history during the 1820s. Its longest river, the River Thames, froze over regularly and townspeople held Frost Fairs, during which they played games and danced on its icy surface.

BIG MOUNTAINS, DEEP HOLES

How many **kinds of rock** does Earth have?

There are three different kinds of rock: sedimentary, igneous, and metamorphic, and each type tells how the rock formed. Sedimentary rocks formed long ago in lay-

U.S. presidents George Washington, Thomas Jefferson, Theodore Roosevelt, and Abraham Lincoln are carved out of a mountain in South Dakota's impressive Mt. Rushmore.

ers, often along the bottom of the sea. They include conglomerate, sandstone, and limestone. Igneous rocks formed from liquid rock like volcano lava, which cooled and became solid. Basalt, granite, and obsidian are all igneous rocks. Metamorphic rocks, such as marble and slate, formed from sedimentary or igneous rocks that were changed by heat, friction, or other natural causes.

Can **mountains grow** and **shrink**?

Yes. Mount Everest, Earth's highest summit, continues to rise. The 29,035-foot-high (8,850-meter-high) mountain grows about 0.16 inch (0.41 centimeters) per year. That's because the Himalayas, the mountain range that includes Mount Everest, was formed 50 million years ago when the Eurasian and Indian plates collided. Today, the plates continue to press against each other, causing the mountains in the range to rise. Other mountains shrink. For example, Mount St. Helens, a volcano in Washington State, erupted on May 18, 1980. The mountaintop was blasted into volcanic ash, shrinking the summit height from 9,677 feet (2,950 meters) to 8,364 feet (2,550 meters).

What is an **avalanche**?

An avalanche is a huge mass of ice and snow that breaks away from the side of a mountain and slides downward at great speed. Most avalanches result from weather conditions, such as heavy winds and earth tremors, that cause snow on a mountain slope to become unstable. A large avalanche in North America might release

What is Mount Rushmore?

Carved into the southeast face of a mountain in South Dakota are the faces of four presidents: George Washington, Thomas Jefferson, Theodore Roosevelt, and Abraham Lincoln. Known as Mount Rushmore, these 68-feet (20.7 meters) high granite sculptures were the brainchild of South Dakota state historian Doane Robinson. In 1923, he conceived the project to attract more people to the Black Hills of South Dakota. Congress passed legislation that authorized the carving in what is today known as Black Hills National Forest. In 1927, the sculptor Gutzon Borglum and 400 workers began the project, using dynamite to remove unwanted rock. Mount Rushmore was completed in 1941.

300,000 cubic yards of snow—the equivalent of 20 football fields filled 10 feet (3.3 meters) deep with snow. Wintertime, particularly from December to April, is when most avalanches occur.

Why is the **Grand Canyon** unique?

Located in Arizona and stretching to Colorado, the Grand Canyon is 18 miles (29 kilometers) wide, 227 miles (365 kilometers) long, and 6,000 feet (1,828 meters) deep in its deepest section. It takes about two days by foot or mule to travel from the top to the bottom. Although it is not the biggest canyon in the world—Barranca de Cabre in northern Mexico and Hell's Canyon in Idaho are deeper—it is known for its amazing landscape. The canyon's walls are made up of rocks, cliffs, hills, and valleys formed millions of years ago, and it is home to hundreds of species of mammals, reptiles, and birds. Although people lived in the canyon some 4,000 years ago, today it is a national park and national landmark.

How are **caves formed**?

Water erosion creates most caves found along coastal areas. Waves crashing against the rock over years and years wear down part of the rock, creating a cave. Inland caves are also created by water erosion; groundwater erodes limestone, creating underground passageways and caverns. Lechuguilla Cave, in Carlsbad Caverns National Park, New Mexico, is the deepest cave in the United States. Unlike most caves in which carbon dioxide mixes with rainwater to produce carbonic acid, these caverns were shaped by sulfuric acid. The sulfuric acid was the result of a reaction between oxygen that was dissolved in groundwater and hydrogen sulfide that came from far below the cave's surface. Since 1984, explorers have mapped 120-plus miles (193-plus kilometers) of passages and recorded the depth of the cave as 1,604 feet (489 meters), ranking Lechuguilla the fifth longest cave in the world. (The longest cave in the world is Kentucky's Mammoth Cave, which is almost 350 miles [560 kilometers] long!)

Where is the **deepest hole**?

The deepest hole ever made by humans is in Kola Peninsula in Russia, where in 1989 geologists dug a hole 7.6 miles (12.2 kilometers) deep. The Kola Superdeep Borehole began in the 1970s. Russian teams used special drilling techniques to dig into the Baltic continental crust, presumed to be about 22 miles (35 kilometers) thick, exposing rocks 2.7 billion years old at the bottom.

WATER, WATER EVERYWHERE

How much of **Earth is covered** with **land and water**?

Only 30 percent of Earth is covered by land, which includes all types of environment, such as the desert, rain forest, and Arctic tundra. Far more of Earth, about 70 percent, is covered with water. Of this, more than 97 percent is salty seawater from our oceans. All of Earth's freshwater makes up the remaining 3 percent. Freshwater includes water from the polar icecaps, lakes, rivers, and groundwater (water from wells and aquifers).

Why is the **ocean salty**?

Today, about 3.5 percent of ocean water is salt. When planet Earth was still young, its atmosphere contained a mix of hydrogen chloride, hydrogen bromide, and other gasses from volcanoes. Oceanographers (scientists who study the ocean) believe that some of these gases dissolved in the early ocean, making it salty. Today, however, most of the salt in the oceans comes from rain. Rain falling on the land dissolves the salts in eroding rocks, and these salts are carried down the rivers and out to sea. The salts accumulate in the ocean as water evaporates to form clouds. The oceans are getting saltier every day, but the rate of increase is so slow that it hard to measure. If the oceans suddenly dried up, there would be enough salt to build a 180-mile- (290-kilometer) tall wall around the equator.

What is the difference between an **ocean, a sea, a gulf,** and a **bay**?

All four bodies of water are different in size and location. Oceans, rich in seawater, are the largest bodies of water. There are four oceans: the Pacific, the Atlantic, the Indian, and the Arctic. At the edges of the oceans are seas, a part of the ocean that is partially enclosed by land. For example, the North Sea borders the Atlantic Ocean. (Not every body of water with the word "sea" in it is a sea: the Caspian Sea, Dead Sea, and Aral Sea are actually saltwater lakes because they lack an outlet to the ocean.) Gulfs and bays are bodies of water that jut into the land; a gulf is larger, sometimes has a narrow mouth, and is almost completely surrounded by land. The world's largest gulf is the Gulf of Mexico, with a total surface area of about 600,000 square miles (1.5 million square kilometers). It is surrounded by Mexico, the southern coast of the United States, and Cuba, and contains many bays, such as Matagor-

A diver watches butterfly fish swim in a coral reef. Coral reefs are like the rain forests of the oceans—beautiful and filled with wildlife.

da Bay in Texas and Mobile Bay in Alabama. The San Francisco Bay, off the coast of northern California, is a well-known bay in the United States.

What is an **iceberg**?

An iceberg is a large block of floating ice. A majority of the icebergs in the North Atlantic come from about 100 iceberg-producing glaciers along the Greenland coast, and a few originate in the Eastern Canadian Arctic Islands. The glaciers of western Greenland—where 90 percent of Newfoundland's icebergs originate—are among the fastest moving in the world, drifting up to 4.3 miles (7 kilometers) per year. Although some Antarctic icebergs are more than 60 miles (100 kilometers) long, they look a lot smaller because most of the iceberg floats underwater. This can be dangerous to ships, whose navigators may underestimate the length or depth of the iceberg.

What are **coral reefs**?

Tropical coral reefs are ridgelike or moundlike structures composed of corals and other aquatic organisms. They border the shorelines of more than 100 countries. Although coral reefs comprise less than 0.5 percent of the ocean floor, it is estimated that more than 90 percent of marine species are directly or indirectly dependent on them—they are home to approximately 4,000 species of fish alone. Reefs protect human populations along coastlines from wave and storm damage by serving as buffers between oceans and near-shore communities. The Great Barrier Reef, locat-

39

Why do planes disappear in the Bermuda Triangle?

The Bermuda Triangle is an area in the Atlantic Ocean bounded by imaginary lines in the shape of a triangle that run from Bermuda down to Puerto Rico, over to southeast Florida, and back up to Bermuda. Over the past century, hundreds of ships and aircraft have either disappeared or crashed in this region. Scientists believe there are many reasons why planes and ships disappear, including strong and unpredictable tropical storms, hurricanes, compass or equipment failure, lack of radios on board, and the structural weakness of the aircraft. Other people believe that ships disappear because of other less scientific reasons—such as unidentified flying objects (UFOs) that may have interfered.

ed in northeast Australia's Coral Sea, measures 1,616 miles (2,000 kilometers) in length. It the largest living structure on Earth, and can be seen from the Moon.

Do **rivers** ever **dry up**?

Some rivers have a lifetime of many thousands of years, but they eventually dry up. As a river flows over land, the water wears away, or erodes, the rock of the riverbed. Over time, the river levels out the land until it is flat, and then it stops flowing. Rivers also need a steady source of water, such as from a mountain's rainwater or snowmelt, or from rainfall. Without it, they will dry up.

What is an **estuary**?

Estuaries are bodies of water along the beaches that are formed when freshwater from rivers flows into and mixes with saltwater from the ocean. Tides may rise and fall in the estuary, making this area a unique ecosystem rich in nutrients. Only certain types of plants, such as saltwort, eelgrass, and saltgrass can grow there, and few animals can live their entire lives there. However, mud shrimp, certain types of mussels, and the Western sandpiper all call estuaries home.

VOLCANOES AND EARTHQUAKES

How do **volcanoes erupt**?

A volcano is a natural opening in Earth's crust through which lava (hot molten, or melted, rock), gases, steam, and ash escape, often in a big, noisy eruption or explosion. These eruptions are thought to act like safety valves, relieving the enormous heat and pressure that exist deep in Earth's interior. A volcano is usually a cone-shaped mountain (its sides built up from solidified lava and ash) that has a hole or crater in its center through which it vents. There are several different kinds or stages of eruptions, many causing no damage to the places or people located near the volcano. But a few eruptions are huge and destructive. During these, lava can pour out and run down the volcano into surrounding areas, and enormous suffocating clouds of steam, ash, hot gases, and shooting rock can travel downhill at great speeds, covering many miles.

What is the **Ring of Fire**?

Many volcanoes occur near the area where two ridges or plates of Earth's crust meet. Circling the Pacific Ocean—where crust plates meet—is a group of volcanoes known as the Ring of Fire. Plate movement in such regions may allow liquid rock, called magma

Volcanoes usually form in places where the Earth's crust is weakened, such as the places where plates of crust meet along the Ring of Fire.

(it's called "lava" only after it rises to the surface), that is located in chambers in Earth's interior to rise, resulting in volcanic activity. (Such conditions often result in earthquakes as well.) Volcanic activity can take place under the ocean as well as on land, and when this happens the formation of islands sometimes results.

How do **earthquakes** happen?

An earthquake is a great shaking of Earth's surface. It is caused by the cracking and shifting of the plates of rock that make up the planet's layered crust. As shifting plates suddenly slide past one another, vibrations in the form of waves are released. These shock waves travel through Earth, gradually weakening as they move farther from the spot (or spots) where the quake began, which is called the epicenter. Regions located near faults (places where cracks in Earth's crust are known to exist), are particularly vulnerable to earthquakes. Earthquakes vary in size and intensity. They may last a few seconds or continue for a few minutes. They may cause no damage, or they can result in widespread destruction and the deaths of thousands of people. Earthquake vibrations can be so violent that they collapse bridges and buildings, destroy highways, cause landslides, and lead to flooding if they occur in shallow water near a coast.

What are **earthquake zones**?

Scientists have learned that earthquakes occur in a number of definite zones, mainly where there are deep trenches in the ocean bed with groups of islands nearby, such as around the Pacific. In these zones, seismologists (people who study earthquakes) try to guess whether stress is building up underneath the surface. If the area has been dormant (quiet) for a long time, it may be that an earthquake is about to happen. They also use seismometers to detect the tiny shock waves that occur right before an earthquake. It is estimated that there are 500,000 detectable earthquakes in the world each year. Of these, 100,000 can be felt, and 100 of them cause damage.

When is **earthquake season**?

There is no such thing as "earthquake season." Earthquakes happen in cold weather, hot weather, dry weather, and rainy weather. Weather, which takes place above Earth's surface, does not affect the forces several miles beneath the surface, where earthquakes originate. The changes in air pressure that are related to the weather are very small compared to the forces in Earth's crust, and the effect of air pressure does not reach beneath the soil.

What are **icequakes**?

The interior of Antarctica has icequakes which, although they are much smaller, are more frequent than earthquakes in Antarctica. The icequakes are similar to earthquakes, but occur within the ice sheet itself instead of the land underneath the ice. Polar observers detect icequakes using South Pole seismometers, located 1,000 feet (304 meters) beneath the surface of the 10,000-foot-tall (3,048-meter-tall) ice cap. These seismometers measure and record the quietest vibrations of Earth.

What is a **tsunami**?

The Japanese word *tsunami* (pronounced soo-NAH-mee) means "harbor wave." It is a huge volume of moving seawater—kind of like a giant wave—that can travel for thousands of miles across the sea and then approach the shoreline with the strength to destroy buildings, trees, wildlife, and people. Tsunamis can be triggered by an undersea earthquake, landslide, or volcanic eruption. The most frequent tsunami-maker is an undersea earthquake, which buckles the seafloor and displaces large volumes of seawater, creating a tsunami. This unique ocean event is not related to tides, although it is sometimes mistakenly called a tidal wave.

GOING GREEN

What is **smog**?

The word "smog" was first used in London during the early 1900s to describe the combination of smoke and fog. Today, the term "smog" is used to describe a mixture of pollutants, primarily made up of ground-level ozone. Ozone can be beneficial or harmful depending on its location. The ozone located high above the surface in the stratosphere protects human health and the environment, but ground-level ozone is responsible for the choking, coughing, and stinging eyes associated with smog. Smog-forming pollutants come from many sources, such as automobile exhaust, power plants, factories, and many consumer products, including paints,

Why is smog bad for us?

Smog causes health problems such as difficulty breathing, asthma, reduced resistance to lung infections and colds, and eye irritation. The ozone in smog also inhibits plant growth and can cause widespread damage to crops and forests, and the haze reduces visibility. The smog or haze is particularly noticeable from mountains and other beautiful vistas, such those in national parks.

hair spray, charcoal starter fluid, solvents, and even plastic popcorn packaging. In many American cities, at least half of the pollutants come from cars, buses, trucks, and boats. Scientists estimate that about 90 million Americans live in areas with ozone levels above the standards for health safety.

What is **climate change**, and how does it differ from **global warming**?

Climate change refers to any significant change in measures of climate (such as temperature, precipitation, or wind) lasting for an extended period (decades or longer). Global warming is an average increase in the temperature of the atmosphere near Earth's surface and in the troposphere, which can contribute to changes in global climate patterns. Global warming and climate change can be caused by a variety of factors, both natural and human-induced.

What is the **greenhouse effect**?

The greenhouse effect is a natural phenomenon that helps regulate Earth's temperature. Greenhouse gases—carbon dioxide, methane, nitrous oxide, chlorofluorocarbons—act like an insulating blanket, trapping solar energy that would otherwise escape into space. Without this natural "greenhouse effect," temperatures would be about 60 degrees Fahrenheit (15.5 degrees Celsius) lower than they are now, and life as we know it today would not be possible. However, human activities, primarily the burning of fossil fuels and clearing of forests, have enhanced the natural greenhouse effect, causing Earth's average temperature to rise.

When was the **greenhouse effect discovered**?

The greenhouse effect was first described in theoretical terms by a Swedish researcher, Svante Arrhenius, in the late 1800s. However it wasn't until the following century that Arrhenius's theory was observed. In the 1930s, scientists realized that parts of the globe had warmed during the previous half-century. Then in the early 1960s scientists discovered that the level of carbon dioxide in the atmosphere was rising. Researchers began to take an interest and found a strong relationship between the increasing levels of carbon dioxide and average global temperature.

How much oil is there left in the world?

The world uses about 80 million barrels of oil per day to keep itself running. Based on this figure, scientists estimate that there may only be enough oil for another 100 years or so. Almost all of the world's oil is found in the Middle East, with Russia, Saudi Arabia, and Iran contributing the most oil to the world.

Are **human activities** responsible for the **warming climate**?

Yes. Careful measurements have confirmed that greenhouse gas emissions are increasing and that human activities (for example, the burning of fossil fuels and changes in land use, such as cutting down forests) are the primary cause. Scientists have confirmed that the recent increase in atmospheric greenhouse gas concentrations is primarily due to human activity. Human activities have caused the atmospheric concentrations of carbon dioxide and methane to be higher today than at any point during the last 650,000 years. Scientists agree it is very likely that most of the global average warming since the mid-twentieth century is due to human-induced increases in greenhouse gases, rather than to natural causes.

When do I send greenhouse gases in the air, and **how can I make a difference**?

You send greenhouse gases in the air during everyday activities, like every time you watch television, use the air conditioner, play a video game, listen to a stereo, turn on a light, use a hair dryer, wash or dry clothes, turn on the dishwasher, or microwave a meal. The trash that we send to landfills produces a greenhouse gas called methane. Methane is also produced by the animals we raise for dairy and meat products and when we take coal out of the ground. And when factories make the things that we buy and use everyday, they too are sending greenhouse gases into the air.

Whenever we use electricity, we help put greenhouse gases into the air. By turning off lights, the television, and the computer when you are through with them, you can help a lot. You can save energy by sometimes taking the bus, riding a bike, or walking. Planting trees is a great way to reduce greenhouse gases. Trees absorb carbon dioxide, a greenhouse gas, from the air. And you can recycle cans, bottles, plastic bags, and newspapers. When you recycle, you send less trash to the landfill and you help save natural resources, like trees, oil, and elements such as aluminum.

What is a **carbon footprint**?

A carbon footprint is a measure of the impact our activities have on the environment, and in particular climate change. It relates to the amount of greenhouse gases produced in our day-to-day lives through the burning of fossil fuels for electricity, heating, and transportation. The carbon footprint is a measurement of all greenhouse gases we individually produce and has units of kilograms of the carbon dioxide equivalent.

Do people still **mine for gold** in **America**?

Yes. Yet unlike a few centuries ago, gold panning today is primarily a recreational activity. Gold nuggets are found in areas where lode deposits and erosion have occurred—for example, in streams, rivers, ravines, and lake areas. All you need is a gold pan, a shovel, and a lot of patience. Both gold mines and gold prospecting sites exist in national parks from near Montgomery, Alabama to Washington, D.C. In addition, North Carolina, South Carolina, Georgia, Virginia, and Alabama have many gold mines and prospecting sites. These states were America's main source of gold for 45 years before the California Gold Rush of 1838, when gold was discovered at Sutter's Mill in Coloma, California. Its news spread like wildfire, resulting in some 300,000 people coming to California to pan for gold. In California, the five counties of Mariposa, Tuolumne, Calaveras, Amador, and El Dorado—nicknamed the "Mother Lode"—still have gold for discovery. In 1837, the U.S. government established gold coin mints in Georgia and North Carolina to avoid transporting the raw gold to the U.S. Mint in Philadelphia, where coins are made.

How much **garbage** do we **throw away** every year?

Each year, Americans create nearly 210 million tons of solid waste. According to the Environmental Protection Agency, the average American produces about 4.4 pounds (2 kilograms) of garbage per day, or a total of 29 pounds (13 kilograms) per week and 1,600 pounds (726 kilograms) per year. With the garbage produced in America alone, you could form a line of filled-up garbage trucks and reach the moon!

What does the slogan **"Reduce, Reuse, and Recycle"** mean?

You may have heard this expression used in school, in television commercials, or on a sign at your local parks and recreation. Basically, the slogan means that there are three key ways to produce less waste:

1. Reduce the amount of trash (and toxicity) you throw away.

2. Reuse containers and products whenever possible.

3. Recycle as much as possible and buy products with recycled content.

As much as 84 percent of all household waste can be recycled—so it makes sense to be conscious of what we use and how we can reuse it.

People make lots and lots of garbage. Americans make more garbage per person than anyone else. It all has to be put somewhere, and most of it ends up in huge landfills.

Why is it **important to recycle**?

Recycling turns materials that would otherwise become waste into valuable resources. Collecting used bottles, cans, and newspapers and taking them to the curb or to a collection facility is the first step in recycling. Recyclables are sent to a materials recovery facility to be sorted and turned into other items for manufacturing. Recyclables are bought and sold just like any other product. Besides reducing greenhouse gases by sending less garbage to the landfill, recycling helps you actively contribute the environment and your community.

You can help the environment if you buy recyclable products instead of non-recyclable ones. Look for the recycle mark—three arrows that make a circle—on the package. Recyclable products are usually made out of things that already have been used. It usually takes less energy to make recycled products than to make new ones. In addition, many consumer products—like computers, TVs, stereos, and VCRs—have special labels on them. The label says "Energy" and has a picture of a star. Products with the ENERGY STAR® label are made to save energy and ultimately help protect the environment. And, if you have the yard space, you can practice composting by using microorganisms (mainly bacteria and fungi) to decompose organic waste, such as food scraps and yard trimmings.

Why is it important to **conserve water**?

Water is vital to the survival of everything on the planet and is limited in supply. Earth might seem like it has abundant water, but in fact only 1 percent is available for human use. While the population and the demand on freshwater resources are increasing (each person uses about 12,000 gallons of water every year), supply remains the same. Water is constantly being cleaned and recycled through Earth's water cycle, yet we still need to conserve it because people use up Earth's freshwater faster than it can naturally be replenished. When you use water wisely, you help the environment. You save water for fish and animals, help preserve drinking water supplies, and ease the job of wastewater treatment plants—the less water you send down the drain, the less work these plants have to do to make water clean again. When you use water wisely, you also save the energy that your water supplier uses to treat and move water to you, and the energy your family uses to heat your water. Your family pays for the water you use, so if you use less water, you'll have more money left to spend on other things.

What is **acid rain**?

Acid rain is a problem that affects us all—whether it is damaging the family car, defacing historical statues, harming trees in a once-beautiful mountainous forest, or destroying the fish population in a lake. Acid rain is rain, fog, or snow from the atmosphere that contains higher than normal amounts of nitric and sulfuric acids. Acid rain comes from both natural sources, such as volcanoes and decaying vegetation, and human-made sources, such as emissions of sulfur dioxide and nitrogen oxides, which come from fossil fuel combustion. In the United States, most of these

What Is Earth Day?

Earth Day is a national holiday that was first celebrated on April 22, 1970. It was created by Senator Gaylord Nelson, a Democrat from Wisconsin who was elected to the U.S. Senate in 1962. Senator Nelson decided to set aside one day aside for the entire nation to focus on environmental issues, learn about ways to improve the environment, and protest against the federal government's unwillingness to help solve problems such as air pollution and the widespread destruction of forests. After lots of hard work and publicity, on the first Earth Day 20 million Americans gathered at different places from the East to West coasts to hear speeches, participate in community-wide cleanup efforts, and demonstrate to the government that the environment is a major national issue. Ever since then, April 22 has been the date for celebrating Earth Day—a time when the United States (and now many countries all over the world) could participate in educational activities that celebrate Earth and think of new ways to preserve our natural resources. On Earth Day 2008, over 100 million people joined in the effort to celebrate and protect our planet.

emissions come from electric-power generation that relies on burning fossil fuels, like coal. Acid rain occurs when these gases react in the atmosphere with water, oxygen, and other chemicals to form acidic compounds. The result is a mild solution of sulfuric acid and nitric acid. When sulfur dioxide and nitrogen oxides are released from power plants and other sources, the wind blows these compounds across state and national borders, sometimes over hundreds of miles.

Which **country pollutes** Earth the most?

The United States is the worst air polluter in the world, contributing about 25 percent of the world's carbon dioxide emissions (which result from burning gasoline, oil, and coal). China is second in line, followed by Russia, Japan, Indonesia, and India. Most of these country's emissions result from industrial waste and automobile emissions. Within the United States, Los Angeles is the most polluted city.

CREATURES BIG AND SMALL

DINOSAURS AND ANCIENT LIFE

What are **fossils**?

A fossil is the hardened remains or an imprint of a plant or animal that lived a very long time ago. Some fossils are thousands of years old, others are several hundred million years old. Most plants and animals died and then decayed without ever leaving a trace. But some were buried under mud, rocks, ice, or other heavy coverings before decaying. The pressure of these layers over thousands of years turned animal and plant remains into rock. Usually fossils preserve the organism's hard parts: the bones or shells of an animal and the seeds, stems, and leaf veins of plants.

Sometimes the fossil is the actual animal part, like a bone or tooth, that has hardened into rock. Some fossils, called trace fossils, show the imprint of parts of the animal or plant. Occasionally these imprints act as a mold, and the sediment that fills the imprint hardens and becomes a cast of, for example, a dinosaur footprint. Sometimes bones or trees are preserved by minerals that seep into the part's pores and then harden, or petrify, that part. Arizona's Petrified Forest contains numerous examples of giant trees that were petrified millions of years ago.

What were the **first primitive plants** to appear on land?

The first primitive plants appeared on land about 470 million years ago. But these plants did not look like the lush greenery we see in the world today. Rather, they were rootless patches of thin, leaflike plants called liverworts, so named because some species look like green livers. Liverworts used a specialized filament (called a rhizoid) to absorb water and stick to rocks. Fossils reveal that the first true plants to colonize land appeared about 420 million years ago. These plants included flowerless mosses, horsetails, and ferns. They reproduced by throwing out spores, or

49

Fossils aren't actually bones, they are stones that formed out of the bones of dead animals or from plants. This is good news for scientists who can learn a lot from uncovering fossils.

minute organisms that carried the genetic blueprint for the plant. The ferns eventually bore seeds, but not until about 345 million years ago. Plants with roots, stems, and leaves (called vascular plants) evolved about 408 million years ago.

What were the **first animals** to appear in water and on land?

Fossils reveal that the first soft-bodied animals appeared about 600 million years ago in the oceans, and included a form of jellyfish and segmented worms. The first land animals to conquer the land may have been the arthropods, such as scorpions and spiders. Many of these creatures have been found in the old rock layers, usually with fossils of the oldest known vascular land plants. The first land animals evolved around 440 million years ago and the dinosaurs evolved around 250 million years ago. So, it took about 190 million years for dinosaurs to appear after the first land animals. These numbers change as scientists discover new fossils.

Have scientists ever discovered an **entire animal fossil**?

Yes, in some cases, an entire animal is preserved in ice, hardened tree sap (called amber), or in dry, desert areas. In these instances, as with woolly mammoths found in Alaska, Siberia, and elsewhere, the whole animal—hair, skin, bones, internal organs—is preserved much as it was when it died thousands of years earlier. During the last Ice Age, there were many large mammals, including mammoths, saber-toothed cats, giant ground sloths, woolly rhinos, and mastodons. These animals, which are now extinct, are known mostly from fossils and frozen, mummified carcasses.

Will animals and plants that die today become fossils?

Yes, if the conditions are right. Many organisms will decay quickly, as sunlight, water, or air interacts with them. This is especially true if the organisms do not have hard parts. If the organisms do have hard parts, those that are quickly buried have the best chance of becoming fossils, as soil stops much of the decay. Most of Earth's future fossils will be from oceans, lakes, and rivers because these are areas in which quick burial and fossilization will most likely happen because dirt and other sediments quickly pile up over dead plants and animals in such places.

When did the **woolly mammoths** live?

Woolly mammoths lived from about 2 million years ago to 9,000 years ago, during the last Ice Age (called the Pleistocene Epoch), and are now extinct. The Ice Age took place millions of years after the dinosaurs became extinct. Mammoths were elephant-like animals that were herbivores, or plant eaters. They ranged in size from about 9 feet (2.7 meters) tall to more than 15 feet (4.5 meters) tall, and had long, dense hair and underfur, large ears, a long nose, and long tusks. Both the males and the females had tusks, which were really incisor teeth. Some species had tusks that were straight, and others had tusks that were curved. Sometimes reaching 17 feet (5.2 meters) in length, the tusks were used in mating rituals, for protection and self-defense, and for digging in the snow for food. Modern-day Indian elephants are related to woolly mammoths.

When did the **dinosaurs live**?

Dinosaurs first appeared about 230 to 250 million years ago, during the Triassic Period. Their large size and vast numbers meant that they dominated animal life on Earth for millions of years. Dinosaurs became extinct around 65 million years ago, at the end of the Cretaceous Period. Earth was much different when dinosaurs roamed the planet. Several hundred million years ago, instead of there being seven continents, or large land masses, there was just one giant mass of land that was surrounded by ocean. This land mass gradually broke apart into separate continents. Areas that are now covered with tall buildings or mountain ranges were once beneath the sea, and scientists believe the climate was fairly warm throughout the year. By the end of the era in which dinosaurs lived, temperatures had cooled and distinct seasons had developed.

Which was the **biggest dinosaur**?

Information about dinosaurs changes all the time as new bones are found and new evidence about their surroundings becomes available. The largest complete dinosaur fossil found by paleontologists (scientists that study dinosaurs) was *Bra-*

What does the word dinosaur mean?

The word dinosaur comes from the term *dinosauria,* which is a combination of the Greek words *deinos* and *sauros. Deinos* means "terrible" and *sauros* means "lizard" or reptile. Thus, dinosaur means "terrible lizard." As dinosaurs are discovered, scientists generally name them after a unique body feature, after the place where the fossils of the dinosaur were found, or after a person involved in the discovery. Usually the name is made up of two Greek or Latin words, or combinations of the two. For example, the Greek and Latin combination *Tyrannosaurus rex* means "king of the tyrant lizards."

chiosaurus (meaning "arm lizard"), a huge dinosaur that lived during the Jurassic Period. It weighed about 80 tons (72,640 kilograms) and reached 75.5 feet (23 meters) in length and 39 feet (12 meters) in height—about the length of two large school buses and the height of a four-story building. Parts of leg bones and vertebrae of even larger dinosaur species have been discovered, and scientists have studied these parts to try and determine their exact size. Several of these—such as *Argentinosaurus* and *Amphicoelias*—might have been one and a half to two times larger than *Brachiosaurus.* The *Argentinosaurus,* thought to weigh as much as 100 tons (90,800 kilograms), was uncovered in the late 1990s in Argentina, which was home to many of the world's largest dinosaurs.

These gentle giants were once thought to live in watery, swampy regions, but recent evidence suggests that most of them were forest dwellers that ate leaves from the tops of trees. They had enormous bodies, very long necks, relatively small heads, and thick, tree-trunk-like legs, much like an elephant's legs. They moved very slowly and did not have many ways to defend themselves, but their tremendous size kept most predators away.

Which was the **smallest dinosaur**?

The smallest dinosaurs were just slightly larger than a chicken. *Compsognathus* (meaning "pretty jaw") was 3 feet (1 meter) long and probably weighed about 6.5 pounds (2.5 kilograms). At one time, scientists thought that *Mussaurus* (meaning "mouse lizard") was the smallest dinosaur, but it is now known to be the hatchling of a dinosaur type that was much larger than *Compsognathus* when fully grown. If birds are advanced dinosaurs, as some scientists believe, then the smallest dinosaur would be the hummingbird!

What did **dinosaurs eat**?

Dinosaurs came in many different shapes and sizes, and they also had a variety of diets. Most dinosaurs ate plants, with the very large dinosaurs eating leaves from the tops of trees and smaller ones eating plants and bushes growing close to the ground. Rocks that contain dinosaur bones also contain fossil pollen and spores that indicate hundreds to thousands of types of plants existed during the Mesozoic Era (70 million to 220 million years ago). Many of these plants had edible leaves, including evergreen conifers (pine trees, redwoods, and their relatives), ferns, mosses, horsetail rushes, cycads, ginkos, and—in the latter part of the dinosaur age—flowering (fruiting) plants. Some dinosaurs were meat eaters, with most hunting other animals for food and some being scavengers who ate the flesh of dead animals they encountered. The hunters preyed on plant-eating dinosaurs and even on each other. Smaller meat-eating dinosaurs fed on other animals, like insects, lizards, and mammals. Evidence suggests that some dinosaurs hunted in packs, while others lived solitary lives.

Would it **hurt** if a **plant-eating dinosaur** bit you?

Absolutely. Being bitten by a plant-eating dinosaur such as *Brachiosaurus,* with its 52 chisel-like teeth, would certainly hurt! The bite of a *Parasaurolophus,* with its interlocking rows of teeth, might take off your fingers. In the *Iguanodon,* numerous sharp teeth were set in rows in the upper and lower jaws, and at steep angles to each other. When the teeth were pressed together, the upper jaw was forced outward, creating a grinding motion between the teeth and its meal of crushed plant tissue.

What did **dinosaurs use** their **teeth** for?

Dinosaur teeth were used for chewing, cutting or slicing plants, or, in meat eaters, tearing apart flesh. Dinosaurs had more teeth than humans do, and they would shed their teeth throughout their life, much like sharks do today. For example, duck-billed hadrosaurs (meaning "bulky lizards") had hundreds of teeth waiting to replace their worn-out teeth. Other dinosaurs, such as the ornithomimosaurs (meaning "bird mimic"), had no teeth at all, but a beak similar to a bird. Some dinosaurs also had a combination of a beak and teeth.

Did all **dinosaurs lay eggs**?

As far as scientists can tell, all dinosaurs nested and laid eggs. From these eggs, their babies hatched. Hundreds of sites with fossil eggs of different dinosaurs have been found all over the world, including in the United States, France, Mongolia, China, Argentina, and India. The largest dinosaur egg fossil found is about 12 inches (30 centimeters) long and 10 inches (25 centimeters) wide, and may have weighed 15.5 pounds (7.0 kilograms). Scientists think the egg came from a giant, 100-million-year-old

Dinosaurs were egg-laying animals, and they left behind many fossilized eggs to prove it.

Did dinosaurs get sunburned?

It was very hot and humid during the time of the dinosaurs, especially during the Mesozoic Era, so there may have been a lot of sunshine. But it's doubtful that a dinosaur would get sunburned. Fossils show that most dinosaur skin was thick, tough, and scaly—similar to that of modern reptiles like turtles and crocodiles.

dinosaur called a *Hypselosaurus*. This is more than twice the size of the eggs of the modern African ostrich, which can lay eggs up to 6 inches (15 centimeters) long and 5 inches (13 centimeters) wide. The smallest fossilized egg found so far came from a *Mussaurus*; it measures about 1 inch (2.5 centimeters) long.

Did **dinosaurs communicate**?

Dinosaurs probably communicated both vocally and visually. Large meat eaters like *Tyrannosaurus rex*, with its loud roar, or a *Triceratops* shaking his head, would have made its intentions very clear. The chambered head crests on some dinosaurs such as *Corythosaurus* and *Parasaurolophus* might have been used to amplify grunts or bellows. Mating and courtship behavior and territory fights probably involved both vocal and visual communication. Scientists believe that the sounds created by dinosaurs like *Parasaurolophus* were so individual that each had a slightly different tone. They also believe that these dinosaurs had different calls, ranging from low rumbles to high-pitched notes, which they used for different situations.

Were **dinosaurs warm-blooded**?

Scientists have conflicting opinions about whether dinosaurs were warm-blooded or cold-blooded. Some paleontologists think that all dinosaurs were "warm-blooded" in the same way that modern birds and mammals are, with a high rate of metabolism (body chemistry). Some scientists think they were "cold-blooded," much like modern reptiles. Some scientists think that very big dinosaurs could have had warm bodies because of their large body size, just as some sea turtles do today. It may be that some dinosaurs were warm-blooded—the problem is that it is hard to find evidence that shows with certainty what dinosaur metabolisms were like.

An understanding of dinosaur metabolism helps paleontologists understand the behavior of dinosaurs. If they were cold-blooded, they were most probably sluggish, with only occasional bursts of quickness. In addition, they probably would not have been very smart creatures. Like modern crocodiles, they probably spent most of their time basking in the sun, moving only to get more food. On the other hand, if dinosaurs were warm-blooded, then they were probably active, social animals. They would have been quick, alert, and intelligent. They would have spent much of their time actively grazing, like the modern antelope, or hunting in packs, like the lion.

Which **dinosaur** was the **fastest**?

Based on the trackways (stride lengths) found, it is difficult to name the fastest dinosaur. But scientists guess that the speediest dinosaurs were probably the small, two-legged, meat eaters, especially those with long, slim hindquarters and light bodies. These swift dinosaurs probably didn't run any faster than the fastest modern land animals. One carnivorous dinosaur called *Ornithomimus* is thought to have run about 43 miles (70 kilometer) per hour—about the speed of a modern African ostrich.

What **other types of animals** lived at the time of the **dinosaurs**?

During the Triassic Period, a lot of plants and animals existed along with the dinosaurs. There were all types of animals (except birds)—crocodiles, turtles, lizard relatives, giant amphibians, and the first mammals. In the oceans, there were many types of reptiles,

What if dinosaurs had never become extinct and lived with us today? Extinction can actually provide an opportunity for other types of animals to evolve.

sharks, and fish, including ichthyosaurs, predatory sea reptiles that ate shellfish, fish, and other marine reptiles. They looked similar to, and probably had some of the same habits of modern dolphins, whales, and sharks. Some animals were closely related to the land-dwelling dinosaurs, like the flying pterosaurs. These creatures were all different sizes—some skimmed the surface of the water while others flew like birds. At the beginning of the Jurassic period, dinosaurs began to dominate the land. But there were still plenty of salamanders, frogs, turtles, lizards, small mammals, and ancient crocodiles, the crocodilians. During the Cretaceous period, many crocodiles became massive, including the *Deinosuchus,* a large land creature that reached 50 feet (15 meters) in length. By this time there were also snakes, birds, winged insects, and mammals.

Why did **dinosaurs become extinct**?

Scientists do not know for sure why dinosaurs became extinct. They have many different theories, some of which explain the extinction as something that happened gradually over a long period of time. Other theories suggest that a single catastrophe, such as fallen asteroid from outer space, caused the dinosaur population to die off rather suddenly. And some scientists believe the dinosaur population had been gradually getting smaller and then was finished off by some dramatic event.

Those who believe gradual changes brought about the dinosaurs' end suggest that, as more and more mammals appeared, the dinosaurs had trouble competing with them for food sources. And these mammals may have eaten dinosaur eggs in such large numbers that fewer and fewer baby dinosaurs were born. Some experts believe that widespread disease killed off dinosaurs. Many suggest that gradual climate changes—from continuously warm, mild weather to seasonal variations with hot summers and cold winters—affected the dinosaurs. Scientists are not sure whether dinosaurs were warm-blooded or cold-blooded (and there may have been some of each). If they were cold-blooded, meaning that their body temperature changed depending on the temperature of their surroundings, it would have been difficult for such large animals to survive extreme temperatures. Smaller cold-blooded creatures can burrow under the ground, for example, to escape both heat and cold. But most dinosaurs were simply too large to do that.

The scientists who believe that dinosaurs became extinct after a major catastrophe point to evidence that suggests a huge asteroid, perhaps several miles wide, hit Earth. The impact of such an object would have created enormous clouds of dust and other debris. The heat of impact would have started fires over a great area. Between the dust clouds and the smoke from the fires, sunlight would have been blocked, maybe for several months. A lack of sunlight would have caused a dramatic drop in temperature, and much plant life would have died. Without plants, the plant-eating dinosaurs and many other animals would have died; without the plant-eating dinosaurs and those other animals, the meat-eating dinosaurs would eventually die as well.

Will the **dinosaurs** ever **come back**?

When the dinosaurs became extinct, the world's environment was already changing. It was stressed by natural events, such as falling sea levels and volcanic eruptions, leading to the decline and disappearance of many plants and animals. Our modern world has continued to create many environmental changes and stresses—most man-made, including pollution and global warming—and our fragile ecosystem could not support the return of dinosaurs. (Imagine a large dinosaur roaming New York City!) However, some scientists argue that not all dinosaurs became extinct. The striking similarities between modern birds and some kinds of dinosaurs have led some people to believe that birds are living descendants of dinosaurs. Although not all dinosaurs were similar to modern birds, some did have features such as bony tails, claws on the fingers, beaks, and feathers.

AMAZING ANIMALS

How **many different kinds** of **animals** are there?

Experts estimate that more than 100 million different kinds of animals have been identified in the world. There may be millions more, particularly insect species, that have not yet been identified or discovered by scientists. Hundreds of years ago scientists began dividing the animal kingdom into categories based on certain characteristics like body type, ways of reproducing, and what the animals can do (fly, swim, walk on two legs, and so on). The animal kingdom, and every other kingdom as well, is divided and subdivided into numerous other categories.

What is a **mammal**?

Mammals are a class of animal. They have certain traits that distinguish them from animals in other classes, such as fish, reptiles, and amphibians. All mammals share two characteristics: they all feed their young with mammary gland milk, and they all have hair. Almost all of them are warm-blooded, which means they try to keep the inside of their bodies at a constant temperature. They do this by generating their own heat when they are in a cooler environment, and by cooling themselves when they are in a hotter environment. Unlike reptiles, who sit in the hot sun to regulate their body temperature, mammals wake up and are ready to go! In general, mammals spend much more time raising and training their young than other animals do. Some examples of mammals include apes, bats, lions, mice, moose, aardvarks, beavers, elephants, gorillas, pandas, hamsters, dogs, cats, horses, whales, and dolphins.

There are three types of mammals: placental mammals, monotremes, and marsupials. Placental mammals are those whose young are born live and at a relatively advanced stage. Before birth, the young are nourished through a placenta. Like the human placenta, it is a specialized embryonic organ that is attached to the mother's uterus and delivers oxygen and nutrients to growing young. Most mammals are placental mammals, including cats, dogs, and horses. The monotremes are egg-laying mammals. These include the echidnas (spiny anteaters) and the duck-billed platypus. Marsupials give birth to their young in an immature state, and most female marsupials have pouches in which to carry and nurse their young. Some marsupials include the koala, kangaroo, and the numbat. Some mammals, such as cows, horses, and pandas, are plant eaters—called herbivores. Others, including tigers, lions, and whales, are meat eaters—called carnivores. Other mammals, including bears, eat a combination of plants and meat.

Which **mammals fly**?

There is only one mammal that flies: the bat. Most bats are nocturnal, which means they sleep during the day and are most active at dawn, dusk, or nighttime. During the day, they sleep by hanging upside down in groups called roots. Most bats, called microbats, eat flying insects, such as moths and flies, but

A fruit bat, like all bats, is a large flying mammal, not a bird.

What is special about the Galapagos Islands?

The Galapagos Islands are a group of 19 islands located in the Pacific Ocean more than 620 miles (1,000 kilometers) off the coast of South America. Located at the confluence of three ocean currents, they are home to thousands of marine species. Ongoing seismic and volcanic activity reflects the processes that formed the islands. These processes, along with the islands' extreme isolation, led to the development of unique animal life, such as the land iguana, the giant tortoise, and the many types of finch. The British naturalist Charles Darwin was one of the first geologists to visit the islands in 1835. His research led to his theory of evolution by natural selection.

others eat small mammals, like mice. Some insect-eating bats can land on the ground and chase insects that live in leaf litter or dirt. One of these bats, the pallid bat, feeds on scorpions and large centipedes. Others eat fish or live on cow's blood. The largest bats are megabats, which feed mostly on fruit.

How are **bats** able to **see in the dark**?

Bats, which are most active at night, have eyesight that ranges from very good to very poor. However, they rely primarily on echolocation to "see" in the dark. Echolocation is the transmission of sound waves to locate objects, including food, and to detect obstacles in an animal's path. These sound waves travel out away from the bat and then bounce off objects and surfaces in the bat's path, creating an echo. The echo returns to the bat, giving it a sense about the object's size, shape, direction, and distance. This high-frequency ultrasound is higher than the range of human hearing and usually comes from the bat's mouth. A few species emit sounds from their noses, freeing their mouths for eating at the same time.

Are there any **poisonous mammals**?

Venomous mammals produce venom, a poisonous chemical in their saliva. They use their venom to kill prey or to defend themselves against predators. They include the male duck-billed platypus, several species of shrews, and the solenodon, a nocturnal, burrowing animal that looks like a large shrew. Venomous mammals are rare: There are many more species of venomous reptiles such as snakes and amphibians. There are no species of venomous birds, however some birds are poisonous to eat or touch, such as the brightly colored pitohui and the ifrita. Both birds live in the rain forests of New Guinea.

Which **mammal** is the **fastest**?

The cheetah can run as fast as 70 miles (110 kilometers) per hour, making it the fastest mammal in the world. They accelerate from 0 to 45 miles (72 kilometers) per hour in just two seconds, reaching top speeds of about 70 miles per hour for up to 300 yards. Its body parts are built for speed: Large nostrils, lungs, liver, heart, and adrenals give the cheetah an ability to respond to its environment and hunt down prey. Its long, slender body is flexible and curls like a whip when it needs to make huge bursts of acceleration—usually to hunt down a small antelope or escape the jaws of a pack of hungry hyenas. Special paw pads and nonretractible claws provide traction for sprinting.

The cheetah (which comes from the Indian name for "spotted one") lives in the open savannas of southwestern Asia and Africa, where it has lots of room to run, roam, and hunt down its prey. Cheetah mothers spend much time teaching their young how to hunt game. The mothers bring small, live antelopes—such as gazelles or impalas—to the cubs and release them, so they can chase and catch them. The cheetah usually hunts during daylight, preferring early morning or early evening, but is also active on moonlit nights. They communicate by purring, hissing, whining, and growling.

Which **mammal** is the **slowest**?

The sloth is the slowest mammal on Earth. It spends most of its time alone hanging upside down from tree branches, where it eats shoots and leaves, sleeps (up to 15 hours per day!), mates, and gives birth. The sloth holds onto tree branches with strong, curved claws that are on each of its four feet. It is a nocturnal creature that moves about slowly, sometimes foraging for insects. Sloths have a short, flat head, big eyes, a short snout, a short tail, long legs, and tiny ears. They live in Central and South America.

Which animal is both the biggest mammal and the **largest living creature on Earth**?

The blue whale, who swims all of the world's oceans, in the largest mammal. The largest blue whale cited was at least 110 feet (33.5 meters) long and weighed 209 tons (189,604 kilograms). The average length is about 82 feet (25 meters) for the males, and 85 feet (26 meters) for the females. A newborn blue whale can weigh anywhere from 2.5 to 4 tons (2,268 to 3,628 kilograms), and can reach 100 to 120 tons in adulthood. Whale calves drink 50 to 150 gallons of its mother's milk per day, adding about 8 pounds (3.6 kilograms) of weight per hour, or 200 pounds (90.7 kilograms) per day. At about eight months of age, when the calf is weaned, it measures close to 50 feet (15.2 meters) long and weighs about 25 tons (22,679 kilograms).

Blue whales do not have teeth. Instead, in their upper jaw they have rows of hundreds of baleen plates—flat, flexible plates with frayed edges, arranged in two parallel rows that look like combs of thick hair. The blue whale feeds on a small shrimp-like animal called krill. Scientists believe that large marine mammals, like whales and dolphins, have brains much like those of humans. They are able to communicate, follow instructions, and adapt to new environments. Throughout history, these gentle giants have been hunted for their baleen and blubber (fat), and are today considered an endangered species. Scientists believe there are about 4,000 or so of them left in the world.

What is an **endangered species**?

There are many organizations in the United States and all over the world that study and research plant and animal species, determining which ones may be headed for extinction (when a species of plant or animal dies out completely). Any species in such danger is described as "endangered." Once a species is endangered, it becomes illegal to hunt that animal or destroy its habitat. In 2008 the U.S. Fish and Wildlife Service, the organization that maintains the nation's list of endangered and threatened plants and animals, listed more than 1,000 animals worldwide ("threatened" species are those that might soon become endangered). The goal of such organizations is to help a species recover to the point that it no longer needs to be listed as endangered.

Which **mammal** spends the **most time sleeping**?

The western European hedgehog—which likes to live in hedges—spends most of its life asleep. It builds a nest of grass and leaves among tree roots or under a bush, and spends about 18 hours a day there during summer months. It wakes up at night to eat, sniffing out worms, insects, snails, and snakes for its evening meal. During the winter months, it hibernates (sleeps all the time). When it sleeps or senses danger, the hedgehog rolls into a tight, spiny ball for protection. Related creatures, including sloths, armadillos, and opossums, sleep almost as long as the hedgehog—accumulating up to 17 hours each day! Other animals that sleep a lot are the dormouse (about 17 hours), koalas (about 15 hours), and all kinds of felines, including pet cats.

Which **mammal** is the **smelliest**?

If you have ever been to the zoo, you might think that some of the large animals, like the elephant, are the smelliest. But this title goes to one of the smaller mammals, the striped skunk. This black and white-striped creature sprays a foul-smelling, musky fluid as a defense against predators. Most wild skunks spray only when injured or attacked, as a defense mechanism. Their scent is composed of a chemical composition that can be released from one or both of their anal glands, located on both sides of their rectum. They can aim their glands at a target up to 15 feet (4.5 meters) away with great accuracy, but fortunately they tend to give a little bit of advanced warning: to signal being angry or scared, they often stamp their front feet, knead the ground like a cat, and hold their tail erect.

Why do **camels** have **humps**?

Camels are the only animals with humps. A camel's hump is a giant mound of fat, which can weigh as much as 80 pounds (35 kilograms). The hump allows a camel to survive up to two weeks without food. Because camels typically live in the deserts of Africa and the Middle East, where food can be scarce for long stretches, their hump is key to their survival. When camels are born their humps are empty pock-

When zebras are together in herds, their striped fur is very confusing to predatory lions.

ets of flexible skin. As a camel grows and begins to form its fatty tissue reserves, the humps begin to fill out and take shape.

The humps also come in handy for humans who have domesticated the camel. For thousands of years, people have used these strong, resilient creatures for transportation and for hauling goods. The two-hump, or Bactrian, camel was domesticated sometime before 2500 B.C.E., probably in northern Iran, northeastern Afghanistan, and northern Pakistan. The one-hump, or Dromedary, camel was domesticated sometime between 4000 and 2000 B.C.E. in Arabia.

Why do **zebras** have **stripes**?

Researchers believe a zebra's stripes help camouflage the animal and protect it from predators. The wavy black-and-white stripes of a zebra blend in with the wavy lines of tall grass in its savanna surroundings. Although the zebra's stripes are black and white and the lines of the grass are yellow, brown, or green, the zebra is still able to roam undetected. Why? Because the zebra's main predator, the lion, is colorblind. In fact, if a zebra is standing still among tall grass, a lion may overlook it completely. Zebra stripes work even more efficiently in a herd. When individual zebras band together, the pattern of each zebra's stripes blends in with the stripes of the zebras around it. This is confusing to the lion, who sees a large, moving, striped mass instead of many individual zebras. The lion's inability to distinguish zebras makes it difficult for the lion to target and track its meal.

But while zebra stripes act as a defense mechanism for predators, individual striping helps zebras recognize one another. Stripe patterns are like zebra finger-

61

Why don't polar bears freeze in the icy Arctic waters?

In a polar bear's Arctic home, winter temperatures can drop as low as –50 degrees Fahrenheit (–45 degrees Celsius). A polar bear spends the winter living on sea ice, but the bear is so well insulated that it doesn't freeze in these extreme temperatures. A layer of fat more than four inches thick, a thick fur coat, and special white hairs that absorb the heat of the Sun keep the polar bear warm. During ice storms—when wind and blowing snow make travel and hunting too difficult—the polar bear curls up and lets the snow cover it completely. Although this stunt sounds chilling, it is warmer under the snow than aboveground, where the animal is exposed to the freezing air.

prints: Every zebra has a slightly different look, helping each member of the herd distinguish one another. This helps human researchers and animal preservationists, too, because unique stripe patterns help them track individual zebras in the wild.

Which **African animal** can **eat** up to **half a ton of plants** each day?

The wild African elephant, the biggest animal on land, can easily consume more than 770 pounds (349 kilograms) of food each day. While that's not technically half a ton, or 1,000 pounds (453 kilograms), it's pretty close to it! The average male weighs 12,000 pounds (5443 kilograms), is 11 feet (3.3 meters) tall, and spends 16 hours of every day foraging for food in herds with up to 1,000 members. To find food, these vegetarians must roam large areas of the forest and jungle, where grass, shrubs, leaves, roots, bark, branches, fruit, and water plants are plentiful. Wild elephants often devour bamboo, berries, coconuts, plums, and sugarcane. An elephant uses its strong tusks (long, curved teeth) to tear bark off trees and to dig up roots and shrubs. It then relies on its trunk—a combined nose and upper lip—as a "hand" for picking up the food and passing it to its mouth.

Do **bears** really **sleep** through an **entire winter**?

No. Denning bears, such as brown and black bears, often retire to their caves for the winter months, but they sleep lightly, and are often active, with females giving birth to cubs during the winter. They don't technically hibernate during these months. Hibernation is when a species passes the winter in an inactive state, conserving their resources and energy until winter passes. Bears are not *true* hibernators because their body temperature drops only a few degrees and they show only a moderate drop in their metabolism. Small animals with high metabolic rates such as rodents, hummingbirds, and bats are true hibernators: their body temperature drops almost to the level of the surroundings and they show little response to nature's sights and sounds. These animals collect and eat a lot of high-calorie foods (such as nuts) to store calories to make it through the hibernation period.

Why are **polar bears white**?

The polar bear lives in the Arctic, the region of the North Pole. Most of its environment is barren, covered year-round with ice and snow and not much else. A polar bear might eat what few plants it can find, but it feeds mostly on water animals like seals and small walruses, which share its frozen home. The polar bear's yellowish-white coat helps it blend into its snowy surroundings as it hunts its prey. After all, there is not much in the Arctic to hide behind! The fur of a polar bear is also extremely thick, allowing it to withstand polar temperatures and swim in Arctic waters, where its prey is often found. Polar bears are excellent swimmers, and their unique paws—with hairy soles—allow them to run very quickly over ice and snow without slipping.

Do **bighorn sheep break** their **horns** when they charge?

No. The wild bighorn sheep, which make their home in the Rocky Mountains from southern Canada to Colorado, are known by the large heavy horns (weighing as much as 31 pounds [14 kilograms]) that the males grow for sparring, or territorial fighting. In the breeding season, they compete for females. Although the males charge at one another with a series of running head-butts that can last several hours, their skull is double-layered and designed to withstand these hard blows. These sheep also have a broad, massive tendon that connects its skull and spine, which helps the head pivot and recoil from blows.

Why is the **walrus** nicknamed "**tooth walker**"?

The walrus's two tusks—which are really two long, sharp teeth—aid the cold-water creature in battling polar bears, fending off other walruses, and walking around the bottom of the ocean while searching for its favorite food, clams. The "tooth walker" temporarily anchors itself to the bottom of the ocean by pushing its tusks into the muddy sand, where it can look for food. It then pulls its tusks out, moves on, and repeats the process.

Is it true that a **shark** can **smell a drop of blood** from a mile away?

No, but they can detect blood from very far away. Sharks are carnivores (meat eaters) known for their keen sense of smell. Sharks have two nostrils through which some species can detect odors up to almost 300 feet (91 meters) away, which is about the length of a football field. Fourteen percent of the Great White shark's brain matter, for example, is devoted to smell. Sharks zig-zag along

Walruses have huge tusks, long teeth that are useful for defending their territory against polar bears and other walruses.

63

ocean currents, using their highly sensitive nostrils to find sources of odors and food. Some species can smell one molecule of blood in over one million molecules of water—which is equal to one drop of blood in 25 gallons (94 liters) of water. A shark can also detect vibrations of passing prey with its "lateral line," a row of sensors along the side of its body.

How long is the **giant anteater's tongue**?

Anteaters are slow-moving mammals with long snouts and claws and no teeth. If you can image it, a giant anteater can grow a tongue up to 2 feet (0.60 meters) long! The anteater uses its long tongue to investigate anthills in South America's tropical dry forests, rain forests, and savannas. It sticks its long, sticky tongue down the anthill, twirls it around, and scoops up a mouthful of ants. Anteaters can eat mouthful after mouthful of ants—up to 30,000 per day! It also eats termites and other insects.

BUG ZOO

How **many** different kinds of **insects** are there?

Insects are small creatures with three pairs of legs, a body with three main parts (a head, thorax, and abdomen), and a tough shell-like outer covering, called an exoskeleton. Insects are arthropods, which means they do not have a backbone. Most have one or two pairs of wings and a pair of antennae. There are 900,000 known species of insects in the world, and entomologists (scientists who study bugs) estimate that there are millions (perhaps up to 10 million!) more yet to be discovered. Insects are everywhere—there are more bugs in 1 square mile (2.59 square kilometers) of rural land than there are human beings on the entire globe.

Insects are divided into 32 orders, or groups. The largest insect order is the beetles (Coleoptera) with 125 different families and approximately 500,000 different species. In fact, one out of every four animals on Earth is some type of beetle. In the United States, there are some 73,000 species of insects: approximately 24,000 beetles, 19,500 flies, 17,500 ants, bees, and wasps, and 11,500 moths and butterflies.

Why are there so many insects?

Entomologists believe that there are so many insects for a few reasons. Their exoskeleton provides protection, they are small, and most of them can fly. These traits help them escape from enemies and travel to new environments. Because they are so small they only need small amounts of food to survive and can live in very small cracks and crevices. Insects have lived on Earth a very long time. The oldest group of insects on Earth are the cockroaches, which first appeared some 300 million years ago.

How do **insects grow**?

Insects grow through the process of metamorphosis, meaning that they undergo change. Insect groups that undergo a complete metamorphosis include beetles, moths, butterflies, sawflies, wasps, ants, bees, and flies. All these groups begin their life cycle as an egg. The egg hatches into a larva—such as a caterpillar, grub, or maggot—that feeds, molts (sheds its skin), and grows larger. The larva goes through an inactive pupa stage—for example, it is wrapped up in a cocoon—and emerges as an adult insect, such as a butterfly or beetle, that looks very different from the larva it once was. Other insect groups do not go through a complete metamorphosis, but rather experience gradual changes as they turn into adults. These include scales, aphids, cicadas, leafhoppers, true bugs, grasshoppers, crickets, praying mantises, cockroaches, earwigs, and dragonflies. Immature forms of these insects are called nymphs. The nymphs grow and gradually change size, shedding their skin along the way. After a final molt, the full adult form emerges.

Why do **butterflies** and other insects fly from **flower to flower**?

Butterflies and other insects fly from one plant to the next to feed on the sweet nectar—and sometimes the pollen—located in the interior of flowers. The sugar in nectar supplies insects with the energy they need, and pollen contains protein, fat, vitamins, and minerals. In the process of feeding, many insects transfer pollen—which sticks to their bodies—from one plant's flower to another. Pollen, which is a fine powdery grain from a flower's male reproductive organ, must be transferred to the female reproductive organ of a flower for fertilization to take place and seeds to form.

Why do **insects** have eyes with **thousands of lenses**?

Most adult insects, including bees and dragonflies, have two large compound eyes, made up of separate, sometimes thousands, of lenses. They all point in different directions to give the insect a very wide field of vision. The lenses also help the insect see movement, enabling it to react quickly to seize its prey or escape danger. You can witness this yourself as you try to swat a fly in your home—it's almost impossible to catch a flying insect!

What do the **spots** on the **wings** of **butterflies and moths** do?

The large round spots on the wings of butterflies and moths, which look like big round eyes, are a defense mechanism. When a bird or other animal tries to eat the insect, it opens its wings and flies off. The wing movement reveals the

Flies and many other types of insects have compound eyes with thousands of lenses, unlike human eyes, which only have one lens.

There are over 3,000 kinds of tropical walking stick insects, some of which are among the largest insects on the planet.

moth's "eyes," confusing the insect's enemy by making it think it has attacked something much bigger with eyes. The predator hesitates, and the insect is able to escape.

Do some **insects use slaves** to survive?

Yes. Ants are social insects that live in colonies, or underground chambers, which may house as many as 500,000 individuals. Ant chambers are connected to each other and to the surface of the earth by small tunnels. There are rooms for food storage, rooms for mating, and nurseries for the young. A queen produces eggs to supply new ants for the colony. The colony is built and maintained by legions of worker ants, who carry tiny bits of dirt in their mandibles (a pair of appendages near the insect's mouth) and deposit them near the exit of the colony, forming an ant hill. While most ant colonies are self-sufficient, Amazon ants, aggressive red ants found in the western U.S., steal the larvae of other ants to keep as slaves. The slave ants build homes for and feed the Amazon ants, who cannot do anything but fight. They depend completely on their slaves for survival.

What is the **largest insect on Earth**?

That depends on what you mean by "large." The *longest* insect is *Pharnacia serritypes,* which lives in western Malaysia. These insects get to be 22 inches (56 centimeters) long! They are related to the group of insects called walking sticks. Walking sticks get their name from the fact that they do, indeed, look like sticks with legs. The largest walking sticks can grow to up to 13 inches (33 centimeters) in length. There are approximately 3,000 tropical species of walking sticks, and 10 species that live in North America. One species, *Megaphasma dentricus,* is the longest insect in the United States, reaching 7 inches (17.7 centimeters) in length.

If you are talking about the *heaviest* insect, then take a look at the giant weta (scientific name *Deinacrida heteracantha*), an endangered insect that can weigh up to two and a half ounces (71 grams). These insects may look ferocious and scary because of their size, but they are actually harmless. Another insect that is often considered the biggest is the acteon beetle (*Megasoma acteon*) because it is very bulky looking and can be as big as 3.5 inches (9 centimeters) long by 2 inches (5 centimeters) wide and 1.5 inches (4 centimeters) thick

Which insect is sometimes called a **"vicious predator"**?

The praying mantis, also called a praying mantid, is a large flesh-eating insect that lives in warm areas of the world. Mantis species from Europe and China were introduced to the northeastern United States about 75 years ago for use as pest exterminators on farms and in gardens. These carnivorous insects—sometimes called "vicious predators"—are among the few insects that can rotate their heads to look over their shoulders, making them extremely effective hunters. They pose in a deceptively humble posture when searching for food, as if their front legs are folded in prayer. Mantises grab their victims with their raptorial front legs, which quickly shoot out from their bodies. Mantises almost always start eating their catch while it is alive, and they often start eating their victim's neck to quickly end the struggle. Praying mantises eat a variety of insects—other mantises, beetles, butterflies, crickets, grasshoppers—and spiders. They also eat small tree frogs, lizards, mice, hummingbirds, and other nesting birds. Because they keep down the populations of "bad bugs" that threaten farms, they are highly useful to agricultural workers.

What's the difference between an **insect** and a **spider**?

Many people think of spiders as insects, but actually they are classified in a separate category. Spiders are part of a group called arachnids, which also includes mites, ticks, and scorpions. Arachnids share many features with their arthropod cousins, but they differ in that they do not have antennae. Also, spiders have eight legs (insects have six), and their bodies are segmented into two parts (insects' bodies have three parts).

How long does it take a **spider** to **spin its web**?

Spiders spin their webs at different speeds, and no two spider webs are the same. It takes about one hour for the average spider to construct an elaborate web of silk thread, called an orb web. An orb web is a series of wheel-shaped, concentric outlines, with spokes extending from a center. Many species of spiders weave orb webs, which are most noticeable in the morning dew.

Like other webs, spiders use orb webs to capture insects for food. The orb web is the most efficient type of spider web, since it covers the greatest area with the least amount of silk. Pound for pound, spider silk is about five times stronger than

67

What is "ballooning"?

Spiders do not have wings and cannot, technically, fly. Several types of spiders, however, can travel long distances through the air by a process called ballooning. The spiders spin long strands of silk that are caught by the wind, carrying the spiders along the currents. Spiders can travel far by this method (as far as hundreds of miles), and in some cases they can "fly" as high as 2,600 feet (800 meters). One spider was even recorded at an altitude of 15,000 feet (4,572 meters).

steel and twice as strong as Kevlar. Spider silk also has the ability to stretch about 30 percent longer than its original length without breaking, making its threads very resilient. Still, a spider usually spins a new orb web every day to help it keep its stickiness and insect-trapping capability. Throughout the day, the spider makes frequent repairs to damaged threads.

What do **spiders** do with their **victims**?

All spiders are predators. They do not eat plants, but only other living things, such as insects, other spiders, and invertebrates (animals without backbones). When a spider catches a bug in its web, it doesn't chew it. Instead, the spider bites the insect and injects its venom, which either paralyzes or kills its prey. Then the venom turns the bug's insides into liquid. While the venom is working, the spider wraps the bug in silk. At that time, the spider may drink the liquid, or tie the little silk bundle to its web to snack on later.

Do doctors ever use **bugs** for **medical reasons**?

As strange it may sound, both leeches and blowfly maggots are used occasionally in the field of medicine. The U.S. federal government's Food and Drug Administration considers both bugs "approved medical devices," the first live animals to be called that name. Maggots are used to eat dead tissue, thus helping to kill bacteria, clean open wounds, and stimulate healing. Leeches suck out excess blood from the body, and their saliva contains a powerful blood thinner. About 5,000 clean, laboratory-grown maggots are delivered to hospitals across the United States every week.

FISH AND SEA CREATURES

How can **fish breathe underwater**?

Living creatures need oxygen to survive, and fish are no exception. Human beings use their lungs to take in oxygen, and fish breathe using their gills. A fish's gills are full of blood vessels that absorb the tiny particles of oxygen from the water. The fish sucks the water in through its mouth and squirts it out through its gills; during this process, the gills take the oxygen from the water into the blood vessels. A fish's gills are not constructed to take oxygen from the air, so they cannot breathe on dry land.

Are there **certain fish** that can **live without water**?

Yes, for a period of time. The mangrove killfish spends several months of every year out of the water, living inside rotting branches and tree trunks. The 2-inch- (5-centimeter-) long fish normally lives in muddy pools and the flooded burrows of crabs in the mangrove swamps of Florida, Latin America, and the Caribbean. When their pools of water dry up, they temporarily alter their gills to retain water and nutrients, while they excrete nitrogen waste through their skin. These changes are reversed as soon as they return to the water. The mangrove killfish is not the only fish able to temporarily survive out of water. The walking catfish of Southeast Asia has gills that allow it to breathe in air and in water. The giant mudskippers of Southeast Asia breathe through their gills underwater and breathe air on land by absorbing oxygen through their skin and the back of the mouth and throat.

Can a **fish fly**?

Flying fish, who live in the warm waters of the Atlantic and Pacific Oceans, can spread and stiffen their large fins like wings and propel themselves into the air for short distances. A flying fish can glide through the air for at least 30 seconds and can reach a top speed of at least 40 miles (64 kilometers) per hour, produced by the quick movement and vibration of its tail fin. The fish extends its "flight" by plunging its vibrating tail into the water, thus adding momentum. Flying fish can be seen gliding over waves when they are trying to escape their predators, such as albacore or blue fish, or to escape collision with a boat.

Which **undersea creatures** are known for **making electricity**?

Certain fish produce electricity to kill their prey or to defend themselves. The electric eel, a South American fish with a long, wormlike body, can grow to a length of 9 feet (2.75 meters) and weigh nearly 50 pounds (22.7 kilograms). The electric eel floats through slow-moving water, searching for fish to eat. It breathes air, which means it must come to the surface every few minutes. The electric eel has organs made up of electric plates that run the length of its tail, which makes up most of its body length. This eel, which has no teeth, uses elec-

The unusual flying fish uses its long fins to actually soar out of the water for hundreds of feet at a time!

tric shocks to stun its prey, probably to protect its mouth from the struggling, spiny fish it is trying to eat. The eel shocks the fish with several brief electrical charges, temporarily paralyzing it so the eel can suck it into its stomach. The electrical charge can be anywhere from 300 to 600 volts, enough of a shock to jolt a human being.

Electric rays have two special kidney-shaped organs that generate and store electricity like a battery. A large Atlantic torpedo ray can produce a shock of about 220 volts, which it uses to stun its prey before eating it. In addition to stunning potential prey and discouraging possible predators, the electric organs of electric rays may be used to communicate with each other. Like the rays, the electric catfish of Africa produces an electric shock of up to 400 volts, which it uses for self-defense and prey capture. Mormyrids, which live in very muddy waters in West Africa, use electrical signals as a form of radar, allowing them to travel safely and to find food.

Which **fishes** blow themselves up **like balloons**?

Porcupine fish and puffer fish look like normal fish most of the time. When they are threatened by another fish or perceive danger, they swallow water and inflate their bodies into a ball shape—up to five times their normal size. Predators see this and are scared away, and the enlarged size makes it difficult for larger predators to eat them. When the fish senses that there is no longer any danger, it slowly deflates.

Which **fish** makes a **nursery out of bubbles**?

Siamese fighting fish, which live in the muddy waters of Thailand and Cambodia in Southeast Asia, have a special way of caring for their eggs. The males of the species build a nest of bubbles among the plant leaves. To make the bubbles, the fish swims to the surface of the water, takes air in its mouth, coats it with saliva, and spits out the bubbles, which stick together on the surface of the water. After the female hatches her eggs, the male catches them in his mouth and spits them into the bubble nest. The male also guards the nest and protects the eggs from being eaten by other fish.

Is it true that a **salmon** will always **return to its birthplace**?

Yes, the salmon is most famous for its life cycle. It is born in tiny streams far from the sea, where it spends the first part of its life in freshwater. In the springtime, it migrates down streams to rivers, sometimes traveling hundreds of miles, until it ends up in the open ocean, where it spends much of its adult life. Then, when it's time to lay its eggs, the salmon makes the journey back to its birthplace to spawn and die. The salmon's body is rich in oils that are picked up during its life in the ocean. The oil helps give the salmon the energy it needs to navigate the journey upriver.

Which **animals** live inside **empty seashells**?

Unlike other crabs, hermit crabs have soft exoskeletons (outer coverings). Their delicate bodies need protection from the harsh elements of undersea life, as well as a place to hide from predators. In order to survive, they crawl into abandoned seashells. The crab's flexible body allows it to twist and turn into a curved shell, leaving only its claws exposed. A hermit crab will carry the shell on its back as it moves along the ocean floor. When it outgrows its home, it moves on to a larger shell.

Is **coral** a **plant or an animal**?

Both. Coral is made up of two living organisms, an animal and a plant that lives inside of the animal. The animal portion is a simple creature called a polyp, a miniature sea anemone that looks a little like a flower. Single cells of algae live inside the cells of the polyp. The polyp needs the algae to provide energy and recycle nutrients. Like most animals, coral has a skeleton, but unlike mammals and fish, its skeleton is formed by the outer skin and is external to the polyp. This "exoskeleton" is made up of limestone, a hard, white chalky material that acts as the animal's protective covering and gives coral its unique shape. The polyps build massive, intricate structures called coral reefs, which can be found in warm waters of more than 100 countries.

Seahorses are fish that really do look like horses! They are also unique because the male seahorse raises its babies in a pouch until they are ready to swim free.

Which **male sea creature** keeps its **young in a pouch**?

The male seahorse takes care of the female's fertilized eggs in a pouch on the front of his abdomen, which works much like the womb of a female mammal. The female seahorse deposits 100 or more eggs into the male's pouch. The male releases sperm into the pouch, fertilizing the eggs. The fertilized eggs grow in the wall of the pouch and are coated in a fluid that provides nutrients and oxygen. After two to six weeks (depending upon the species), the eggs hatch and the male seahorse gives birth to live offspring as tiny as 0.04 inches (1 centimeter) long—the only male in the animal kingdom to do so.

What is the difference between a **porpoise** and a **dolphin**?

At first glance, it's hard to tell a porpoise and a dolphin apart from one another. Both are fascinating undersea creatures, both are carnivores, and both belong to the same scientific group: Cetacea. However, there are slight physical differences between the two: Porpoises tend to be smaller than dolphins and do not have pronounced beaks. Dolphins have cone-shaped teeth, while porpoises have spade-shaped teeth. Dolphins usually have a hooked or curved dorsal fin, and porpoises usually have a triangle-shaped dorsal fin. (Some have no dorsal fin at all.) There are over 30 species of true dolphins, including familiar species like the bottlenose, spinner, and spotted dolphins.

REPTILES AND AMPHIBIANS

Why does a **lizard** need to **lie in the sunshine** to get energy?

The lizard is a reptile, a cold-blooded animal that is unable to internally control its own body temperature. In order to warm up or cool down, lizards and other reptiles—such as snakes, turtles, and crocodiles—move to different areas of their environment. They also use certain other behavioral traits to keep their body temperatures constant. For instance, if a lizard is starting to feel the intensity of the tropical sun, it might head into the shade or take a dip in a pool of water. The same lizard might also bask in the sun to warm up. Frilled dragons and collared lizards run on their hind legs in the heat of the day, making an artificial breeze to help cool themselves off. And another reptile, the crocodile, holds its jaws open to cool down on hot days. The blood vessels in its mouth are close to the skin surface, and help transfer heat. Lying quietly is another technique the crocodile uses to warm its body and help digest its food. Because they are cold-blooded, reptiles can survive on much less food, compared to warm-blooded small mammals and birds, which burn much of their food to keep warm.

How do **lizards and snakes smell**?

Lizards and snakes smell by licking the air with their tongues. The tongue picks up scents in the form of airborne molecules that the animal then draws back into its mouth. The forked tips of the tongue are inserted into two openings of a special organ, called Jacobson's organ, which identifies the molecules and passes it on to the brain. Thanks to this unique organ, both lizards and snakes have a sharp sense of smell, which they use to track prey and find potential mates.

Which **snake builds a nest** to care for its young?

Generally, snakes show little or no parental care. But a male and female King Cobra—the world's largest venomous snake—often cooperate to find a safe nesting spot for their young. In April, the female builds her nest of dead leaves by scooping them up with her large body. She then lays approximately 20 to 50 eggs, with an incubation period ranging from 60 to 80 days. The female lies on her nest until just before the eggs hatch, at which point instinct causes her to leave the young so she does not eat them. The male king cobra guards the nesting area until the young hatch.

Why do **snakes** have **scaly skin**?

Snake bodies are covered with plates and scales, which help them move over hot surfaces like tree bark, rocks, and desert sand. Rough belly scales help the snake

This is an American alligator. Alligators are different from crocodiles in several ways, but the easiest way to tell them apart is their snouts. Alligators have wider snouts compared to a crocodile's narrower, V-shaped snout.

keep its grip on rough branches and push off of surfaces when it needs to move. The scales are also waterproof, helping keep water away from the snake's body. The scales are made up of many layers of cells. The outer cells are dead and protect the living ones underneath them. Several times each year a snake sheds a layer of its dead skin, allowing a new layer to emerge. Before the skin peels, the snake is sluggish, its colors become dull, and its eyes turn cloudy. When a snake is ready to shed its old skin it rubs up against a rough surface, like a rock, to rip its skin. Then it glides out. Snakes shed their skin so they can grow, as well as to remove parasites along with their old skin.

Are **crocodiles** living **dinosaurs**?

Crocodilians—scaly, carnivorous reptiles that include crocodiles, alligators, caimans, and gharials—are descendents of the archosaurs who lived on Earth with the dinosaurs 200 years ago. Today's modern crocodiles are semi-aquatic predators that have remained relatively unchanged since the Triassic period. Besides birds, they are the dinosaurs' closest living relatives.

What is the difference between an **alligator** and a **crocodile**?

Alligators are slightly larger and more bulky than crocodiles. A wild alligator can reach up to 13 feet (3.9 meters) in length, and weigh up to 600 pounds (272 kilograms). Besides the two animals' size difference, the easiest way to tell them apart

73

is by their snout. A crocodile has a very long, narrow, V-shaped snout, while the alligator has a wider, U-shaped snout. The alligator's wide snout delivers more crushing power to eat prey like turtles, which make up a large part of the animal's diet. The crocodile's upper and lower jaws are nearly the same width, so its teeth are exposed all along the jaw line in an interlocking pattern, even when its mouth is closed. An alligator, on the other hand, has a wider upper jaw, so when its mouth is closed the teeth in the lower jaw fit into sockets of the upper jaw, hidden from view. South Florida is the only known place in the world where crocodiles and alligators live together in the same area.

What's the difference between a **lizard** and a **salamander**?

Lizards and salamanders may look alike, but they are very different from one another. Lizards are reptiles, and salamanders are amphibians. Both are cold-blooded animals that use the environment to help regulate their body temperature. And both animals are vertebrates, which means they have a backbone. An amphibian needs moist conditions in which to live, has smooth and moist skin without scales, and stumpy toes. Salamanders can be found under leaves in the forest, or under rocks in a stream. Lizards have dry and scaly skin, have longer toes that can be used for climbing, and live in a dry, hot environment. They can go long periods of time without water. Salamanders lay eggs without shells, and must lay them in a moist environment. Many salamander eggs need to be laid completely underwater, because when the larvae hatch they soon develop gills and are dependent on water. These aquatic salamanders go through metamorphosis—from tadpole to adult—just as frogs do. Lizard eggs have shells and their nests are typically in the sand. Upon hatching, young lizards are small versions of their parents and do not change or morph.

How do **frogs** make their loud **croaking sound**?

Frogs are able to make their croaking noises because they have simple vocal cords that have two slits in the bottom of the mouth. These slits open into what is called a vocal pouch. When air passes from the lungs through the vocal cords, a sound is produced. The inflating and deflating vocal pouch makes the sound louder or quieter. That sound changes depending on the kind of frog—there are as many different kinds of croaks as there are frogs! Frogs croak for the same reasons that many animals make noises: to track down and then select a mate, and to protect their territory from other male frogs.

BIRDS

How do **birds fly**?

Birds have one major feature that distinguishes them from all other animals: feathers. These strong but lightweight feathers, in combination with the structure of their bodies, allow birds to fly with amazing skill and speed. Many birds have hollow bones, making their bodies very lightweight, and the muscles that move their wings are extremely powerful. Birds fly, basically, by flapping their wings and using their tails to steer. A bird's wing is a very complicated instrument that can be adjusted in many different ways to control the flight's speed, angle, height, and direction. The wider base of the wing (the part closer to the bird's body), gives it support, while the tip of the wing propels the bird forward. The way the bird's body is built, particularly the shape and structure of the wing, determines the way the bird flies. Some fly at high altitudes, while others stay low to the ground. Some fly quickly with small, rapid wing movements, others flap their wings slowly but powerfully.

Ostriches are the biggest bird on the planet. While they can run very fast with their powerful legs, they cannot fly.

Can **all birds fly**?

Most birds fly. They are only incapable of flight during short periods while they molt, or naturally shed their old feathers for new ones. There are, however, several birds that do not fly, including the African ostrich, the South American rhea, and the emu, kiwi, and cassowary of Australia. The penguins of the Southern Hemisphere are also incapable of air flight. They have feathers and insulation for breeding purposes, but use a different form of motion: their sleek bodies "fly" through the ocean using flipper-like wings. All of these flightless birds have wings, but over millions of years of evolution they have lost the ability to fly, even though they probably descended from flying birds. These species may have lost their ability to fly through the gradual disuse of their wings. Perhaps they became isolated on oceanic islands and had no predators; therefore, they had no need to fly and escape danger. Another possibility is that food became plentiful, eliminating the need to fly long distances in search of food.

Why do birds **fly south** for the **winter**?

Birds migrate—or move regularly from one place to another—for several reasons, including warmth and the availability of food and water. Many species of birds mate and nest in specific areas of the world. Most of these areas are only comfortable during the warmer months of the year, so when the cold weather arrives birds migrate to warmer climates. These trips can be as long as thousands of miles. For example, the American golden plover breeds north of Canada and Alaska during the Northern Hemisphere's spring and summer. In the Northern Hemisphere's fall, the

The bald eagle's head is covered with white feathers. So why is it called the bald eagle?

Because one meaning of the word "bald" that is not commonly used anymore refers to white markings. "Bald" used to refer to people with white hair. Due to excessive hunting, environmental pollution, and loss of habitat, the bald eagle population became dangerously low at one point, prompting the U.S. Congress to pass a law protecting it. Bald eagles were once listed by the U.S. Fish and Wildlife Service as an endangered species, meaning they were close to being extinct. Thanks to the laws protecting it, these birds have rebounded a bit. They are now listed as threatened, which means they are not as close to being extinct as they once were, but their numbers are still few (only about 50,000 in the United States), and it is illegal to hunt them.

plovers travel to southeastern South America to spend the "winter"—which is the summer season in the Southern Hemisphere—allowing the birds to find plenty of food. When spring arrives again in the Northern Hemisphere, the trip is reversed, and the plovers migrate back to the northern nesting grounds to breed.

Why is a **bird's beak** important?

Bird beaks, which vary greatly in size, form, and color, are important to the animal's survival. The beak is the "instrument" that a bird uses to gather and break apart food. They also use their beak to clean themselves, itch, collect material for nesting, and protect their territory. A strong, cone-shaped bill, used for cracking seeds, is found in many birds such as finches and grosbeaks. Thin, slender, pointed beaks are found mainly in insect eaters, such as the warbler. Woodpeckers have strong beaks that form a chisel at the tip, which is used for pecking holes in trees for food or nests. Hummingbirds have long, tubular bills that look like drinking straws, which they use to sip nectar from flowers. Although these birds are all different, they have one thing in common: without their beaks, they would not survive long.

How do birds **replace their feathers**?

Birds replace their feathers by molting, the periodic shedding of old feathers and the growing of new ones. They do this one to three times each year, although different birds molt at different times of the year. Male goldfinches, for example, molt from a dull greenish yellow to bright yellow during spring. The periodic shedding of feathers and their replacement with new ones makes perfect sense in the animal kingdom. Feathers are incapable of further growth, and may get worn down, broken, and faded over the year from normal wear-and-tear. Molting replaces these damaged feathers and helps the males look attractive to females, which is why many molts take place during the mating season.

Why do **birds** often **crash into windows**?

Birds don't see the way mammals do, and a reflection in a window might look like another bird. Most birds that are active during the day have eyes on either side of their heads, which gives them a wide field of view but little depth perception. In the springtime, many birds are territorial and when they establish territories they become aggressive and chase off intruders. Unfortunately, they don't distinguish between their own reflection in a window (or car mirror) and they try to chase that reflection off. People sometimes add awnings and window screens to eliminate the reflection and stop birds from colliding into their homes or office buildings. Although a bird can crash into glass at any time, the behavior is seen less often when nesting season begins.

What do **worms** eat?

While some birds eat mostly insects, others, like penguins, eat seafood. Beach birds, like seagulls, eat shellfish as well, but they are also scavengers that will eat discarded people food. Some birds, such as ducks and geese, float on the water, dipping or diving to nibble on plants from oceans, lakes, and rivers. Others, such as raptors, swoop out of the sky to capture and eat small mammals, such as mice or rabbits. Some birds also prey on each other, such as large predatory birds like eagles and hawks. Many birds, like crows, jays, and magpies, eat the eggs and young of others. Individual bird species eat the foods from their local environment, but they have also developed physical characteristics that help them harvest food. Specific birds have adapted to feasting on plants as well, including algae, lichen, grass, herbs, flower nectar, leaves and buds of trees, ferns, acorns, nuts, corn, rice, and seeds of all kinds.

Which birds are called **"birds of prey"**?

Birds of prey, also known as raptors, are meat eaters that use their feet, instead of their beak, to capture prey. They have exceptionally good vision, a sharp, hooked beak, and powerful feet with curved, sharp talons. Birds of prey include falcons, hawks, eagles, kites, osprey, and vultures. Most of these birds capture live prey, including reptiles, insects, fish, birds, mammals, mollusks, and carrion (the dead and decaying remains of an animal). In general, birds of prey feed on game that average 12 to 50 percent of their own body weight; however, larger species will catch prey their own weight or larger. For example, bald eagles have been seen carrying mule deer fawns, which can weigh 15 to 20 pounds (6.8 to 9 kilograms).

Can an **eagle see a mouse** from two miles away?

Yes! The expression "eagle eyes" is taken from the golden eagle, whose incredible eyesight allows it to see a rabbit or mouse from 2 miles (3.2 kilometers) away. For comparison purposes, a human being could not see the same rabbit from one-quarter of a mile (0.40 kilometers) away. As a bird of prey, an eagle has eyes that are designed for clear vision in daylight, from early morning light to early evening. Its pupil is not big enough for night vision. The bony ridge above the eagle's eyes helps protect them from sunlight and assist in effective hunting.

Why does a **peacock spread its tail**?

The peacock is a male Indian peafowl. An adult peacock has an average of 200 tail feathers, which are shed and regrown each year. When it spreads its long feathers above its tail, it makes a large fan of glossy, bluish-green plumes that have large eyespots. They are iridescent and contain many intricate patterns. This site attracts the female peahen, and may encourage her to breed with him. The decorative feathers are also called display feathers, because the male "displays" them as part of its mating ritual.

Golden eagles are a type of bird of prey, also known as a raptor, a word that means "hunting with the claw."

How **fast** can a **hummingbird** fly?

Hummingbirds are very tiny birds, about 4 inches (10 centimeters) long, with long bills and tongues to sip nectar from tubular flowers. Because they are light—they only weigh about one-tenth of an ounce—they are skilled air acrobats. They can fly in every direction, even upside down, reaching speeds of up to 60 miles (96.5 kilometers) per hour. To keep up its energy level, a hummingbird eats every 15 to 20 minutes and may visit up to 1,000 flowers per day.

PLANT LIFE

PLANT BASICS

How are **plants different** from **animals**?

Plants and animals make up almost all of the living things in the world. They are alike in a lot of ways. Both are made up of cells, tiny building blocks of life that produce chemicals that control growth and activity. Often these cells become specialized in a plant or animal, with different types of cells doing particular jobs. In addition, both plants and animals use gases, water, and minerals to carry on life processes. Both experience life cycles in which they are created, grow, reproduce, and die.

But plants are very different from animals in one big way: most do not move around and thus cannot go and get food. Instead, plants are able to perform a special process called photosynthesis. For this remarkable process, plants use energy from sunlight, a gas in the air called carbon dioxide, and water and minerals from soil to produce their own food. Animals cannot do this. They must look for food, eating plants or other animals in order to get the energy they need to live.

How are **plants and animals related**?

The waste product produced by photosynthesis is oxygen, the gas that all animals need to breathe. So without plant life, there would be no animal life on Earth. And without plants around to absorb carbon dioxide, an excess amount of this gas would linger in our atmosphere, trapping the Sun's heat and causing an unwanted increase in the planet's average temperatures. Plants, then, are essential not only because they provide so much of the food people eat (and provide nourishment for many of the animals we eat), but because they make the air healthier, using up carbon dioxide and releasing oxygen. In addition, we depend on plants to provide us

What is plant food from the nursery made of?

The plant food that we buy in garden stores and nurseries is simply a mixture of minerals that plants need to grow well. These include nitrogen, phosphorus, and potassium. Usually a plant is able to get these things from the soil in which it grows, drawing them up with water through its roots. But gardeners, farmers, and other plant growers add to this natural mineral supply so plants can thrive.

with other things we need, like wood for building, fibers for making clothes, and medicines to improve our health.

How do **plants** get their **nutrients**?

Green plants get nourishment through a chemical process called photosynthesis, which uses sunlight, carbon dioxide, and water to make simple sugars. Those simple sugars are then changed into starches, proteins, or fats, which give a plant all the energy it needs to perform life processes and to grow.

Generally, sunlight (along with carbon dioxide) enters through the surface of a plant's leaves. The sunlight and carbon dioxide travel to special food-making cells (palisade) deeper in the leaves. Each of these cells contain a green substance called chlorophyll. Chlorophyll gives plants their green color and traps light energy, allowing food making to take place. Also located in the middle layer of leaves are special cells that make up a plant's "transportation" systems. Tubelike bundles of cells called xylem tissue carry water and minerals throughout a plant, from its roots to its outermost leaves. Phloem cells, on the other hand, transport the plant's food supply—sugar dissolved in water—from its manufacturing site in leaves to all other cells.

How do **plants grow**?

Special cells in plants produce hormones, chemical messengers that tell different plant cells to perform certain activities. Plant hormones are responsible for things like fruit development, the death of flower petals and leaves, and, most importantly, for growth. Cells in stem tips, new leaves, and buds, for instance, produce various growth hormones that tell plant cells to multiply by division or to become larger. The pattern of growth in plants is an important example of how they differ from animals. While animals eventually become fully grown (and live for a long time after that point), plants never stop growing throughout their life cycles. In other words, there is no such thing as an adult plant that no longer grows but continues to live.

How many **different types of plants** are there?

Scientists have found and described more than 275,000 kinds of plants, but they believe that many more are yet to be discovered. Plants vary greatly in size and appearance. Some, like single-celled algae, are so small that you can only see them with the help of a microscope. Others, like giant sequoia trees, are so big that you cannot even see the tops of them. Plants are very different from one another because they have developed features—over millions of years—to help them live in the world's many different environments.

Who is called the **"father of botany"**?

Botany is the scientific study of plants. The ancient Greek Theophrastus (371–286 B.C.E.) is known as the father, or founder, of botany. He wrote two large books, *On the History of Plants* and *On the Causes of Plants*. These books contained so much information about plants that 1,800 years went by before any new discovery in botany was made. Theophrastus was the first person to include the practice of agriculture (growing plants for food) into botany. He also developed a theory of plant growth and wrote about how plants were structured. He identified and described 550 different plants. Theophrastus spent most of his time in Athens, Greece, where he was in charge of the first existing botanical garden.

Do **all plants** have **leaves**?

Most plants have leaves, even if they do not look like leaves. For example, blades of grass are really leaves. Mushrooms and other fungi do not have leaves, and seaweeds and lichens do not have leaves. Seaweed, a type of algae, also does not have flowers or roots. As an underwater plant, it usually clings to stones, shells, and rocks with its holdfast, a part of the plant that looks like roots. Unlike other plants that feed through their roots, seaweed takes its nutrients from the water in which it grows.

How are a **water lily's leaves** different?

A water lily is a floating aquatic plant with large, fragrant, white or pink flowers and flat, round, floating leaves. The leaves have long stems and are bright green above and reddish or purplish underneath. The underside of the leaf contains air spaces; the air that traps beneath the leaf makes it float on water. The leaves' strong stems help them grow and stay upright in the water—which allows the leaves to absorb sunlight and stay alive.

Do **all plants** have **flowers**?

No. Although most of the world's plants are flowering plants called angiosperms (from the Greek words for "vessel" and "seed"), there are hundreds of plants that do not make flowers. Seed plants that do not have flowers—such as cycads, ginkgo, and conifers—are called gym-

Water lilies have specialized leaves that allow them to easily float on water.

81

nosperms. Conifers, for example, are common gymnosperms; instead of flowers, conifers have cones that produce pollen or eggs. Well-known examples are cedars, cypresses, Douglas firs, junipers, pines, redwoods, and spruces. Male cones are small and soft, and female cones are large and hard. Wind carries pollen from the male cone to the female cone. As the eggs are pollinated and seeds develop, the scales of the cone open up to release the seeds. Once the seeds take root, a new plant grows. Other plants that do not have flowers are mosses; although they sometimes look like they are blooming, the flower-like part is a little capsule full of spores at the end of a small stem.

SEEDS AND GROWTH

What is a **seed**?

A seed contains all that is needed to create a new plant. It holds the embryo, from which the seedling develops. It also holds enough food to help the plant through its first stages of growth—either packed around the embryo or stored in special internal leaves called cotyledons. When conditions are right—for example, when it has been exposed to water for a period of time—the seed germinates. As the young plant develops, stems and roots grow. The plant reaches maturity when it is able to reproduce by creating new seeds.

How do **seeds become plants**?

Once seeds are fully developed, they need a good place to grow. If they just fell to the ground beneath their parent plant, they would struggle, competing against each other for sunlight, water, and minerals. Most seeds need to travel—by wind, water, or with the help of insects and other animals—to better places to germinate, or start to grow into new plants. Some seeds, like those from conifer and maple trees, have wings attached. Others, like those of dandelions, have parachutes made of tiny hairs. Both features allow the seeds to be carried great distances by the wind, and they sometimes land in spots that are good for germination. Water carries other seeds to good growing places; the hard, watertight shell of a coconut, for instance, allows it to travel many miles at sea before finding a beach where conditions are suitable for growth.

Seeds sometimes have to wait a long time before they find good places to grow, places where the sun, moisture, and temperature are right. Most seeds are designed for the wait, protected by a hard outer pod (except those of conifers). Some seeds wait years to germinate, and some just never do. But inside each seed pod is a baby plant, or embryo, and endosperm, a supply of starchy food that will be used for early growth if germination takes place. Then a tiny root will reach down into the soil, and a tiny green shoot will reach up, toward the light.

Do **animals** ever **carry seeds**?

Yes, animals are great seed carriers. They take them from one place to another in their mouths (as does a squirrel preparing for winter), or sometimes seeds stick on

Dandelions are considered weeds, but they have a clever strategy for survival. Kids—and even a lot of adults—find it very irresistible to blow their seeds off their stems, helping them to populate lawns everywhere.

their fur or feathers. But most often seeds travel in animals' digestive systems. Some plants grow colorful and tasty fruits, which are really just fleshy seed coverings meant to attract hungry animals. When creatures like birds, bats, raccoons, or bears eat berries and other fruits they usually swallow the seeds whole. Safe inside a hard coating, the seeds pass through unaffected by digestive juices, appearing many hours later in animal waste. The seeds sometimes emerge in places far from their parent plants, in locations better for germination.

Which **plant spreads** its **seeds** with the **help of children** at play?

The dandelion, of course! A dandelion is really many tiny flowers bunched together in one plant. After a dandelion blooms yellow, each of its tiny flowers produces a seed. Each seed is attached to a stem with white fluffy threads. Children who pick up and blow dandelions—even if they do not make a wish—are spreading their seeds. Dandelion seeds are carried away by the wind and travel like tiny parachutes—often miles away from the parent plant—eventually landing and taking root. The dandelion seeds are also a tasty treat for many small birds, and its pollen is an important food source for bees.

How do **flowering plants** make their **seeds**?

Most flowers contain both male and female sex cells. The typical flower has four main parts: an outer cup of leaflike sepals, a ring of petals within the sepals, and

**Does the expression "Open sesame!"
have anything to do with sesame seeds?**

S esame seeds burst open when they ripen, so the phrase may be related to that fact. The English word sesame traces back to the Arabic word simsim. Sesame seeds are believed to be one of the first condiments as well as one of the first plants to be used for edible oil, and its usage dates to 3000 B.C.E. The earliest recorded use of the sesame seed comes from an Assyrian myth that claims that the gods drank sesame wine the night before they created the earth. More than 5,000 years ago, the Chinese burned sesame oil as a light source and also to make soot for their ink blocks. Today, sesame seeds are a source of food and oil in different parts of the world, including the United States. Sesame seed oil is still the main source of fat used in cooking in the Near East.

inside, male reproductive organs surrounding female parts. Male cells develop in structures called stamens and travel enclosed in the hard shell of pollen grains. Female cells, or ovules, develop deep in a flower's ovary, enclosed in a structure called a pistil. The top of the pistil—known as the stigma—is long and sticky and a good target for pollen. After it reaches the stigma, a small tube grows out of the pollen grain. The male cells travel down the pollen tube, eventually reaching female ovules. Then fertilization occurs and seeds start to grow.

What is the difference between **self-pollination** and **cross-pollination**?

Since flowers possess both male and female parts, some flowers can fertilize themselves—or fertilize another flower on the same plant—which is called self-pollination. Or the ovules of one flower may be fertilized by the pollen of a different flowering plant of the same species, a method called cross-pollination. The wind, water, insects, and other animals help to carry pollen from one flower to another. Cross-pollination usually produces a better plant: the offspring of cross-pollination possesses the genetic traits of two parents, which may give it new characteristics that will help it survive in an always-changing environment. Cross-pollination is so desirable, in fact, that many flowering plants have developed different ways to keep self-pollination from happening. In the flowers of a spiderwort plant, for example, the stamens are ready to release pollen grains before the pistils are ready to accept them, so the pollen has to travel to other spiderwort plants in search of a ripe pistil.

Are there **plants** that **do not grow from seeds**?

Yes. Not all plants are seed plants. Some plants, such as ferns and mosses, reproduce with spores instead of seeds. Spores, like seeds, can survive harsh conditions and develop into new plants. However, unlike seeds, spores are produced without fertilization and contain neither a plant embryo nor endosperm. Some plants can reproduce without spores or seeds through vegetative reproduction, in which a part of the stem or root gives rise to a new plant.

What is the difference between a **bulb, a corm**, and a **tuber**?

Bulbs, corms, and tubers are all parts of a plant that grow underground. They are each a storage unit for food that gives the plant the energy it needs to grow, bloom, and complete its life cycle each year. A bulb is an underground stem and leaf. It grows in protective layers, much like an onion. At the very center of the bulb is a small version of the flower itself. The bulb's basil plate—a round and flat hairy mass (the beginnings of roots) on the bottom of the bulb—helps the bulb stay together. Examples of bulbs include tulips, daffodils, lilies, narcissus, and amaryllis. A corm is an underground stem. It has the same type of protective covering and basal plate as the bulb, but it does not grow in layers. Instead, the corm is the base for the flower stem and has a solid texture. Crocuses and gladiolus are both corms. The tuber is an underground stem or root. Just like a potato, it has leathery skin, lots of "eyes," and no basal plate. The eyes are the growing points where the plants eventually emerge. Dahlias, begonias, and anemones are all tubers.

FRAGRANT FLOWERS, BEAUTIFUL BLOOMS

When did the **first flowers** bloom?

Mosses and fungi probably appeared about 400 million years ago. By about 200 million years ago, the earth sprouted sweeping forests of giant cycads, conifer trees, huge horsetails, and ferns. But the first flowering plants did not appear until the dinosaurs, sometime in the middle of the Cretaceous period, about 100 million years ago. Before this, most of the trees had been gymnosperms, or plants with cones. Magnolias are among the oldest of all flowering plants, appearing about this time, along with orchids. With flowers came many insects, including butterflies, ants, termites, and bees. The flowering plants provided food for these insects, who spread the pollen from flower to flower to produce the seeds that would keep the flowers reproducing.

What is the difference between **annual, perennial,** and **biennial** flowers?

An annual grows from seed, blooms, sets seed, and dies in just one growing season. Petunias, marigolds, and poppies are examples of flowers widely grown as annuals. Most annuals bloom continuously from spring through fall, and need to be replanted every spring. A perennial flower is a "permanent" one, as it lives for three or more seasons. Perennials need to be fed plant food and/or replaced about every three to five years. Most perennials, such as roses and tulips, offer a burst of color for only a few weeks once a year. A biennial grows its first year, lives over the win-

Some flowers we have to plant every year in our gardens because they are annuals and only survive until the next winter.

ter, and then blooms in the second season, before dying. Foxgloves and hollyhocks are examples of biennials.

Why are so many **flowers brightly colored**?

Flowers are brightly colored to attract insects and other animals to them, which help the plant's fertilization by carrying pollen from one plant to another. Butterflies, bees, and hummingbirds are attracted to bright colors like reds, oranges, pinks, yellows, blues, and purples. A flower's fragrance is another method of attracting pollinating visitors, especially at night when moths are out. The way in which a flower is shaped also attracts pollinators. For instance, butterflies prefer flowers with flat petals that act like a landing strip for them to sit on. Long, tubular flowers, such as honeysuckle, daylilies, and salvia are just a few of the flowers that attract hummingbirds because their long beaks can easily fit into the flower when gathering nectar.

What makes a **plant bloom** at the **right time of year**?

All flowering plants have a mechanism to make sure that their blooms develop at just the right time of year, whether in the springtime or autumn. Most respond to the amount of sunlight, and can distinguish between 16 hours of light and 8 hours of light. Some flower only when days are long and nights are short, such as radishes, asters, petunias, and beets. Others, such as chrysanthemums, goldenrods, and poinsettias, flower only when nights are long and days are short.

Do all **flowers close** up at **night**?

Although many flowers close up at night, not all of them do. Those that open their petals during the day and then close them at night are reacting to light or temperature changes. Some flowers, such as tudaylilies, remain open for twenty-four hours. Other flowers have unusual opening and closing habits. Crocuses, poppies, and morning glories, for example, open as the temperature increases during the day and close as the day gets cooler in the late afternoon. The flower called the four-o'clock closes in the morning and opens again late in the afternoon, right around four o'clock. Moonflower, night-blooming jasmine, evening primrose, angel's trumpet, night phlox, and night-blooming cereus open only at dusk or at night. Some plants also react to touch and close up their leaves and "play dead" if a hand or twig brushes against them. For example, if you touch a mimosa plant, it will fold its leaves and the stalk will droop.

Flowers close their petals at night because they are protecting the pollen and other reproductive parts of the plant that are inside from the cold and rain. Also, many flowers are pollinated by insects and birds that are active during the day, so there is no reason to be open at night. However, some types of flowers—such as some types of tropical fruit plants and varieties of cactus flowers and related plants—are pollinated by bats at night, and these flowers will be open at night and closed during the daytime.

Can you **eat flowers**?

Yes, flowers can be eaten or used to garnish a dish. Cooking with flowers dates to Roman times, and to Chinese, Middle Eastern, and Indian cultures. Edible flowers were especially popular in the Victorian era during Queen Victoria's reign. Today, many restaurant chefs decorate their entrees with flower blossoms, such as pansies and violets. Dandelions, arugula, watercress, lilac, nasturtiums, and garlic blossoms are often used in salads. In fact, you are probably eating flowers for dinner tonight. Broccoli, cauliflower, and artichokes are all flowers. The spice saffron, often used to flavor rice dishes, is the stamen from the crocus flower. And capers are the unopened flower buds from a bush that grows in the Mediterranean.

What it the **largest flower** in the world?

The flower with the world's largest bloom is the rafflesia, which grows in the rain forests of Indonesia. It can grow to be 3 feet (0.91 meters) across and weigh up to 15 pounds (6.8 kilograms). It is a parasitic plant, with no visible leaves, roots, or stem. It attaches itself to a host plant to obtain water and nutrients. When in bloom, the rafflesia gives off a repulsive odor, similar to that of rotting meat. Although people do not want to come near it, the strange odor attracts insects that pollinate the plant.

Which is the **smallest flower** in the world?

The smallest individual flowering plant is watermeal, a member of the duckweed family. The plant itself is 1/32 of an inch in width, or about the size of a pinhead. The light green free-floating, rootless plant grows in lakes and ponds, and weighs about 1/190,000 of an ounce, equivalent to two grains of table salt. They are very hard to see; in fact, you would need about 5,000 plants to fill up one thimble. However, because they grow in colonies, these plants look like algae spreading across the water. Their

The rafflesia, which is found in Indonesia, is the world's biggest flower, though certainly not the prettiest.

Which flowering plant can you float on?

Known as the "Giant Water Platter," South America's giant Amazon water lily has strong leaves that reach 6 to 8 feet (1.8 to 2.4 meters) across and can support the weight of a child. The water lilies produce flowers that open at night and are the size of a dinner plate. The first night they are white female flowers; on the second night they turn to pink male flowers. Beetles and sphinx moths that live in the Amazon River region pollinate the flowers and the seedpods—that are the size of a baby's head—sink beneath the water, where they lay dormant in the mud for up to four years before germinating. The plant lays dormant for a period every year before producing more leaves that increase in size before it flowers again. However, the giant water lily's leaves are not the biggest on Earth. Palm trees can grow leaves up to 65 feet (20 meters) long!

capacity to reproduce very quickly can cause a pond to be completely covered in the green plants in just a few weeks.

Are all **flowers fragrant**?

Unlike the fragrant blossoms that attract bees, carrion flowers simulate the odor of a rotting animal carcass and attract carrion beetles and different types of flies, including blowflies, flesh flies, and midges. The stapelia flower, which is shaped like a starfish and grows in Africa, has fine hairs around its petals, perhaps to imitate the appearance of a small dead animal. When the bloom opens it gives off a rotting smell, imitating dead animal meat. The smell attracts flies, which collect pollen before they fly away. Some carrion flowers, such as the European and Brazilian Dutchman's pipe, lure insects into dark openings that lead to the foul-smelling interior where they become trapped. When the flower "releases" the insect, it is coated with fresh pollen to be taken to a different plant. The lantern stinkhorn, a fungus that releases a feces-like odor, attracts green bottle flies to spread its spores.

POISONOUS, MEAT–EATING, AND OTHER EXTREME PLANTS

What are **carnivorous plants**?

Carnivorous plants are plants that receive some or most of their nutrients from trapping and eating insects, other arthropods, and sometimes small frogs and mammals. (They are sometimes called insectivorous plants because insects are the most common prey.) Like other plants, carnivorous plants need sunlight, soil, and water to grow. Carnivorous plants generally grow in places where the soil is thin or poor in nutrients, especially nitrogen, such as bogs. Today, there are more than 600 plant species around the world that attract and trap prey, produce digestive enzymes, and absorb parts of the insect as its nutrients.

How do **carnivorous plants digest** their prey?

Carnivorous plants use enzymes to digest their prey. Most of them, including Venus flytraps, butterworts, sundews, and many types of pitcher plants, all make their own digestive enzymes. These enzymes help them digest their prey. After their insects have been digested, all that remains is a mass of dead insect parts. Other carnivorous plants do not make their own digestive juices. Instead, they rely on bacteria to produce their enzymes. Once captured, the insect rots, and the carnivorous plants absorb the decomposed mole-

Some plants, like this Venus flytrap, have turned into meat eaters because they live in soil that does not have enough nutrients to sustain them otherwise.

cules. Many plants, such as sarracenia, use both their own enzymes and bacteria-generated enzymes. This is called a symbiotic relationship because both organisms benefit from this unique feature: The plant enjoys the bug-soup digested by the bacteria, while the bacteria get a comfortable place to grow. Bacterial digestion is no stranger to the animal kingdom: termites have bacteria inside them that help them digest wood, for example; and humans have *Escherichia coli* (*E. coli*) in their intestines to help them digest food.

Which **plants drown bugs**?

The pitcher plant drowns small insects, who are attracted to the colorful leaf rosettes that resemble flowers. At the ends of the leaves are traps shaped like small pitchers, with a leafy "lid" to keep the rain out. Insects love the sweat nectar the plant produces around its slippery rim. When an insect lands on the rim, it slips inside, and drowns in the fluid at the bottom—a mixture of rain, dew, and a digestive enzyme that soon dissolves the insect. The pitcher plant's meals include not only insects but also mites, spiders, and, occasionally, a small frog. The pitcher plant grows in bogs, savannas, and wooded areas of the South—from Florida to Mississippi, and north to Virginia and Maryland—where insects are plentiful!

Is the Amazing Flynapping Arum of Sardinia a circus performer?

No, it is a fly-trapping flower that grows in the rocky Mediterranean island soil of Sardinia and Corsica. It is sometimes called the "dead-horse arum" because it smells like a horse carcass. Blowflies are lured into the funnel-like flower, then force their way into the neck and its pitch-dark chamber. Carrying pollen from another plant, they unknowingly pollinate the female flowers at the base of the chamber. Unable to escape from the chamber because it is filled with stiff hairs, the flies remain prisoners until the male flowers above the stiff hairs start to release pollen. Then the hairs wilt and the flies are able to escape, getting dusted with pollen as they fly away.

Does a **Venus flytrap** really snap up live flies?

Indeed, it does. A Venus flytrap is a carnivorous plant that attracts, captures, and kills insects and digests and absorbs their nutrients. The leaves of the Venus flytrap, which can open wide, have short, stiff hairs called trigger hairs. When anything touches these hairs enough to bend them, the two lobes of the leaves snap shut, trapping whatever is inside. The "trap" will shut in less than a second, capturing flies and other insects. When the trap closes over its prey, finger-like projections called cilia keep larger insects inside. In a few minutes the trap shuts tightly and forms an air-tight seal in order to keep its digestive fluids inside. These fluids help the plant digest prey. At the end of the digestive process, which takes from 5 to 12 days, the trap reabsorbs the digestive fluid and reopens. The leftover parts of the insect blow away in the wind or are washed away by rain.

How do **plants defend themselves**?

Because plants cannot move to escape danger, many have developed defense mechanisms. Most plants today have one or more defenses that include poisons, physical structures (tough branches; sharp, pointy leaves; spikes; or thorns), irritants (such as hairs, prickles, or oils that annoy the skin), and bad flavors (that can cause stomach pain and diarrhea). These defenses ward off predators (animals that want to eat them) and some defenses protect them from invading diseases. For example, waxy or tough leaves make it hard for bacteria or fungi to get into the plant. In addition, many bacteria and fungi rely on water to live, move, and reproduce. If the plant's leaves shed water quickly, it is less likely that a disease-causing pathogen will be able to make its way into the plant.

How many **poisonous plants** are there in the world?

Thousands of plants around the world contain varying amounts of poison, or those properties that can injure animals or people. Plants may be poisonous to the touch (such as poison ivy and poison sumac) or toxic if swallowed (such as deadly amanita or poison hemlock). Sometimes the entire plant is poisonous, and other times a certain part of the plant such as the seeds, leaves, berries, and flowers—is poisonous. For example, the leaf blades of rhubarb are poisonous, but not the stalks. Many times, there is not enough poison to affect humans, and sometimes cooking the plant destroys its poisonous substance. Some plants have substances that are dangerous to some animals, but not others. For example, onions occasionally poison horses or cattle, but are widely used for human food. Poison ivy or poison oak can affect some people's skin, but not others, and goats eat it regularly without any side effects. Some of the more common poi-

"Leaves of three, let it be," is an easy rhyme to remember to identify poison ivy.

sonous plants found in the United States and Canada are belladonna, daffodil, foxglove, holly, iris, lily-of-the-valley, mistletoe, morning glory, and rhubarb.

Is **poison ivy** really poisonous?

A popular summer-camp rhyme is "Leaves of three, let it be." Poison ivy, the three-leaved plant that grows wild in all regions of the United States, is aggravating to the skin, though not lethal if swallowed unless you are very allergic. After brushing up against the poison ivy plant, a red rash usually develops. Rubbing the rash will not spread poison ivy to other parts of the body (or to another person) unless urushiol oil—the sticky, resin-like substance that causes the rash—has been left on your hands. Other plants that usually irritate the skin upon contact include cowhage, poison oak, poison sumac, rengas tree, and trumpet vine.

How was **hemlock used** to poison in ancient times?

In ancient times, small doses of the plant were used to relieve pain, with a great risk of poisoning. One species, *Conium maculatum,* was used to carry out the death sentence in ancient times. The Greek philosopher Socrates was condemned to death in 329 B.C.E.; he killed himself by drinking a potion made from hemlock. The hemlock plant was introduced to North America from Europe, and has often been mistaken for a pretty garden plant. All parts of the weedy hemlock plant are poisonous, especially leaves and seeds. Hemlock is a member of the wild carrot family, and it grows along roadsides and waterways in North America.

How do **nettles sting**?

Certain kinds of nettles have tiny, sharp hairs on them that stick into your skin if you touch them. As they stick, they inject a stinging liquid called formic acid, which produces a stinging pain, followed by redness and skin irritation. Despite its unique defense mechanism, which stops animals from eating the plant, stinging nettle has a long history of use in both European and North American communities. The tough fibers from the plant stem have been used to make cloth, and cooked nettle leaves were eaten as vegetables. Since ancient Greek times, stinging nettle has been used to treat coughs, tuberculosis, and arthritis, and to stimulate hair growth.

Why do **cacti and desert plants** have **spines**, and not leaves?

Most cacti do not have leaves because they grow in a hot, dry environment, with little water. They are able to survive by storing water for long periods of time; they do this through their extensive root system, which absorbs water from the soil when it rains. In a typical leaf, there is a large amount of water loss through small openings at the leaf surface (called the stomatas). This water loss, called transpiration, is speeded up with warm temperatures. Cacti have adapted by being leafless, storing water in their stems, developing waxy skin to seal in moisture, and growing spines, a form of leaf modification. Spines help shade the rounded or ribbed stems from the blazing sun of their desert habitat. They also protect desert animal species by providing them with shelter.

Why do **tropical rain forests** grow so many plants?

Rain forests—thick forests of trees and other plants found in the lowland areas of the Tropics around the world—exist in parts of Australia, Indochina, India, the Malay Peninsula, the East Indies, in central and western Africa, and in Central and South America. Unlike forests in many other parts of the world, which have been affected by global climate changes like the Ice Age, tropical rain forests have been growing uninterrupted in some places for millions of years. During that time an unimaginable number of different types of plants and animals have evolved to use every food source and live in every spot there.

Tropical rain forests have more plant and animal species than the rest of the world combined, and scientists continue to discover new species. Because tropical rain forests are located near the equator, their climate is warm. The name "rain forest" comes from the fact that they receive a lot of rain—between 160 and 400 inches (4 and 10 meters)—throughout the year. Plants grow very quickly under such ideal conditions. In order to get the sunlight that they need for photosynthesis (the process by which they and other green plants make their own food), rain forest trees grow very tall, up to 130 feet (40 meters) high. Their tops form a huge canopy that shades most of the ground, protecting plants on the ground from excessive sunshine as well as wind. Rain forest trees have very shallow roots, for the soil in which they grow is poor, having long been depleted of nutrients by the needs of thick plant life over millions of years. But the abundant life all around contributes organic matter (the decomposed remains of plants and animals) to the surface of the soil, which is enough to nourish these grand, ancient forests.

Which plants grow in the rain forests?

More than two-thirds of the world's plant species are found in the tropical rain forests of the world. In this environment—where there is abundant plant growth with little ground space for roots and plenty of moisture—some plants grow high up in trees. These epiphytes, or air plants, have fibrous, spongy, aerial roots that get moisture from the frequent rains and take minerals from the surface of the tree on which they grow, or from the plant debris that gathers around their roots. Many orchids and bromeliads are epiphytic plants. Other plants that grow in this unique environment include bamboo, which is one of the fastest growing plants in the world. Found in Asian rain forests, the plant can grow 6 to 15 inches (15 and 38 centimeters) a day, reaching as tall as 120 feet (36.5 meters). The hearty grass, which is hard like wood, is used in the tropics to build houses, rafts, and bridges, and to make mats, hats, fish traps, chopsticks, and musical instruments. Other unique plants, many of which provide food and products for local populations, include Brazil nut trees, cacao trees, palm trees, kapok trees, rubber tree plants, and climbing plants called lianas.

Can a plant grow in ice and snow?

It is difficult for plants to survive in the coldest regions of the world, where snow covers the ground for most of the year. In the Arctic tundra that circles the North Pole, once the snow melts in the spring the growing season is short (50 to 60 days), and flowers have little time to make their seeds. Even in the summer it is cold and windy, with just a few months of sunshine. Yet, many different types of plants have adapted to this cold area, where winter temperatures dip below –30 degrees Fahrenheit (–34 degrees Celsius) and the average summer temperature is 37 to 54 degrees Fahrenheit (3 to 12 degrees Celsius). In fact, there are about 1,700 kinds of plants in the arctic and subarctic, including low shrubs, sedges, reindeer mosses, liverworts, and grasses; more than 400 types of flowering plants; and lichen.

Most plants, such as purple saxifrage, are small, and grow close together and close to the ground. This protects them from the cold temperatures and the strong winds, which can soar up to 100 miles (161 kilometers) per hour. Others, such as the arctic crocus, have fuzzy coverings on the stems, leaves, and buds to protect them from the wind. Plants like the arctic poppy have cup-shaped flowers that face up to the Sun, so the Sun's rays can easily reach the flower's center. These plants stay warmer than the air around them. The Alpine soldanella uses its food stores to keep warm, producing enough "heat" to melt the snow near its roots. Other plants are dark-colored so they can absorb more solar heat. Often, small leaves help the plants retain moisture. Certain plants, such as edelweiss, have a thick coat of hair on them, which traps heat and cuts down water loss. And lichen is super-hardy. It can grow on bare rock and survive long droughts and extremely cold temperatures.

What is lichen?

Thought to be among the oldest living things on Earth, lichen is a unique growth that is made up of a fungus and either green algae or bacteria called cyanobacteria.

The algae or bacteria live underneath the sheltering fungus, and provide it with sugars (food) from photosynthesis. In return, they receive protection from the sunlight and are able to live without drying out. In this way, lichen represents one of the most unique living "partnerships" on Earth. Lichen is a hardy plant that grows on all kinds of bare surfaces in extreme environments, such as rocks, tree trunks, desert sand, cleared soil, and living bark. Most kinds grow very slowly—often less than 1 millimeter per year.

FERNS, MOSSES, AND MUSHROOMS

What are **ferns**?

Ferns are an ancient group of plants that first appeared on Earth about 325 million years ago. They are most closely related to mosses and liverworts. There are more than 12,000 species of ferns that grow around the world, and many live in moist, shady, tropical regions such as rain forests. Ferns are called vascular plants because they have internal vein structures that help spread water and nutrients throughout the plant. Ferns do not have flowers or fruit. They reproduce by spores, microscopic dustlike particles that are released by the hundreds and spread by wind and water. They are typically produced on the lower side of the fronds or "leaves." When released, each spore grows into a tiny heart-shaped structure called the thallus, which makes male sperm cells at the pointed end and female cells in the notch. After a heavy rainfall, the sperm burst free from the thallus and swim to the female cells, where they are fertilized.

Are **fiddleheads** and **ferns** related?

Yes. Fiddleheads are young fern fronds that have not yet opened up. Fiddleheads are named for their appearance, which resembles the scroll at the head or top of a fiddle. They often appear on menus in the eastern United States during springtime. Many fern species produce these edible shoots, which have a unique texture but taste a bit like asparagus. They include the ostrich fern, the bracken fern, the royal fern, and cinnamon and flowering ferns.

A Boletus mushroom (a type of fungus) grows in a patch of dense, green moss.

What is **moss**?

Moss is a type of plant that does not have traditional roots, stems, or leaves. Because they have no true roots, mosses use delicate growths called rhizoids to anchor them to soil, rocks, or tree

94

bark. Moss grows along the ground where it is moist, absorbing water and nutrients from the air. Like their cousins the ferns and liverworts (leafy mosses), mosses reproduce from spores, not seeds, and need to be moist in order to reproduce. They grow in soft cushions or small clumps, and can spread out like a blanket along the ground.

What is **fungi**?

Fungi are neither plants nor animals, and include mushrooms, toadstools, molds, and yeast. Fungi do not have chlorophyll (the green food-making compound found in plants), so they cannot make their own food. To survive, they release enzymes that break down living or dead plants, animals, or other fungi, and live off of their nutrients. All fungi reproduce by spores. In many mushrooms, spores are located on the underside of the mushroom cap and released from vertical plates or flaps called gills. The stinkhorn is a tall fungus that shoots up out of the ground, and produces a foul, stinking smell as it ripens. Its slimy body is covered with spores, and its foul smell attracts flies, which help deliver the stinkhorn's spores to new locations in the forest.

Why are some **mushrooms** called **toadstools**?

The word "toadstool" dates to the Middle Ages when it was associated with the toad, which was thought to be poisonous. Toadstools, with their stool-like shape, are really mushrooms that are poisonous or inedible. For example, the bright red "fly agaric" toadstool's juice was once used to make a remedy for killing bugs. It is a very poisonous mushroom that still lives today and should be avoided.

What is a **giant puffball**?

The giant puffball is an edible mushroom that grows in meadows, forests, and fields all over the world. Big and white, the giant puffballs look like a large ball of thick whipped cream that has been dropped on the ground. The giant puffball is one of the biggest mushrooms—it can grow as large as a basketball and weigh up to 40 pounds (20 kilograms). When it reaches its full size, the giant puffball starts to crack slightly, revealing a white interior. Within days, the spores in the interior mature and are released through a hole in the top of the puffball's cap. The mushroom then begins to rot, and touching it will cause it to—puff!—burst into a cloud of dust.

What is **bracket fungus**?

Bracket fungus is a type of fungus that grows on both living and dead trees. It looks a lot like a hard mushroom, and is called bracket fungus (or sometimes shelf fungus) because it grows like a bracket or shelf in horizontal rows. Some forms grow so thick they may speed up the death of the tree, and then feed off the wood for years afterwards.

TREES

What are the **longest-living trees** in the **United States**?

Of the 850 different species of trees in the United States, the oldest is the bristle-cone pine, which grows in the deserts of Nevada and southern California. Scientists think that some of these trees are more than 4,600 years old. They believe they can live as long as 5,500 years. Although this seems old, it is actually very young when compared to the oldest surviving species in the world, the maiden-hair tree, or *Ginkgo biloba,* of China. This tree first appeared during the Jurassic era some 100 million years ago. Also called icho, or ginkgo, meaning "silver apricot," this species has been grown in Japan since 1100 B.C.E..

How can you tell **how old a tree is**?

Scientists can tell the age of a tree by examining it. Researchers call this area of study dendrochronology, which is a combination of several Greek root words: *dendro,* meaning "tree"; *chrono,* meaning "time"; and *ology,* meaning "the study of." Scientists have several ways to tell how old a tree is. First, they count the whorls around it. A whorl is the circular growth of branches in the same spot around the tree trunk. As the tree gets older, it will loose its whorls and markings will be left behind. They count from the bottom whorl up to tell how old it is. Sometimes, they will use a boring tool to drill into the core of the tree to tell its age. (A boring tool is a T-shaped tool with a long, thin hollow plug that drills into the tree to take a sample of the core.) Scientists count the rings on the sample to determine the age of the tree and then cover the hole to keep the tree alive. If a tree is cut down, they look inside the core for circles, called annual circles. The circles start off very small in circumference and get larger with each ring. Each ring represents one year of life for the tree—researchers begin with the inner-most part of the core (called the pith) and count outward toward the bark until they determine the age.

What else do the **tree rings** tell us?

Scientists also use a tree's annual rings to tell what the climate was like and what happened in the area where the tree grew. Every year the tree produces an annual layer of cells that appear as one wide, light ring (during spring and early summer) and one narrow, dark ring (during the winter). Very thick rings mean it was a good growing season with plenty of rainfall. Darker areas mean that the tree was not growing much because of lack of nutrients, less water, and less sunlight. Other markings reveal information about fires, floods, deforestation, and insect damage.

Which **tree** is the **biggest and tallest**?

Living species of sequoias are some of the biggest and widest trees in the world. The tallest trees are the coastal redwoods of California, while the widest ones are the giant sequoias, which have much larger trunks and branches. These trees grow in the Sierra Nevada mountains of Central California at elevations of about 6,500 feet (1,981 meters). The trees have survived for 2,000 or 3,000 years. Some of the largest sequoia trees measure 35 feet (10.6 meters) in diameter and up to 300 feet (91 meters) in height. Their bark can be 4 feet (1.2 meters) thick! Many are found in California's Sequoia National Park. The General Sherman, for example, is one of the tallest giant sequoias in the world, with a height of about 275 feet (85 meters).

Which tree can have more than 2,000 trunks?

The banyan tree, which grows in tropical Asia, is a member of the ficus or fig family. As the massive limbs spread horizontally, the tree sends down roots that develop into secondary, pillar-like supporting trunks. Over many years a single tree may spread to take over an entire area. The Great Banyan Tree, in the Botanical Gardens in Calcutta,

A redwood forest can make you dizzy just by looking up. Redwoods are among the tallest trees on the planet and can live for thousands of years.

India, has more than 2,000 trunks. It became diseased after it was struck by lightning, so in 1925 the middle of the tree was removed to keep the remainder of the tree healthy. But still it kept growing, thanks to its elaborate root system. The Great Banyan is about 250 years old and is spread over an area of 3.7 acres (1.5 hectares).

What is the Joshua tree?

The Joshua tree is a desert tree that grows in southwestern North America, in California, Arizona, Utah, and Nevada. A native of the Mojave Desert, these drought-tolerant trees thrive in the open grasslands of California's Joshua Tree National Park. The Mormon pioneers named this tree after the prophet Joshua, because its extended branches resembled the outstretched arm of Joshua as he pointed with his spear to the ancient city of Ai. The trees are twisted and spiky, with tough leaves, and look a little bit like a tree from a Dr. Seuss book. Joshua trees can grow from seed or from an underground rhizome of another Joshua tree. They grow very slowly, sometimes 3.9 to 7.8 inches (10 to 20 centimeters) in their first few years. The tallest trees reach about 49 feet (15 meters) tall. The trunk of a Joshua tree is made of thousands of small fibers and does not have yearly growth rings, which makes it hard for scientists to tell the tree's age. Although the fragile tree

Which tree grows on stilts?

Mangrove trees live in estuaries near the ocean's edge where freshwater and saltwater mix. Most mangrove estuaries are found in tropical and subtropical climates near the equator, including coastal Florida, Central America, the Caribbean, South America, and parts of Africa. These trees have waxy leaves and an elaborate root system that branches from the stem and helps prop up the tree, which appears to be growing on stilts. The protected waters between the mangrove roots are a breeding ground for fish, crabs, and birds. The tree's decaying leaves fall into the water and provide nutrients for animals and plants. Mangroves help protect coastlines by trapping soil and sediment and reducing erosion caused by waves and tides.

has shallow roots, if it survives the harsh desert environment, it can live hundreds—even thousands—of years.

Why do **leaves change color** in the autumn?

Tree leaves change color as autumn approaches because the days are shorter and the temperatures are cooler. As the length of the days shortens, the leaves stop their production of chlorophyll, a pigment that provides the leaves' green color. Other pigments in the leaves, mostly yellow, are then able to show through. The yellow color is mostly seen in aspen, birch, hickory, willow, and yellow poplar trees. Sugars that are trapped in the leaves as the trees prepare for winter form red pigments, also called anthocyanins. Some trees with red leaves are the dogwood, red and silver maple, oak, sumac, and sassafras.

Why are these trees called **deciduous**?

After turning shades of yellow, orange, and red, deciduous trees shed their leaves. Trees such as birch, oak, and maple lose water quickly from their wide, flat leaves. In wintertime, it is hard for them to absorb water from the cold, often frozen ground, so their leaves die and fall off. In the springtime, leaf and flower bud return, burst open, and come into full foliage by summer.

Is it true that **hundreds** of wild **things live** in **oak trees**?

Oak trees—with their broad leaves that provide shelter and shade—provide a home for more than 300 species of insects, birds, and mammals. Their bark is crawling with a wide variety of insects, including ants, ladybugs, weevils, wasps, oakworms, caterpillars, and moths. Blue jays, hummingbirds, magpies, finches, sparrows, wrens, and woodpeckers feed off of the insect life and make their nests in the branches. The oak's acorns are an important food source for mice, squirrels, chipmunks, deer, bears, foxes, quails, blue jays, crows, and turkeys. Oaks can live more than 200 years; by the time they are 70 years old they produce thousands of acorns per year.

What do **fir and pine trees** tell us about the **weather**?

Firs and pines are coniferous trees, which have tall, straight trunks and either flat narrow leaves or sharply tipped needles. Conifers bear their seeds inside dry, woody, female cones. In cool or damp weather the scales of the cones close up tightly, protecting the seeds inside with a waterproof layer of waxy resin. When the weather is warm and dry, the resin softens, and the cone's scales open to release their seeds. Some species, like the lodgepole pine, need the heat of a forest fire to melt the wax that seals their cones.

What is **bonsai**?

Bonsai means "tree in a pot" in Chinese and is pronounced BONE-sigh. It is a special method for growing trees or

Some people think that bonsai trees are dwarf trees, but they actually are regular trees and bushes that have been specially pruned to look like miniature versions of themselves.

shrubs in a pot, tray, or dish, which results in an artificially dwarfed plant. Bonsais are regular trees or shrubs, such as juniper or cypress, that are stunted by pruning their roots and tying their branches with wire. The art originated in China around 200 C.E., and was adapted by the Japanese early in the sixth and seventh centuries.

What is a **fruit**?

A fruit is the part of the plant that nourishes and protects new seeds as they grow. The plant's ovaries develop into fruit once the eggs inside have been fertilized by pollen. Some plants produce juicy fruit, such as peaches, pears, apples, lemons, and oranges. Others produce dry fruit, such as nuts and pea pods. If an animal doesn't eat the fruit, or a human doesn't pick it off, it falls to the ground and decays and fertilizes the soil where a new seed will grow.

Which fruit tree makes the **heaviest fruit**?

The jackfruit tree, which grows in southern Asia, produces the largest fruit in the world. The fruit, which grows directly from the trunk, may reach nearly 3 feet (0.9 meters) in length and weigh up to 75 pounds (34 kilograms). Jackfruit and its close relative, breadfruit, belong to the mulberry family. Asians eat the fruit raw or preserved in syrup, and they eat the seeds after boiling or roasting them.

Did Johnny Appleseed really plant apple trees?

Yes. John Chapman, a pioneer nurseryman who lived in the 1800s, was also called Johnny Appleseed because he planted orchards in the Midwest United States. He also encouraged the development of fruit-tree orchards farther west by giving away free seedlings to pioneers. In drawings, he is often shown as a barefoot tramp roaming the countryside scattering seeds from a bag slung over his shoulder. The real Appleseed, however, was a curious figure who often preached from the Bible and from religious texts to passersby. At the time of his death in 1845, he was a successful businessman who owned thousands of acres of orchards and nurseries.

Which tree produces the **largest nut**?

The coco de mer tree, a palm that only grows today on two islands in the Seychelles, produces both the largest seed (each weighs about 44 pounds [20 kilograms]) and the largest nut in the world. The nut, which takes six to seven years to mature and another two years to germinate, is sometimes called the sea coconut or Seychelles nut. When early explorers first discovered the nut, they thought it came from a mythical tree at the bottom of the sea. Sixteenth-century European nobles decorated the nut with jewels as collectibles for their private galleries. Today, the coco de mer is a rare protected species.

How do **coconuts swim**?

The coconut palm, or coconut tree, grows in many tropical areas of the world, including the coastal regions of Indonesia, the Philippines, India, Brazil, and Sri Lanka. When the tree is four or five years old, it begins to produce male and female flowers, followed by nuts. The coconuts reach full size in about six months and, as they mature, drop from trees. The fallen coconuts, which are light and able to float, get scooped up by waves. The ocean currents carry the "sea-beans" across oceans, until they land on another shore, ready to sprout new trees. Scientists believe this why coconut trees appear in so many faraway regions of the world.

PLANTS THAT HELP AND HEAL

Which tree was used in the **fledgling shipbuilding industry**?

During colonial times the U.S. Navy used the oak tree's hard wood to build its ships. The *U.S.S. Constitution* received its nickname, "Old Ironsides," during the War of 1812 because its live oak hull was so tough that British war ships' cannonballs literally bounced off it. Because the *Constitution* was built before shipbuilders learned to bend or steam wood into shape, the live oak's long, arching branches were used as braces to connect the ship's hull to its deck floors. Throughout the years, oak wood has been used as lumber, railroad ties, fenceposts, veneer, and fuel wood. Today it is manufactured into flooring, furniture, and crates.

Which plant is used to **make linen**?

Linen, one of the oldest human fabrics, is woven from fibers of the flax plant. The fibers are located in the stalk, which is picked by hand. After the fibers have been separated from the stalk and processed, they are spun into yarns and woven or knit into linen textiles. However, many years ago linen was used for sheets and is still used for household items such as tablecloths and personal items such as handkerchiefs. Slacks, dresses, suits, and blazers are all common clothing items made from linen today.

How is **cotton harvested**?

Cotton, which comes from flowering Gossypium plants, is a key vegetable fiber used for making clothes, and oil from its seeds can be used in cooking or for making soap. The cotton plant grows in 17 states that make up the U.S. "Cotton Belt": California, Arizona, New Mexico, Texas, Oklahoma, Arkansas, Missouri, Mississippi, Alabama, Louisiana, Florida, Tennessee, North Carolina, South Carolina, Virginia, Georgia, and Kansas.

In the United States, where cotton is no longer picked by hand, machines called pickers or strippers harvest the crops. Cotton-picking machines have spindles that pick (twist) the seed cotton from the burrs that are attached to plants' stems. Doffers—a series of circular rubber pads—then remove the seed cotton from the spindles and knock the seed cotton into a conveying system. Conventional cotton stripping machines use rollers equipped with alternating bats and brushes to knock the fluffy white bolls, which contain seeds and hairs, from the plants into a conveyor. After harvest, most of the cotton is pressed into large blocks for storage. These cotton bundles are then transported to the cotton gin, a machine that pulls out the seeds from the cotton bolls.

What is **paper made of**?

Around the world, people have made paper from a wide variety of plant materials, such as wood pulp, rice, water plants, bamboo, cotton, and linen clothing. The ancient Egyptians made paper from papyrus reeds that grew abundantly along the Nile River. Today's paper fiber comes mainly from two sources: pulpwood logs and recycled paper products. In fact, much of the paper today is a blend of new and recycled fiber. To make paper commercially, companies mash up these wood fibers and mix them with water. This mixture is mashed into a thin sheet. The sheet is dried and pressed flat into large rolls, cut into different sizes, and converted into paper products. Recycling paper and paper products helps save trees and support the paper-making process. According to the American Forest and Paper Association

The sap from the aloe vera plant has long been known to have healing properties.

more than half—53.4 percent—of the paper used in the United States was recovered for recycling in 2006.

What is **aloe vera**?

A cactus-like plant of the lily family, aloe vera grows wild in Madagascar and on the African continent. It also is cultivated in Japan, the Caribbean, the Mediterranean, and the United States. People around the world have used its gooey, jelly-like sap for healing and cosmetic purposes. Aloe extracts can be used to treat digestive problems, including constipation, and aloe oils are used in cosmetic creams to help keep skin soft and to treat minor skin irritations.

Are **marine plants** used in **toothpaste**?

Yes, and lots of other products, too. Substances from marine plants and animals are used in many home products, including ice cream, toothpaste, fertilizers, gasoline, and cosmetics. If you read the labels of some of these products, you may find the words carrageenan and alginate. Carrageenans are compounds extracted from red algae that are used to stabilize and jell foods. Brown algae contain alginates that make foods thicker and creamier and add to shelf life. They are used to prevent ice crystals from forming in ice cream, for example. Alginates and carrageenans are often used in puddings, milkshakes, and ice cream. The remains of diatoms (algae with hard shells) are used to make pet litter, cosmetics, and pool filters. The kelp plant is often used in lipstick, toothpaste, and clothing dye.

Why do people plant **marram grass** on **sand dunes**?

Marram is a tough perennial grass that is often planted in shifting sand dunes to help stabilize them. Between the edge of the water and the beginning of the dunes, dry sand is constantly shifting and floating. One of the few plants that can take root in this windy environment is marram grass. It spreads its tuberous roots just under the surface of the sand, and forms an underground web that helps hold the sand in place. This allows the soil to stabilize and the dune to grow higher.

What were **ancient spices** used for?

Spices are dried and ground up plant seeds, fruits, root, or bark. Grown for centuries in the Middle and Far East, spices have been used for their antibacterial properties, to flavor foods, and to aid in digestion. In ancient times, spices were used as a way to mask the unpleasant tastes and odors of food, and later to keep food fresh.

They were very important commodities. As early as 1000 B.C.E., a handful of cardamom was worth as much as a poor man's yearly wages, and many slaves were bought and sold for a few cups of peppercorns. During the time of the Ancient Greeks, the spice trade flourished between the Mediterranean region and the Far East. Arab merchants brought spices such as cinnamon, cassia, black pepper, and ginger by camel caravan to Europe. During this time, spices were used for cooking, in medicine, and in luxury items such as perfumes, bath oils, and lotions. During the fifteenth and sixteenth centuries, European explorers introduced spices to the New World. During the days of American colonization the most popular cooking spices were pepper, cinnamon, vanilla, nutmeg, ginger, cloves, and allspice. Colonial families experimented with exotic spices to flavor dishes, including chili peppers, cardamom, cumin, saffron, and turmeric (which was also used as a food preservative). Today, most spices are grown on large plantations in China, India, the Middle East, South America, and North Africa, where they are often picked by hand.

Are there **plant species** that are **endangered**?

Yes. According to scientists, at least 34,000 of the world's 275,000 fern, conifer, and flowering plant species—or about one in eight—is endangered with extinction. Researchers think that the true number of these plants is actually much higher because many plants species have not yet been identified. In the United States, 29 percent of its 16,000 plant species are considered endangered. Throughout the world, the main threats to plants are habitat destruction, the spreading of towns, and modern farming techniques that use pesticides. Some plants, such as rare orchids and cacti, are threatened because they have been overcollected. In addition, climate changes, disease, and plant-eating animals, such as goats, have destroyed many rare pants.

Why are **rain forests** so important to the **health of our planet**?

In 1800 there were 7.1 billion acres of rain forest in the world. Now—a little more than 200 years later—less than half, or 3.5 billion acres, remain. Over 100,000 acres of the world's rain forests are destroyed each day, with trees cut down for their valuable wood and land cleared for farming. While covering just two percent of Earth's surface, the dense vegetation of these forests plays an important role in the health of our planet. The destruction of rain forests threatens the health of our planet by reducing the amount of oxygen in our air and increasing carbon dioxide. Too much carbon dioxide in our atmosphere keeps the Sun's heat from radiating back into space, increasing global temperatures (called the greenhouse effect). Global warming, in turn, could bring about major climate changes. Melting glaciers and rising sea levels, for example, could cause the flooding of coastal regions.

The plants in rain forests produce natural chemicals that fight off destruction by insects, and scientists have learned how to make plant-based insecticides from rain forest plants (without destroying the rain forests) to spray on crops. These natural insecticides are far less toxic than synthetic, or human-made, chemicals. Numerous medicines, as much as one-quarter of all prescription drugs, have been made from materials gathered in rain forests, and many more life-saving medicines may await discovery there. Many products, like natural rubber, essential oils used in cosmetics and perfumes, and rattan, a material weaved together to make furniture, can be taken from rain forests without causing widespread destruction. In addition, rain forests can absorb huge amounts of water. When rain forests are destroyed, the vast amounts of rainfall in those regions cannot be absorbed, resulting in widespread flooding. International efforts have begun trying to save what remains of the rain forests by helping the people who destroy them find other ways to earn a living. Still, the destruction of these important forests continues at a rapid pace.

PEOPLE AROUND THE WORLD

LOTS OF PEOPLE!

How many people are there in the world?

The world's population, or the total number of humans on Earth, reached 6.6 billion in 2008. Different regions have different rates of population growth, but in the twentieth century, the world saw the biggest increase ever in its population due to medical advances and increasing agricultural productivity. In 2000, the United Nations estimated that the world's population was growing at the rate of 1.14 percent (or about 75 million people) per year, and by the year 2050 there may be as many as 9.2 billion people in the world!

Why did people begin exploring?

For many hundreds of years, adventurous travelers have explored the far reaches of the earth. They traveled for many reasons: some were looking for new areas to trade with; others were looking for new areas to conquer, settle, and farm; some desired to spread their religion; and others hoped to achieve fame and become wealthy. Some of the earliest oceanic voyages were made by the Polynesians of New Guinea more than 3,500 years ago. They traveled the Pacific Ocean in small boats the size of canoes. Around this time, Egyptians sent their large trading ships to the land of Punt, south of Egypt at the tip of the Red Sea. Hanno the Navigator was one of the first known explorers. A Carthaginian explorer who lived about 450 B.C.E., Hanno was best well known for his naval exploration of the African coast. Around 1000 C.E. Leif Eriksson and his Viking explorers became the first Europeans to sail across the Atlantic Ocean to North America. These early explorers used ancient maps and the stars' position at night to guide them—but they would often get lost or shipwrecked. It would take hundreds of years of trial and error

How many kids are there in the world?

In 2000, one out of every three people was under the age of 15; which means there were about 1.8 billion kids in the world. About 70 million of these children lived in the United States.

before Italian-born explorer Christopher Columbus set sail from Spain in 1492, hoping to find a western sea route to China. Like other Europeans of his time, Columbus did not know that North and South America, and the islands of the West Indies, lay between Europe and China. When he landed in the West Indies, he believed it was part of China.

What is the **U.S. Census**?

The U.S. Census is a survey that the United States government takes every ten years, according to Article 1 of the U.S. Constitution. The survey asks questions about you, your family, your friends and their families, and all the other families or individuals who live in the 105 million households that are in the United States. The survey gathers information about how many people live in your house, how old you are, if you are male or female, and what race you are—white, black, American Indian, Asian, or Hispanic. In 1790 the first census counted 4 million people living in the United States. Today, there are more than 281 million.

The census count tells a state how many people it can send to represent it in the U.S. Congress, which includes both the Senate and the House of Representatives. Every state sends two people to the Senate. But the House of Representatives is different—the number of people a state sends to the House is based on that state's population. According to the 2000 Census, the state with the smallest population is Wyoming, while the state with the largest population is California. Wyoming can send only one person to the House, but California can send 53 people to the House of Representatives.

The census also gives information about everyday things, so that the government can tell which states and regions of the country need improvements. If a town has more children living in it than it had ten years ago (when the last census count was taken), this would be a good place to build another school. Or, if workers in a city are spending too much time getting to work, this would be a good place to build more roads or increase public transportation like subways and buses.

Which parts of the world have the **fastest growing populations**?

From the three billion people that will be added to the world population between now and 2050, Asia will contribute some two billion, mainly because of the already massive size of its population and high fertility rates. Most of Asia's growth will occur in the next three decades. The 10 countries which will contribute most to the world's

The world's population is soaring, and some cities, such as New Delhi, India, are crowded with millions of people. China and India are home to over a third of our planet's 6.6 billion people.

population growth over the next 30 years are India, China, Pakistan, Nigeria, Ethiopia, Indonesia, the United States, Bangladesh, Zaire, and Iran—in that order.

Where in the world do people live the longest?

The Japanese have the longest lifespan in the world. Japanese men live to be 78 years old on average while Japanese women live to be about 85. Okinawa, Japan, has a population of one million and of those 900 are centenarians, or people who are at least 100 years old. Scientists believe this is because the Okinawans eat more soy products than any other population in the world, as well as a wide range of different vegetables and fruit all rich in antioxidants. After Okinawa, the Sardinian mountain town of Ovodda has the most centenarians, on average 5 out of its small population of 1,700. For hundreds of years families in Ovodda have lived in isolation from the rest of the world, marrying into each others' families, which may result in few genetic diseases.

Where are people suffering from disease and poverty?

Disease and poverty exist all over the world. The areas with the most disease and poverty are countries in sub-Saharan Africa and the Asia-Pacific region. In these areas, people do not have enough food to eat, water to drink, or money to live. They have diseases like AIDS, which weakens the immune system, and cholera, an intestinal infection. In the United States, about 33 million people live in poverty, according to government statistics. Almost 12 million of these people are children, and about 3.5 million were age 65 or older.

107

LANGUAGES AND CULTURES

What is a country's **culture**?

A culture is made up of many complex parts of the country—its traditions, beliefs, art, music, clothing, food, holidays, languages, family and marriage rules or laws, games, folktales, and mythology. Culture is "the way of life" of a country or society, and these ways of living together—including value systems, traditions, and beliefs—are passed down from generation to generation. While all cultures have universal traits, different cultures have developed their own specific ways of expressing them. For example, people around the world are similar in that we communicate with each other, live by eating food and drinking water, and dream when we sleep. Yet we speak different languages, eat different foods, and dream different dreams. Anthropologists (people that research different cultures and how they develop) say that culture is made up of at least three parts: what people think, what they do, and the products they produce. In complex cultures such as the United States, culture is what knits us together as human beings living in one country, but also separates us into our different ethnic communities.

Why do people speak **different languages**?

While some animals have demonstrated the ability to communicate with other animals and with humans, people are the only creatures on Earth who communicate through language, which is a system of vocal symbols. Scientists don't know exactly when humans first spoke, though they know that it happened a very long time ago, in prehistoric times. Different languages arose when groups of people—separated by things like deserts, mountains, or great oceans—developed their own systems of communicating that reflected their unique ways of life. These new languages were passed on when children learned to speak the same way the people around them did.

As groups of people spread out to settle different parts of the world, they took their languages with them. They began to pronounce some words differently as time passed and had to add words to describe the new things and situations they found in distant lands. Languages gradually changed from their parent languages, though they still shared some characteristics. Today, English and French are languages that seem very different from one another, but they came from the same parent language (Indo-European) a long time ago. All languages that share a parent language belong to the same "family." There are 13 large language families in the world today, from which most languages have descended.

Which **language** is most **widely spoken**?

There are more than 6,000 languages spoken in the world today. In some large countries, several languages are spoken. (India has more than 800!) In other large countries, different versions or dialects of the same language are spoken in different areas. In both cases, an "official" language is usually chosen for the country. That language is used in schools, by the mass media (like television), and by the government. It is not surprising that Chinese—the language spoken in the world's most populous country is the world's most widely spoken language. Although many different versions or dialects of Chinese are spoken in the country, the standard or official language, Mandarin Chinese, is spoken in its northern and central regions. It is the native language of nearly 900 million people. Spanish is the second most widely spoken language, and English is the third. English is the most common international language, which means it is spoken in more places around the world than any other.

How does a **person's clothing** tell where he or she **comes from**?

In all countries, climate, usefulness, and customs (including religion) all influence the way people dress. When people immigrate or move to another country, they sometimes keep their style of national dress as a marker of their ethnicity and culture. In Saudi Arabia, which has a hot, desert-like climate, men and boys wear the *thawb,* an ankle length piece of clothing, sometimes made of cotton, which is long and fits loosely. Men also wear a *ghutra an iqal* on their heads—a square head cloth with a double circle of black rope or cord to hold it on the head, which keeps them cool. Women wear a long dress with long sleeves, called a *jallabia,* which covers every part of their body because their religion (Islam) does not permit them to show any body parts. Women in Japan sometimes wear kimonos, a traditional, full-length garment that wraps around the body like a robe, and is secured by a wide belt called an *obi,* usually tied in the back. In Japan, professional sumo wrestlers are often seen in kimonos because they are required to wear traditional Japanese dress whenever they appear in public. Nigerians often wear traditional Nigerian clothing, both in Africa and when they travel, which is made from lace, jacquard, and ankara, and sometimes tie-dyed. It usually consists of a shirt, long, flowing skirt (that can be tied in different ways), and a headpiece for women and cap for men. And American-made Levi's Jeans are worn across the globe by everyone from Americans to Europeans and South Americans, so it might be hard to tell where a person wearing jeans really comes from!

Why do **women** in some countries **wear veils**?

A veil is a piece of cloth that is usually worn to hide a person's hair or face. Women have worn veils since ancient times—mostly in Middle Eastern countries—primarily to keep men from looking at them. Many women of the Muslim faith still wear veils of some type when they are out in public. In some Muslim countries, only a woman's eyes are allowed to show. Although Westerners (people from North America and

Wearing veils is an important tradition in many cultures, especially among Muslim women, who wear them as a sign of modesty and obedience to their faith.

Western Europe) may find these veils symbolic of women's restricted freedoms in many Muslim societies, Muslim women wear them to honor long-held traditions of modesty and to show respect for their religion and the men in their lives.

Why are there **different religions** and how did they spread?

From our earliest days, many people have believed in a power or powers greater than themselves. This belief is known as religion. In ancient times, it was a way to make sense of the mysteries of the natural world; evil spirits were thought to be responsible for bad weather and disease, for instance. Ancient peoples felt that they had a measure of control over their lives when they made offerings and prayed to friendly spirits, whom they believed could help them win battles or grow better crops. Even today, when people know the scientific explanations for such things as thunder or the eruption of volcanoes, many look to religion to explain some of the other hard-to-understand things that we experience as humans—things like the purpose of life or the reasons for tragedies.

While most religions spring from the same basic human need to believe in a great power or powers, the ideas, practices, and traditions that religions involve can be very different. Long ago, groups of people—separated by things like deserts, mountains, or great oceans—developed special religious beliefs and forms of worship that fit their unique ways of life. Some, like the ancient Greeks, built their religions around the belief in several gods (a practice called polytheism), while others, like the Jews, believed in a single god (monotheism). Great temples, shrines, and churches were built to honor these gods, and believers showed their faith through ceremonies, sacred writings, prayers, and other forms of worship. As civilizations developed and ways of traveling long distances improved, explorers, traders, settlers, and missionaries spread different religions to other parts of the world. As religions spread, they were often changed into different forms that better fit the conditions and people of various lands. All the major religions of the world began in Asia before they gradually spread to other parts of the world—Judaism, Christianity, and Islam in the Middle East; Buddhism, Hinduism, and Sikhism in India; Taoism and Confucianism in China; and Shinto in Japan.

Which **religions** are the **most widely practiced** around the world?

Today there are some 4,300 religions in the world. Nearly 75 percent of the world's population practices one of the five most influential religions of the world: Christianity, Buddhism, Hinduism, Islam, and Judaism. Christianity, which is based on the teachings of Jesus Christ, who preached in Palestine about 2,000 years ago, is the most widely practiced religion in the world today, with 2.1 billion followers. The second most practiced religion is Islam, with 1.3 billion followers.

Why is America called a **"melting pot"**?

Except for Native Americans and slaves from Africa, the United States is a nation of people who left their home country looking for a better life (called immigrants). As a result, the population of the United States is made up of a mixture of people from different countries, such as France, Ireland, China, Brazil, and Mexico. For this reason, the United States is sometimes called the "melting pot." The next time you are in class, look around. Everyone around you is different. Although your classmate may have been born in the United States, at some point, that person's family left their home country and came to the United States.

CITY LIFE

What is the difference between a **metropolitan area, a city**, and a **megalopolis**?

A metropolitan area includes a core city as well as nearby communities, making it a larger settlement of people than just a city. A city is any urban settlement that is larger than a town (which generally has between 2,500 and 20,000 residents), and that is able to function on its own, with a government and other public services. A megalopolis is any multicity area with more than 10 million people. For example, in the United States, the third largest metropolitan area is the Chicago-Gary-Kenosha area, with 8.8 million residents, which also houses the third largest U.S. city, Chicago.

Which **city** is the **largest**?

There are many cities around the world that are "big," meaning they have more than 10 million people living in them. Tokyo, Japan, ranks the largest, since it has 33.2 million people living in the city, according to 2005 estimates. The next biggest cities in order of size are São Paulo, Brazil (17.7 million), Seoul-Incheon, South Korea (17.5 million), Mexico City, Mexico (17.4 million), Osaka-Kobe-Kyoto, Japan (16.4 million), and New York City (about 8 million people). Most of these cities are located in different places around the globe. In the United States, after New York, Los Angeles is the biggest city (with almost 4 million people), and then Chicago (with almost three million people). Populations of cities are constantly changing as people move in and out of them, according to the U.S. Census Bureau, a government organization that estimates how big or small cities are based on their populations, or the number of people living in them.

Which **city** is the **smallest**?

Ferdania, in Saudi Arabia, is probably the world's smallest city: it has one police station, one school, one market, one gas station, one health center, and about 10 houses. According to the *Guinness Book of World Records,* Hum, Croatia, is the smallest town in the world, with a population of only 23 citizens. The tiny town, which rose during the Middle Ages, is closed off on one side by high towers and a system of walls; the other side is closed off by the outer walls of houses. The smallest city in the United States is Maza, located in Towner County, North Dakota. Established in 1893, the city had a population of 5 when the 2000 Census was taken.

Which U.S. city has the most **public landmarks**?

New York City has the most landmarks in the United States. Landmarks are permanent structures, such as trees, bridges, buildings, and statues that contribute to the historic, cultural, or architectural heritage of a city. In New York, there are 1,116 designated landmarks, 104 interior landmarks, 9 scenic landmarks, and 84 historic districts, resulting in the largest number of designated landmarks and the most valuable real estate in any city in the United States. Some of the most famous landmarks include the Empire State Building, which is 1,250 feet (381 meters) high from the ground to its tip. There is an observatory on the 86th floor of the building that overlooks the city, but you have to either take the elevator or climb more than 1,000 steps to reach it. Another famous New York City landmark is the Statue of Liberty, which was built by French sculptor Auguste Bartholdi, with the help of many laborers working ten hour days, seven days a week for nine years! The statue was finally finished in July 1884, and shipped to America in 350 individual pieces that were finally assembled many months later.

Where are the **largest factories** located?

Factories, also called manufacturing plants, are large buildings where workers create and assemble all types of useful things, or supervise machines to make them, including airplanes, cars, shoes, clothing, household appliances—even chocolate. Today's factories usually have large warehouses that hold heavy equipment used for assembly-line production. Most industrial cities—like Shanghai, China; Seoul, South Korea; St. Louis, Missouri; and Detroit, Michigan—have factories. Hershey, Pennsylvania, has the largest chocolate factory in the world, where it makes one billion pounds of chocolate products each year. Other areas—such as the Garment Districts in New York and Los Angeles—make many of the clothes we wear. Recycling plants, found in every major city, take millions of old aluminum cans, plastic bottles, and glass containers and make new ones. The world's largest plastic bottle recycling plant is in Spartenburg, South Carolina.

Which city has the most **elaborate subway system**?

London, England's underground subway system, called the Underground, is the world's largest metro subway system and the world's oldest underground system (it was inaugurated in 1863). Its 253 miles (407 kilometers) of track and its 11 lines transport more than three million people around the city each day. Londoners beware: If the Chinese capital is successful with its plans to expand its Beijing subway system to 348 miles (561 kilometers) by 2020, it will surpass London as the city with the world's most extensive underground subway system. After London, the most substantial system is New York City's rapid transit system. Built in 1904, its 229 miles (369 kilometers) of routes carries 4.9 million people around the city every day, making it one of the ten busiest systems in the world, with more boardings than systems in London, Paris, Tokyo, Moscow, and Mexico City.

The London subway system—commonly called the Underground—has over 250 miles (400 kilometers) of track and services three million people daily.

Other extensive subway systems include the Paris subway system which is the second oldest in the world (the initial system was completed in 1900), with more than 133 miles (214 kilometers) of track and 380 stations; and the Moscow subway system, which boasts the largest ridership of all metro systems throughout the world, with about 8.2 million passengers per day. While most of the Moscow trains run underground, some lines cross bridges and provide scenic views of the Moskva River and the Yauza River.

Which **airport** is the **busiest** in the world?

The biggest airport is not necessarily the busiest one. If you were to measure all the airports around the world, the King Khalid International Airport in Riyadh, Saudi Arabia, would be the largest: It takes up some 81 square miles (209 square kilometers), an area larger than many cities! But the Hartsfield-Jackson Atlanta International Airport is the busiest airport in the world, handling about 1,121,000,000 passengers annually. Atlanta overtook Chicago's O'Hare International Airport in 1998, which handled 66.6 million passengers in 2002. London's Heathrow Airport accommodates the most international passengers, but ranks third behind Atlanta and Chicago in total number of passengers.

Why do cities have **dams**?

Dams, which are structures that hold back water, have been built since ancient times. They are usually made of earth, rock, brick, or concrete—or a combination of these things. They are constructed to control the flow of water in a river, and they are built for a number of reasons. One reason is to prevent flooding. Heavy rains in high country may cause water levels in a river to rise. As the river flows downhill, it may overflow its banks, flooding communities located downstream. A dam can prevent this by stopping or slowing rushing water, allowing it to be released at a controlled rate. Dams are also frequently used to store water for general use and farming. When a river's flow is restricted by a dam, water often spreads out behind the dam to form a lake or reservoir in the river valley. That water can then be used as needed, preventing water shortages and crop damage during long periods of dry weather.

A great number of dams today are used to make electricity. Such hydroelectric dams are built very tall, to create a great difference in the height of the water level behind and in front of it. High water behind a dam passes through gates in the dam wall that allow it to fall to the river far below. As the water falls, it flows past huge blades called turbines; the turbines run generators that make electricity. One of the world's largest and most productive hydroelectric dams is the Hoover Dam, located on the Colorado River between Nevada and Arizona. Built in the 1930s, it is 726 feet (221 meters) high and 1,244 feet (379 meters) long. Its reservoir (Lake Mead)—the world's largest—supplies water to several states, allowing huge regions of naturally dry terrain in southern California, Arizona, and Mexico to flourish. Many modern dams are used for all three purposes: flood control, water storage, and hydroelectric power.

How does **nuclear energy** work to make a **city run**?

We usually make heat energy by burning fuels—oil, gas, coal, or wood. In large quantities, such energy can be used to heat water, and the resulting steam can be used to run generators that make electricity for a city. Burning fuel (combustion) is a chemical reaction that converts one form of energy into another: it recombines elements from the fuel and the oxygen in the air into things like ash, smoke, and waste gases, as well as heat.

A fission-generated nuclear reaction produces heat in a different way: it breaks apart elements themselves, turning them into waste products with less mass, which creates a great amount of energy. The tiniest particles of matter—atoms—of heavy elements like uranium or plutonium provide the fuel for nuclear reactors. At the center of each atom is a nucleus, which is made up of even tinier particles called protons and neutrons. A nucleus is held together by a powerful force, and breaking up the nucleus releases that force. A nuclear reaction starts when fast-moving neutrons strike the nuclei of fuel atoms, causing them to break into smaller nuclei. These in turn release neutrons that break up more fuel nuclei. All this movement produces great heat, which can be used to make steam to run electric generators.

Why is **nuclear power dangerous**?

The good thing about fission-generated nuclear energy is that very little fuel is needed to produce huge amounts of energy. (Two pounds of nuclear fuel could produce as much energy as 6.5 million pounds of coal, for instance!) The challenging part is that the process must be very carefully controlled. (In a nuclear reactor, control rods that absorb neutrons are moved in and out of the core to control the process.) If it isn't controlled, the result could be a build up of pressure within the reactor. If this continues, radioactive gases might be released along with steam. It was a situation like this that happened at the Chernobyl plant in the Soviet Union in 1986, resulting in radioactive pollution that still exists today.

An uncontrolled nuclear reaction can cause harmful radioactive materials (such as iodine isotopes that can cause thyroid cancer) to be released into the environment. This by-product of nuclear fission is a problem connected with nuclear power. Nuclear reactors are encased in thick layers of steel and con-

Nuclear energy currently provides about 15 percent of the world's energy needs. As of 2009, there were 104 operating nuclear power plants in the United States.

crete to keep radiation from escaping. And because leftover nuclear fuel is highly radioactive, it must be carefully stored far away from people for decades or even centuries before it is safe again. Transporting and disposing of dangerous waste is another challenge presented by nuclear power; at present, used fuel is sealed in safety containers and buried deep underground.

The nuclear process that we get our power from is called fission, where atomic nuclei that break apart produce great energy and heat. But nuclear power can also be created by a process called fusion, where atomic nuclei join together. Scientists are still working on creating a satisfactory fusion reactor. The Sun produces its great energy and heat through the nuclear fusion of its hydrogen gases.

FARM LIFE

Where does our food come from?

People in industrialized nations like the United States eat food that comes from all over the world. Such countries have the wealth to buy food products that are brought by plane or ship from far away. A wide variety of canned and packaged foods are available from every corner of the globe. And even fresh foods like fruits, vegetables, fish, and meats can now be sped across oceans in refrigerated boats. So foods that were once rare treats are now available at nearly every time of the year, arriving from places with different climates and seasons. That means that the asparagus and strawberries you eat may be grown nearby—or halfway across the world! Today, when you look in your cupboards, it can be like taking a trip around the world: you will see tea from India, coffee from Brazil, olive oil from Italy, and much more. In the past, people ate only the food that they could produce on their farms or find at their local markets. That is still true of many people who live in developing nations.

How has **farming changed** in the **United States**?

In the 1700s, English farmers settled in New England villages; Dutch, German, Swedish, Scotch-Irish, and English farmers settled on Middle Colony farmsteads; English and French farmers settled on plantations in tidewater and on isolated Southern Colony farmsteads in Piedmont; Spanish immigrants, mostly indentured servants, settled the Southwest and California. Farmers endured a rough pioneer life while adapting to their new environments, and by the 1800s small family farms grew and sold crops such as wheat, cotton, corn, and rice. But the work was hard and slow going: In 1830, it took 250 to 300 hours of labor using very basic tools to produce 100 bushels (5 acres) of wheat. The growth of farming brought many labor-saving devices to nineteenth- and early-twentieth-century farm life, including reaping and threshing machines, which replaced work done by hand. Today, with modern methods of agriculture that include complex machinery, scientific breeding, and chemical pesticides, farms require far fewer workers.

Before the Industrial Revolution (which began in the 1800s in the United States), most people lived and worked on farms. In 1935, there were 6.8 million farms in the United States, and the average farmer produced enough food each year to feed about 20 people. In 2002, the number of farms dropped to about 2.1 million, yet the average U.S. farmer produced enough food to feed almost 130 people. Average farm size in 1935 was smaller than it is today, about 155 acres (63 hectares) compared to about 467 acres (189 hectares) today.

Which states are the **biggest farm states**?

California produces the most agriculture (animal and plant foods) for the United States, contributing about two-thirds of the nation's fruits, nuts, berries, and melons. Almost one-quarter of the state's land—about 27.7 million acres (11.2 million hectares)—is dedicated to farming. Other states that grow a large percent of the nation's agriculture include Texas, Iowa, Kansas, Nebraska, North Dakota, and Arkansas. Texas, for example, produces the most cattle; Iowa raises the most hogs and grows the most corn; and North Dakota grows the most wheat, followed by Kansas. Arkansas tops the list as the state with the largest poultry production.

How does the **combine harvester** help farmers?

The combine harvester saves the farmers time and labor. Before modern machinery, harvesting crops was a painstaking process. Gathering and removing mature plants from the field had to be done by hand. Farm workers used sharp-bladed, long-handled scythes and curved sickles to cut down cereal crops like wheat. Even the fastest reaper could only clear about a third of an acre a day. Because rain could ruin harvested wheat, workers called sheaf-makers quickly tied it into bundles, so that it could be safely stored if the weather turned stormy. During the long winter months farm workers used jointed wooden tools called flails to thresh or beat the dried wheat in order to separate its edible grain seeds from its stalks. But in 1786 a machine that threshed wheat by rubbing it between rollers was invented, replacing human threshers. And around 1840 a reaping machine—whose revolving wheel pressed grain stalks against a sharp blade that cut them down— replaced human harvesters. Today, farm machines called combine harvesters do this work in much the same way. These machines are very efficient and combine all three jobs of cutting, collecting, and threshing a crop. A single combine harvester can process five acres of wheat in less than an hour!

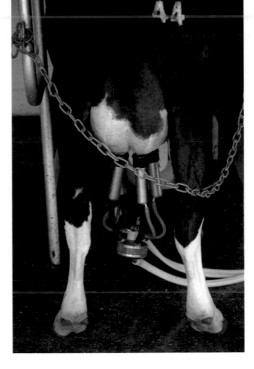

Farmers used to milk cows by hand, but now most dairy farms use milking machines like this one.

Who invented the **earliest milking machines**?

There are reports that primitive milking machines were used around 300 B.C.E. by the ancient Egyptians, who used hollow wheat stems inserted in the teats to milk cows. But hand milking was popular in the United States until about the 1860s, when American inventors began finding more efficient ways to milk cows. In 1860, Lee Colvin invented the first hand-held pump device. In 1879, Anna Baldwin patented a milking machine that used a large rubber cup connected to the cow's udder and to a pump lever and bucket. Working the pump lever pulled the milk out of the udder and into the bucket. Baldwin's was one of the earliest American patents, but it was not successful. Her invention, like others of the time, created a continuous suction on the udder, damaging the cow's fragile mammary tissue and causing the cow to kick. These ideas laid the groundwork for the successful milking machines that started to appear in later decades, and today modern milking machines use a computerized vacuum suction to gather milk.

What is a **seed drill**?

A seed drill was a device that allowed farmers to plant seeds in the soil and then cover them up. The instrument, created in 1701 by the English farmer Jethro Tull, allowed farmers to sow seeds in well-spaced rows at specific depths at a specific rate. Before this, farmers cast seeds to the ground in a haphazard fashion by hand, allowing them to grow where they landed (called "broadcasting"). The seed drill allowed farmers more control over their crops and less waste, and was one of Tull's several inventions,

117

which included the horse-drawn hoe and an improved plough. Seed drills are still in use today, although they are more sophisticated mechanisms that allow farmers to cultivate many more acres of land than the machines of yesterday.

What are **windmills** used for?

Windmills, mechanisms that look like giant pinwheels, have been used to generate power and grind wheat since ancient times. American colonists used windmills to power machinery that could then grind wheat into flour and corn into cornmeal. Windmills also powered tools to saw wood and make typical household items, such as oil, paper, spices, chalk, and pottery. Through the 1920s, Americans used small windmills to generate electricity in rural areas. When power lines began to transport electricity to these areas in the 1930s, local windmills were used less and less, although they can still be seen in some parts of the western United States. When the oil shortages of the 1970s created an interest in alternative energy sources, windmills became fashionable again, especially in states like California whose governments encouraged renewable energy sources.

Today, clusters of giant windmills—with blades up to 200 feet (61 meters) long—sit atop windy hillsides in great numbers to make electricity. The force of the wind pushes the slanted blades, which causes them to rotate because they are bound by a shaft. This spinning shaft runs an electrical generator, which creates power. They are sometimes called wind power plants or wind farms. The world's largest wind farm, the Horse Hollow Wind Energy Center in Texas, has 421 wind machines that generate enough electricity to power 230,000 homes per year. The states with the most wind production are California, Texas, Iowa, Minnesota, and Oklahoma.

What are **barns** used for?

Today, the huge, airy farm structures we know as barns are used mostly to store modern farm machinery and house farm animals. But before modern farming, they had a greater number of important uses. Before the invention of threshing machines (which separate cereal grains like wheat from their stalks), the grain harvest had to be stored in barns, where it would await threshing or pounding by hand during winter months. The structures had to be large and drafty for the process of winnowing, which separated straw dust from the grains after threshing.

Before farmers began to raise special crops to feed their livestock during

The tradition of painting barns red in America began for no other reason than because the chemical used to make paint red was inexpensive.

118

0

Why are barns usually painted red?

Paint coats wood, protecting it from sunlight and rain damage and making it last longer. When early farmers had enough money to paint their barns, they usually used inexpensive paint because the structures were so large. Ferrous oxide, a chemical powder that gives paint its red color, was readily available and cost little. Thrifty farmers in New England, New York, and the upper Midwest region painted their barns red. In those places, red barns remain a tradition.

But there are plenty of barns in other parts of the country that are not red. Early farmers that were poor—especially in regions like Appalachia and the South—left their barns unpainted because they did not have the money to do the job. Unpainted wood usually weathers to a soft gray color. And in places like Pennsylvania, Maryland, and some southern Midwestern states, the most frequently seen barn color is white. Some people think that white barns grew popular when dairy farming became more important after the Civil War; white suggests cleanliness and purity, desirable qualities to be associated with milk production. Special farms where fancy horses or prize livestock were raised sometimes had barns painted unusual colors, like yellow, green, or black.

the winter, they used hay, which is dried grass (grown wild or taken from the stalks of cereal crops). Huge amounts—enough to last several months—had to be stored away. Hay was usually kept in barn lofts located above the main floor, where farm animals spent the winter. This high storage place allowed air to circulate around the hay, keeping it from rotting. It was convenient, too, because hay could be pulled down as needed to feed the livestock.

Because farmers had to store their harvest crops in barns, they wisely cut entrance holes near their roofs, inviting barn owls to make nests there. The birds would hunt the rats and mice that liked to feed on the grain.

What is a **silo**?

The tall, cylinder-shaped farm structures known as silos are used to store silage, which is animal feed. Silage is moist feed made from green crops that ferment when stored in an airtight place. This fermentation process preserves the feed, which is used along with or instead of hay (dried grasses) to feed livestock like horses, cattle, and sheep during the winter when they cannot feed in green pastures. Silage gives farm animals needed nutrients. Before farmers started to raise food crops to feed their livestock (during the eighteenth century), they had to kill most of their animals when winter approached, because grass in pasturelands stopped growing and the creatures faced starvation. But herds of livestock could be kept year-round once farmers began to grow crops for winter feed. Root crops like turnips, as well as leafy crops, were sometimes used. Today, corn is the crop most often used for silage.

Why are **crops sprayed** with **pesticides**?

Farmers and state governments use chemical pesticides to protect their crops from insect pests, weeds, and fungal diseases while they are growing. They also spray their crops with pesticides to prevent rats, mice, and insects from contaminating foods while they are being stored. While these actions are meant to benefit human health and bring a wide variety of fruits and vegetables to the supermarket, they can also harm people, wildlife, and the environment. This is why there are strict controls in place over their sale and use.

What is **organic farming**?

While most large farms today use chemicals to control weeds and insects and to produce increased amounts of vegetables, milk, or eggs, some farmers have chosen to run their farms without chemicals. Organic farmers believe that the chemicals many farmers use can be damaging to the environment and to the people that eat the food grown on such farms. They feel that natural fertilizers and pest-control methods are just as effective and far healthier.

A British farmer and scientist named Albert Howard began the practice of organic farming as an alternative to modern chemical-based methods in the 1930s. His ideas have spread all over the world, taking hold in the United States in the late 1940s. A basic principle of organic farming is to focus on keeping the soil rich with nutrients by feeding it natural fertilizers like cow manure. Such fertile soil can help create stronger plants that are better able to resist disease and insects. Organic farmers also prevent insect damage by putting up insect traps or by bringing in beneficial insects that feed on the harmful ones that are causing the problem. In extreme cases, they need to use pesticides, but to continue being certified as organic farmers in the United States, such farmers need to use botanical pesticides (those that are made from plants) rather than synthetic, or manmade, chemicals.

Does **organic farming** contribute to **less pollution**?

Yes. Organic farmers also try to do more tasks using human power rather than gas-powered vehicles, thereby using less fuel and cutting down on pollution. Organic farms that raise livestock like dairy cows or chickens feed the animals with natural food, avoiding pollution-causing chemicals and growth hormones that make cows produce more milk and chickens produce more eggs. Some organic farmers also allow their animals to roam in a large area (such animals are described as "free range") rather than keeping them in small, climate-controlled pens for their entire lives.

What is a **fish farm**?

Fish farms are businesses that produce a limited number of fish for sale in restaurants and supermarkets. The business is called aquaculture, which includes the farming of fish, shrimp, shellfish, and seaweed. Fish can be grown in natural

Why does a rooster crow when the Sun comes up?

A farm rooster is an adult male chicken. Long ago, when chickens had not yet been tamed or domesticated by people and lived in the wild, roosters crowed to call female chickens to mate. This loud crowing caused problems for roosters, though, because it attracted predators as well as female chickens. So to avoid being eaten, roosters began to do most of their crowing when they couldn't be easily seen, like at dawn or at nightfall, when light was dim. Today's roosters continue the habit, crowing mostly in the early morning or early evening. But it is usually most noticeable at dawn because there aren't a lot of other activities and noises to distract your attention.

waters—such as ponds, lakes, rivers, and streams—or artificial environments, like tanks, pools, and special cages. Fish species such as salmon, catfish, rainbow trout, tilapia, and cod grow in fish farms. Fish farms around the world supply almost half of the world's total food fish supply. The United States has fish farms in California, Idaho, Alabama, Arkansas, Louisiana, Mississippi, and along the southeastern U.S. coast. However, it imports about 80 percent of its seafood—and half of these imports come from fish farms in Asia and Latin America.

Can **farm animals** be **cloned**?

Yes. In 1997 a team of scientists at the Roslin Institute in Edinburgh, Scotland, announced the birth of Dolly the sheep, the first clone (identical copy) of an adult mammal. The process used to create Dolly, called somatic cell nuclear transfer, began with an egg cell from one sheep. The scientists destroyed that egg cell's nucleus and then injected the nucleus from the cell of another sheep into the egg cell. With a little encouragement from electronic stimulation, the donated nucleus fused with the egg cell, and the new cell began to divide. The cluster of cells was then implanted into the uterus of the sheep that had provided the egg cell, and five months later Dolly was born—an exact replica not of the sheep that had carried her in the womb but of the sheep that had supplied the nucleus. While cloning mammals is very controversial, some scientists argue that cloning farm animals has advantages to livestock farmers, who could use the technology to breed only high-quality animals that produce the most milk or the finest wool.

How can **cows** make so **much milk**?

A cow, like all mammals, produces milk to feed its young. If its calf nurses regularly, the mother cow's mammary glands will produce enough milk to give the baby animal all the food it needs. Gradually a calf will nurse less as grass and other feed makes up more of its diet. A mother cow, in turn, will produce less milk until it is no longer needed.

121

Why do flies like cow poop?

Flies like animal feces—such as dog, cat, cow, or horse poop—because these warm, moist areas are the ideal spots for laying eggs and give the larvae something to eat while they develop into pupa. Flies land on the piles of excretion looking for mouth-watering bacteria, which provides them with a meal. Although it sounds disgusting, it's the fly's job to take the disease-causing bacteria and eat it up. However, because of their habits of being attracted to feces and decaying meat, flies often carry diseases such as dysentery, typhoid fever, and cholera.

But by milking the cows regularly—two or three times a day—dairy farmers can cause the cows to continue producing milk. Certain breeds of cows are particularly good at milk-making, producing 18–27 pints (around 2–3 gallons, or 10–15 liters) each day. A cow's large, round udder, located on its underside, has four nipples, or teats, that are squeezed to release stored milk. While once done by hand, milking is done on modern dairy farms by machines with suction hoses, which do the job more quickly and cheaply. Tank trucks collect milk from farms daily and take it to processing plants where it is pasteurized (made germ-free) and used to make dairy products like cheese, butter, and ice cream.

Why do **cows** stand around in fields **eating all day**?

In order to produce four or more gallons of milk each day, dairy cows have to eat a lot. Producing milk requires additional calories in the form of extra food. A large dairy cow may eat up to 150 pounds (about 68 kilograms) of grass each day, and all that munching takes time!

Cows have special stomachs, too, that make eating a slow process. Instead of having one chamber like a human's, a cow's stomach has four chambers. When a cow takes a bite of grass it swallows it right away without chewing it. The food goes into the first chamber of its stomach, called the rumen (animals that have such stomachs are called ruminants), where it mixes with fluid to form a soft mass. The mushy grass is regurgitated or brought back up again later, when the cow is resting. This "cud" is thoroughly chewed, swallowed, and digested as it passes through all the other chambers of the stomach. A cow spends nearly nine hours each day chewing its cud. Scientists think that when animals like cows lived in the wild they had to snatch grass in a hurry before predators attacked them. Their special stomachs allowed them to store food for later chewing and digestion once they were hidden and out of danger. Goats, sheep, camels, and antelope are other examples of ruminants.

Why do **horses sleep standing** up?

Horses sleep standing up for a number of reasons. Their legs can lock in place, enabling them to fall asleep without falling over. Because they are prey animals, hors es often do not feel comfortable sleeping on the ground, and most of their sleeping is done during the day rather than at night when the predators are out hunting. Horses have straight backs, so they cannot get up quickly. If a predator were to come while a horse was on the ground, it might not be able to get up fast enough to escape. However, horses do occasionally take short naps laying down during the day, which helps them rest their legs. When horses are in groups, they will often take turns guarding each other as they rest, with one horse standing up near the sleeping horse.

Pigs like to roll in the mud to protect their skin from the sun and from insects, not because they are filthy animals.

Why are **pigs so dirty**?

Because pigs will eat almost anything, they have traditionally been fed farm leftovers and waste. This unappealing diet—commonly known as slop—may contain food waste from a farm household or the unusable by-products of the manufacturing processes for things like butter and cheese and even beer brewing. Pigs are natural foragers, frequently using their snouts to dig up roots or grubs for food when they are in the wild. On farms they are fed from low troughs, but their big snouts and foraging habits still make them very messy eaters. Adding to the dirty reputation of pigs is the fact that they have usually been kept in pens, or sties, close to farm buildings to make their feeding quick and easy. They—and their messes—have been confined to small spaces, unlike cows and sheep, which are free to roam pastureland. Because pigs are raised mainly for their meat and fat, they are given a lot of food and spend most of their time eating. Piglets that weigh only a few pounds at birth can reach more than 200 pounds (90 kilograms) in less than half a year.

POLITICS AND GOVERNMENT

COUNTRIES

How many countries are there?

There are about 195 countries in the world today. But because the political world is constantly changing, that number never stays the same for very long. The number 195 includes Taiwan. Although Taiwan operates as an independent country, many countries (including the United States) do not officially recognize it as one. Of these countries, 192 belong to the United Nations (UN), an international organization that aims to get countries to cooperate with one another. The exceptions are Taiwan (in 1971, the UN disqualified Taiwan and replaced it with the People's Republic of China), Vatican City, and Kosovo. The newest UN members are Switzerland (2002) and Montenegro (2006).

What are the world's **newest countries**?

The world's newest country is Kosovo, which declared independence from Serbia in February 2008. Before that, the newest country was Montenegro, which became a country in June 2006, after splitting off from Serbia. Since 1990, 28 new nations have come into being. Many of these emerged from the collapse of the Soviet Union (14 countries) and the breakup of the former Yugoslavia (7 countries).

Which **country** is the **biggest**?

Russia is the largest country in the world, with 6,592,812 square miles (17,075,383 square kilometers) of area. It stretches across two continents, Europe and Asia. It is far bigger than the next largest country in the world, Canada, which has 3,851,809 square miles (9,976,185 square kilometers) of area.

Which **country** is the **smallest**?

The smallest country in the world is Vatican City. It is located on 108.7 acres (44 hectares) in the city of Rome, Italy. Vatican City is where the central government of the Roman Catholic Church is located. The home of the pope, who is leader of the Church, is also located there. About 850 people are citizens of Vatican City, which is ruled by the pope, though a governor and a council actually run it. Vatican City has its own money, postage stamps, flag, and diplomatic corps. Monaco, which is less than 1 square mile (around 2 square kilometers) in area, is the second smallest country in the world.

How does the **United States's size compare** with that of other countries?

The United States has an area of 3.79 million square miles (9.83 million kilometers) and a population of more than 303 million people, making it the third or fourth largest country by total area, and third largest by land area and by population. The United States is one of the world's most ethnically diverse nations.

How are **countries formed**?

Often it is a group of people with something in common, whose members identify with one another, that makes up a country. It may be a shared race, religion, language, history, or culture that makes people feel that they belong together as a nation. Because of its uniqueness, the group feels that it should govern itself as an independent country. This feeling of shared identity and loyalty to the group is frequently behind the rise of nations. Some countries are so large and have such complicated histories of war and conquest that they are home to many different groups of people who have their own separate beliefs, languages, and customs. The differences between these groups sometimes make it difficult for them to get along. A nation is weakened by such groups if they put their own interests ahead of those of their country. But a population of many different groups can also enrich a country with diverse ideas and cultures if a spirit of acceptance and cooperation exists.

Which countries have the **most neighbors**?

Except for island nations, every country in the world touches at least one neighbor, and most touch three or four. China has the most neighbors, 13 in all: Afghanistan, Bhutan, Burma, Hong Kong, India, Laos, Macao, Mongolia, Nepal, North Korea, Pakistan, Russia, and Vietnam. Russia is next in line, with 12 neighbors: Afghanistan, Czechoslovakia, China, Finland, Hungary, Iran, Mongolia, North Korea, Norway, Poland, Romania, and Turkey. Five countries—Austria, Mali, Niger, Yugoslavia, and Zambia—share borders with 7 neighbors.

What is a **"landlocked"** country?

A landlocked country is one that has no coastline, meaning it has no direct access to a sea or ocean. As of 2007, there are 43 landlocked countries. Africa includes a total of 15 landlocked countries; Asia has 12; Europe has 15; and South America has 2. The largest landlocked country is Kazakhstan, the ninth largest country in the

Is there really a place called Atlantis?

Historians are still debating that question. Atlantis is the name of an island that supposedly sank long ago, and on which was a great civilization. The city of Atlantis has been mentioned in many stories and religions, and the great philosopher Plato wrote about a great, technologically advanced sunken continent in his book *Critias* in 360 B.C.E. Plato believed that Atlantis was approximately the size of Libya and Asia put together, had a vast army with chariots, and was located somewhere in the Atlantic Ocean. Although historians agree there was no island like this in the Atlantic, in the Aegean Sea in Greece, a volcanic island exploded in about 1645 B.C.E. The center of the island, today called Santorini or Thera, sank. Excavations of this island show an advanced civilization that may have been Atlantis. Archaeologists have found sophisticated multistory buildings with wall paintings, furniture, and stone and bronze pottery and an elaborate drainage system for the city.

world covering just over 1 million square miles (2.65 million square kilometers). Two countries in the world are double landlocked, which means that they are surrounded only by other landlocked countries: Lichtenstein and Uzbekistan.

Does **every country** have its **own flag**?

Every country has a national flag, including the United States. Flags date back to around 1000 B.C.E., when the Egyptians used primitive versions of flags—some were even made out of wood or metal—to identify themselves and to signal to others. Ships started using flags at sea to signal to each other and to harbors, often to let them know they had a diseased crew aboard. Flags are still used today to let sailors know what weather conditions await at sea. The military also made use of flags to rally its troops. During the ancient wars, capturing an enemy's flag was considered an honorable seizure. Today, the most popular use of flags is to identify and symbolize the world's countries, which became commonplace in the 1700s. When new lands are discovered—and, for example when Mount Everest and the Moon were conquered—explorers raise their country's flag as a sign of their being the first to set foot on these unchartered lands.

WARS

Why are there **wars**?

Wars have taken place since the beginning of recorded history, and they surely occurred before that as well. A war begins when one group of people (the aggressors) tries to force its will on another group of people, and those people fight back. War frequently springs from the differences between people, or from the desire of

127

one group to increase its power or wealth by taking control of another group's land. Often the aggressors feel that they are superior to the group they want to dominate: they believe that their religion, culture, or even race is better than that of the people they wish to defeat. This sense of superiority makes them feel that it is acceptable to fight to take the land, possessions, and even lives of the "inferior" group, or to force their ways on the dominated people.

Because countries can be very different from one another in government, religion, customs, and ideology (ways of thinking), it is not surprising that nations disagree on many things. But great efforts are usually made to settle the disagreements through discussion and negotiation—a process called diplomacy—before they result in anything as destructive as a war. War usually occurs when diplomacy fails. Because science and technology have allowed us to create such powerful and destructive weapons that can result in such devastating wars, we now have international organizations that work all the time to try to keep peace among nations.

Which wars has the United States been involved in?

America has been involved in war since its beginnings, and American colonists or U.S. citizens officially participated in more than 25 major conflicts. When Europeans settled North America, for example, the Native Americans who lived there fought a series of wars with them for the next 250 years, trying to keep their land and preserve their way of life. They eventually lost the battle and were forced to either live like their European conquerors or relocate to parcels of land set aside for them called reservations. The Americans also fought in the Revolutionary War from 1775 to 1783, which the 13 early colonies fought with Great Britain in order to overthrow Britain's royal rule and declare their independence as a new nation, the United States of America. Civil wars take place between groups of people within a single country. The U.S. Civil War, which took place between 1861 and 1865 was a war between the Northern states (called the "Union") and the slave-holding Southern States (the "Confederacy") over the expansion of slavery into Northern territories. In the twentieth century, the United States was involved in several major international wars—wars occur between nations—including World War I (1914–1918), World War II (1939–1945), the Vietnam War (1959–1975), and the Persian Gulf War (1990–1991).

Why did soldiers once wear armor?

Since ancient times, soldiers have worn special clothing or armor to protect themselves during warfare. Hard materials like leather, wood, shells, and even woven reeds were used to give soldiers extra protection against enemy arrows. Metal started to be used for armor about 3,500 years ago, by warriors in the Middle East. By the time of the ancient Greeks, about 1,000 years later, soldiers were well protected, wearing large pieces of metal on their chests and backs, shin guards, and metal helmets, and they carried metal shields.

Soon armored clothing, garments with metal strips and plates attached, began to be made for soldiers. Then chain mail, a type of metal cloth, was developed. Made of

Suits of armor were often worn by soldiers centuries ago when fighting was done with swords and arrows. Such metal armor would not deflect today's bullets, however.

small metal rings linked together, chain mail was much more flexible than metal plates, but could not withstand the force of larger weapons, like lances. So full suits of armor made of steel plates, hinged at the knees and the elbows, came into use around the fourteenth century. Soldiers were covered with steel from head to toe, with heavy metal helmets covering their faces, heads, and necks. A warrior could see and breathe through small slits or openings in the helmet's visor, a movable metal flap that could be lifted up. (Only important or wealthy warriors could afford this kind of elaborate armor.) Suits of armor weighed so much that the soldiers or knights who wore them usually could not move around in them very well; they wore such armor mostly when they fought on horseback. Even the horses sometimes wore armor.

As the methods and weapons of warfare changed, clumsy personal armor was no longer useful. It became far more important for soldiers to be able to move quickly and easily. Today's soldiers usually wear cloth uniforms, body armor, and steel helmets. But armor is used on war vehicles like tanks, naval vessels, and aircraft. The bulletproof vests that police officers use are also a type of armor.

GOVERNMENTS

Why does **government exist**?

Governments exist for many reasons, but most importantly they exist to provide a sense of order in the land. All governments tax, penalize, restrict, and regulate their people. A democracy exists to give voice to the people and to protect their basic human rights. In contrast, a totalitarian government exists to benefit the state or those in charge, and this type of government empowers its leaders to rule in any way they see fit. In this type of government, the people's personal freedom is not recognized. In the United States, the purpose of the government is outlined in the Constitution: to form a more perfect union, to establish justice, to insure tranquility; to provide for the common defense, to promote the general welfare, and to secure the blessings of liberty. As a whole, our government provides us with an organized system by which we can live as a nation in peace.

What **types of government** are there in the world?

There are three general forms of government, based upon who rules: (1) those governments in which the authority is placed in one single person, (2) those dominated by several people, and (3) those controlled by many. In some nations, governing is done by a single individual, such as a king, queen, or dictator. This form of government is known as an *autocracy*. An autocratic government is called an *oligarchy* if a small group, such as landowners, military officers, or wealthy merchants, make up the government. If the country's people make up the government and contribute to its decision-making process, that nation's government is known as a *democracy*.

There are also several ways in which governments do their governing. Limited governments, such as the United States and most countries in Western Europe, are known as *constitutional* governments, since these governments are limited as to what they are permitted to control. In other words, they have limited power, and this limited power is enforced by a separation of powers. Most of these nations have constitutions that define the scope of governmental power. In contrast to a constitutional government, a government is called *authoritarian* when it has no formal limits; the government is limited by other political and social institutions in the land—such as churches, labor unions, and political parties. While these governments are sometimes responsive to these sources of limitation, there is no formal obligation for the government to represent its citizens. Examples of recent authoritarian governments include Spain from 1936 to 1975 under General Francisco Franco.

Totalitarian governments attempt to control every area of political, economic, and social life and are usually associated with dictators who seek to end other social institutions that might challenge the government's complete, or total, power. Some examples of totalitarian governments include Nazi Germany from 1933 to 1945 under dictator Adolf Hitler, the Soviet Union from 1928 to 1953 under dictator Joseph Stalin, and Cuba from 1959 to 2008 under Fidel Castro.

What is a **democracy**?

The word democracy comes from the ancient Greek word *demokratia*. *Demo* means "the people" and *kratia* means "to rule." A democracy, then, is a form of government in which the people rule. The power lies in the hands of the people, who may either govern directly or govern indirectly by electing representatives. The American government is a democracy, and the Constitution of the United States ensures this. Under this "social contract" the people of the United States established a government, gave it its powers, placed upon it certain limitations, set up its structure, and provided the means of control over it. At the heart of democracy lies the concept of "popular sovereignty"—the idea that the people are the supreme authority, or sovereignty, and that authority rests in the body of citizens, not one supreme ruler.

AMERICAN GOVERNMENT

What does the **U.S. government do**?

The government is the institution that enforces our public policies. Public policies are all the things that the government decides to do, such as impose an income tax, service its armed forces, protect the environment, and hold businesses to certain standards. In the democratic United States, the people elect representatives to the government to carry out the popular will. The people who exercise the powers of the government include legislators, who make the law; executives and administrators, who administer and enforce those laws; and judges, who interpret the law.

Each year, Congress enacts about 500 laws and the state legislators enact about 25,000 laws. Local governments enact countless ordinances, or city laws.

What is the **federal government**?

The federal government is the national government of the United States of America. It includes the executive, legislative, and judicial branches. The executive branch is responsible for enforcing the laws of the United States. Its main components include the president, the vice president, government departments, and independent agencies. The president is the leader of the country and commander in chief of the armed forces; the vice president is the president of the Senate and the first in line for the presidency should the president be unable to serve; the departments and their heads (called Cabinet members) advise the president on decisions that affect the country; and independent agencies help carry out the president's

A U.S. president is not all powerful, but as head of state he has great influence on the country. Some presidents, such as Abraham Lincoln, have been credited with changing the course of American history.

131

How can the average person get involved in the government?

The average person can get involved in the government by first educating him- or herself about current issues. This can be done through reading the paper daily, reading a weekly newsmagazine, or watching the evening news. In order to make a difference, a person needs to have a working understanding of the U.S. government—indeed, a democratic system of government assumes there is a knowledgeable, interested public body of citizens. Next to education, other very practical methods of involvement include attending a city council meeting, volunteering at a local politician's office, working with voter registration drives, or registering to vote. Often, people call or write legislators to voice their opinion on a certain topic, or participate in nonviolent protest demonstrations or marches.

policies and provide special services. The legislative branch is the lawmaking branch of the federal government. It is made up of a bicameral (or two-chamber) Congress: the Senate and the House of Representatives. The judicial branch, made up of the Supreme Court and other federal courts, is responsible for interpreting the meaning of laws, how they are applied, and whether or not they violate the Constitution.

What is the **president's job**?

The president's chief duty is to protect the Constitution and enforce the laws made by Congress. However, he also has a host of other responsibilities tied to his job description. They include: recommending legislation (laws) to Congress, calling special sessions of Congress, delivering messages to Congress, signing or vetoing legislation, appointing federal judges, appointing heads of federal departments and agencies and other principal federal officials, appointing representatives to foreign countries, carrying on official business with foreign nations, acting as commander in chief of the armed forces, and granting pardons for offenses against the United States.

What is the difference between a **senator** and a **representative**?

The U.S. Congress consists of the Senate and the House of Representatives. Both senators and representatives are responsible for representing the people of the states they serve. This involves voting on and writing bills in the U.S. Congress. There are, however, some major differences between a U.S. senator and a representative. While both senators and representatives are permitted to introduce bills, senators are restricted from introducing bills that raise revenue, such as tax bills. There are 100 senators in Congress; two senators are allotted for each state. This number is independent of each state's population. However, the number of U.S. representatives a state has is determined by the population of that particular state. There are 435 representatives in Congress and each state has at least one representative. Another difference involves the length of time a senator and a representative are permitted to serve. A senator represents his or her state for a six-year term. A representative, on the other hand, serves for a two-year term.

How is **state government** organized?

Like the national government, state governments have three branches: the executive, legislative, and judicial. Each branch functions and works a lot like its national branch. The chief executive of the state is a governor, who is elected by popular vote, typically for a four-year term (New Hampshire and Vermont have two-year terms). Except for Nebraska, which has a single legislative body, all states have a bicameral (two-house) legislature, with the upper house usually called the Senate and the lower house called the House of Representatives, the House of Delegates, or the General Assembly. The sizes of these two legislatures vary. Typically, the upper house is made up of between 30 and 50 members; the lower house is made up of between 100 and 150 members.

What is a **governor's job**?

The governor is responsible for the well-being of his or her state. The details of this job include many hands-on tasks and leadership duties. The governor's executive powers include the appointment and removal of state officials, the supervision of thousands of executive branch staff, the formulation of the state budget, and the leadership of the state militia as its commander in chief. Law-making powers include the power to recommend legislation, to call special sessions of the legislature, and to veto measures passed by the legislature. In 43 states, governors have the power to veto (or reject) several parts of a bill without rejecting it altogether. The governor can also pardon (excuse) a criminal or reduce a criminal's sentence.

What does a **mayor do**?

The mayor-council is the oldest form of city government in the United States. Its structure is similar to that of the state and national governments, with an elected mayor as chief of the executive branch and an elected council that represents the various neighborhoods, forming the legislative branch. The mayor appoints heads of city departments and other officials. The mayor also has the power to veto the laws of the city (called ordinances), and prepares the city's budget. The council passes city laws, sets the tax rate on property, and decides how the city departments spend their money to make the city a better place.

What is a **town meeting**?

The town meeting is one aspect of local government that still exists today, although it was created in the early years of the republic. At least once a year the registered voters of the town meet in open session to elect officers, debate local issues, and pass laws for operating a government. As a group, or body, they decide on road construction and repair, construction of public buildings and facilities (such as libraries and parks), tax rates, and the town budget. Having existed for more than two centuries, the town meeting is often called the purest form of direct democracy because governmental power is not delegated, but rather exercised directly by the people. However, town meetings cannot be found in every area of the United States. They are mostly conducted in the small towns of New England, where the first colonies were established.

What is the **Bill of Rights**?

The Bill of Rights is made up of the first 10 amendments to the U.S. Constitution. The Bill of Rights guarantees rights and liberties to the American people. These amendments were proposed by Congress in 1789, and ratified (approved) by three-fourths of the states on December 15, 1791, thereby officially becoming part of the Constitution. The first eight amendments outline many individual rights guaranteed to all people of this nation, while the Ninth and Tenth Amendments are general rules of interpretation of the relationship among the people, the state governments, and the federal government.

How does the **Bill of Rights protect individual** liberties?

The Bill of Rights limits the ability of the government to intrude upon certain individual liberties, guaranteeing freedom of speech, press, assembly, and religion to all people. Nearly two-thirds of the Bill of Rights was written to safeguard the rights of those suspected or accused of a crime, providing for due process of law, fair trials, freedom from self-incrimination and from cruel and unusual punishment, and protection against being tried twice in court for the same crime. Since the adoption of the Bill of Rights, only 17 additional amendments have been added to the Constitution. While a number of these amendments revised how the federal government is structured and operates, many expanded individual rights and freedoms.

What happens when a person breaks the law?

Laws are enforced by the courts and the judicial system. If an adult breaks a law in the community or a business or organization does something illegal, they go to the judicial branch of government for review of their actions. The judicial branch is made up of different courts. The court leader, or judge, interprets the meaning of laws, how they are applied, and whether they break the rules of the Constitution. If a person or group is found guilty of breaking a law, the judicial system decides how they should be punished.

In the United States, several laws have been written to protect the rights of someone accused of committing a crime. He or she is considered innocent until proven guilty in a court of law. Someone suspected of a crime is usually arrested and taken into custody by a police officer. Sometimes, the case is presented before a grand jury (a group of citizens who examines the accusations made). The grand jury files an indictment, or a formal charge, if there appears to be enough evidence for a trial. In many criminal cases, however, there is no grand jury. While awaiting trial, the accused may be temporarily released on bail (which is the amount of money meant to guarantee that the person will return for trial instead of leaving the country) or

Why do we need to follow the law?

Almost everything we do is governed by some set of rules. There are rules for games, for sports, and for adults in the workplace. There are also rules imposed by morality (or ethics) that play an important role in telling us what we should and should not do. However, some rules—those made by the state or the courts—are called "laws." Laws are designed to control or alter our behavior, and to help make society a more ordered place. If people were allowed to choose at random what to do and how to behave, our country would be dangerous and chaotic. Laws that govern business affairs help businesses to operate properly, and laws against criminal behavior help to protect personal property and human life.

kept in a local jail. Trials are usually held before a judge and a jury of 12 citizens. The government presents its case against an accused person, or defendant, through a district attorney, and another attorney defends the accused. If the defendant is judged innocent, he or she is released. If he or she is found guilty of committing a crime, the judge decides the punishment or sentence, using established guidelines. The lawbreaker may be forced to pay a fine, pay damages, or go to prison.

What is a **citizen**?

Citizens of the United States enjoy all of the freedoms, protections, and legal rights that the Constitution promises. However, living in the United States doesn't automatically make a person an American citizen. Only those people born in the United States or born to U.S. citizens in foreign countries are citizens of the United States. Persons born in other countries who want to become citizens must apply for and pass a citizenship test. Those who become citizens in this way are called naturalized citizens.

Why is it **important to vote**?

Republics such as the United States are based upon a voting population. If the citizens of the country do not vote, then politicians do not necessarily need to heed their interests. It is necessary for the people of a democratic country to constitutionally voice their opinions, and they do this by voting for state propositions and for their city, state, and country's leaders.

Why is the **Statue of Liberty** such an important symbol of the United States?

The Statue of Liberty stands for many of the nation's most cherished ideals: freedom, equality, and democracy. Perhaps most importantly to the millions of immigrants for whom the statue was one of their first sights of the United States, it stands for the ideal of opportunity—the chance to begin a new life, in a new land. While their lives in the United States were frequently difficult, for millions of immi-

135

The Statue of Liberty, which has stood as a symbol of American freedom since 1886, was a gift from France. The statue was designed by sculptor Frederic Auguste Bartholdi.

grants America offered the chance to escape from grinding poverty and abusive governments in other lands.

Standing in the midst of New York Harbor, the point of entry into the United States for so many immigrants arriving on ships from other countries, the Statue of Liberty has been a powerful symbol of opportunity for more than 100 years. A poem called "The New Colossus," written by Emma Lazarus, was mounted on the statue's pedestal in the early 1900s. Its famous lines include these words that Lazarus imagined Lady Liberty to be saying:

Give me your tired, your poor,
Your huddled masses yearning to
   breathe free,
The wretched refuse of your teeming
   shore;
Send these, the homeless, tempest-tost
   to me,
I lift my lamp beside the golden door!

Why is the **bald eagle** the official **national symbol** of the United States?

In 1782, six years after the end of the Revolutionary War, leaders of the newly independent United States were designing a national seal, an image that would appear on official documents and elsewhere. Eventually these men settled on the bald eagle for the Great Seal of the United States. The bald eagle was chosen in part because it was believed to be found only in North America. The bald eagle was also admired for its strength, its noble appearance, and the freedom of its life spent soaring through the sky. While the eagle became an important American symbol when it was adopted for the U.S. seal in 1782, it wasn't until 1787 that it officially became the national emblem. The bald eagle has been used for the official seals of many states, and it has appeared on stamps, currency (or paper money), and several coins, including the quarter.

What do the **stars and stripes** on the United States **flag mean**?

When the first United States flag was adopted in 1777, it had 13 alternating red-and-white stripes (seven red, six white) and, in the upper left portion, 13 white stars on a blue background. The number 13 was chosen because that was the number of original states that formed the United States. For several years after that design was adopted, a new stripe and a new star were added each time a new state joined the

Union, but in 1818 Congress decided to keep the number of stripes at 13 and simply add a new star for each new state. The U.S. flag has several nicknames: the Stars and Stripes, the Star-Spangled Banner, and Old Glory.

At the time the U.S. flag was designed, the stars and stripes (and the colors of each) were given no specific meaning. The ideas for the design most likely were based on other countries' flags. In 1782, when the national seal was designed and the flag was incorporated into it, national leaders decided that each color and symbol should have a meaning. As reported in the book *Our Flag,* published by the U.S. House of Representatives in 1989, it was decided that red symbolized "hardiness [strength] and valour [bravery]"; white symbolized "purity and innocence"; and blue represented "vigilance, perseverance, and justice." It has also been said that the stars are symbols of the heavens, and the stripes represent rays of light coming from the Sun.

How did we get the **United States national anthem**?

In September 1814, the United States and Great Britain were in the midst of fighting what is known as the War of 1812. The British had taken over Washington, D.C., and planned to attack Baltimore, Maryland. A few American citizens, including a lawyer and poet named Francis Scott Key, approached the British fleet, which was anchored in Chesapeake Bay, to request the release of an American who had been taken prisoner. The British agreed to let the prisoner and the others return to American shores, but only after the British were done attacking Fort McHenry, which was defending Baltimore.

Throughout the night of September 13–14, Key heard the explosions of the battle, anxiously awaiting morning to see whether the Americans had won the battle. In the early morning light, Key could see that Fort McHenry's enormous American flag was still waving, indicating that the Americans had been triumphant. Relieved and inspired by the sight, Key composed a poem called "Defence of Fort M'Henry." Its opening lines recalled his first glimpse of the flag that morning: "Oh, say can you see, by the dawn's early light / What so proudly we hailed at the twilight's last gleaming?" Key may have had a popular tune in mind when writing the poem. That tune, called "To Anacreon in Heaven," had been an English drinking song, but it soon became linked with Key's poem, and the title of the new song became "The Star-Spangled Banner."

"The Star-Spangled Banner" (which actually has four verses, though usually only the first is sung) spread quickly throughout the country and became extremely popular. It was played at important ceremonies and military functions for many years before being officially declared the national anthem by Congress in 1931.

U.S. STATE FACTS AND TRIVIA

How did the **United States begin**?

The United States of America (USA), or United States for short, is a country that takes its name from the fact that it is made up of states that are joined together, or

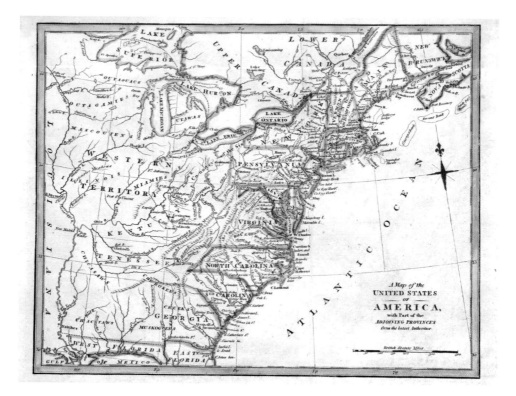

A 1795 map made in England of the United States shows the original 13 colonies.

united, by the U.S. Constitution to form one nation. The country began as 13 colonies of England, which were spread out along the central Atlantic Coast of North America. The original 13 colonies were Connecticut, Delaware, Georgia, Maryland, Massachusetts, New Hampshire, New Jersey, New York, North Carolina, South Carolina, Pennsylvania, Rhode Island, and Virginia. The first colony, Virginia, was founded in 1607, and the thirteenth colony, Georgia, was founded in 1733. More than 40 years passed before the colonies joined together, rebelled against England, and declared themselves free, independent states on July 4, 1776, in the famous Declaration of Independence.

To gain freedom, the colonies fought the Revolutionary War against the British. The set of peace treaties that ended the war, called the Peace of Paris, was signed in 1783. With this treaty, England gave up its claim to the 13 colonies, along with all land east of the Mississippi River from Canada to Florida. The original 13 colonies became the first U.S. states, with additional states added into the Union over time. Today there are 50 states, and one district, the District of Columbia.

The U.S. Constitution provided that new states can be admitted into the Union by the U.S. Congress. Before they gained statehood, most of the other 37 states passed through a period of time when they were known as territories, organized by Congress. When the people of a territory felt they were ready to form a state government, they elected delegates, prepared a state constitution, and then voted to

Which states were not organized as territories first?

A few U.S. states outside of the original 13 have been admitted that were never organized territories of the federal government. The most notable are Vermont, an unrecognized, independent republic until its admission in 1791; Kentucky, a part of Virginia until its admission in 1792; Maine, a part of Massachusetts until its admission in 1820 following the Missouri Compromise, an agreement that regulated slavery in the Western territories; Texas, a recognized independent republic until its admission in 1845; California, created as a state out of the unorganized territory of the Mexican Cession in 1850 without ever having been a separate organized territory; and West Virginia, created from areas of Virginia that rejoined the Union in 1863, after the 1861 secession of Virginia during the Civil War era.

decide whether they would accept the constitution and ask Congress to approve their admission into the Union. The dates that these territories were admitted into the Union as states are their official birthdays.

Is the **District of Columbia** a state?

No, it is not a state or a part of any state. The District of Columbia, or D.C. for short, is a district in the national capital, Washington, D.C. The district, named after explorer Christopher Columbus, sits on the Potomac River on land that once belonged to the state of Maryland. Because the city of Washington—which was named after the nation's first president, George Washington—covers the entire area, the names "Washington, D.C." and "District of Columbia" have the same meaning. The area is 69 square miles (178 square kilometers) and a federal district, meaning it is an area reserved as the seat of the U.S. government. So, Washington, D.C. is almost like two cities in one—a federal city with government monuments, buildings, and parks (including the White House, the Capitol, and the Supreme Court), and an everyday city more than half a million people call home.

Why do **states** have names and **nicknames**?

When people initially founded the states of the nation, the first thing they did was choose a name for their area of land. The name helps establishes the identity of the state. Almost half of the states have names of that come from Native American languages; for example, Arizona probably came from the Indian word *arizonac*, meaning "small springs" and Connecticut came from the Indian *quinnitukq-ut*, meaning "at the long river." Other states were named for people or places—the Spanish explorer Juan Ponce de León named Florida after the Spanish words *Pascua florida*, meaning "flowery Easter." He discovered Florida during the Easter season, in March 1513, when his ships landed on Florida's east coast near present-day St.

By dog sled, of course! The native people of Alaska's icy terrain have been traveling by dog sled for hundreds of years. Dog racing is such a part of the state's history that Alaskans hold an annual event, the Iditarod (dubbed "The Last Great Race on Earth"), a competitive dog-sled race over 1,150 miles (1,850 kilometers) of sub-zero terrain. From Anchorage, in south central Alaska, to Nome on the western Bering Sea coast, each team of 12 to 16 dogs and their musher cover over more than 1,000 miles (1,609 kilometers) in 10 to 17 days.

Augustine. "La Florida" had a lavish landscape, abundant flowers, and beautiful beaches, so the state name embodies both aspect of de León's discovery.

Similarly, the people give nicknames to their states to further establish their identities. Alaska is called "Land of the Midnight Sun," because the Sun shines almost all night long during Alaskan summers; Colorado is nicknamed the "Centennial State" because it became a state in the year 1876, 100 years after the signing of our nation's Declaration of Independence; Georgia is called the "Peach State" because of the growers' reputation for producing delicious peaches; and Wyoming is known as the "Equality State" because of the civil rights women have traditionally enjoyed there.

In addition to naming their states, founders design a flag, using colors and symbols that have special meaning. They also choose mottoes (words or phrases), often in Latin, that help express the state's character. For example, New York's motto is *Excelsior,* Latin for "Ever upward!" Oklahoma's motto, *Labor omnia vincit,* means "Labor conquers all things." Another important emblem is the state seal, which is placed on all official documents and usually bears the state motto.

Which is the **largest state** (in area), and which is the **smallest**?

Alaska, the northernmost and westernmost state of the United States, is the largest state of the Union, covering 571,951 square miles (more than 1.4 million square kilometers). It makes up the extreme northwestern region of the North American continent and is separated from Asia by the 51-mile- (82-kilometer-) wide Bering Strait. Alaska has been a part of the United States since 1867, when it was bought from Russia by Secretary of State William H. Seward for $7.2 million. The smallest state is Rhode Island, which covers just 1,045 square miles (2,706 square kilometers). Rhode Island—officially named the State of Rhode Island and Providence Plantations—was the first of the 13 original colonies to declare independence from British rule (on May 4, 1776) and the last to ratify the United States Constitution (on May 29, 1790).

Which **state** has the **most people**?

California, a state on the West Coast of the United States, along the Pacific Ocean, is the third largest state by area and the most populous U.S. state. By 2007, California's population reached about 37.7 million people, making it the most populated state, and the thirteenth fastest-growing state in the nation. Almost 12 percent of all American citizens live in California.

Where can you **stand in four states** at the same time?

The Four Corners, located 40 miles (64 kilometers) southwest of Cortez, Colorado, is the only place in the United States where four states come together at one place. Arizona, New Mexico, Utah, and Colorado meet at the Four Corners. Here, a person can put each of his or her hands and feet in four states at the same time. The unique landmark is on Navajo Nation land and is open for visits from the public. The area surrounding the monument is also Indian land, which includes part of New Mexico, Utah, and Arizona and covers 25,000 square miles (64,750 square kilometers).

The Four Corners Monument was originally established by the U.S. Government Surveyors and Astronomers in 1868 with the survey of Colorado's southern boundary. Surveys followed of New Mexico's west boundary and Utah's east boundary in 1878. The northern boundary of Arizona was surveyed in 1901. A small permanent marker was made in 1912 to show where the boundaries of the four states intersect. The Monument was refurbished in 1992 with a bronze disk embedded in granite. The disk shows the state boundaries and each state's seal rests within that state's boundary.

Which **state** was once an **independent kingdom**?

Hawaii is the only U.S. state that was once a kingdom with its own monarchy. From 1810 to 1893, Hawaii was an independent kingdom, ruled by King Kamehameha I and his successors, including David Kalakaua, the last king of Hawaii. It was formally annexed by the United States in 1898, became a territory in 1900, and was admitted to the Union as a state in 1959. The state of Hawaii is made up of eight main islands—Niihau, Kauai, Oahu, Maui, Molokai, Lanai, Kahoolawe, and the Big Island of Hawaii—and is America's 50th state.

A statue of King Kamehameha stands in front of Honolulu's Judiciary Building. Hawaii was an independent kingdom before it became America's fiftieth state.

HOW THINGS WORK

NUTS AND BOLTS

What is the difference between an **invention** and a **discovery**?

An invention is something that is made by human beings and that did not exist in the world before. Inventions include items, devices, processes, materials, machines, and toys—from AstroTurf® to zippers. A discovery is something that existed before, but was not yet known or "discovered"; for example, the concept of black holes in outer space. Inventions and discoveries usually come about by bringing together existing technologies in a new way, and they may take centuries to take shape. They usually are created in response to a specific human need, such as a medicine to heal sickness; as a result of the creator's desire to complete a task more efficiently or effectively, such as a tool or machine; or even by accident, such as the Slinky. Sometimes just one person makes the discovery or invention; other times the end result is the product of a team effort. Sometimes different people have made the same invention independently at the same time. In very rare cases different people have made the same invention on the same day.

What is a **patent**?

According to the United States Patent and Trademark Office, a patent for an invention is the grant of a property right to the inventor. A patent gives the inventor the right to exclude others from making, using, offering for sale, or selling his or her invention in the United States or importing the invention into the United States. According to the Patent and Trademark Office, any person who invents or discovers any new and useful process, machine, manufacture, or composition of matter may obtain a patent. The American inventor Thomas Edison filed more than 1,000 patents in his lifetime, including 141 patents for batteries and 389 for electric light and power.

What was the **Industrial Revolution**?

The Industrial Revolution was an era of sweeping change, as the focus in different societies changed from agricultural to mass-producing and industrial. It began in Great Britain in the 1700s. By the early 1800s it had spread to western Europe and the United States. It was brought about by the introduction of steam-power-driven machinery to manufacturing. As inventors made new machines that could take over manual labor, sweeping changes in agriculture, textile and metal manufacture, transportation, economic policies, and social structures took place. By the end of the eighteenth century, most finished goods—which had once been made by hand or by simple machines—were produced in quantity by technologically advanced machinery. Factories were built to house the new machines, causing a population shift from rural areas to urban ones.

What is the **Nobel Prize**?

The Nobel Prize is the most famous international science award. Three science prizes, for chemistry, physics, and physiology or medicine, are awarded every year to people who have made significant contributions to these fields. The prize was created by the Swedish chemist and industrialist Alfred Nobel, who made a fortune from his invention of dynamite and left much of his money to fund the prize. Since 1901, the Nobel Prize has been honoring men and women from all parts of the world for their discoveries and inventions in these areas, as well as in the fields of literature and peace. Some famous scientists and inventors who have been awarded the prize include Ivan Pavlov (in 1904), Albert Einstein (1921), and Linus Pauling (1954). Eleven women, from a total of 500 scientists, have been awarded a Nobel Prize in the sciences from 1901 to 2008. Among them, Marie Curie is the only person ever to have twice received a Nobel Prize in the sciences, each time in a different field of specialization: in Physics, in 1903, and in Chemistry, in 1911.

BUILDINGS

How is **steel used** in **skyscrapers**?

Tall, multistory structures called skyscrapers are made of steel, which is sturdier and lighter in weight than other building materials, such as brick and stone. In the late 1800s, when steel production became common, architects experimented with steel, forming it into long, thin pieces called girders. The first skyscrapers, built in the United States in the 1880s, were constructed using vertical columns and horizontal beams made from steel girders. This supporting skeleton allowed buildings to rise to 10 or more stories. Skyscrapers grew taller when designers began using bundled steel tubes instead of heavy girders. Tube buildings, like Chicago's Sears Tower, get most of their support from a stiff grid of steel columns and beams in their outer walls. The lighter weight pieces need less support, and so architects can add more height. Additional beams can be placed diagonally for additional support while adding little extra weight. The girders and beams are bolted together and welded on all sides so that the building will not sway from side to side as a unit when there is wind.

What is the **tallest building** in the world?

When its construction is completed, the Burj Dubai skyscraper in the United Arab Emirates will be the world's tallest skyscraper at 2,064 feet (629 meters) high. As of early 2009, the world's tallest *completed* skyscraper was still the Taipei 101, located in the Hsinyi district of Taipei, Taiwan. With 101 stories, it reaches 1,671 feet (509 meters) high. Taipei 101 became the world's tallest building when it was finished in 2003, surpassing the Petronas Towers in Kuala Lumpur, Malaysia, the world's tallest twin towers. The Sears Tower in Chicago, Illinois, is the world's third tallest building that people can live and work in. Built from 1970 to 1974 for Sears, Roebuck &

The Burj Dubai skyscraper, located in the United Arab Emirates, will be the world's tallest skyscraper when it is completed.

Company, it rises 110 stories to a height of 1,450 feet (442 meters). (If you count the tower's antenna, it actually reaches 1,730 feet [527 meters]) high. Another very tall structure (though it is not a skyscraper building where people can live and work) is the CN Tower in Toronto, Canada. This transmission tower is 1,815 feet (553 meters) tall and was built in 1976.

How do **elevators** work?

An elevator moves things or people from one level to another, and is important to tall structures like skyscrapers. The car of an elevator, in which people ride, is attached to guard rails inside a tall, empty space called a shaft. It is moved by a steel cable that is attached to a large weight that counterbalances it. An electric motor raises and lowers the cable, changing the positions of the car and weight as the elevator moves from floor to floor. (Usually posted inside an elevator are numbers that indicate the car's weight limit; an elevator motor cannot do its job if a car is a lot heavier than the weight that balances it.)

Why are they called skyscrapers?

Some buildings are called skyscrapers because they are of great height and have an iron or steel frame inside that supports its floors and walls. Before builders figured out how to make such frames, stone or brick walls had to bear the weight of structures, which could not stand up if they were made too high. And tall stone or brick buildings had to have very thick walls on lower floors to bear the weight of the walls and floors above them. These thick walls wasted a lot of useful space. Because cities have limited land, builders experimented with materials and construction methods in an effort to construct taller buildings that were more practical. Finally, in 1885, William Le Baron Jenny built the first modern skyscraper in Chicago. While just 10 stories high, which seems short by today's standards, the Home Insurance Company Building was the first structure to have an internal steel skeleton bear all of its weight. From that point on, tall buildings began to soar into the air, scraping the sky. Just 30 years after the first skyscraper was built, buildings were erected that reached 60 stories high.

The first elevators in use were not especially safe because once in a while a cable would break, and a car, pulled by gravity, would come crashing down. Safety devices were soon added, though, to keep such disasters from occurring. (American inventor Elisha Otis invented the first "safety" elevator in 1853.) Additional ropes attached to cars and powerful metal "jaws" that grip guard rails keep elevators from falling if their main cables break. Other safety devices keep elevators from moving when their doors are still open and from traveling too fast. Automatic switches in the shaft allow an elevator to hurry past unwanted floors, or to slow and stop when a chosen floor is reached, unlocking its doors to admit and release passengers. Very long elevators are not always practical, so some buildings use one set of elevators to take passengers part way up the building and another set to service the upper floors.

How does an **escalator** work?

The escalator is a set of moving stairs that transports people from one floor to another in a department store, airport, or other public place. Underneath the stairs is a continuous belt that moves around wheels. The stairs are attached to two side belts or to one central belt, which is driven by electricity. The moving handrails on both sides of the escalator work the same way and are timed at the same speed as the steps. At the top and bottom of the escalator, the steps fold flat so they can move underneath the floor, and after traveling around the belt they open up and start again. The same set of steps can be used to run up or down, depending on the direction in which the belt is driven.

MOVING ON THE GROUND

How does a **cable car stop** and **go**?

Also called an "endless ropeway," the cable car was invented by Andrew S. Hallidie, who first operated his system in San Francisco, California, in 1873. A cable car moves because of its cable, which runs continuously in a channel, between the tracks located just below the street. The cable is controlled from a central station, and usually moves about 9 miles (14.5 kilometers) per hour. Each cable car has an attachment, on the underside of the car, called a grip. When the car operator pulls the lever, the grip latches onto the moving cable and is pulled along by the moving cable. When the operator releases the lever, the grip disconnects from the cable and comes to a halt when the operator applies the brakes.

Who **invented** the **automobile**?

The history of the automobile is complex and dates back to the fifteenth century when the Italian inventor and engineer Leonardo da Vinci was creating designs and models for transport vehicles. However, two men, Karl Benz and Gottlieb Daimler, are both credited with the invention of the gasoline-powered automobile, because they were the first to make their automotive machines practical to people. Both German engineers living in the nineteenth century, Benz and Daimler worked independently, unaware of each other's efforts. Both built compact, internal-combustion engines to power their vehicles. Benz built his three-wheeler in 1885; it was steered by a tiller (a farming tool used to prepare the soil for planting). Daimler's four-wheeled vehicle was produced in 1887.

What were some of the earliest **steam- and gasoline-driven** vehicles?

Before Benz and Daimler, there were earlier, self-propelled road vehicles, including a steam-driven contraption invented by Nicolas-Joseph Cugnot. The French inventor rode the Paris streets at 2.5 miles (4 kilometers) per hour in 1769. Richard Trevithick, a British inventor and mining engineer, also produced a steam-driven vehicle that could carry eight passengers. It first ran in 1801, in Camborne, England. Londoner Samuel Brown built the first practical four-horsepower gasoline-powered vehicle in 1826. And the Belgian engineer J.J. Etienne Lenoire built a vehicle with an internal combustion engine that ran on liquid hydrocarbon fuel in 1862, but he did not test it on the road until September 1863, when it traveled a distance of 12 miles (19.3 kilometers) in three hours.

How does an **electric car** work?

On the outside, most electric cars look exactly like gas-powered cars. An electric car does not have a tailpipe or a gas tank, but the overall structure is basically the same. Instead of a huge engine, an electric car uses an electric motor to convert electric energy stored in batteries into mechanical energy. Different combinations of generating mechanisms—solar panels, generative braking, internal combustion

147

engines driving a generator, fuel cells—and storage mechanisms are used in electric vehicles.

When did people **first use electric cars**?

During the last decade of the nineteenth century, the electric vehicle became especially popular in cities across America. People had grown familiar with electric trolleys and railways, and technology had produced motors and batteries in a wide variety of sizes. The Edison Cell, a nickel-iron battery, became the leader in electric vehicle use. By 1900, electric vehicles were the most popular car. In that year, 4,200 automobiles were sold in the United States. Of these, 38 percent were powered by electricity, 22 percent by gasoline, and 40 percent by steam. By 1911, the automobile starter motor did away with hand-cranking gasoline cars, and Henry Ford had just begun to mass-produce his

Many people hope that electric cars will help reduce pollution, as well as America's dependence on oil from other countries.

Model T's. By 1924, not a single electric vehicle was exhibited at the National Automobile Show, and the Stanley Steamer was scrapped that year.

Because of "Clean Air" legislation, the energy crises of the 1970s, and concern for the well-being of the environment, car manufacturers have again marketed several all-electric cars and "hybrid" vehicles. Hybrid cars use two or more different power sources to propel them, such as a gasoline engine and an electric motor. General Motors sold the Impact, an electric vehicle. And Honda offered people two hybrids, the Insight and a Civic sedan. The Toyota Prius is a hybrid that first went on sale in Japan in 1997, making it the first mass-produced hybrid vehicle. According to the United States Environmental Protection Agency, the 2008 Prius is the most fuel-efficient car sold in the United States. Because of this, electric cars and hybrid vehicles may be the new cars of the future, eventually replacing all-gasoline-powered cars.

What are the **types of bridges**, and how do they work?

There are more than half a million bridges in the United States. They transport people across valleys, streams, and railroads, and they are constructed as one of four basic types: a beam bridge, an arch bridge, a suspension bridge, and a cantilever bridge. The simplest and most common form of bridging, the beam bridge has straight slabs or girders carrying the roadbed. Its span is relatively short (often not more than 250 feet [76 meters]) and its load rests on its supports or piers. The arch

What is the importance of America's interstate highways?

Today, two million trucks travel the interstates and move more than 10 billion tons of goods across the United States. It is possible for them to drive more than 2,400 miles (4,000 kilometers) from the East Coast to the West Coast, or more than 1,200 miles (2,000 kilometers) from the Canadian border to the Mexican border—all thanks to the interstate ("between states") highways. People in passenger cars can also drive these distances, making it possible for them to travel easily and quickly from one part of the country to another. The highways, which have no traffic signals or stop signs, cross more than 55,000 bridges and can be found in 49 of America's 50 states. (Only Alaska has no interstate highways, although Hawaii's "interstate" highways don't cross state lines either). The Interstate Highway system is usually two roads, one in each direction, separated by an area that is planted with grass and trees. Each road holds two lines of cars that can travel at speeds between 65 and 75 miles per hour (104 to 120 kilometers per hour).

The Interstate Highway system—signed into law in 1956 by President Dwight Eisenhower—set off a highway-building boom that produced nearly 47,000 miles (75,639 kilometers) of interstate highways as of 2004. It has been an important part of the nation's economic growth since the 1950s, as trucks using the system carry about 75 percent of all products that are sold in the country. Jobs and new businesses have been created near the busy interstate highways, including hotels, motels, diners and fast-food restaurants, gas stations, and shopping centers. At the end of the twentieth century, the U.S. government renamed the Interstate Highway system to the Eisenhower Interstate System.

bridge, usually made of steel or concrete, looks like an arch, and thrusts outward on its bearings at each end. They can span up to 800 feet (244 meters). In the suspension bridge, the roadway hangs on steel cables, with the bulk of the load carried on cables anchored to the banks. Suspension bridges can span great distances—2,000 to 7,000 feet (610 to 2134 meters)—without intermediate piers. A cantilever bridge is a bridge built using cantilevers—structures that are built horizontally into space, supported on only one end. The cantilevers may be simple beams; however, large cantilever bridges made to handle road or rail traffic use trusses, an interconnected framework of beams, built from structural steel.

Where is the **longest bridge**?

The longest bridge in the United States—and the world, for that matter—consists of two parallel bridges called the Lake Pontchartrain Causeway, near New Orleans, Louisiana. The Causeway runs over water, is 23.87 miles (38.42 kilometers) long, and is supported by more than 9,000 concrete pilings. The south end of the Causeway is in Metairie, Louisiana, a suburb of New Orleans, and the north end is in Mandeville, Louisiana.

The historic Brooklyn Bridge in New York was completed in 1883 and is still heavily used by traffic today.

New York City houses the Verrazano-Narrows Bridge, the longest suspension bridge (a type of bridge where the main load-bearing elements are hung from suspension cables) in the United States. Its total length is 4,260 feet (1,298 meters). The ends of the bridge are at historic Fort Hamilton in Brooklyn and Fort Wadsworth in Staten Island, both of which guarded New York Harbor at the Narrows for over a century. The bridge was named after Giovanni da Verrazano, who, in 1524, was the first European explorer to sail into New York Harbor. Next in line is San Francisco's Golden Gate Bridge, which is 4,200 feet (1,219 meters) long. The third longest suspension bridge in the United States is Michigan's Mackinac Straits suspension bridge, which connects the upper and lower peninsulas of the state. Nicknamed "Big Mac," the bridge spans 3,800 feet (1,158 meters).

Other cities around the world with long suspension bridges include Japan, Denmark, China, and England: The Akashi Kaikyo Bridge, for example, also known in Japan as the Pearl Bridge, is the longest suspension bridge in the world with a main span of 6,532 feet (1,991 meters). By comparison, the bridge is almost one-quarter mile longer than the previous record holder, the East Bridge (StoreBaelt) in Denmark, which opened the same year, in 1998.

Who built the **Brooklyn Bridge**?

John A. Roebling, a German-born American engineer, constructed the first truly modern suspension bridge in 1855. Its characteristics included towers supporting massive cables and a roadway suspended from main cables. In 1867, Roebling was

What is a "kissing bridge"?

"**K**issing bridges" are covered bridges with roofs and wooden sides. They are called kissing bridges because people inside the bridge cannot be seen from the outside, making them good places to kiss discreetly. They were first built in the nineteenth century by engineers who designed coverings to protect the structures from the effects of the weather. More than 10,000 covered bridges were built across the United States between 1805 and the early twentieth century. As of January 1980, only 893 of these covered bridges remained—231 in Pennsylvania alone, where the first one was erected.

given the ambitious task of constructing the Brooklyn Bridge. In his design he proposed the revolutionary idea of using steel wire for cables rather than the less-resilient iron. Just as construction began, Roebling died of tetanus when his foot was crushed in an accident, and his son, Washington A. Roebling, took over the bridge's construction. Fourteen years later, in 1883, the bridge was completed. At that time, it was the longest suspension bridge in the world, spanning the East River and connecting New York's Manhattan with Brooklyn. The bridge has a central span of 1,595 feet (486 meters), with its masonry towers rising 276 feet (841 meters) above high water. Today, the Brooklyn Bridge is among the best-known of all American civil engineering accomplishments.

How are **tunnels built**?

Bored through mountains or burrowed beneath oceans, tunnels provide spaces for cars and trains, water and sewage, and power and communication lines. Although tunnels have existed for thousands of years—Roman engineers created the most extensive network of tunnels in the ancient world—they have been perfected by today's technology. To build a stable tunnel, engineers dig through the earth, or excavate, using special tools and equipment. If the ground is unstable, engineers must support the ground around them while they dig. For the support work, they often use a tunnel shield, a cylinder pushed ahead of tunneling equipment to provide advance support for the tunnel roof. For harder, mountainous rock, engineers use humungous rock-breaking devises called tunnel-boring machines. Once the tunnel is structurally sound, engineers line tunnels with final touches, like the roadway and lights. If builders are working underwater, pre-made tunnel segments are often floated into position, sunk, and then attached to other sections.

How does a **roller coaster** work?

A roller coaster works the same way as a bicycle coasting down a hill. When you ride your bike to the top of a hill, you pedal to get there. Then, to coast down the hill, you take your feet off the pedals and glide down the other side. If the slope is steep enough, you can go very fast. Similarly, a roller coaster is only powered at the beginning of the ride, when the coaster, or train, is pulled up the first hill. When it goes over the top of the hill, the weight of the train itself, pulled downward by gravity, is what keeps the entire unit moving. There are no cables that pull the train around the track. This conversion of potential energy (stored energy) to kinetic energy (the energy of motion) is what drives the roller coaster, which often reaches 60 miles (96.5 kilometers) per hour. Running wheels guide the train on the track, and friction wheels control the train's movement to either side of the track. A final set of wheels keeps the train on the track even if it is upside down. Air brakes stop the car as the ride ends.

FLYING HIGH

How do **airplanes fly**?

Airplanes function according to a complex mix of aerodynamic principles—theories that explain the motion of air and the actions of bodies moving through that air. Airplanes get their power from engines. Small planes generally use piston engines, which turn propellers that push aircraft through the air in the same way that boat propellers push vessels through water. But bigger planes use jet engines, powered by burning fuel. These engines expel great amounts of air that thrust a plane forward and up. An airplane must be in constant motion— its wings slicing through rushing air to create lift—in order to stay up; moving air is also required to steer it. In order to get enough lift to rise into the air on takeoff, an airplane has to travel along the ground first at great speed.

Airplanes are able to lift into the air and stay there because of the shape of their wings. An airplane wing is flat on the bottom and curved on the top. When a plane's engines push it forward, air divides to travel around its wings. The air that passes over the larger curved top moves faster than the air that passes under the flat bottom. The faster-moving air on top becomes thinner and has lower pressure than the air below, which pushes the wing up. Uneven air pressure caused by the shape of an airplane's wings, then, creates a force called lift, which allows an aircraft to fly.

How do **pilots steer** an airplane?

The force of moving air steers an airplane. Steering is done through a system of moveable flaps—working much like boat rudders—that are located on the plane's wings and tail. When set at an angle, they push at flowing air that pushes back, turning or tilting an airplane. To descend, for instance, a pilot lowers a plane's tail flaps, causing airflow to direct its nose downward. Turning requires changing the direction of wing flaps and the tail rudder.

Who were the **Wright brothers**?

The Americans Wilbur and Orville Wright, known as the Wright brothers, were the first people to successfully build and fly an airplane. The owners of a bicycle shop in their hometown of Dayton, Ohio, Wilber and Orville were interested in mechanics from early ages. After attending high school, the brothers went into business together and, interested in aviation, began experimenting with gliders in their spare time. The brothers consulted national weather reports to figure out the best place to conduct flying experiments. They determined that the ideal location was Kitty Hawk, North Carolina. So in 1900 and 1901, on a narrow strip of sand called Kill Devil Hills, they tested their first gliders. Back in their bicycle shop in Ohio, they built a small wind tunnel in which they ran experiments using wing models to determine air pressure.

The Wright brothers use their research to design and build an airplane, which they tested in Kitty Hawk in 1903. On December 17 of that year, they made the world's first flight in a power-driven, heavier-than-air machine. Orville piloted the craft a distance of 120 feet (36.5

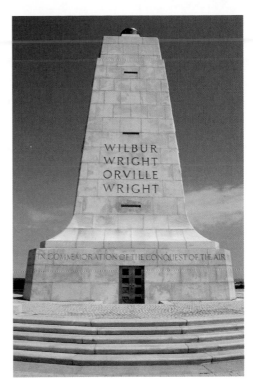

A 60-foot-tall memorial to Orville and Wilbur Wright's historic airplane flight was dedicated at Kill Devil Hills, North Carolina, in 1932.

meters) and stayed in the air 12 seconds. The brothers made a total of four flights that day, and Wilbur made the longest: 59 seconds of flight time that covered just more than 850 feet (259 meters). They received little media attention for their efforts, until 1908, when they signed a contract with the Department of War to build the first military airplane. A year later, they set up the American Wright Company to manufacture airplanes.

What is a **supersonic airplane**?

A supersonic airplane is shaped quite differently than a regular, "subsonic" plane, or commercial plane. It is usually shaped like a dart, with a long pointed nose and wings that swing back and hug the plane body. This slim shape causes less friction as it races through the air. The close-set wings also stay within the shock waves the plane creates, which is necessary to maintain control of the aircraft. While the special wings of supersonic planes don't provide as much lift as those of regular planes, the aircraft get the lift they need for takeoffs and landings by traveling at very high speeds.

How do **helicopters** fly?

Although a helicopter doesn't have wings like an airplane, it uses the same principle of lift to rise and maneuver in the air. The blades of a helicopter's propeller-like top rotor are shaped just like a plane's wings—flat on the bottom and rounded on the top—and are likewise adjustable. Instead of rushing forward through the air like a plane does to gather enough lift to fly, a helicopter moves only its (three to six) rotor blades, which are attached to a central shaft driven by an engine. The rotor blades slice through enough air—creating the changes in surrounding air pressure that produce lift—to achieve flight. Adjusting the angle at which the rotor blades are set helps control a helicopter's lift and manner of flight. Because the angle of the rotor is adjustable, too, a helicopter has far greater maneuverability than an airplane: besides moving up, down, and forward, it can fly backward and hover in the air.

THE WATER HIGHWAY

How do **boats float**?

The weight of an object pulls it down into water. It displaces or pushes water aside. But if the object's density (its weight in relation to its size) is less than the density of the water it displaces, it will float. That principle explains why a heavy wooden raft can float in water, while a small stone will sink to the bottom: the raft spreads its weight over a large area, while the stone's weight is concentrated.

Boats, which are hollow, float because of this principle. The air inside them makes them less dense than they appear. Large ships that transport heavy material, though, have less air inside when they are carrying a big load. Such ships must be careful about weight limits and have load lines on their hulls that show how low they can ride in the water and still maneuver safely. Weight limits vary with the kind of water the boats are traveling through: they can carry more weight when in salt-water seas, which are denser than freshwater, and in cold water, which is denser than warm water.

How are **boats powered** to move through the water?

Boats need a power source to move them forward in the water. In small vessels this power can be provided by people, who use oars to paddle along. Muscle power cannot move boats very fast or very far, though. The wind can be used, too, to move boats equipped with sails. But for a large boat that needs to go a long distance, the most reliable source of power is a motor-driven engine.

Depending on the size of the boat, a gasoline engine, diesel engine, or steam engine does the job. Nuclear power is even used to run some boat engines, like those found in submarines. Motors rotate boat propellers, which have large twisting blades that radiate around a central hub. These blades push water backward, and the boat moves forward as the disturbed water pushes back. Rotating propellers also create lower water pressure in the space in front of them, which sucks them forward, along with the vessel to which they are attached. (Using these same prin-

Submarines fill or empty their ballast tanks with water in order to float or sink under water.

ciples of movement, propellers can also power aircraft.) A boat is steered by a rudder, which is a flat, upright, movable piece of wood or metal that is attached to its stern, or rear. When turned, the rudder changes the direction of the water around it, which pushes back, forcing the stern, and gradually the rest of the boat, to change direction, too.

How do **submarines sink** below the water and **then rise**?

The body of a submarine is uniquely constructed. Under its strong outer hull are huge ballast tanks that surround its working core. The tanks can be filled with and emptied of seawater and air, which allows the submarine to sink or rise in the water.

When a submarine travels on the surface, its ballast tanks are filled with air, which makes it less dense than the seawater it displaces, and it floats. But when a submarine needs to submerge or dive below the surface, its ballast tanks are flooded with seawater. This action makes the submarine sink; now equal in density to the water that surrounds it, it can move about below the surface. Motor-driven propellers are used to move the vessel along (its streamlined shape creates as little water resistance as possible), and swiveling fins (called hydroplanes) located on its sides direct it up and down. When a submarine needs to return to the surface, compressed air stored in tanks is blown into the ballast tanks. This air forces out the seawater, and the vessel begins to rise, aided by the hydroplanes. Once again lighter than the seawater it displaces, the submarine is able to float on the surface.

How do **submarine pilots know** where they are **going** when they are **underwater**?

Submarine pilots use a periscope to navigate their direction if they are not too far below the water's surface. This tall, rotating, tube-shaped instrument can be raised above the water's surface to view surroundings, using a series of mirrors and lenses inside to relay images. Beyond that, submarines use sonar (sound waves) to make

155

echo soundings of their surroundings. Transmitted sound waves are reflected off objects or the ocean floor; the time it takes for these sound waves to be reflected back indicates how far away things are located. The echoes are then converted into electrical signals that appear on a display screen, which gives a picture—similar to that of an airport's radar screen—of surrounding waters.

COMMUNICATIONS AND ELECTRONIC DEVICES

How are **newspapers made**?

People usually read newspapers to get information about current events, things that are happening at the present time or have just occurred. When a good news story breaks, reporters are immediately sent out to gather as much information about the situation as possible and photographers take pictures that add visual information. When they return to the newspaper office, the reporters type their story into a computer, and camera film is developed into photos in a darkroom.

The photographs are put into the computer with a device called a scanner. Increasing numbers of photographers use digital cameras, which means their photos do not have to be first developed on paper. They are automatically in digital, or computer-ready, format and can be transmitted over phone lines or via satellites just like e-mail or other electronic files. Once the photos are in digital format, the printed story and the pictures that illustrate it are arranged together. The story may take up part of a newspaper page or may extend for a few pages. Designers arrange all the stories and photos that make up a newspaper into visually appealing, easy-to-read pages on the computer screen. They are then printed out on pieces of clear film.

Next, the film print of each newspaper page is laid on a light-sensitive metal plate. When it is exposed to a flash of bright light, shadows of the film's letters and pictures are left on the plate. The shadows are permanently etched or marked into the plate when it is soaked in acid, which eats some of the metal away. What is left is a perfect copy of the film print of the newspaper page, with its words and pictures appearing as grooves in the metal.

The newspaper page is now ready to be printed on paper. The metal plate is first wrapped around a roller on a motor-driven printing press and coated with ink. After being wiped clean, ink still stays in the grooves. When paper (in big rolls) is passed under the roller, it is pressed into the grooves, and perfectly printed pages appear. This process is repeated for each newspaper page. As you can imagine, printing plants are enormous, with some presses standing three stories tall. These expensive machines (costing tens of millions of dollars) can print and sort up to 70,000 copies of a newspaper per hour. Once the press is done printing and sorting, the newspapers are bundled for delivery the next day to homes and newsstands.

What is a hornbook?

A hornbook is a flat, wooden board with a handle that students used in English and American classrooms from the fifteenth to the eighteenth centuries. A sheet of paper was pasted on the board. It contained the alphabet, the Benediction (a special prayer from the Book of Numbers), the Lord's Prayer, and the Roman numerals. A thin, flat piece of clear animal horn covered the whole board to protect the paper, which was scarce and expensive at the time. Hornbooks were used as early as 1442 in England and became standard equipment in English schools by the 1500s. They were discontinued around 1800, when books became cheaper to produce.

How was **printing done before computers** and motor-driven **presses**?

Long before computers and motor-driven presses, printing was done by hand with wooden blocks of letters and figures dipped in ink and pressed onto paper. Historians believe that this method of printing was invented in China around the year 700. A hand-operated printing press—with moveable type or letters—was first used in Europe in the mid-fifteenth century. Johannes Gutenberg printed the first book, a Bible, in what is now Germany, in 1455. Until that time all books and other manuscripts were written out by hand.

Why do **newspapers fade** and yellow within a few months?

Most commercial cellulose paper manufactured in the last century, including newsprint, is acidic. The acid makes paper brittle and eventually causes it to crumble with only minor use. The problem comes from two features of modern paper: the paper manufacturing process results in cellulose fibers that are very short and acid is introduced (or not removed by purification) during manufacture. Acid in the presence of moisture degrades the fibers, and the acidic reaction splits the cellulose chains into small fragments. The reaction itself produces acid, accelerating the degradation. Ironically, the older the paper the longer it lasts. Paper manufactured up until about the mid-nineteenth century was made from cotton and linen. These early papers had very long fibers, the key to their longevity. Today's newspaper print is the weakest paper; it is unpurified and has the shortest fibers. Consequently, newspapers generally fade and yellow within a few months.

What is the **Morse code**?

In 1835, the American painter-turned-scientist Samuel F.B. Morse devised a code composed of dots and dashes to represent letters, numbers, and punctuation. Telegraphy—the long-distance transmission of a message—uses an electromagnet, a device that becomes magnetic when activated and raps against a metal contact. A series of short electrical impulses repeatedly can make and break this magnetism, resulting in a tapped-out message.

157

Morse code messages used to be transmitted to and from telegraph offices like this one. In larger cities, big telegraph exchange rooms were filled with telegraph machines manned by large staffs.

Morse secured his patent on the code in 1837, and several years later established a communications company with machinist and inventor Alfred Vail. In 1844, the first long-distance telegraphed message was sent by Morse in Washington, D.C., to Vail in Baltimore, Maryland. This was the same year that Morse took out a patent on the telegraphy, although he did not acknowledge the unpatented contributions of Joseph Henry, who invented the first electric motor and working electromagnet in 1829 and the electric telegraph in 1831. Still in use today by the military, the maritime service, and by amateur radio operators, the International Morse Code now uses sound or a flashing light to send messages.

Who **invented radio**?

Guglielmo Marconi, of Bologna, Italy, was the first to prove that radio signals could be sent over long distances. Radio is the radiation and detection of signals spread through space as electromagnetic waves to convey information. It was first called wireless telegraphy because it duplicated the effect of telegraphy without using wires. On December 21, 1901, Marconi successfully sent Morse code signals from Newfoundland to England.

What was **"the Audion"**?

In 1906, the American inventor Lee de Forest built what he called "the Audion," which became the basis for the radio amplifying vacuum tube. This devise made voice radio practical, because it magnified the weak signals without distorting them. The next year, de Forest began regular radio broadcasts from Manhattan, New York. As there were still no home radio receivers, de Forest's only audience was ship wireless operators in New York City Harbor.

How does television work?

Television works through a series of complicated processes. It starts with a television camera, which takes pictures of scenes. Photo cells inside the camera change the pictures to electrical signals. At the same time, a microphone records sounds that are occurring during the scenes. A vibrating magnet in the microphone changes these sounds into electrical signals, too. Some television shows, like news reports, are recorded live, which means that they are broadcast to homes as they occur. But most of the television programs that we watch are recorded, which means that they are put on videotape and sent out later. The electrical signals of sound and pictures are stored as magnetic signals on videotape, which are converted back to electrical signals when played.

Before a program is broadcast, its electrical picture and sound signals are run through a device called a television transmitter. With the help of strong magnets, the transformer turns the electrical signals into invisible bands of energy called radio waves (similar to visible light waves), which can travel great distances through the air. They can travel directly to outdoor television antennae, which catch the waves and send them to television sets that change them into pictures and sounds again. Cable companies send electrical picture and sound signals through cables directly to homes. When broadcasting to distant places, communication satellites that orbit Earth are used to bounce or return the waves back to Earth, extending their travel distance. Satellites are necessary because radio waves move in straight lines and cannot bend around the world.

When an antenna or satellite dish receives radio waves, it changes them back into electrical signals. A speaker in a television set changes some of the signals back into sound. The pictures are reproduced by special guns at the back of a television set that shoot electron beams at the screen, causing it to glow with tiny dots of different colors. Viewed together, the dots look like a regular picture. The individual pictures that make up a scene are broadcast and received, one after another, at a pace so quick that it looks like continuous action is occurring on the screen. The entire process happens very fast because television stations and broadcast towers are all around and because radio waves travel very quickly, at the speed of light. Radio programs broadcast talk and music across the airwaves using the same technology.

What is high-definition television?

High-definition television (HDTV) is a digital television broadcasting system with higher resolution than traditional television systems. The amount of detail shown in a television picture is limited by the number of lines that make it up and by the number of picture elements on each line. The latter is mostly determined by the

Kids today really take telephones for granted. Phones are an everyday part of our lives, but do you know how they work?

width of the electron beam. To obtain pictures closer to the quality of 35-millimeter photography, HDTV has more than twice the number of scan lines with a much smaller picture element. American and Japanese HDTVs have 525 scanning lines, and Europe has 625 scanning lines.

How does a **telephone** work?

All sound is made by the back and forth movement, or vibration, of objects. When an object vibrates, it makes the molecules around it vibrate too, causing a ripple of motion known as a sound wave, which can travel through air, water, and solid materials. A telephone has vibrating parts—a disc in the mouthpiece and one in the earpiece—that turn voice sounds into electrical signals that can travel along telephone wires and then turn back into sound again.

Phones are usually connected to wires because they run on electricity. When you pick up a phone, a low electrical current allows you to dial the series of numbers that will connect you to the phone of a friend, for example. Each number on the phone has its own special electrical signal, and when the right numbers are combined, they can exactly identify your friend's phone line. A local telephone office receives this information when you dial and sends your call in the right direction. Call signals to places close by travel along wires or cables buried underground or strung high in the air between supports. But when the person you call is very far away, the electrical signals sent from your phone are changed into invisible waves of energy called microwaves, which can travel long distances through the air. These waves are sent through space to communication satellites that orbit the world, which bounce them back to Earth, extending the waves' travel distance. An antenna at a receiving station near the home of your friend picks up the waves and changes them to electrical signals once more. They travel by cable to the telephone office that services your friend's neighborhood, where his or her number is identified. A signal is then sent to your friend's phone to make it ring. The entire process from dialing to ringing takes just a few seconds!

When your friend answers the phone, a microphone in its mouthpiece contains a plastic disc that vibrates, turning his or her message into electrical signals that travel along the same path as before. A speaker in the earpiece of your phone receives the electrical signals, which vibrate another plastic disc that changes them back into sound. Two circuits—from microphone to speaker—are created, and you can talk back and forth with your friend. The next time you use the phone, think of the remarkable process that makes it possible!

How did people communicate from their cars before cellular phones?

Before portable cellular phones, people like police officers or taxi drivers communicated from their cars using two-way radios. All of the radios in one city transmitted signals via a large, central antenna located on top of a tall building. With all callers sharing one antenna, the number of calls that could be made at any one time was very limited. Consumers, like you and me, had an old type of cell phone that was permanently attached to the car and powered by its battery. The first transportable cellular phones had their own battery packs that allowed owners to detach them from the car and carry them in a pouch. However, most weighed about 5 pounds (2.25 kilograms) and were not very practical when used this way.

How does a **fax machine** work?

A fax machine, also called a telefacsimile, transmits (carries) graphic and textual information from one location to another through telephone lines. A transmitting machine uses either a digital or analog scanner to convert the black-and-white representations of the image into electrical signals that are transmitted through the telephone lines to a receiving machine. The receiving unit converts the transmission back to an image of the original and prints it. In its broadest definition, a fax terminal is simply a copier that can transmit and receive images. Although the fax was invented by Alexander Bain of Scotland in 1842, it wasn't until 1924 that it was first used to transmit wire photos from Cleveland to New York as part of the newspaper industry.

How does a **cellular phone** work?

Cellular, or cell, phones first became available to consumers in the early 1980s, but the technology that made them small and truly portable evolved gradually over the next 10 years or so. By the beginning of the twenty-first century, millions and millions of people in countries all over the world were using cell phones on a daily basis. And it isn't just adults who enjoy the benefits of completely mobile phone capabilities: in the United States alone, more than 20 percent of teenagers have a cell phone. That translates to at least one in five American teens.

The cellular system divides each city into many small cells (a large city can have hundreds). Each cell has its own tower (which contains an antenna as well as transmitters and receivers that send and receive signals). Each tower can handle numerous callers at a given time, and their small size and weaker signal (compared to the radio antennae) means that their signals don't interfere with those of nearby towers.

When you call someone using a cellular phone, your phone is sending and receiving signals via radio waves, invisible bands of energy that work like light rays.

161

In other words, your cell phone is a fancy, high-tech radio. After you dial a friend's number, your phone must find the closest tower by searching for the strongest signal. Once that signal is located, your phone transmits certain information—like your cell phone number and serial number—that help your service provider make sure you are one of their customers. Then the mobile telephone switching office (MTSO) finds an available channel where your conversation can take place. The MTSO then completes the connection (all of this happening in a few short seconds) and you are chatting with your friend, without wires or cords to hold you down. If you are sitting in the back seat of the car while talking, and your mom is driving you from one end of town to the other, your call will be switched automatically from one cell tower to the next without any pause in your conversation.

What is a **"smartphone"**?

A smartphone is a mobile, or cellular, phone that offers advanced capabilities beyond a typical mobile phone, such as e-mail or Internet capabilities, and/or a complete keyboard. The BlackBerry®, Trio®, and iPhone™ are all called smartphones. For example, the iPhone™, which was introduced by Macintosh in 2007, blends five devices—a mobile phone, an iPod® portable media player, a camera, a personal organizer, and a widescreen mobile Internet device—into one.

How does a **computer** work?

Like all digital machines, a computer changes writing, images, and sound into a special numerical language. It is a binary (or two-part) language that has just two numbers: 0 and 1. These numbers are called "binary digits," or bits for short. In a digital machine, the numbers take the form of electric signals. With a 1 the electricity is switched on and with a 0 it is switched off. Information of all kinds, then, is turned into electrical on-off signals arranged in countless individual patterns.

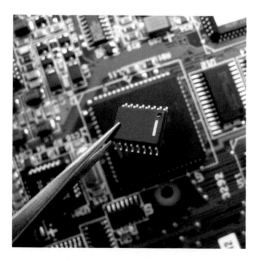

These patterns can be stored, sent along digital pathways, or converted back into forms that we can use and understand with extraordinary speed and accuracy. Bits enter a personal computer from the keypad, mouse, microphone, and scanner. They are received and sent out by cable or broadband modem technology, as well as stored in various memory devices. The computer screen, printer, and speakers convert the bits into forms of information that we can use.

What is a **silicon chip**?

Today's computers contain millions of transistors placed in a tiny piece of silicon, some so tiny that they can fit in an

Far smaller than the vacuum tubes that were used decades ago, modern silicon chips allow us to have computers small enough to rest on our laps or fit in our hands.

How many computers are there in the world?

According to statistics from technology research companies such as Gartner Inc., in April 2002 the billionth personal computer (PC) was shipped. The second billion mark (some being ordered as replacements for older PCs) was reportedly reached in 2007. With personal computers becoming more popular around the world, research companies estimate that there will be more than two billion PCs in active use by 2015. In the United States, more than half of the people who use a computer are also connected to the Internet.

ant's mouth. The transistors (devices that control the flow of electric current) are packed and interconnected in layers beneath the surface of the chip, which is used to make electrical connections to other devices. There is a grid of thin metallic wires on the surface of the chip. This silicon chip was independently co-invented by two American electrical engineers, Jack Kilby and Robert Noyce, in 1958–1959. The chip, along with the invention of the microprocessor, allowed computers to get smaller and more efficient. Silicon chips are also used in calculators, microwave ovens, automobile radios, and video cassette recorders (VCRs).

Who invented the **first computer**?

In 1823, the English mathematician Charles Babbage originated the concept of a programmable computer. At this time, he persuaded the British government to finance what he called an "analytical engine." This would have been a machine that could undertake any kind of calculation. It would have been driven by steam, but the most important innovation was that the entire program of operations was stored on a punched tape (a long strip of paper in which holes are punched to store data). Babbage's machine was not completed in his lifetime because the technology available to him was not sufficient to support his design. However, in 1991 a team lead by Doron Swade at London's Science Museum built the analytical engine (sometimes called a "difference engine") based on Babbage's work. Measuring 10 feet (3 meters) wide by 6.5 feet (2 meters) tall, it weighed three tons and could calculate equations down to 31 digits. The feat proved that Babbage was way ahead of his time, even though the device was impractical because one had to a turn a crank hundreds of times in order to generate a single calculation. Modern computers use electrons, which travel at the speed of light.

Which types of **computers predated Babbage's** "analytical engine"?

Computers developed from calculating machines. One of the earliest mechanical devices for calculating, which is still widely used today, is the abacus—a frame for carrying parallel rods on which beads or counters are strung. The abacus originated in Egypt in 2000 B.C.E. It reached the Orient about a thousand years later, and arrived in Europe in about the year 300 C.E. In 1617, the Scottish scholar John Napier invented "Napier's Bones"—marked pieces of ivory for multiples of numbers. In the middle of the same century, the French mathematician Blaise Pascal produced a simple mechanism for adding and subtracting. Multiplication by repeated addition was a feature of the stepped drum or wheel machine of 1694, invented by the German mathematician Gottfried Wilhelm Leibniz.

When was the **earliest programmable computer** built?

In 1943 and 1944, the British government developed two Colossus computers. These huge machines were electronic computing devices used by British code breakers to read encrypted German messages during World War II. Dubbed "Colossus Mark 1" and "Colossus Mark 2" these devises were the world's first programmable, digital, electronic, computing machines. Based on concepts of the British mathematician Alan M. Turing, the mathematician Max Newman and engineer Tommy Flowers designed and built the machines, which used vacuum tubes (thermionic valves) to perform the calculations. The Colossus hardware and blueprints were destroyed as part of an effort to keep the project secret. However, based on notes in engineers' logs and other information, in 2007 a functional replica of a Colossus computer was completed. The computer is on display at the Bletchley Park Museum in Milton Keynes, Buckinghamshire, England.

What is the **Internet**?

The Internet is the world's largest computer network. It links computer terminals together via wires or telephone lines in a web of networks and shared software. With the proper equipment, an individual can access vast amounts of information and search databases on various computers connected to the Internet, or communicate with someone located anywhere in the world as long as he or she has the proper equipment. According to various sources, including the International Telecommunications Union, in 2008 approximately 1.4 billion people around the world were in some way using the Internet. About 578 million are in Asia, 384 million are in Europe, and 248 million are in North America.

How does the **Internet work**?

Just as telephones are connected by a worldwide phone system, home and work computers can connect with a global computer communications network known as the Internet. Each computer that is linked to the system has its own Internet address, as individual as a phone number. Home computer users buy the services of an Internet provider, which is an organization with powerful computers that link all its subscribers to the Internet. Many large organizations and companies have computers that link them directly to the network. Internet users can visit the World Wide Web, which is a global network of Web sites providing information, entertainment, products, and other services.

Tiny MP3 players allow us to carry thousands of songs with us everywhere we may go.

How does a **search engine** work?

Internet search engines are like computerized card catalogs at libraries. Viewed through a Web browser with an Internet connection, they provide a hyperlinked listing of locations on the World Wide Web according to the requested keyword or pattern of words submitted by the searcher. Search engines use computer software called "spiders" or "bots" to search out, inventory, and index Web pages automatically. The spiders scan each Web page's content for words and the frequency of words, then stores that information in a database. When the user submits words or terms, the search engine returns a list of sites from the database and ranks them according to the relevancy of the search terms.

How is an **MP3 player** related to a computer?

An MP3 player—an electronic device that weighs less than one ounce (28 grams)—allows music to be copied from the Internet, organized, and stored into a computer's memory. An MP3 player plays MP3 files, a compressed digital audio file. With an MP3 player, like Apple's iPod®, a consumer can create personalized music lists and carry thousands of songs wherever he or she goes.

What is **e-mail**?

People can use the Internet to send electronic mail, known as e-mail, to one another in just a few seconds. Once you type a message into your computer to send to your cousin, let's say, who lives miles from you across the country, it travels through the wires of your phone line as a series of electrical signals (or, for some people, the signals travel through the same cables that bring them cable television).

How was mail delivered before there were mail carriers?

In early colonial times, correspondents depended on friends, merchants, and Native Americans to carry messages among the colonies, either by foot or on horseback. However, most correspondence ran between the colonists and England, the Netherlands, or Sweden—their mother countries. These letters were carried overseas on ships. It was largely to handle this mail that, in 1639, the first official notice of mail service in the colonies appeared. The General Court of Massachusetts designated Richard Fairbanks's tavern in Boston as the official repository of mail brought from or sent overseas, and people gathered there to collect letters from loved ones and business associates from faraway places.

These signals travel to a station run by your service provider, where a big computer sends them to an Internet routing center. Located all over the world, routing centers, which are linked to organizations and Internet providers, send the countless computer communications that come to them each second along the quickest possible routes to their destinations. A giant computer there reads the address on your e-mail and sends it farther: depending on the distance it must travel, it may continue along phone lines, be changed into light signals that can travel with great speed along thin glass strands called fiber-optic cables, or be converted into equally speedy invisible bands of energy known as radio waves and transmitted to a communications satellite that will bounce it back to Earth, to a ground station located close to where your cousin lives. Once your message reaches the routing center nearest your cousin, it will be sent to the station of his or her service provider. From there it will be sent along regular phone lines to his or her computer. And all of this happens in a matter of moments.

What is "snail mail" and how does it travel?

The term "snail mail" is used for regular mail that is sent through the United States Postal Service. Once you address a letter, affix postage stamps, and drop it in the mailbox, a complex process begins that requires the efforts of many people and machines—sometimes located in different parts of the world. Mail carriers visit mailboxes in your town or city a few times each day to pick up their contents. The mail collected by carriers is taken to a local postal sorting office, where it joins all the other letters that have been mailed in the area that day. High-speed machines take over then, preparing your letter to reach its destination.

Mail is dumped onto a moving conveyor belt that brings it to a machine that separates it by size. Another machine checks to make sure that all the mail is properly stamped, and then it cancels, or prints over, the stamps so that they cannot be used again. A postmark is also printed on each envelope, which tells the time, date, and place where it was processed.

A machine reads the zip codes written in the addresses of letters, which tell exactly to which part of the country, or the world, they are headed. (Postal services around the globe work together to distribute mail and most have similar code systems.) Postal workers process by hand the letters that have missing or unreadable zip codes. The zip code machine prints a bar code (a machine-readable series of lines, more reliable than written numerals) on each letter, and a second sorting machine reads and separates them by destination. Mail is grouped by city and country. Local mail is prepared for delivery the next day. Other mail travels by truck, express train, or plane, depending on where it is going. Each delivery day, the Postal Service sorts and delivers more than 700 million pieces of mail. Because of this complex process, and that it takes longer to reach its destination than email, it is referred to as snail, or slow, mail.

What happens to the mail when it gets close to its destination?

Once mail travels close to its destination, it is unloaded at another postal sorting office. A bar code–reading machine scans the letters again, separating them further for delivery to districts, neighborhoods, and streets. The letters are sent to local post offices, where carriers are given the mail for their delivery areas. Routes may include homes, shops, and office buildings. Carriers who work in farm country, where people live very far apart, may have to travel many miles to deliver the mail each day.

When was the first post office in the United States established and how did the system grow?

Governor William Penn established Pennsylvania's first post office in 1683. Central postal organization came to the colonies after 1692, when Thomas Neale received a 21-year grant from the British Crown, whose settlements dominated the Atlantic seaboard, for a North American postal system. It wasn't until 1774, however, that William Goddard, a newspaper publisher and former postmaster, set up the Constitutional Post for intercolonial mail service. Colonies funded it by subscription, and net revenues were used to improve mail service rather than to pay back to the subscribers. By 1775, when the Continental Congress met in Philadelphia, Goddard's post was flourishing, and thirty post offices operated between Williamsburg, Virginia, and Portsmouth, New Hampshire. The Constitutional Post provided security for colonial messages and created a communication line that played a vital role in bringing about American independence during the Revolutionary War.

PICTURES, LIGHTS, AND LASERS

Why do I see my shadow on the sidewalk on a sunny day?

Whenever light hits an object, it casts a shadow. A shadow forms when an object blocks light from its light source, creating an area behind the object that the light cannot reach. A screen placed behind the object will be dark where it lies in the

167

shadow. When you stand on the sidewalk, the screen is the cement surface on which you are standing. The Sun is your light source. As the Sun moves in the sky, the shadow—since it is the part of space "behind" you as viewed from the Sun—will move as well.

Because the sidewalk touches your feet, the shadow will always form an image connected to your feet. It will extend from there in a direction opposite to the direction to the Sun. When the Sun is in the East, in the morning, the shadow will extend to the West, and when the Sun is in the West, in the evening, the shadow will extend to the East.

How does a **light bulb** work?

An incandescent light bulb, like the ones on your desk lamp, use heat caused by an electrical current. When electrical current passes through a wire, it causes the wire to heat. The wire, or filament, gets so hot that it glows and gives off light. Light bulbs for everyday usage have a filament made of tungsten. Since the hot tungsten would quickly burn away if it were exposed to oxygen, it must be placed in a sealed glass bulb, which is either evacuated or filled with a gas that won't let it burn. Thomas Edison, the creator of the light bulb, thought that it would take him six weeks to develop it, but instead it took more than one year. Of this experience, he famously said, "I have not failed … I have just found 10,000 ways that will not work." When he finally got it right, in 1879, it was due to two important factors: First he put the filament in a glass bulb and then he removed the air (including oxygen) from inside the bulb. Edison tested more than 1,500 materials to find the right filament, including coconut fibers, fishing line, and facial hair.

How does an **ear thermometer** read **body temperature**?

An ear thermometer reads the spectrum of thermal radiation given off by the inner surfaces of a person's ear. All objects give off thermal radiation (including the light emitted by a glowing incandescent light bulb) and that radiation is characteristic of their temperatures. The hotter an object is, the brighter its thermal radiation and the more that radiation shifts toward shorter wavelengths. The thermal radiation from a person's ear is in the invisible infrared portion of the light spectrum, which is why you can't see people glow. But the ear thermometer can see this infrared light and it uses the light to determine the ear's temperature. The thermometer's thermal radiation sensor is very fast, so it can measure a person's body temperature in just a few minutes.

Ear thermometers, unlike other thermometers, read body temperature by detecting invisible infrared light.

Why do certain items **glow-in-the-dark**?

Glow-in-the-dark stickers, stars, toys, and clothes, all work by absorbing light and emitting it later. These items contain phosphors, substances such as zinc sulfide that radiate visible light after being energized by natural light. Phosphorescent materials continue to glow after the energizing light is removed. They have electrons that are easily excited to higher energy levels when they absorb light energy. In phosphorescent materials—such as glow-in-the-dark objects—the excited electrons drop to a lower, but still excited intermediate level and stay there for a period of time before returning to their ground state (original energy level) and emitting the excess energy as visible light.

How does a **camera take pictures**?

When you press the picture-taking button on a camera, you open the shutter and let light inside for a fraction of a second. The light passes through a lens that focuses it on film, leaving a record there of what the camera "saw" during that button-pressing instant. The film is coated with light-sensitive chemicals that save the impression, but it usually has to be placed into a bath of other chemicals to make an image appear and remain permanently. The film is developed into negatives, on which appear images that look very different than those that were photographed: dark shades appear light, light shades appear dark, and colors are the opposite of what they should be. But when light passes through these negatives onto special photo paper, which is also developed using chemicals, the images that appear are normal again—exact copies of the photographed scenes. With "instant" cameras, developing chemicals are contained inside, treating the film right away. A picture pops out on photo paper, its image forming while you wait. Digital cameras work the same way that television cameras do: Instead of using film, they make electronic pictures. The pictures are loaded onto a computer, where they can be altered in size, shape, and color, and printed out.

What was the **daguerreotype**?

The daguerreotype was the first successful type of photograph. It was named after the French chemist Louis Daguerre, who announced his invention to the public at a meeting of the French Academy of Sciences in Paris in 1839. His photographic process created a highly detailed image on a sheet of copper, plated with a thin coat of silver, without the use of a negative. The process was complex. First, the silver-plated copper plate had to be cleaned and polished until the surface looked like a mirror. Next, the plate was sensitized in a closed box over iodine until it took on a yellow-rose appearance. The plate, held in a lightproof holder, was then transferred to a simple camera. After exposure to light, the plate was developed over hot mercury until an image appeared. To fix the image, the plate was immersed in a special chemical and then toned with gold chloride. Exposure times for the earliest daguerreotypes ranged from 3 to 15 minutes. American photographers quickly capitalized on this new invention, and portraits based upon daguerreotypes, such as those of President Abraham Lincoln, appeared in popular periodicals and books.

The popularity of the daguerreotype declined in the late 1850s when the ambrotype, a faster and less expensive photographic process, became available.

How does an **X-ray** take **pictures of bones**?

X-rays are similar to visible light in that both are forms of electromagnetic energy, which travels in waves. But X-rays have much shorter wavelengths than light, so they are invisible. Just as light can pass through some things, like glass, X-rays can pass through certain materials. They can pass through your skin, muscles, and organs, for example, but not through dense things like your bones (which contain heavier atoms). When you have an X-ray taken, the waves are projected through you onto a film or plate that is coated with special chemicals. Most X-rays are stopped when they hit a bone but pass through other body parts, which appear dark on the X-ray after it is developed. Bones stand out light and clear. When organs like the stomach or intestines need to be X-rayed, the patient drinks a special liquid that stops the rays. That liquid coats the organ, and a picture can be taken.

What are **lasers**?

First built in 1960 by American physicist Theodore Maiman, lasers are machines that produce intense beams of high-energy light. Laser light is more powerful than ordinary light because all its rays have the same wavelength and move together in exactly the same direction, allowing them to be focused in a narrow beam with great precision. Laser light beams vary in strength, depending on the materials and amount of energy used to make them. Lasers can melt, burn, or cut through a variety of different surfaces, from hard metal to the delicate human body, which is why they are often used in surgery today. Lasers can be used to make precise measurements, to reshape corneas to correct poor vision, to transmit telephone signals, to guide weapons, and to read supermarket bar codes.

What are **bar codes**?

Bar codes are numerical product codes that appear on the labels of merchandise. A full-length bar code has 12 digits. Each digit is coded by two black and two white stripes that range in width. Each digit represents something different; for example, the first digit indicates the type of product it is; other digits form the manufacturer's identification number and price. Bar codes were originally created to help grocery stores speed up the checkout process and keep better track of inventory, but the system quickly spread to all other retail products because it was so successful. Barcodes are read by laser scanners called bar code readers or scanned from an image by special software.

How does **a laser make musical sound off** of a **CD**?

Music is stored on a compact disk (CD) as digital data. On the bottom side of a CD is a thin metal sheet. Tiny round depressions called pits, which represent sound, fill its spiral track. A beam of laser light is used to change a CD's pitted track back into sound.

Unlike ordinary light, which spreads out in all directions once it leaves its source, laser light can be focused with great accuracy. It moves along the track of a CD, and sensors detect the pattern of shiny flat parts (which reflect light back) and pits (which do not). These on-and-off flashes of reflected light turn into electrical signals. A computer in a compact disc player, which has an enormous memory that stores every possible combination of on-and-off patterns, converts the signals to musical notes with different pitches and volumes in the player's speakers. And then the music plays!

How do **mirrors** use light to create a **reflection**?

We see objects in a mirror, because a mirror, when hit by particles of light called photons, reflects the photons back to us and some reach, and enter, our eyes. Photons that hit a rough surface will bounce off of the surface in a haphazard manner, while those that hit a smooth surface, such as a mirror, only bounce off of the surface at the same angle at which they hit the object. The scientific term for this phenomenon is reflection. Photons that bounce off of any part of our bodies and hit the mirror reflect back to our eyes from only one place on the mirror, and at only one angle. Therefore, each point on our bodies that reflects back to our eyes from one point on the mirror produces an image in the mirror. All of the images together make up our body's reflection.

How does a **magnifying glass** work?

A magnifying glass is a convex lens, which means that it is curved outward, much thicker in the middle than around its edges. This shape bends the light waves of objects viewed through it, causing us to see them in unusual ways. When you hold a magnifying glass close to an object, its light waves are widened before they are focused on your eyes, causing the object to appear very large. But when you hold a magnifying glass out and view a distant object with it, the item appears smaller and upside down. This effect is due to the image being beyond the focus of the lens. The more curved a convex lens is, the greater its ability to bend light and magnify. Microscopes (which allow us to look at things that are too small to be seen with our eyes), binoculars, and telescopes (which make far away things look bigger and nearer to us) also use convex lenses.

Because light waves change speed when they pass through material like glass, we can bend light and even magnify objects through a lens.

HANDY THINGS
AROUND THE HOUSE

Who **invented** the **zipper**?

Like many inventions, the development of the modern zipper can be traced to a series of events. In 1893, Whitcomb Judson patented and marketed a "clasp locker," a complicated hook-and-eye shoe fastener. Together with businessman Colonel Lewis Walker, Whitcomb launched the Universal Fastener Company to manufacture the new device. He did not use the word "zipper," although many people often credit him as the zipper's creator. Instead, it was Swedish-born Gideon Sundback, an electrical engineer who was hired to work for the Universal Fastener Company, who gets the credit. He was responsible for improving Judson's fastener, and by December 1913, he had designed the modern zipper. Sundback increased the number of fastening elements from four per inch to ten or eleven, had two facing-rows of teeth that pulled into a single piece by a slider, and increased the opening for the teeth guided by the slider. Sundback also created a machine that was able to manufacture the zipper.

What do many **household appliances** have in **common**?

Despite their varied uses and different systems of wires, pipes, and vents, household appliances use electricity to run. They also rely on a transformer, a nineteenth-century invention that made it possible to transmit power for home use. In the early 1900s two major engineering innovations—resistance heating and small, efficient motors—led to electric stoves and irons, vacuum cleaners, washers, dryers, and dishwashers. In the second half of the twentieth century advances in electronics made the way for appliances that could be set on timers and even programmed, further reducing the workload necessary to complete simple tasks.

How does a **vacuum cleaner** pick up dirt?

James Spangler, a janitor at an Ohio department store who suffered from asthma, invented his "electric suction-sweeper," in 1907 as way of picking up the dust and debris that triggered his health condition. His invention was the first practical domestic vacuum cleaner. It used an electric fan to generate suction, rotating brushes to loosen dirt, a pillowcase for a filter, and a broomstick for a handle. Because it was heavy and hard to handle, Spangler sold the rights of his invention to his relative, William Hoover, whose redesign of the appliance coincided with the development of the small, high-speed universal motor, in which the same current (either AC or DC) passes through the appliance's rotor and stator. This gave the vacuum cleaner more horsepower, higher airflow and suction, better engine cooling, and more portability than was possible with the larger, heavier induction motor. Hoover's model has since been refined, but the mechanics of his vacuum cleaner are still used in vacuum cleaners today.

How does a **washing machine** clean our clothes?

All washing machines work by using a mix of mechanical energy, thermal energy, and chemical action. Mechanical energy is employed by the rotation of an agitator (a simple device that moves back and forth) in top loaders, or by the tumbling action of a drum in front loaders. Thermal energy is used in the temperature of the water. Chemical action involves the detergent and water mix that works to remove dirt. Once you load your clothes, add laundry detergent, and push the buttons or dials to select a temperature, agitation strength, rinse cycle, and time duration, the machine does the rest of the job. It stirs (or washes) clothes with its agitator or drum, drains the dirty water, and follows it with a spin of clothes to remove the remaining water. In order to do its job, a washing machine has an inner and outer tub. The inner tub, which contains the agitator, holds the clothes and helps in the removal of water. It is attached to a gearbox, which in turn is attached to a black metal frame, which holds the machine's motor as well. The outer tub is bolted to the washer's body. The back of the machine has hook-ups for a hot and cold water line. After the machine has performed the washing, rinsing, and spinning processes, the clean clothes are ready for the dryer.

How does a **refrigerator** work?

In the 1870s the German engineer Carl von Linde invented a continuous process of liquefying gases in large quantities, which led to his invention of the first efficient compressed-ammonia refrigerator. His revolutionary machine paved the way for the modern technology of refrigeration. Modern refrigerators run on ammonia gas, which liquefies when it is under high pressure using thermodynamics—a scientific law that says when two different temperatures of things touch or are near each other, the hotter surface cools and the colder surface warms up. Through the use of a compressor, small valves, and a coil, the liquid ammonia hits a low pressure, boils, and changes to a vaporizing gas. The coils go through the coldest part of the fridge, the freezer, as well as the main body of the refrigerator. The colder ammonia in the coil absorbs the heat out of the freezer and fridge, keeping the whole appliance cold. The compressor then takes back the ammonia gas and recycles it continuously. The thermometer inside the fridge regulates the temperature to make sure it is always the same.

How does a **thermos** keep **cold things cold** and **hot things hot**?

A thermos is also called a vacuum bottle because it uses a vacuum—a space that has no air in it—to keep heat from escaping from hot things inside; it also keeps heat from getting inside to make cold things warmer. The vacuum is located in a thin space between the thermos liner and its outer wall, where it stops the movement of heat to and from the outside air. A vacuum works in a thermos because it is empty of air (and molecules) and therefore has no conductivity. (Heat is caused by the motion of molecules.) Because the opening of a thermos is also tightly sealed with a stopper or lid made of a nonconductive material, no heat can escape or enter there, either. Hot food stored in a thermos can keep its heat for many hours; in the same way, cold food can remain cold because the vacuum insulates it from the warm air surrounding the thermos.

The linings of thermoses used to be made of glass, which is a good insulator. The linings were also coated with silver, which made them shiny and reflective. Such mirrored liners worked very well—they were able to efficiently bounce back the invisible rays of heat energy (radiation) given off by all hot things. But there was one problem: glass thermos bottles broke easily. Today, most thermos containers are made of metal or plastic, which don't break easily but also generally don't work quite as well. Also, because vacuums in thermoses aren't perfect—they contain some air—and because their lids don't seal perfectly, they cannot keep cold things cold and hot things hot forever.

Thermoses keep hot things hot and cold things cold because they use insulation and store things within a vacuum.

How does a **coffeemaker** cook up the morning's brew?

With the most common coffeemaker, the drip coffee machine, hot water drips down freely onto ground coffee beans to make coffee. The water inside the machine's water bucket is heated as it passes along a heat-resistant tube. The tube goes into the drip area and releases heated water, just below boiling temperature (212 degrees Fahrenheit [100 degrees Celsius]). The water is heated by a heating element (a resistive heating coil that gives out heat when electricity is passed through it). The heating element has direct contact with the water inside the water bucket, and also heats the heating pad on which the glass coffee container is rested. Today, most models of coffee machines are either semi-automatic or automatic. Buttons and switches have replaced the manual coffee straining and lever-pushing of espresso machines. And some machines now have special features, such as built-in coffee bean grinders and froth makers.

How does a **toaster** work?

Inside a toaster are thick wires arranged in panels that heat up and toast your food. When you push down the lever that lowers your bread, it catches on a hook inside, turning on the heater. While your bread turns brown and crispy, a special metal switch inside the toaster gets hot, too, and bends. After a certain amount of time it bends so much that it pushes on a bar that releases the lever from the hook, and the toasting stops. This action also releases a spring, which pushes the lever up again—and your toast pops up.

How does the metal switch in a toaster bend?

It bends because it is made of two metals that are joined together, something called a bimetal switch. One metal (usually brass) expands quickly when heated, while the other expands much more slowly. This difference causes the switch to bend toward the low-expansion metal. Bimetal switches are used in other appliances that switch electricity on and off to keep their temperatures even, like irons and refrigerators. The thermostat that regulates the temperature of your home by turning your furnace and air conditioner on and off also uses a bimetal switch.

How can a **microwave oven** cook food so **fast**?

Unlike other ovens, which cook food with heat waves made from burning gas or electric currents, microwave ovens use special bands of electromagnetic energy called microwaves (similar to light waves) to cook food. While heat waves gradually work their way inside food to cook it, microwaves can travel right through food in an instant. In a microwave oven a device called a magnetron produces a beam of microwaves that pass through a spinning fan, which sends the waves bouncing in all directions. As they travel through food their energy is absorbed by molecules of water. The water molecules vibrate at the same high speed as the microwaves (2.45 billion times per second!) and rub against other molecules. All this movement and friction causes a great deal of heat, cooking the food inside and out. Microwaved food is cooked through a process similar to steaming, which explains why it doesn't turn brown. But some microwave ovens have traditional heating elements to make food look more appealing—giving it the outer color that we expect in cooked food.

Certain materials allow microwaves to pass through (meaning they are not heated by the waves) while other materials absorb the waves and still others reflect them, or bounce them back. For this reason it is important to be careful about the containers and coverings we use in microwave ovens. Microwaves pass through glass and plastic wrap, for example, which are safe to use, as are paper products and most sturdy plastics. But metal containers and coverings like aluminum foil are reflective. Such surfaces keep food from absorbing microwaves, allowing the waves to bounce around so much inside an oven that it may break.

Why do **burning** things make **smoke**?

During a fire, the air around the fire becomes heated. The heated air sweeps up water vapor (molecules of water that float in the air) and tiny specks of the fuel (the material being burned) into a dark cloud of smoke. The more incompletely something burns, the more smoke it produces, because more particles are left to be swept up into the air. Smoke gradually spreads out and drifts away, with gravity pulling the heaviest bits back to the ground. When a fire first starts to burn, there

Fire extinguishers should only be used by adults or under adult supervision—and only during a fire emergency!

is usually a lot of smoke, which decreases as more of the fuel is burned completely. Smoke detectors take advantage of the fact that fires cause a lot of smoke in their early stages. The detectors sense the small particles in smoke before a fire really starts to burn. An optical smoke detector uses a light beam and light sensor that sounds an alarm when smoke particles get in the way of the beam. An ionizing smoke detector can sense even smaller particles; they disturb a low electric current inside, which sets off an alarm.

How does a **fire extinguisher** work?

In order for something to burn, high heat and oxygen are needed. All fuels have their own particular temperatures at which they begin to burn when exposed to high heat (called their flash points). Removing heat or oxygen from fuel will put out a fire. Water is frequently used to extinguish fires. Large supplies of water can be found almost anywhere, an important condition when dealing with large fires, like those in burning buildings. Water works in two ways to put out a fire. First, it sharply reduces the temperature of the burning material. Second, it covers the material, keeping oxygen-filled air from reaching the material.

But water cannot put out oil fires. Because oil floats on the surface of water, an oil fire's oxygen supply can't be cut off by water. Other substances—liquids, gases, or powders that don't burn—must be used to smother the fire and remove its oxygen supply. Most fire extinguishers are filled with carbon dioxide, a heavy gas that prevents burning. When released, the gas forms a type of snowy foam that both covers and cools a fire. Powdered sodium bicarbonate (what we know as baking soda) is also used in extinguishers, usually for use on oily chemical fires. It quickly melts in heat, forming a crust that keeps oxygen out. (If you do not have a fire extinguisher on hand you should always throw baking soda on a cooking fire that involves grease;

water will only spread the fire by causing splattering.) Because the substance in a fire extinguisher must cover a large area very quickly, it needs to be released in a powerful spray. The extinguishing substance is stored inside the tank under high pressure, which drives it out of a nozzle with great force once it is released.

Has a **robot** been invented to **help with housework**?

Yes! Robots already do a lot of the jobs that humans cannot or do not want to do. In 1986, the Honda Motor Company introduced ASIMO, which stands for Advanced Step in Innovative Mobility, the most advanced humanoid robot in the world. At 4 feet 3 inches (1.3 meters) high and weighing 119 pounds (54 kilograms), ASIMO is the first humanoid robot in the world that can walk independently and climb stairs. In addition to ASIMO's ability to walk like humans, it can also understand preprogrammed gestures and spoken commands, recognize voices and faces, and interface with communication cards. ASIMO has arms and hands so it can do things like turn on light switches, open doors, carry objects, and push carts. Rather than building a robot that would be another toy, Honda wanted to create a robot that would be a helper for people—a robot to help around the house, assist the elderly, or help someone confined to a wheelchair or bed. In 2008, researchers at the Korea Institute of Science and Technology unveiled Mahru, a humanoid robot that can dance and do household chores. In some countries, robots have already replaced jobs, like at help desks in a few Japanese businesses.

How do robots like **ASIMO** and **Mahru** work?

Robots like ASIMO and Mahru are sophisticated, expensive, highly technologically advanced machines that are built upon major components found in humans. Robot technicians use the inner workings of the human body as the model for the robots that they make. This modeling ensures that their robots are as lifelike as possible. First, the robot technician designs the five major components he or she will put into the robot: a body structure, a muscle system, a sensory environment, a power source, and a brain system. Next, they build an intricate machine made up of electrical circuits, electrical valves, piston cylinders, electric motors, solenoids, hydraulic systems, and more—each plays a specific role in getting the robot to work. Every robot has a computer that controls everything else within its body. Many robots can talk and some can even smell, taste, and hear. To get the body of a robot moving, the computer must "tell" the specific part to move. If the technician wants the robot to do something new once it has been made, he or she writes a new computer program. In some cases, if the task is too big for the robot's wiring system, new parts need to be installed.

MATH, MEASUREMENT, AND TIME

NUMBERS AND COUNTING

Where and when did **numbers originate**?

Thousands of years ago there were no numbers to represent one, two, or three. Instead, people used fingers, rocks, sticks, or eyes to represent numbers. There were neither clocks nor calendars to help keep track of time. The Sun and the Moon were used to distinguish between 1:00 P.M. and 4:00 P.M. Most civilizations did not have words for numbers larger than two so they used terminology familiar to them such as flocks of sheep, heaps of grain, piles of sticks or stones, or groups of people. People had little need for a numeric system until they formed clans, villages, and settlements and began a system of bartering and trade that in turn created a demand for currency.

The Babylonians, who lived in Mesopotamia, between the Tigris and Euphrates rivers, began a numbering system about 5,000 years ago. It is one of the oldest numbering systems in the world. The ancient Egyptians used special symbols, known as pictographs, to write down numbers more than 3,000 years ago. The Babylonians and the Egyptians were the first to complete a system for arithmetic based on whole numbers and positive rational numbers. About 500 B.C.E. the Romans developed a system of numerals that used letters from their alphabet rather than special symbols (for example, III represented three). Roman Numerals was the standard numbering system and method of arithmetic in ancient Rome and Europe until about 900 C.E., when the Arabic numbering system, which was originated by the Hindus, came into use. Today, we use numbers based on the Hindu-Arabic system. We can write down any number using combinations of up to 10 different symbols (0, 1, 2, 3, 4, 5, 6, 7, 8, and 9).

Who was **Pythagoras**?

Pythagoras was one of the first Greek mathematical thinkers. He is known for proving and teaching the Pythagorean Theorem, which says that in a right triangle, the sum of the squares of the two right-angle sides will always be the same as the square of the hypotenuse (the long side). He lived in the 500s B.C.E., and spent most of his life in the Greek colonies in Sicily and southern Italy. He had a group of followers who studied with him and taught other people what he had taught them. The Pythagoreans were known for their pure lives (they did not eat beans, for example, because they believed that beans were not a pure food). They wore their hair long, wore only simple clothing, and went barefoot. Both men and women Pythagoreans were interested in philosophy, but especially in music and mathematics, which they believed were two ways of making order out of chaos. Nichomachus of Gerasa was a Pythagorean of the first and second centuries. His ideas about arithmetic built upon Pythagoras's ideas of the harmonic sounds of the motions of the planets and the proportional relationships of numbers.

What is Euclid's *Elements*?

Euclid's *Elements* is a series of 13 geometry and mathematics books written by the Greek mathematician Euclid in Alexandria about 300 B.C.E. It is a collection of definitions, postulates (axioms), theorems, and mathematical proofs of the propositions. The 13 books cover Euclidean geometry and the ancient Greek version of elementary number theory. Along with the Greek mathematician Autolycus's *On the Moving Sphere,* the *Elements* is one of the oldest Greek mathematical treatises to have survived, and is the world's oldest continuously used math textbook. Historians do not know a lot about Euclid's life, but his work has proven important to the development of logic and modern science. Most of the theorems in the *Elements* were not discovered by Euclid himself, but were the work of earlier Greek mathematicians such as Pythagoras, Hippocrates of Chios, Theaetetus of Athens, and Eudoxus of Cnidos. However, Euclid is credited with arranging these theorems in a logical manner.

What is a **"perfect" number**?

Approximately 2,500 years ago the Pythagoreans defined a "perfect" number as one for whom the sum of its divisors, excluding itself, equals the number itself. For example, 6 can be divided by 1, 2, 3, and 6. If you add these numbers together, excluding 6 itself, the total is 6. Therefore 6 is a perfect number. Over the centuries, many mathematicians from all over the world have contributed to finding and defining perfect numbers.

Why is the **number 10** important?

One reason is that the metric system is based on the number 10. The metric system emerged in the late eighteenth century out of a need to bring standardization to measurement. But 10 was important before the metric system. For example, Nichomachus of Gerasa, a second-century mathematician from Judea, considered

How long will it take me to count to one billion?

Probably longer than your lifetime. Most of the numbers between one and one billion are long and challenging to pronounce. When you start counting the larger numbers like 482,051,341, you will likely start to slow down. If you allow just three seconds to say each number, which is probably faster than most people can count, and you take no breaks at all, it will take you three billion seconds to finish counting. How many years is that? More than 95 years! Here's how you arrive at that figure: three billion seconds divided by 60 (seconds per minute) = 50,000,000 minutes; 50,000,000 minutes divided by 60 (minutes per hour) = 833,333.333 hours; 833,333.333 hours divided by 24 (hours per day) = 34,722.22 days; 34,722.22 days divided by 365 (days per year) = 95.1 years.

10 a perfect number, the figure of divinity present in creation with humankind's fingers and toes. Pythagoreans believed 10 to be "the first-born of the numbers, the mother of them all, the one that never wavers and gives the key to all things." And shepherds of West Africa counted sheep in their flocks by colored shells based on 10, and 10 had evolved as a "base" of most numbering schemes. Some historians believe the reason 10 developed as a base number had more to do with ease: 10 is easily counted on figures and the rules of addition, subtraction, multiplication, and division for the number 10 are easily memorized.

What is so **special** about the **number 2**?

The number 2 is called the "oddest" even prime number. 2 is a unique even prime number because all even numbers are divisible by 2. But any number apart from 2 that is divisible by 2 is not a prime number.

What are **Roman numerals**?

Roman numerals are symbols that stand for numbers. They are written using seven basic symbols: I (1), V (5), X (10), L (50), C (100), D (500), and M (1,000). Sometimes a bar is placed over a numeral to multiply it by 1,000. A smaller numeral appearing before a larger numeral indicates that the smaller numeral is subtracted from the larger one. This notation is generally used for 4s and 9s; for example, 4 is written IV, 9 is IX, 40 is XL, and 90 is XC.

Roman numerals were developed around 500 B.C.E. at least partially from primitive Greek alphabet symbols that were not incorporated into Latin. Using mainly addition, they are read from left to right. Historians believe the long usage of Roman numerals is due to a number of factors, including the widespread influence of the Roman Empire, tradition, and the fact that the system had many advantages over other European systems of the time. For example, the majority of users had to memorize only a few symbols and their values. You can see Roman numerals every-

The abacus can be thought of as an old-fashioned adding machine. It uses beads to represent numbers that can be added and subtracted by moving them back and forth along columns.

where today—in the appendices in books, in the credits of feature films, on building faces for dates, and on watches and clocks.

What is an **abacus**, and how long has it been used?

An abacus, also called a counting frame, is a calculating tool used for mathematical problems. Abaci are often constructed as a wooden frame with beads sliding on wires, but originally they were beans or stones moved in grooves in sand or on tablets of wood, stone, or metal. These early abaci were documented in Mesopotamia around 3500 B.C.E. The modern form, with beads sliding on rods, dates back to at least fifteenth-century China. Before the use of decimal number systems, which allowed the familiar pencil-and-paper methods of calculation, the abacus was used for almost all multiplication and division. The abacus is still used in many countries where modern calculators are not available. It is also widely used in Japan and China, both of which have long traditions of abacus use.

Is **zero** a number?

Yes. 0 (zero) is both a number and the numerical digit used to represent that number in numerals. The idea to use zero as a number was probably not recognized until the early centuries C.E., when the Hindus and Arabs tried to solve mathematical equations and organized a systematic study of the properties of operations on numbers. In about 850 C.E. Mahavir, a Hindu mathematician, wrote in his book *The Compendium of Calculation*: "A number multiplied by zero is zero, and that number remains unchanged which is divided by, added to, or diminished by zero." Today's mathematicians agree with most of what this ancient thinker wrote. We can add or subtract zero to a number and get back that number. When we multiply a number by zero the answer is zero. However, division by zero is undefined.

Why is **learning math** important?

Galileo once said, "The great book of nature can be read only by those who know the language in which it was written. And that language is mathematics." Math is one way we understand the world around us. Math is the most widely used subject in the world, and every career—from retail work to rocket science—uses some sort of math. More importantly, doing math helps the mind to reason and organize complicated situations or problems into clear, simple, and logical steps. Thus, as students learn more math, they become critical thinkers and problem solvers

For some, learning math is fun, while other kids might not enjoy it so much. Still, math is used in everyday life and is important for everyone to learn.

that can resolve difficult situations in everyday life. Taking math is important if you are considering attending a college, university, or technical school—nationwide studies have found that students who take algebra and geometry in high school have about an 80 percent chance of attending college regardless of race, religion, and family income.

What is a **googol**?

A googol is a very large number: the number 1 followed by 100 zeros, or 10^{100}. Unlike most other names for numbers, it does not relate to any other numbering scale. The American mathematician Edward Kasner first used the term in 1938; when searching for a term for this large number, Kasner asked his nephew, Milton Sirotta, then about nine years old, to suggest a name. The googolplex is 10 followed by a googol of zeros. The popular Web search engine Google.com is named after the concept of a googol.

Is it possible to **count to infinity**?

No. Very large finite numbers are not the same as infinite numbers. Infinite numbers are defined as being unbounded, or without boundaries or limits. Any number that can be reached by counting or by representation of a number followed by billions of zeros is a finite number.

WEIGHTS AND MEASURES

How are **measuring units** related to the **human body**?

In all traditional measuring systems, short-distance units are based on the dimensions of the adult human body. The inch represents the width of a thumb; in fact, in many languages, the word for "inch" is also the word for "thumb." The foot (12 inches) was originally the length of a human foot, although today it is longer than most people's feet. The yard (3 feet) is the name of a 3-foot measuring stick in England, but it is also approximately the distance from the tip of the nose to the end of the middle finger of the outstretched hand. Finally, if you ask an adult to stretch their arms out to the sides as far as possible, their total "arm span," from one fingertip to the other, is called a fathom (6 feet).

Other early measures were derived from physical activity, such as a pace, a league (the distances that equaled an hour's walking), an acre (the amount of land plowed in a day), a furlong (the length of a plowed ditch). The ell, based on the distance between the elbow and the index finger, was used to measure out cloth. It ranged from 20 to 91 inches (0.513 to 2.322 meters) depending upon where it was used and the type of goods measured.

What is a **cubit**?

In ancient Egypt and Mesopotamia, the basic unit of length was the cubit, based on a forearm measured from the elbow to the tip of the outstretched middle finger. Indeed, the word cubit comes from the Latin word *cubitum,* meaning "elbow." This distance is approximately 18 inches (roughly 45 centimeters). In ancient times, the cubit was usually defined as equal to 24 digits or 6 palms. The Egyptian "royal" or "long" cubit, however, was equal to 28 digits or 7 palms.

How were **stones** used as weights and measures?

Babylonians made important improvements upon the invention of weights and balance using stones. Instead of just comparing the weights of two objects, they compared the weight of each object with a set of stones kept just for that purpose. In the ruins of their cities, archaeologists have found some of these stones finely shaped and polished. It is believed that these were the world's first weight standards. The Babylonians used different stones for weighing different items. In modern English history, the same basis has been used for weight measurements. For the horseman, the stone weight was 14 pounds (6 kilograms). In weighing wool the stone weight was 16 pounds (7.3 kilograms). For the butcher and fisherman, the stone weight was 8 pounds (3.6 kilograms). The only legal stone weight in the king's legal system was 14 pounds.

Is a **mile** the **same distance** on **land and at sea**?

No. A mile on the ocean and a mile on land are not the same distance. On the ocean, a mile is called a nautical mile and measures 6,076 feet (1,852 meters). A land mile

How can you know that the pound used to weigh your apples is the same whether you are in New York City or Los Angeles?

The weights and measures officials in each U.S. state use standards that are checked against the national standards in Washington, D.C. The standards are kept at the National Institute of Standards and Technology (NIST), an agency of the U.S. Department of Commerce. The NIST (previously known as the National Bureau of Standards between 1901 and 1988) was established by Congress as the central measurement laboratory of the federal government. So no matter where you are in the United States, 16 ounces will always equal 1 pound; 8 fluid ounces will always equal 1 cup; 2 cups will always equal 1 pint; 2 pints will always equal 1 quart; and 4 quarts will always equal 1 gallon.

(or statute mile) is 5,280 feet (1,609 meters). Queen Elizabeth I of England established the statute mile. This measure, based on walking distance, originated with the Romans, who designated 1,000 paces as a land mile.

How are **carats** and **carob seeds** related?

The weight of a carat (200 milligrams), the standard unit of measurement for gemstones, is based on the weight of the carob seed, which was once used as a weighing standard by jewelers in Africa and the Middle East. Historians believe the word "carat" is derived from an Arabic word meaning "bean" or "seed."

How can **U.S. money** be used to **measure items** around the house?

All U.S. paper currency is 6 1/8 inches wide by 2 5/8 inches long. The diameter of a quarter is approximately one inch. The diameter of a penny is approximately three-quarters of an inch. So if you want to measure the length of your pencil, simply line up some coins and begin measuring!

What is an **acre** used to measure?

An acre is a unit of area used for measuring real estate. The word "acre" is an Old English word meaning "a field." The acre was originally defined as the area that could be plowed in a day by a yoke of oxen. An acre is 43,560 square feet (4,840 square yards). There are exactly 640 acres in a square mile.

What is a **cord** used to measure?

A cord is a traditional unit of volume used to measure stacked firewood. In the United States, the cord is defined legally as the volume of a stack of firewood 4 feet (1.2 meter) wide, 8 feet (2.4 meter) long, and 4 feet (1.2 meter) high. (In Maryland, the law specifies that the wood be stacked "tight enough that a chipmunk cannot run through it.") The name comes from an old method of measuring a stack of firewood using a cord or string. In the U.S. timber industry, the cord is also used as a unit of weight for pulpwood. The weight varies with tree species, ranging from about 5,200 pounds (2,358 kilograms) for pine to about 5,800 pounds for hardwood.

How is a **baker's dozen** different from a standard dozen?

A dozen is a unit of quantity, equal to 12. A baker's dozen is an informal unit of quantity, equal to 13. Bakers often toss in an extra item for each dozen bought, making a total of 13. This custom is very old, dating at least from the thirteenth century, when the weights and prices of loaves of bread were strictly regulated by royal proclamations called assizes, and bakers could be jailed if they failed to provide fair weight at the listed prices.

Are the terms **"gnat's eye"** and **"hair's breadth"** true units of measure?

Yes, but both are slang units of distance and diameter. The eyes of typical gnats tend to have diameters similar in size to a hair's breadth—roughly 100–150 micrometers. An item would have to be *very short* in order to be gnat's eye in length! A hair's breadth is an informal unit of distance: it is used to denote a measurement of approximately 70 to 100 micrometers in diameter, or 0.1 millimeter, which is similar in thickness to real human hair.

What is **horsepower**?

Horsepower is a unit of power representing the power exerted by a horse when it pulls an object. James Watt, the inventor of the steam engine, defined the term horsepower after determining through careful measurements that a horse is typically capable of a power rate of 550 foot-pounds per second. This means that a horse, harnessed to an appropriate machine, such as a plough or wagon, can lift 550 pounds at the rate of one foot per second. Today the standard unit of power is named for Watt, and one horsepower is equal to approximately 745.6999 watts. Outside the United States, the English word "horsepower" is often used to mean the metric horsepower, a slightly smaller unit.

What is the **metric system**?

The metric system is a decimalized system of measurement. Designed during the French Revolution of the 1790s, the metric system brought order out of the conflicting and confusing traditional systems of weights and measures that were being used in Europe at the time. Prior to the introduction of the metric system, it was common for units of length, land area, and weight to vary, not just from one country to another but from one region to another within the same country. As the modern nations gradually developed from smaller kingdoms and principalities, confusion multiplied. Length, for example, could be measured in feet, inches, miles, spans, cubits, hands, furlongs, palms, rods, chains, and leagues. Merchants, scientists, and educated people throughout Europe realized that a uniform system was needed, and in 1790 the French National Assembly commissioned the Academy of

Science to design a simple decimal-based system of units.

The horsepower number used to describe engine power literally relates to the strength of an average horse. The man in this picture is using a four-horsepower plow!

The three most common base units in the metric system are the meter, gram, and liter. The meter is a unit of length equal to 3.28 feet; the gram is a unit of mass equal to approximately 0.0022 pounds (about the mass of a paper clip); and the liter is a unit of volume equal to 1.05 quarts. Temperature is expressed in degrees Celsius; 0 degrees Celsius equals 32 degrees Fahrenheit.

Why is the **metric system** called a **decimal-based system**?

The metric system is a called a decimal-based system because it is based on multiples of 10. Any measurement given in one metric unit (such as a kilogram) can be converted to another metric unit (such as a gram) simply by moving the decimal place. For example, if your father told you he weighed 82,500.0 grams (181.8 pounds), you can convert this to kilograms simply by moving the decimal three places to the left; in other words, your father weighs 82.5 kilograms.

How big is a **hectare**?

The hectare (abbreviated ha) is a unit of area equal to 10,000 square meters and used exclusively for measuring land. To get a sense of how big this is, imagine a football field. A football field is almost exactly 100 meters from one end line to the opposite goal line. Imagine a square of that length on each side, and you've got an area of one hectare. There are 100 hectares in one square kilometer, so one square kilometer is the same area as a square that is ten football fields on one side.

Which countries of the world have **not formally begun converting** to the **metric system**?

In 1960, the metric system was officially named the Système International d'Unités (or SI) and is now used in nearly every country in the world except the United

Which is heavier, a pound of gold or a pound a feathers?

A pound of feathers is heavier than a pound of gold because gold is measured in troy pounds, while feathers are measured in avoirdupois pounds. Troy pounds are made of 12 ounces and avoirdupois pounds have 16 ounces. A troy pound contains 372 grams in the metric system, and an avoirdupois pound contains 454 grams.

States, Burma (also known as Myanmar, in Southeast Asia), and Liberia. As early as 1790, Thomas Jefferson, then the U.S. secretary of state, proposed adoption of the metric system. It was not implemented because Great Britain, America's major trading source had not yet begun to use the system.

What is the difference between **avoirdupois** measurements and **troy measurements**?

Troy weight is a system of mass units used primarily to measure gold and silver. A troy ounce is 480 grains, or 31.1 grams. Avoirdupois (pronounced AV-er-deh-POIZ) weight is a system of units that is used to measure mass, except for precious metals. It is based on the pound, which is approximately 454 grams. In both systems, the weight of a grain is the same: 65 milligrams.

CALENDARS AND TELLING TIME

How did **ancient civilizations** develop **calendars**, or ways for tracking days, months, and years?

Celestial bodies, such as the Sun, Moon, planets, and stars, provided peoples of ancient civilizations a reference for measuring the passage of time. Ancient civilizations relied upon the apparent motion of these bodies through the sky to determine seasons, months, and years. Historians know little about the details of timekeeping in prehistoric eras, but wherever archaeologists dig up records and artifacts, they usually discover that in every culture some people were preoccupied with measuring and recording the passage of time. Ice-age hunters in Europe over 20,000 years ago scratched lines and gouged holes in sticks and bones, possibly counting the days between phases of the Moon. Five thousand years ago, Sumerians in the Tigris-Euphrates valley (in present-day Iraq) developed a calendar that divided the year into 30-day months, divided the day into 12 periods (each corresponding to two of our hours), and divided these periods into 30 parts (each like four of our minutes). Historians have no written records of Stonehenge, built over 4,000 years ago in

England, but its alignments show one of its reasons for existence was to determine seasonal or celestial events, such as lunar eclipses and solstices.

Was one of the early **Egyptian calendars** a 365-day calendar?

Yes. The earliest Egyptian calendar was based on the Moon's cycles, but later the Egyptians realized that the "Dog Star" in Canis Major (which today's astronomers call Sirius), rose next to the Sun every 365 days, about when the annual inundation of the Nile began. Based on this knowledge, they devised a 365-day calendar that seems to have begun around 3100 B.C.E., which thus seems to be one of the earliest years recorded in history.

The Mayans, who once had a thriving civilization in Central America, developed a sophisticated calendar for tracking time.

Before 2000 B.C.E., the Babylonians (in today's Iraq) used a year of 12 alternating 29-day and 30-day lunar months, giving a 354-day year. In contrast, the Mayans of Central America relied not only on the Sun and Moon, but also the planet Venus, to establish 260-day and 365-day calendars. This culture and its related predecessors spread across Central America between 2600 B.C.E. and 1500 C.E., reaching their apex between 250 and 900 C.E. They left celestial-cycle records indicating their belief that the creation of the world occurred in 3114 B.C.E. Their calendars later became portions of the great Aztec calendar stones.

What is the **basis** for **modern timekeeping**?

Modern society has adopted a 365-day solar calendar with a leap year occurring every fourth year (except century years not evenly divisible by 400). The modern clock is based on the number 60. In about 3000 B.C.E. the Sumerians used a base 10 counting system and also a base 60 counting system. The timekeeping system inherited this pattern with 60 seconds per minute and 60 minutes per hour. Ten and 60 fit together to form the notion of time: 10 hours is 600 minutes; 10 minutes is 600 seconds; 1 minute is 60 seconds.

How **long** is each **year**?

Each calendar year is exactly 365 days, 5 hours, 48 minutes, and 46 seconds. This is the amount of time between two successive crossings of the celestial equator by the Sun at the vernal equinox (the first day of spring). The fact that the year is not a whole number of days has affected the development of calendars, which over time generate an error. The current calendar we use, called the Gregorian calendar, attempts to fix this by adding an extra day to the month of February every four years. These years are called "leap years."

When and why were **leap years** introduced?

The use of a 365-day calendar year with occasional leap years was introduced in 46 B.C.E. with the Julian calendar. The Julian calendar was formed by Julius Caesar, who had commissioned the Alexandrian astronomer Sosigenes to revise the calendar system. Sosigenes used a tropical solar year, which calculates to 365.25 days per year. This was slightly off, because the actual tropical solar year is 365.242199 days. This discrepancy caused there to be 10 days missing by the year 1582. That year, Pope Gregory XIII issued a papal bull (decree) to fix the Julian calendar. The Jesuit astronomer Christoph Clavius undertook the Pope's decree and designed what is now known as the Gregorian calendar. In order to correct for the loss of one day every 130 years, the Gregorian calendar drops 3 leap years every 400 years. According to this system, years are leap years only if divisible by 400—thus, 1600 and 2000 are leap years; 1700, 1800, and 1900 are not. Because the solar year is shortening, today a one-second adjustment—called a leap second—is made (usually on December 31 at midnight) when necessary to compensate.

When was the last **leap second** added, and why?

Scientists added an extra second—called a leap second—to 2008 to make up for the slowing down of Earth's rotation. The International Earth Rotation and Reference Systems Service (IERS) in Paris, France, keeps track of time by measuring Earth's rotation, which has been slowing down over time, and by an atomic clock, which never changes. When a difference in the two clocks shows up, the IERS adds or subtracts a second to the year. Time has been measured by the planet's rotation for thousands of years; however, it was not until 1949 that scientists developed a clock that kept perfect time. The IERS atomic clock keeps time by viewing the fundamental vibrations of atoms. As far as scientists know, the cesium atom—which vibrates 9,192,631,770 times per second—does not change over time and is the same everywhere on Earth and in space.

What is the **Chinese lunar calendar**?

The Chinese lunar calendar is based on the cycles of the Moon, and is constructed in a different fashion than the Western solar calendar. In the Chinese calendar, the beginning of the year falls somewhere between late January and early February, and contains 354 days. Each year is given an animal designation, such as "Year of the Ox." A total of 12 different animal names are used, and they rotate in the following sequence: Rat, Ox, Tiger, Hare (Rabbit), Dragon, Snake, Horse, Sheep (Goat), Monkey, Rooster, Dog, and Pig. The Chinese have adopted the Western calendar since 1911, but the lunar calendar is still used for festive occasions such as the Chinese New Year. Many Chinese calendars print both the solar dates and the Chinese lunar dates.

What is the difference between B.C. and A.D.?

The term B.C. stands for "Before Christ," and is used to date events before the birth of Jesus Christ. A.D. is the abbreviation for the Latin phrase *anno domini*, which means "in the year of our Lord," and is used to date events after Jesus's birth. This system of dating has been used for many years by Western archaeologists. Today, however, with a growing understanding that not all archaeologists are Christians, some archaeologists prefer to use the terms B.C.E. (meaning Before the Common Era) and C.E. (meaning Common Era). These terms are exactly the same as B.C. and A.D., but are not related to Christianity.

What is the difference between a **millennium** and a **century**?

A millennium is an interval of 1,000 years. A century is 100 consecutive calendar years. The first century consisted of years 1 through 100. The twentieth century started with 1901 and ended with 2000. The twenty-first century began on January 1, 2001.

How are the **months** of the year **named**?

The origins of our calendar came from the old Roman practice of starting each month on a new moon. Roman bookkeepers would keep their records in a ledger called a *kalendarium,* from which comes the English word "calendar." The original Roman calendar was 304 days long and had 10 months that began with March and ended with December. The Roman political leader Julius Caesar reorganized the calendar year to start with the month of January. Thus, the first month was named for Janus, the Roman god of beginnings and endings. February was named for the god

of purification, Februus. March was named for Mars, the Roman god of war. April comes from the Roman word *aperire,* meaning "to open"; this is the month when the trees and flower buds open. May is named for Maiesta (Maia), the Roman goddess of honor and reverence. June is named for Juno, the Roman queen of the gods. July is named after Caesar himself, who was born in this month, and August is named for Augustus, the Roman emperor. And the last four months of the year have numerical meanings: September comes from the word *septem,* meaning "seven"; October from the word "octo," meaning "eight"; November from the word *novem,* meaning "nine"; and December from the word *decem,* meaning "ten."

The Roman emperor Julius Caesar was responsible for reorganizing the Western calendar so that years began with the month of January.

How are the **days of the week named**?

The English days of the week are named after a mixture of figures in Roman and

Anglo-Saxon mythology. The English language has inherited and changed those names a bit, but the ones we use today resemble those names. For example, Sunday is named after the Sun, and it was originally called "Sun's Day." The Sun gave people light and warmth every day. Monday is named after the Moon, and it was originally called "Moon's Day." The Moon was considered very important in the lives of people and their crops. Tuesday was Tiw's Day. Tiw (sometimes spelled Tiu or Tyr) was a Norse god known for his sense of justice. Wednesday was Woden's Day; Woden (or Odin) was a powerful Norse god. Thursday was Thor's Day, named for Thor, the Norse god of thunder. Friday was Frigg's Day, named for Frigg, the Norse god of love and fertility. Saturday was Seater's Day (or Saturn's Day); Saturn was the Roman god of agriculture.

Is there a **simple rhyme** to help **recall how many days** are in each **month**?

Yes. Many children learn this simple poem to help them remember how many days are in each month. Although the origin of the lyrics to "Thirty Days Hath September" is unclear, the use of old English dates this poem to at least the sixteenth century:

> Thirty days hath September,
> April, June and November
> All the rest have thirty-one,
> excepting only February
> Which hath but twenty eight-days clear
> And twenty-nine in each leap year.

What is the **International Date Line**?

Located at 0 degrees longitude, the prime meridian passes through Greenwich, England. Halfway around the world in the middle of the Pacific Ocean (180 degrees from Greenwich) is the International Date Line (IDL), where the date changes across the boundary of the time zone. The entire world is on the same date only at the instant when it is noon in Greenwich, England, and midnight at the IDL. At all other times, there are different dates on each side of the IDL.

When and why were **time zones established**?

Earth is divided into 24 time zones so that everyone in the world can be on roughly similar schedules. Until about 100 years ago, each city set its clocks to local time. Noon was the time when the Sun was at its highest in the sky, as viewed from that city. In order to make this happen, however, even neighboring cities needed to set their clocks differently. For example, when it was 8:00 in New York City, it was 8:12 in Boston (because Boston is about three degrees east of New York). Before modern transportation and communication, this time difference did not really affect society. As railroads were being constructed in the late 1800s, however, the Canadian railway planner and engineer Sir Sandford Fleming proposed a world time zone system. He did this so that train schedules could be written using common time settings. In November 1883 the U.S. and Canadian railroad companies instituted standard time in time zones. (Standard time in time zones was established by U.S. law with the Standard Time Act of 1918.) The concept was soon adopted internationally, with the world being divided into 24 time zones, each one a long strip from North Pole to South Pole, about 15 degrees of longitude wide. All the people in one time zone set their clock the same way, to the local time in the center of the time zone. Today, most countries use this time zone system.

When do the **seasons officially start**?

There are four traditional seasons on Earth—spring, summer, fall (or autumn), and winter—and each is marked by the movement of the Sun in the sky. In the Northern Hemisphere, spring starts at the moment the Sun is directly over the equator, going from south to north, called the vernal equinox. Summer starts the moment the Sun is farthest north, called the summer solstice. Fall begins the moment when the Sun is directly over the equator, going from north to south, called autumnal equinox. Winter starts the moment the Sun is farthest south, called the winter solstice.

What is **Daylight Saving Time**?

Sometimes called "fast time" or "summer time," Daylight Saving Time (DST) temporarily extends the length of daylight because we move our clocks forward an hour in the spring, creating longer days. In the United States, we change our clocks in March. Most of the United States begins Daylight Saving Time at 2:00 A.M. on the sec-

ond Sunday in March and reverts to standard time on the first Sunday in November (when we set our clocks back one hour). In the United States, each time zone switches at a different time. Different countries have different change dates. Although DST was first proposed by Benjamin Franklin in 1784, it began in the United States during World War I, primarily to save fuel by reducing the need to use artificial lighting. Although some states and communities observed DST between the wars, it was not observed nationally again until World War II. Today, most Americans continue to participate in DST to save energy, although Arizona and Hawaii are the two states that are exceptions to the rule.

What is a **sundial** and how does it work?

The sundial, one of the first instruments used to measure time, works by

Sundials tell time by casting a shadow on a base plate marked with the different hours of the day.

193

simulating the movements of the Sun. The Sun shines on a gnomon (pronounced NO-men), a triangle or device set perpendicular to a base plate, and casts its shadow on the appropriate hour line, thus displaying the time of day. The angle on the gnomon has to be parallel to the Earth's axis and must be equal to your location's latitude if it is to display accurate clock time.

What is a **water clock**?

Water clocks were among the earliest timekeepers that didn't depend on the observation of celestial bodies. One of the oldest was found in the tomb of the Egyptian pharaoh Amenhotep I, buried around 1500 B.C.E. Later named clepsydras ("water thieves") by the Greeks, who began using them about 325 B.C.E., these were stone vessels with sloping sides that allowed water to drip at a nearly constant rate from a small hole near the bottom. Other clepsydras were cylindrical or bowl-shaped containers designed to slowly fill with water coming in at a constant rate. Markings on the inside surfaces measured the passage of "hours" as the water level reached them. These clocks were used to determine hours at night, but may have been used in daylight as well. Another version consisted of a metal bowl with a hole in the bottom; when placed in a container of water the bowl would fill and sink in a certain time. These were still in use in North Africa in the twentieth century.

When and how did the **first modern clocks** develop?

In Europe during most of the Middle Ages (roughly 500 to 1500 C.E.), simple sundials placed above doorways were used to identify midday and four "tides" (important times or periods) of the sunlit day. By the tenth century, several types of pocket sundials were used. One English model even compensated for seasonal changes of the Sun's altitude. Then, in the first half of the fourteenth century, large mechanical clocks began to appear in the towers of several large Italian cities. Historians do not have any evidence or record of the working models that preceded these public clocks, which were weight-driven. Another advance was the invention of spring-powered clocks between 1500 and 1510 by Peter Henlein of Nuremberg. Replacing the heavy drive weights permitted smaller, portable, clocks and watches. Although they ran slower as the mainspring unwound, they were popular among wealthy individuals due to their small size and the fact that they could be put on a shelf or table instead of hanging on the wall or being housed in tall cases. These advances in design were precursors to truly accurate timekeeping.

What is a **grandfather clock**?

A grandfather clock, also called a long case clock or floor clock, is a freestanding, weight-driven, pendulum clock. Its pendulum, which swings back and forth, is kept inside its tower. Clocks of this style are commonly 6 to 8 feet (1.8 to 2.4 meters) tall. The case often features carved ornamentation on the hood, called a bonnet, which surrounds and frames the dial, or clock face. These clocks have a long history. In 1582 the Italian astronomer Galileo Galilei discovered that a pendulum could be used to keep time. He studied pendulum clocks, and drew the first designs for a grandfather clock. In 1656 the Dutch mathematician Christiaan Huygens applied what Galileo had discovered and built the first working grandfather clock (he also patented a pocket watch in 1675.) The first grandfather clocks did not keep time well, often losing as much as 12 minutes a day. In 1670 the English clockmaker William Clement noticed that by making the pendulum in the clock longer he could make the clock keep better time. His longer pendulums required longer cases, which led to the name "long case" clock, and later grandfather clock. Most grandfather clocks are "striking" clocks, which means they sound the time on each hour.

When was the **wristwatch invented**?

The wristwatch, today the most common watch available, was first manufactured by the Swiss watch manufacturer Patek Philippe in 1868. During World War I, military personnel found that the wristwatch was far more beneficial on the battlefield than the day's popular pocket watches. Soldiers fitted their watches into primitive "cupped" leather straps so they could be worn on the wrist, thereby freeing up their hands to operate weaponry. It is believed that the Swiss watchmaker Girard-Perregaux equipped the German Imperial Navy with similar pieces as early as the 1880s, which they wore on their wrists while synchronizing naval attacks. Many European and American officers kept their wristwatches once the war was over, thus popularizing wristwatches in America and Europe. In 1926, the Swiss watch manufacturer Rolex patented the first waterproof and dustproof wristwatch, the Oyster.

Who invented the **alarm clock**?

The clockmaker Levi Hutchins of Concord, New Hampshire, invented an alarm clock in 1787. His alarm clock rang at only one time—4:00 A.M. He invented his device so that he would never sleep past his usual waking time. It was his "firm rule" to awaken before sunrise, whatever the season. But sometimes he slept past that hour, and was distraught the rest of the day. Although he lived to the age of 94, Hutchins never patented or manufactured his clock. He wrote about his clock: "It was the idea of a clock that could sound an alarm that was difficult, not the execution of the idea. It was simplicity itself to arrange for the bell to sound at the predetermined hour." The French inventor Antoine Redier was the first person to patent an adjustable mechanical alarm

Alarm clocks are a pain when we want to sleep. You can thank eighteenth-century American clockmaker Levi Hutchins for waking you up.

195

What is a jiffy?

A jiffy is a unit of time—about 1/100 of a second. A jiffy is often used in chemistry and physics to discuss time equal to a "light centimeter," that is, the time required for light to travel a distance of one centimeter. The definition of the jiffy was proposed by the early-twentieth-century American physical chemist Gilbert N. Lewis, who was one of the first scientists to apply principles of quantum physics in chemistry.

clock, in 1847. In 1876, a small mechanical wind-up clock patented in the United States by Seth E. Thomas was the most inspirational of those invented in this era—soon all the major U.S. clockmakers were making small alarm clocks and the German clockmakers soon followed. The electric alarm clock was invented around 1890.

What do A.M. and P.M. stand for?

The initials A.M. stand for *ante meridian,* which is Latin for "before noon." The initials P.M. stand for *post meridian,* which is Latin for "after noon."

How long is a **fortnight**?

The word fortnight is a unit of time that equals fourteen days. It comes from the Old English word *feorwertyne niht,* meaning "fourteen nights." The term is used in Great Britain, where salaries and most social security benefits are paid on a fortnightly basis, but in the United States people use the term "two weeks." In many languages, there is no single word for a two-week period and the equivalent of "fourteen days" has to be used. In Spanish, Italian, French, and Portuguese, the terms *quince días, quindicina, quinzaine,* and *quinzena*—all meaning "fifteen days"—are used.

ALL ABOUT MY BODY

BONES AND JOINTS

How **many bones** are there in the **human body**?

Babies are born with about 300 to 350 bones, but many of these fuse together between birth and maturity to produce an average adult total of 206. Bone counts vary according to the method used to count them, because a structure may be treated as either multiple bones or as a single bone with multiple parts. There are four major types of bones: long bones, short bones, flat bones, and irregular bones. The name of each type of bone reflects the shape of the bone. The shape of the bone also tells about its mechanical function. Bones that do not fall into any of these categories are sesamoid bones and accessory bones.

How do **bones grow**?

Bones are made of a network of calcium laid down by cells. As children grow, special cells at the end of bones add new calcium to the network of bone. Children have layers of these cells in the shape of plates at the ends of their bones. These are called "growth plates," and they close up when kids reach their full adult height. To grow in a healthy way, bones need protein, calcium, and other minerals. In addition, bones need the hormones that increase at puberty, including estrogen and testosterone. Bones also need vitamin D, to help absorb calcium, and regular exercise to keep bones strong.

Are **bones hard** as a rock?

Yes and no. Bones are hard connective tissue, made up of bone cells, fat cells, and blood vessels, as well as nonliving materials, including water and minerals. Some bones have a very hard, heavy outer layer made out of compact bone. Under this

197

layer is a lighter layer called spongy bone, which is located inside the end, or head, of a long bone. Spongy bone is tough and hard, but light, because it has lots of irregularly-shaped sheets and spikes of bone (called trabeculae) that make it porous (full of tiny holes). The soft, jelly-like inner core of bone is called the bone marrow. It is where red blood cells, certain white blood cells, and blood platelets are formed. The jawbone is the hardest bone in your body. Although bones are hard, they are not the hardest substance in the human body: the enamel on your teeth is harder.

Which are the **biggest** and **smallest bones**?

The femur, or thighbone, is the biggest bone in the body. The average femur is 18 inches (45.72 centimeters) long. The longest bone ever recorded was 29.9 inches (75.95 centimeters) long. It was from an 8-foot-tall (2.45 meters) German who died in 1902 in Belgium. The stirrup (also called the stapes) in the middle ear is the smallest bone in the body. A tiny, U-shaped bone that passes vibrations from the stirrup to the cochlea, it weighs about 0.0004 ounces (0.011 grams) and can measure just one-tenth of an inch.

Where is my **rib cage**?

The ribs are thin, flat, curved bones in your upper body that form a protective "cage" around the heart and lungs. The ribs are comprised of 24 bones arranged in 12 pairs that form a kind of cage that encloses the upper body and gives the chest its familiar shape. The ribs serve several important functions. They protect the heart and lungs from injuries and shocks that might damage them. Ribs also protect parts of the stomach, spleen, and kidneys. The ribs help you to breathe. As you inhale, the muscles in between the ribs lift the rib cage up, allowing the lungs to expand. When you exhale, the rib cage moves down again, squeezing the air out of your lungs.

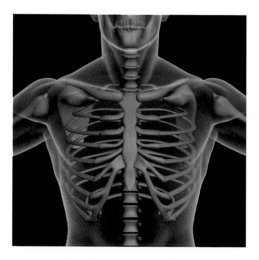

The "rib cage" includes the curved ribs in your chest that protect vital organs like the heart and lungs.

Where is my **spine**?

Your spine, also called the backbone, runs down the length of your back from the base of your neck to your pelvis. The spine has 25 joints connecting 33 individual bones. (The bottom four bones of the spine are fused together to form the terminal vertebrae called the coccyx, or tailbone—and the five bones above that are fused together to form the sacrum. They are caged within the bones of the pelvis.) Each bone in the spine is called a vertebra and they are grouped together to perform specific tasks. The spine supports your head, lets you twist and bend, and holds your body upright. It

Is there such a thing as a funny bone?

The funny bone exists in your body, but it's not a bone at all! The funny bone is a part of the ulnar nerve located at the back of the elbow. If you accidentally bump this area it can cause a tingling sensation toward the front of your forearm. This tingling or dull pain is caused by the ulnar nerve bumping up against the humerus, the long bone that starts at your elbow and goes up to your shoulder. Although it might feel weird, tapping your funny bone doesn't do any damage to your elbow, arm, or ulnar nerve.

also protects the spinal cord, a large bundle of nerves that sends information from your brain to the rest of your body.

How is the **body able to bend**?

The human skeleton moves at its more than 230 joints, which are the places where bones connect. Those joints give you a basic range of motion. For example, everyone's shoulder joints can rotate 360 degrees, and elbows can open and close to just under a 180 degree arc. The pull of ligaments—ropelike connective tissues that anchor one bone to the next around a joint—lengthen a bit to allow a joint to move, but keep the range of motion limited so that you don't hurt yourself. So, the next time you are tempted to do a backbend or stretch your leg up to your ear, think of your joints and ligaments!

Why do my **knuckles** sometimes make a **cracking sound** if I bend them?

Knuckles—as well as your knees, back, and neck—sometimes make a popping or grinding sound thanks to the body's synovial fluid, which acts as a lubricant in your bone joints. This fluid contains the gases oxygen, nitrogen, and carbon dioxide. When you pop or crack a joint, the joint capsule is stretched, gas is rapidly released, and bubbles form. If you want to crack the same knuckle again, you have to wait until the gases return to the synovial fluid. Other sounds, like snapping or the plucking of a rubber band, sometimes happen when your ligaments temporarily slide off your bone as you move your joints.

MUSCLE POWER

What are **muscles made of**?

Our muscles, which make up about half of our body mass, control the way the body moves. Muscles work together all the time, whether we are actively playing sports, or quietly reading and writing. Muscles lie in bands just beneath the surface of the

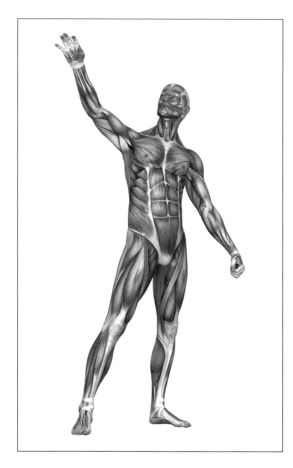

The human body contains about 660 different muscles that are used to move our bodies as well as control our organs.

skin. A muscle is made up of thousands of fibers bundled together within a protective sheath that consists of blood vessels and nerves. These nerves can be up to 12 inches (30 centimeters) long. A muscle becomes stronger when you work it, which is why people who regularly exercise have more defined muscle tone than those who do not exercise.

There are about 660 muscles in the human body. The three types of muscle tissue are skeletal, cardiac, and smooth. The main and most unique characteristic of muscle tissue is its ability to contract, or shorten, making some type of movement possible. Skeletal muscles hold the bones together, and are often called "voluntary" muscles because the brain controls them. The cardiac muscle, which is found only in the heart, contracts to send blood from the heart into the arteries. The brain sends signals to the cardiac muscle to speed up or slow down its contractions, called the heartbeat. Smooth muscles, located in the internal organs such as the stomach and intestines, help these organs or tissues do their job, such as help you digest and eliminate your food.

What's an **Achilles heel**?

Muscles are attached to bones by tendons, the longest and strongest of which is called the Achilles tendon in your heel. This thick band of tissue attaches the muscles of the calf to the heel bone and is the key to the foot's ability to flex. The Achilles tendon allows you to push off of your foot when walking or running. In ancient Greek myth, the hero Achilles died from a wound to his heel, so the popular expression "Achilles heel" often refers to a physical weakness or limitation.

Which **muscles** are the **largest**, and which ones are the **smallest**?

The largest muscle is the buttock muscle (gluteus maximus), which moves the thighbone away from the body and straightens out the hip joint. It is also one of the stronger muscles in the body. The smallest muscle is the stapedius, in the middle

> ## Is it easier for my face to laugh or frown?
>
> It is much easier to smile. Smiling takes about 17 facial muscles while you use 43 muscles to make a frown. Smiling also makes you feel happier!

ear. It is thinner than a thread and 0.05 inches (0.127 centimeters) in length. It activates the stirrup that sends vibrations from the eardrum to the inner ear. The longest muscle is the sartorius, which runs from the waist to the knee. Its purpose is to flex the hip and knee.

What's a charley horse?

A charley horse a muscle cramp, or sudden, uncontrolled contraction of a muscle. This type of pain is generally felt in the legs, sometimes after heavy exercise, and usually lasts just a few minutes. The expression probably came from the word "charley," which is used to describe a horse that is lame.

What causes "growing pains"?

"Growing pains" usually refers to the aches and pains that children feel in their legs at night when they are lying in bed. Kids seem to get them during growth spurts, times when they are growing a lot. Doctors think that the tendons—the tough elastic straps, or bands, that attach muscles to bones—of affected children do not grow quite as fast as their bones do. The tendons eventually catch up, but in the meantime this condition puts muscles under extra stress during an active day and causes them to ache and even spasm (contract abnormally) when they are finally at rest at night. Growing pains are not dangerous. They don't bother children during the day, and they usually come and go at nighttime. Regular stretching exercises—keeping the muscles and tendons relaxed—often solve the problem for good. But if the pains are very bad and continue for a long time, a doctor should be seen. In rare cases, an infection, disease, injury, or unnoticed malformation of the legs is causing the problem.

MY BUILDING BLOCKS

How is the human body a living machine?

The human body is a complicated living machine in which various systems work together as a functioning whole. All the parts of the body—including hundreds of rock-hard bones and quarts of blood—are made up of cells, about 100 trillion (100,000,000,000,000) cells in all! Twenty-two internal organs—the large body parts like the heart, lungs, liver, and kidneys—perform special jobs and work together to form the different body systems. There are eight key systems in the body. The muscu-

Millions of sperm cells try to fertilize a single egg, but (usually) only one sperm will complete its mission.

lar system, made up of more than 600 muscles, enables our bodies to make all of their movements. The circulatory system carries oxygen-rich blood throughout the body. The skeletal system is made of the bones that form the skeleton and give the body its shape. People breathe using the respiratory system. The body's heat-control system is called the integumentary system, which is made up of skin, hair, nails, and sweat glands. The reproductive system creates new life. The nervous system processes information from both inside and outside the body and sends messages, via its nerves, to different parts of the body. And the digestive system helps us digest our food and nutrients and gives us energy to go through the day. There are other systems, too, that help the body sustain life, including the immune system, which fights off invading viruses and diseases, and the urinary system, which helps keep the inside of the body clean and eliminates waste. The endocrine system, made up of glands, sends hormones around the body to trigger growth and to control other activities. These body systems work together to keep all human beings alive and healthy.

How did my life begin?

All living things are made up of cells. They are so small that you need a microscope to see them. Your body contains trillions and trillions of cells. Each person begins life as a single fertilized cell. This single cell contains all the information needed for a new human being to grow and live. The information—coded chemical instructions known as genes—is found on 23 pairs of chromosomes in the nucleus, or control center, of the cell.

That special fertilized cell began with a single egg cell from your mother. Each month a woman releases a mature, or ripe, egg cell from reproductive organs called ovaries. This egg contains half the genes needed to create a new life. A man produces millions of sperm cells in reproductive organs called testes. Each sperm cell contains half the genes needed to create a new life. When a sperm cell from your father joined with and fertilized the released egg cell inside your mother's body, the cell that would become you was complete. It had all the coded instructions it needed to begin dividing and growing into a baby. Within a few hours, the fertilized cell split into two complete cells, each with a full set of genes inside. Before long the cells divided again. After five or six days a ball of hundreds of cells existed. The size of the head of a pin, this ball of cells attached to the lining of your mother's uterus, or womb, the reproductive organ in which babies grow. There, in the nourishing lining of the uterus, the cells continued to multiply. Gradually the cells began to specialize, turning into nerve cells, muscle cells, and so on. A tiny baby began to take shape.

As you grew, you received nutrients and oxygen from your mother's blood through a special tube that was attached to your abdomen called the umbilical cord. After 40 weeks (between nine and ten months), all of your organs and body systems were developed enough to work on their own, and you were ready to enter the world. Then you made your grand entrance and were born!

How do I grow?

Just as the tiny fertilized egg cell from which you began divided again and again to become a baby, the trillions of cells now making up your body continue to divide as you grow. The more cells you have, the bigger you become. Some cells divide to replace worn out cells and others divide to increase the size and change the shape of your body as you mature. Hormones—chemicals that are produced by glands and circulate in your blood—help direct the growth of cells in your body during the process of growing up. Usually people are fully grown by the time they reach the age of 20. By the time a person is 30, however, the rate at which body cells renew themselves begins to slow down, and signs of aging appear. As time goes on, certain body cells—like those of the brain and nerves—are not replaced when they wear out and die.

How big will I become?

Several different factors determine how big a person will grow. The most important one is heredity, the passing of physical traits from parents to children. When you began as a single fertilized cell, your mother and father each contributed half the genes—coded chemical information—needed for you to live and grow. These genes are responsible for your physical traits, like the color of your eyes and hair, how your body will be shaped, and how tall you will become. That is why children look a lot like their parents, or even their grandparents: they have inherited family characteristics that may have been passed on for several generations. If your parents are big or tall, chances are good that you will be big or tall, too. The average height of a

203

woman in the United States is about 5 feet, 4 inches (1.6 meters), and the average height for an American man is 5 feet, 9 inches (1.75 meters). In spite of genetic coding, certain conditions can keep people from growing as large as their genes say they should. Bad nutrition keeps a body from reaching its maximum size. Poor health and disease do the same. That is why people who lived in generations before us, when food was sometimes scarce and health care was poor, were quite a bit smaller than we are today. Taking good care of your body, then, helps it become the best it can be.

Why are **cells** called **building blocks**?

All living things are made up of cells, which are the basic units of life. The human body contains about 100 trillion cells, which live in our brain, bones, muscles, nerves, skin, and blood. Humans have about 200 different types of cells that come in different shapes and sizes, and each has a specific job to do in the human body. However, no matter what job they perform, all cells have a similar structure. Holding the cell together around its outside is the cell membrane. Openings in the membrane allow certain chemicals to travel in and out. The membrane is made up of a watery fluid called cytoplasm, which contains structures called organelles, specialized subunits that play specific roles in making the cell work. The nucleus is the cell's control center, which sends the organelles chemical instructions and which also contains chromosomes, the packaging for our genetic material, or DNA (deoxyribonucleic acid).

What is **DNA**?

DNA, or deoxyribonucleic acid, is a very important molecule found in all living cells. It contains information used in everyday metabolism and growth and influences most human characteristics, including the color of our skin, the color of our eyes, and whether we have curly or straight hair. DNA is often called the blueprint of an organism because it enables various cells to develop and work together to form a fully functional body. When an egg and sperm met to form the first cell that was to become a life, you were given the complete genetic code that all of your cells will use for the rest of your life. The information that DNA contains is passed from one generation to the next. Using gene technology, DNA can be modified or transferred from one animal, plant, or human to another. Genes are made up of short lengths of DNA and modern gene technology is able to make changes at the level of individual genes.

BLOOD

How much blood is inside my body?

The human body contains approximately 6 quarts (5.6 liters) of blood. Blood acts as your body's transportation system—in one day, your blood travels nearly 12,000 miles (19,312 kilometers). Pumped along by your heart, blood brings oxygen from the air you breathe and nutrients from the food you eat to all the cells of your body. (Your heart pumps 1 million barrels of blood during your lifetime—enough to fill three

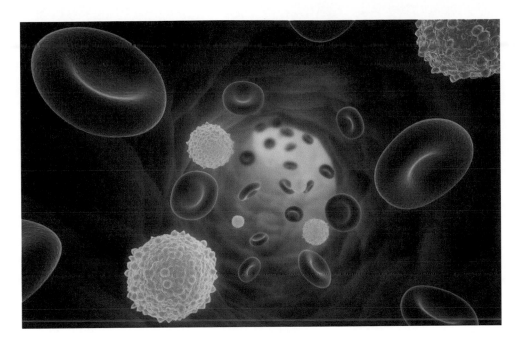

Our blood contains a variety of cells, including red cells for transporting oxygen and white cells that help defend against germs.

supertankers.) Blood also keeps cells clean and healthy by taking waste products away after the nutrients and oxygen have been used for processes like growth and repair. In addition, blood transports hormones—chemicals made in glands that control a variety of processes—throughout your body. Blood also carries heat throughout your body.

What do **plasma, red blood cells**, and **white blood cells** have to do with blood?

More than half of your blood is a light yellow watery liquid called plasma. Plasma contains things like nutrients and waste products, along with chemicals and matter needed for clotting, or sealing a wound before too much blood escapes. The rest of blood is made of tiny cells. Most are red blood cells, which distribute oxygen throughout your body and carry away the waste gas carbon dioxide, which is released from your lungs. The remaining cells are white blood cells, which protect you from infection by attacking and destroying disease-causing germs that enter your body. Red blood cells are the smallest cells in your body. But what they lack in size they make up for in number: in a drop of blood the size of the head of a pin there are 5 million red blood cells. In that same drop there are 10,000 white blood cells and 250,000 platelets, small ovals of matter that gather wherever a blood vessel is injured to plug the hole and help form a clot.

Why is **blood red**?

As the young red blood cell grows and takes on an adult form in the marrow of the bone, it loses its nucleus, and it increases its production of hemoglobin. Hemoglobin

205

is the red pigment, or color of blood, and contains iron, combined with protein. (Oxygen combined with iron is red; the more oxygen iron has bound to it, the redder it is.) When blood passes through the lungs, oxygen attaches itself to the hemoglobin of the red cells. From there, the red cells carry the oxygen through the arteries and the capillaries to all other cells of the body. The arteries appear reddish because the iron in the blood gives up its oxygen to the cells that need it as the red blood cells travel throughout the body. By the time the blood is back on its way to the heart and then to the lungs it has less than half as much oxygen as it did before. The veins, therefore, do not get as much oxygen as the other tissues and they appear bluish.

ORGANS

What does my **brain do**, besides think?

The brain is the body's command center; everything we do—eating, talking, walking, thinking, remembering, sleeping—is controlled and processed by the brain. As the most complex organ in the human body, the brain tells us what's going on outside our bodies (whether we are cold or hot, for instance, or whether the person we see coming toward us is a friend or a stranger) as well as what's going on inside our bodies (whether we have an infection or a broken bone, or whether we feel happy or sad).

The key to the body's nervous system, the brain contains between 10 billion and 100 billion nerve cells, or neurons. Neurons combine to form the body's nerves, thin cords that spread from head to toe and all parts in between. Neurons take in and send out electrical signals, called impulses, that control or respond to everything your body does and feels. The brain is like a very busy, high-speed post office, constantly receiving messages and sending them out all the time; it handles millions of nerve impulses every second.

How many **parts** are there to the **brain**?

The human brain is divided into three main parts: the cerebrum, the cerebellum, and the brain stem. The cerebrum is the largest part of the brain (about 85 percent of its total weight). It controls emotions, thought, memory, and speech. It is divided into a right and left side, called hemispheres, and each side is divided further into parts called lobes. Its thick outer covering, called the cortex, is made up of a type of tissue called gray matter. The cerebellum coordinates the kinds of movements we don't usually think about: it helps us walk upright and in a straight line, it keeps us balanced so we don't tip over, and it gives us coordination so we can run and play. The brain stem connects the brain with the spinal cord. It controls our body's vital processes, like breathing, digestion, and heart rate.

How can you **measure a heartbeat**?

Doctors measure heart rate—the number of contractions of the heart (or heartbeats) in one minute—by taking a person's pulse or listening to the heart with a

Does the brain feel pain?

Technically, no. While it is responsible for receiving and transmitting all messages of pain for the whole body, the brain itself does not have pain receptors. That means that, if you could somehow gain access to another person's brain, you could poke it or pinch it and that person would not feel the pain.

stethoscope. Your heart rate can be taken at any spot on the body at which an artery is close to the surface and a pulse can be felt, such as the wrist or the neck. When resting, the average adult human heartbeats at about 70 beats per minute (for males) and 75 beats per minute (for females), although this rate is often less for athletes. A toddler's heart beats about 100 to 130 times per minute; the older child's about 90 to 110 times per minute, and the adolescent's about 80 to 100 times per minute. If you add it all up, 75 beats per minute translates to 4,500 beats an hour, 108,000 beats per day, or about 39.4 million beats in a year!

How do people **breathe in and out**?

You usually don't have to think much about your breathing because your brain controls it automatically. When you have a lot of carbon dioxide—the waste gas produced by body processes—in your blood, your brain gets the message and tells your lungs to exhale and get rid of it. This action then causes you to inhale, drawing in air that eventually delivers oxygen to every cell in your body. This carefully regulated exhaling and inhaling takes place about 10 to 14 times each minute when you are breathing calmly.

When you need more oxygen than usual, your brain takes care of that, too. When you are exercising or working hard, your brain tells you to breathe more quickly, taking in 15 to 20 times more air. If that still doesn't deliver all the oxygen that your muscles need, you may "run out of breath," which forces you to rest. You will still breathe hard at that point—every second or so—until your muscles are able to work again.

Are the **lungs connected** to my **voice**?

Yes. The human voice, whether singing, speaking, or yelling, is made by a combination of factors. It all begins with air. Air from your lungs rushes through your trachea (also called the windpipe) and vibrates your vocal chords, a tiny, two-part muscle located in the larynx (also called the voice box) in your throat. The pitch of the note depends on the distance between the vocal chords: if you almost close the space between your vocal chords, the result is a high-pitched sound. If you open the space, the result is a low-pitched sound. And the speed of your breath determines just how loud the note is. Your lips and tongue shape these sounds into words.

207

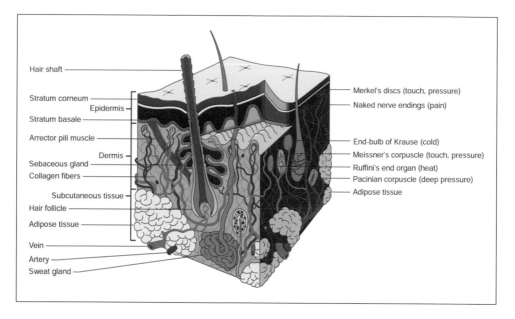

Our skin is a lot more complicated than it looks at first glance. Skin contains cells that sense touch and temperature, grow hair, excrete perspiration, and perform other functions, too.

How **much air** does a **person breathe** in a **lifetime**?

During a person's life, he or she will breathe about 75 million gallons (284 million liters) of air. Every minute, the human body needs 2 gallons (7.5 liters) of air when lying down, 4 gallons (15 liters) when sitting, 6 gallons (23 liters) when walking, and 12 gallons (45 liters) or more when running.

Which is the body's **biggest organ**?

Your skin is your body's largest organ and acts as a barrier to the outside world. It covers your entire body and has a surface area of around 21.5 square feet (2 square meters). Its thickness ranges from .02 inches (0.5 millimeters) on your eyelids to 0.16 inches (4 millimeters) or more in "tougher" areas, like on the palms of your hands and the soles of your feet. In total, it accounts for around 16 percent of your body weight. Your skin protects your internal organs from infection and helps control body temperature.

Many people say that your skin is like layers of an onion, but your skin really consists of three main layers. The outer layer, called the epidermis, contains skin cells, pigment, and proteins. The middle layer, called the dermis, contains blood vessels, nerves, hair follicles, and oil glands, and provides nutrients to the epidermis. The layer under the dermis, called the subcutaneous layer, contains sweat glands, some hair follicles, blood vessels, and fat. Each layer also contains connective tissue with collagen fibers to give support and elastin fibers to provide flexibility and strength. Cells in the deepest layer of your epidermis are constantly dividing to make new cells, providing your skin with a durable overcoat, which protects deeper cells from damage, infection, and dryness. Cells on the surface of your epidermis flake off and are continuously replaced with new ones, so that about every 30 days your body produces a whole new set of skin. A human body sheds about 600,000 particles of skin every hour—that's about 1.5 pounds (0.68 kilograms) a year. By age 70, an average human will have lost 105 pounds (47.6 kilograms) of skin.

What causes a **bruise**?

A bruise is a common skin injury that causes discoloration of the skin, usually yellowish, brownish, or purplish spots. Blood from damaged blood vessels deep beneath the skin collects near the surface of the skin, resulting in a "black and blue" mark. You can get a bruise by bumping into something or someone, or by something or someone bumping into you.

Why do **scabs** form?

As soon as you scrape or break the skin anywhere on your body, special blood cells called platelets get to work. Platelets stick together like glue at the cut site, forming a clot. This clot is like a protective bandage over your cut that keeps more blood and other fluids from flowing out. The clot is also full of other blood cells and thread-like matter called fibrin that help hold the clot together. As the clot starts to get hard and dries out, a scab forms. Crusty and dark red or brown, the scab protects the cut by keeping germs out and giving the skin cells underneath a chance to heal. All by itself, usually after a week or two, a scab falls off, revealing pinkish, new skin underneath.

What is **pus**?

Pus is a thick, whitish-yellow fluid that oozes from a cut because white blood cells, bacteria, and dead skin cells have accumulated there. Eventually the white blood cells eat up all the bacteria and dead skin cells and the puss clears up on its own. Sometimes antibiotics are needed to kill off bacteria and help the wound heal more quickly. If a pimple gets infected with bacteria, the result is a pustule, or small amount of pus.

HAIR, SKIN, AND NAILS

How **many hairs** do I have on my **head**?

Scientists estimate that both children and adults have about 100,000 strands of hair on their heads. Redheads have fewer because their individual strands are thicker. Although you may lose an average of 40 to 100 strands of hair every day, it's hard to notice because you have so many!

Which **hair grows** the **fastest**?

The fastest growing hairs on the human body are men's beard hairs. If the average male never trimmed his beard, it would grow to almost 30 feet (9 meters) long in his lifetime.

Why do people have **different color skin**?

Skin color—which ranges from light pink to dark brown—is determined by the amount and type of the pigment melanin there is in the skin. Melanin comes in two types: phaeomelanin (red to yellow) and eumelanin (dark brown to black). Both amount and type are determined by four to six genes. One copy of each of those genes is inherited from your father and one from your mother. Each gene comes in several coding sequences, which results in a variety of skin colors around the world.

Why do some people have **freckles**?

People with light skin and eyes are more likely to have freckles because they have less melanin, a chemical in the skin that protects it from sun damage by reflecting and absorbing ultraviolet (UV) rays. Instead of tanning, they freckle. Some people's freckles fade away almost com-

Freckles tend to form more easily on the skin of kids who have pale skin.

pletely in the winter, and then return in the summer, when the person is more likely to sunburn. Sunscreen can help protect everyone (freckled or not) from the Sun's harmful rays.

How does the **body cool off**?

The human body cools off by utilizing its three million sweat glands. Nerves in your skin tell your brain that your body is getting hot, and the brain signals the sweat glands to get busy. Each gland is like a little pump that draws water from nearby capillaries and delivers it to the skin, cooling it off. Since up to 60 percent of the body is water, sweat glands are like wells tapping into a giant ocean. There are two types of sweat glands: eccrine glands and apocrine glands. The eccrine glands are specifically designed for cooling the body off, and can pump up to 2 quarts (1.9 liters) of water an hour during intense activity or exercise. The apocrine glands are triggered by emotional stimuli, not heat. These glands secrete sweat in the hair follicles of the armpit, groin, and nipples, where the sweat mixes with bacteria and oils, giving it color and odor. As the sweat dries up, your skin cools off, and your body temperature drops.

Why do my **fingers** get all **"pruney"** in the bathtub?

During long baths (or while swimming in a lake or pool) our fingers and toes soak up water like a sponge, which makes them swell. This happens because the top layer

Why doesn't it hurt to cut my hair?

Haircuts don't hurt because your hair is not alive. Hair is made out of a protein called keratin. Only the root of the hair—the part that grows inside the skin on your head from tiny holes called follicles—is alive and growing. So if you pluck out a hair by the roots, it hurts. But trimming or cutting your hair is painless. And that is also the same reason why it doesn't hurt to trim your fingernails or toenails, which are also made of keratin. And because fingernails grow faster than toenails, you need to trim them more often!

of skin (called the *stratum corneum*) on fingers and toes is more porous than the layers of skin underneath, and thus better at absorbing water. But instead of ballooning up, our fingers and toes shrivel like raisins because of the way the layers of skin are connected: The top, swelling layer of skin is connected underneath to tissue that does not swell, so the skin buckles to accommodate the increased surface area. Once you dry off, the water from your skin evaporates into the air and your skin quickly returns to normal.

My grandmother has a **lump** on her **chin** that **sprouts hair**. What is this?

Chances are that your grandmother has a mole, a spot on the skin that is usually round or oval in shape. Moles can be small or large, smooth or lumpy, and range in color from pink, brown, red, or black. Skin moles can occur on any area of the body and even sprout hair. Moles are melanocytes—or cell factories that make pigments to give skin its color—that have grown in clusters rather than spreading throughout the skin. Moles can appear at any time or at any age; even babies are born with them occasionally. In fact, if you look carefully enough, you may find between 10 and 50 moles on your own body!

Will a **wart go away** if I wrap it in **duct tape**?

Maybe. Warts are skin infections caused by a common virus called HPV (human papillomavirus). They are perfectly "normal," in that health researchers estimate that three out of four people will develop a wart some time in their lives, usually on their hands or feet. It can take months or years for a wart to disappear on its own. To speed up the process, some skin doctors recommend wrapping the wart in duct tape until it disappears. The duct tape removes dead skin from the wart, thereby gradually killing off the wart virus that lives in the skin. It may also trigger the body's immune system to attack the wart virus. Otherwise the wart can be removed by a doctor with a laser or liquid nitrogen, a substance that freezes the skin, killing the cells.

Why is the **skin between my toes** sometimes **red and itchy**?

Itchy, red skin may be the sign of athlete's foot, a skin infection caused by a mold-like fungus. The fungus needs a warm, moist environment to live and often grows

211

on the floors of locker rooms and public showers and in swimming pools and whirlpools. It also loves stinky old tennis shoes. When a foot comes in contact with the fungus, it becomes red and itchy. Sometimes, moist, white, scaly lesions or sores develop between the toes and spread to the soles of the feet. In boys, sometimes athlete's foot fungus spreads to the groin area, where it is called "jock itch." The fungus sometimes spreads from one location to another as it is picked up on a bath towel, and the groin area, which is warm and moist, helps the fungus flourish.

Why do I have a **belly button**?

Your belly button, or navel, is a scar where your umbilical cord once was. The tube-like cord connected you to your mother when you were inside her uterus, growing into a baby. It carried oxygen and nourishment to you from the placenta, an organ that develops in the uterus during pregnancy, connecting you to your mother's blood supply. (It also carried away waste products from your blood.) Once you were born, the umbilical cord was no longer needed, because you began to breathe and eat on your own. The cord was clamped off and cut, and what was left of it withered and dropped off about a week after your birth. Doctors clamp the cord and cut it, leaving a remnant two to three inches long that eventually shrivels up and falls away. Skin grows over the area, and it then becomes the belly button shape you have for life.

What causes **goose bumps**?

Goose bumps or goose pimples are little bumps on your skin that appear when you are cold or afraid. They are named that because they look like the bumpy flesh of a goose that has had its feathers plucked. When you are cold the muscles in your skin raise the hairs on your body so that they can trap a thicker layer of air next to your skin, which may keep you a bit warmer. And, as with all muscular activity, this contraction of the skin muscles also produces heat.

Why do **zits** always form in the **middle of the forehead**?

Acne, a red, irritating skin rash, that mostly affects children approaching puberty, usually appears in the oil-producing areas of the body. These include the face (forehead, nose, and chin), chest, and back. Hyperactive glands produce oil (sebum) at a faster than normal pace due to tweens' rapid changes in hormone levels. Excessive oil clogs pores and creates acne, or pimples. Many times hair—which hangs down onto the forehead or sides of face—contains grease-like gels and styling products that contribute to acne.

Why do people get **wrinkles** and **gray hair** as they **get older**?

As people age, their bodies change in many ways that affect the ways their cells and organ systems function. These changes occur little by little, progress over time, and are different for every man and woman. We all lose height as we age, and by the time we reach 80 years old, our height may have decreased by two inches (five centimeters). Changes in posture, in the growth of our spine's vertebrae, and joint changes all contribute to our loss of height. With aging, the hair follicles produce less melanin, the pigment that gives hair its color. Hair becomes lighter, gray, and eventually turns white. The nails also change with aging: they grow slower, may become dull and brittle, and may become yellowed and opaque. With aging, the outer skin layer (epidermis) thins and the number of pigment-containing cells (called melanocytes) decreases, but the remaining melanocytes increase in size. Aging skin thus appears thinner, more pale, and translucent. Changes in the connective tissue reduce the skin's strength and elasticity, resulting in a wrinkly, leathery skin.

MY SENSES

What are the **five main senses**?

The five main senses of the human body—the ways in which people perceive stimuli from outside the body—are sight, hearing, taste, smell, and touch. But there are many other senses, like balance, hunger, thirst, and fatigue. No one sense is more important than another; *all* your senses work together to allow you to gather information from the world around you.

How **often** does a **person blink**?

Humans blink once every five or six seconds, and each blink lasts about one-sixth of a second. If you add it up, you blink more than three million times per year. The main purpose of blinking is to moisten and clean the cornea and the conjunctiva, two membranes of the eye. In fact, your eyes would dry out if they stayed open all the time. But the eye also blinks if an object or person approaches quickly.

What do **eyelashes** do?

Eyelashes protect our eyes. They help keep small particles and dust out of our eyes, especially when the wind is blowing. Eyelashes are also super-sensitive, and they alert the eyelids to shut when something touches them. If you rub your finger against your eyelashes, you will find that your eyelid automatically shuts. But be careful not to rub too hard—if you lose a lash it will take about four to eight weeks to grow back! Fortunately, your upper eyelid has between 100 and 150 lashes.

Are **tears** good for me?

Absolutely! Tears, which flow from tear glands into your eyes through tiny tear

Tears form when we are sad, but tears have another purpose, too: they help keep dirt and dust out of our eyes.

213

Why can't I see just after I turn off the lights?

It is hard to see in the dark immediately after you turn out the lights, just as it can take a few minutes for your eyes to adjust when you walk from a dark place into a bright, sunny day. Why? Your eyes' pupils are responsible. The size of your pupil—the black circle in the center of your eye controlled by the iris—determines the amount of light that enters the eye and adjusts to light and darkness. Pupils dilate (widen) in dim light or darkness to let more light into the eyes; they constrict (narrow) in bright light to prevent too much light from entering the eyes. When you move from dark to light, pupils widen, and the retinas become six times more sensitive after one minute in darkness than they are after the first few seconds. After a half hour, they are even more sensitive, and you can begin to see more comfortably in the dark.

ducts, wash the eyeballs and carry away dust and dirt. Tears, which contain salt, kill germs and keep the cornea (the transparent front part of the eye) moist. Some of the tears drain out of your eyes through tear ducts, which are tiny tubes that run between your eyes and your nose. That is why people almost always blow their nose after they cry.

Why do our **ears** sometimes **pop in airplanes**?

Your ears sometimes pop in airplanes, while driving through high mountainous areas, and at other high altitudes because of air pressure changes. As you ascend in an airplane, for example, and the air pressure decreases, the air trapped in your inner ear will cause your eardrums to push outward. This expansion causes the discomfort you feel before your ears "pop." Your hearing ability also decreases because the pressure on your ear drums makes the sound harder to transmit. When you yawn or swallow, your body can equalize the pressure between your inner ear and the atmosphere by allowing some air from your inner ear to escape through the Eustachian tubes, two small channels that connect the inner ears to the throat. When they open, you feel the pressure release and you hear a popping sound.

Why do I have **two ears**?

You have two ears so that you can hear which direction sounds are coming from. The brain detects long lines of sound waves or sound patterns that we hear by comparing the information coming from each of our ears. If a dog is barking on the left side of you, the sound will arrive to your left ear a little faster than to your right ear. Also, the sound of the barking will be louder in your left ear than in your right ear. Your brain notes the miniscule difference in time and loudness, and lets you know where the sound is coming from.

Why do I get **dizzy** after **spinning around?**

The fluid in your inner ear is responsible for dizziness. After you spin around, your ear fluid keeps spinning, sending conflicting messages to your brain. These mixed signals cause dizziness, lack of balance, and lightheadedness. After a few seconds, the liquid levels out and the dizziness goes away.

Why do some **people get sick** when they **read in the car?**

Motion sickness happens when your body is feeling the sensation of movement. This can happen when you are riding in a school bus, sailing on a boat, or riding in the backseat of a car. When you are reading a book, your eyes do not see the movement, which confuses your brain and causes some people to feel sick. If you get car sick, the solution is to look out the window, not down at your book, so your brain and body will be in sync.

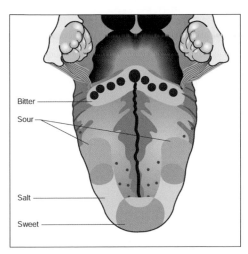

Different parts of our tongues are used for tasting bitter, salty, sweet, and sour flavors.

What are **taste buds?**

The human tongue contains about 10,000 tiny bumps (called papillae), and every bump has about 250 taste buds. Each taste bud has a pore that opens out to the surface of the tongue, which allows molecules going into the mouth to reach the receptor cells inside. Receptor cells live for only one to two weeks and then are replaced by new receptor cells. Taste buds detect the four basic flavors of salty, sweet, bitter, and sour, and work together with other taste buds on the roof of your mouth to give you the taste of your food.

But taste buds also need help from your nose. While you're chewing, the food releases chemicals that immediately travel up into your nose, triggering your nose's olfactory receptors. Your nose is at least 20,000 times more sensitive than your tongue—and it can remember about 50,000 different scents! Smell cells work with your taste buds to create a rich taste experience. In fact, you may notice that if your nose is stuffed and you can't smell your food you also can't taste it very well!

Is it true that people have **"tongue prints"?**

Yes. All human beings have some traits that are the same, but each individual person also has a set of traits that are different from any other. Among these individual traits are fingerprints, tongue prints, patterns in the iris of the eye, and voice patterns. Because fingerprints and tongue prints are unique in every person (even identical twins), they can be used to identify an individual. (But next time someone calls out your name, it's best to answer rather than stick out your tongue!)

How do you stop a **brain freeze**?

Quickly gobbling up cold ice cream may result in "brain freeze," also know as an ice cream headache. When the cold object touches the roof of your mouth, the blood vessels contract in order to prevent loss of body heat. As the coldness stops, the blood vessels relax again, quickly increasing blood flow to the brain. This sudden release is what causes the intense headache sensation. You can relieve brain freeze by quickly warming the roof of your mouth: Touch your tongue to the top of your mouth or, if you can roll your tongue in a ball, press the underside of your tongue (which is warmer) to the roof of your mouth. Slowly sipping room-temperature water or pressing a warm thumb against the roof of the mouth also works for some people.

How do **dust mites** make a **person sneeze**?

Dust mites are microscopic organisms that live in dust. These unwelcome visitors invade your nose and can irritate your mucous membranes, triggering nerve cells that signal the lungs to fill with air. When the air passages close and pressure builds up, your nose tingles and twitches, and you sneeze—forcing mucus (the slimy, moisturizing substance), dust, pollen, and mites out of your nose at speeds of up to 525 feet (160 meters) per second! Sneezing is one of the body's reflexes, an automatic way it rids itself of harmful substances like bacteria and germs. It also keeps the tubes that carry the air from your nose to your lungs healthy.

What is a **booger**?

The mucous membrane that lines your nose is moist and sticky. That environment helps trap dust and other things in the air before they can pass into your lungs. When moisture evaporates from the thick film of mucus that covers the lining of your nose—which happens all the time as air passes over it—the mucus, combining with the particles you've breathed in, becomes dried and crusty, forming boogers.

EATING AND DRINKING

Do I have to **brush my teeth**?

Absolutely! Strong, healthy teeth help you speak clearly, chew harder vegetables and meats, and help you look your best. Brushing your teeth helps prevent plaque, a clear film that sticks to your teeth. The sticky film acts like a magnet for bacteria and sugar. Bacteria eats the sugar on your teeth, breaking it down into acids that deteriorate tooth enamel, causing holes called cavities. Plaque also causes the gum disease gingivitis, which make your gums red, swollen, and sore. At around age six, you lose your baby teeth and a larger set of teeth begin to surface. Eventually, 32 new teeth will line your growing jaws, the last coming in around the age of 18. These permanent teeth will perform all of your eating tasks for the rest of your life, so they are worth taking care of! Your four front teeth (on top and bottom) are sharp

> ## What did people use before toothbrushes were invented?
>
> **E**arly in human history, people used anything that they could find to keep their teeth clean. Usually a thin, sharp object, like a stick, was used to pick out food left between teeth. Chewing on the end of certain sticks would fray the wood, making a kind of brush, which could then be rubbed across the teeth. (Even today, members of primitive tribes chew sticks to keep their teeth clean. The constant chewing produces more saliva than usual, which helps wash food away.) Later, people found that if they rubbed abrasive elements, like salt or chalk, across their teeth, they could get rid of grime. They also used water and pieces of rough cloth to clean their teeth. Toothpicks made of all kinds of materials also became popular. Rich people had jeweled toothpicks made of gold and silver. Toothbrushes for the wealthy, with fancy handles and hog bristles, came into use in the eighteenth century. Only much later, when cheaper, wooden-handled toothbrushes were made, and the importance of good dental hygiene became known, did most people start to regularly use them.

incisors that cut and tear off food when you bite, along with your four pointed canine teeth. The flat-topped bicuspids (premolars) and molars near the back of your mouth crush and chew your food.

What is a **healthy diet**?

Although everyone eats different foods, doctors and nutritionists (people who plan food and nutrition programs) generally agree that a healthy diet is one loaded with fruits, vegetables, whole grains, and fat-free or low-fat milk and milk products; one that includes lean meats, poultry, fish, beans, eggs, and nuts; and one that is low in saturated fats (like those fats found in butter), trans fats (also called partially hydrogenated oils, found in foods like French fries and donuts), cholesterol, salt (sodium), and added sugars. Foods like processed cheese that squirts from a can, frosted pastries filled with sugary jam, and deep-fried fish, nuggets, or French fries do not provide the types of nutrients your body needs to grow, and are sometimes called "empty" foods. For example, 1 ounce of potato chips has 152 calories and 10 grams of fat (3 grams of which are saturated fat).

Why does the body need **vitamins and minerals**?

Vitamins are chemicals that the body needs to function well; minerals are metals and salts that the body also needs in tiny amounts to run properly. Both help the human body grow. Different foods, like vegetables, contain different amounts of vitamins and minerals, so it is important to have variety in your diet so you can get a good balance. When it comes to vitamins, each one works differently in your body. Vitamin D in milk helps your bones grow; vitamin A in carrots helps you see at

217

> ## Why is Jell-O® so wobbly?
>
> Jell-O® is made from gelatin, a processed protein that makes it wobbly. Gelatin is made from the collagen in cow or pig bones and skins. Gelatin melts when heated and solidifies when cooled again. When you add the Jell-O® powder to boiling water, the powder dissolves and the weak bonds that hold together the protein chains start breaking apart. The chains float around in the mixing bowl until you add cold water. As the Jell-O® cools, the chains start bonding again. The chains become tangled when they are stirred, and water gets into gaps between the chains. Once it is refrigerated, the gelatin "chains" harden and the trapped water and flavor make Jell-O® wobbly.

night; vitamin C in oranges helps boost your immune system and helps your body heal if you get a wound; and the B vitamins in leafy green vegetables help your body make protein and energy. And although some vitamins like A (which helps your eyesight) and D are stored in your body (for several days or up to several months), others, like C and the B vitamins, quickly pass through your bloodstream. So it's important to replace your vitamins every day.

How **much food** does the **average person eat** in a **year**?

Some doctors say that the average American adult eats about 525 pounds (238 kilograms) of food each year of his or her life! If a person lives to be 70 years old, he or she will eat about 35 turkeys, 12 sheep, 880 chickens, and 770 pounds (349 kilograms) of fish.

Why **should I drink lots** of **water**?

All living things need water to survive. Without water, the human body stops working properly. Water makes up more than 50 percent of your body weight and a person cannot survive for more than a few days without it. Water flushes toxins out of your organs, carries nutrients to your cells, and provides a moist environment for ear, nose, and throat tissues. Water is also in lymph, a fluid that is part of your immune system, which helps you fight off illness. You need water to digest your food, to get rid of waste, and to sweat. Too little water in your body leads to dehydration, and it can make you tired and unable to function. Your body gets water from drinking it, but lots of foods, such as fruits and vegetables, contain water too.

What does the **esophagus** do?

It takes about 4 to 8 seconds for food to travel from your mouth to your stomach, and your esophagus plays a big part in that action. The esophagus is part of your body's digestive system, which is about 30 feet (9 meters) in length and runs from the mouth to the anus. The main part of the digestive system is the alimentary canal, a long tube that is made up of the mouth, esophagus, stomach, small intestine, and large intestine. Other parts of the body are also linked to the canal, such as your teeth, tongue, salivary glands (which make saliva to help break down food), pancreas, liver, and gallbladder. Food and liquids from your mouth pass down through the esophagus, an 11-inch- (25-centimeter-) long tube, into the stomach, where a wave of gastric juices helps break down food into smaller parts, or molecules, which are small enough to be absorbed into the bloodstream and carried throughout the body.

It is the gelatin in Jell-O® that makes this fun dessert wobble and jiggle.

Does the **red color** in **fruit juice** really come from a **beetle**?

Yes. The red coloring that makes many juices and jams red is from a natural dye called carmine. Carmine is derived from conchineal, or conchineal extract, which comes from the bodies of a female beetle (*Dactylopius coccus*) that lives on the Opuntia cactus. The insect is boiled and the scales of the insect are crushed into a red powder. It takes about 70,000 insects to make one pound of cochineal. The ancient Aztecs used cochineal as a dye for cloth and other items, and today it is widely used as a coloring agent for food, beverages, and cosmetics.

Are **soap, booger,** and **earwax** really **jellybean flavors**?

Yes! And so are dirt, earthworm, vomit, and grass. It's not really clear how the folks at the jelly belly company figured out the flavor recipe for each bean, but those that have tried them say they are authentic tasting! Jellybeans, a type of candy made from sugar, corn syrup, and food starch, have traditionally been made with fruit flavoring. One company, called Jelly Belly, made flavors like butter popcorn, cotton candy, and watermelon in the 1980s. These jellybeans were endorsed by U.S. President Ronald Reagan, who kept a jar of them on his desk in the White House, and who also made them the first jelly beans in outer space, sending them on the 1983 *Challenger* shuttle as a surprise for the astronauts.

Why do some people **throw up** when they eat **spicy food**?

Throw up, also called vomit, puke, and upchuck, is half-digested food and liquid that gets mixed up with your stomach juices and comes out of your mouth. Vomit

219

What do potato chips have to do with the heart?

Potato chips often contain saturated fats, which over time can clog the arteries that carry blood to the heart. The oils used to cook the chips are made up of saturated fats, which increases cholesterol production in the body, a known risk factor for heart disease. Heart disease results from a condition known as atherosclerosis, which happens when a waxy substance forms inside the arteries that supply blood to your heart.

happens when your stomach starts to feel queasy (or nauseated), sometimes after you exercise or run around too much after eating, eat too much food, or eat food that is spicy and therefore irritating to your stomach. Normally, your stomach processes your food well through the digestive system, but if you eat food with lots of bacteria or if you have a virus in your stomach, the quickest way for your body to get rid of the irritants is to vomit them out. Your brain tells the muscles in your stomach walls to spasm (contract abnormally); it also tells your diaphragm—the large sheet of muscles that separates your chest from your abdomen and is most responsible for your breathing—to press downward on your stomach. These activities combine to force the contents of your stomach up and out.

Why do people sometimes **burp**?

A burp, sometimes called a belch, is gas that your body needs to get rid of. When you eat or drink, you swallow air at the same time you swallow food or liquid. The air contains gases such as nitrogen and oxygen. The extra gas you ingest is forced out of the stomach, up through the esophagus, and out of the mouth as a burp. Some kids discover that drinking soda or other carbonated beverages makes them burp more, and this is because these drinks contain carbon dioxide, the gas that makes them fizzy. Sometimes eating or drinking too fast, which sends more air into the stomach, can make a person burp. The same thing happens when you drink through a straw: the straw brings extra air into your stomach, causing you to burp.

What causes **hiccups**?

A hiccup is a noise that your body makes when your diaphragm, the muscle barrier between your stomach and lungs, gets irritated and has spasms. The "hic" part of the sound is caused when air is sucked into your lungs, and the "cup" part of the sound happens when a special flap called the epiglottis, located between your tongue and vocal cords, slams closed over your windpipe. Your diaphragm can become irritated from eating too much food, which causes an enlarged stomach to press against the wall of the muscle. Your diaphragm can also become irritated from lifting a heavy object or from breathing in too much air, which affects your normal breathing pattern. Hiccups may last a minute or two, but generally go away with time. Holding your breath, drinking a glass of water, or having someone scare you generally does not work to get rid of hiccups, since your diaphragm needs time to relax again.

What causes people to **pass gas**?

When there is too much air in your digestive system, there are two ways to get rid of it. It can exit from the top, through your mouth, in the form of a burp. Or it can exit from the bottom, through your anus, in the form of passed gas, better known as a fart.

Some of the gas in your digestive system comes from the air you swallow when you eat, while some of it is a natural by-product of food digestion in your large intestine. When your intestine encounters foods that are difficult to digest—including greasy or high-fat foods—it produces more gas than with foods that are digested easily. This gas travels through your intestine to your rectum and eventually passes out through your anus. While some may not like to admit it, everyone passes gas several times a day.

What is **constipation**?

Constipation occurs when your body has a hard time having a bowel movement, or going poop. When you digest your food, it collects in the last part of the colon, or the end of the large intestine. If the feces doesn't have lot of fiber or bulk to it, it stays in the colon longer than it normally would. Water continues to draw out of the feces, making it hard and compact instead of squishy and moveable. The rectum has to push extra hard to get your poop out. Constipation usually resolves itself, but your body can avoid constipation by eating plenty of fresh fruit, vegetables, and bran, and drinking plenty of water each day.

SICKNESS AND HEALTH

Why do I get **sick**?

When you get sick, part or all of your body is not working as it should. The cause of sickness can come from inside your body or from the outside world. Diseases that start on the inside are usually inherited in the genes that you receive from your parents, which make up the master plan that determines how your body will grow and run. Abnormal development or functioning of different body systems is the cause of many chronic (long-lasting) diseases.

Things in the outside world can cause sickness, too. Poisons in the environment can cause illnesses in people. Not eating the right foods, with their important nutrients, can also cause diseases. But the most common cause of sickness from the outside world is infectious agents. These agents are usually microscopic organisms (living things so small that they can only be seen with the help of microscopes) like bacteria and viruses, which we commonly refer to as germs. Bacteria and viruses and

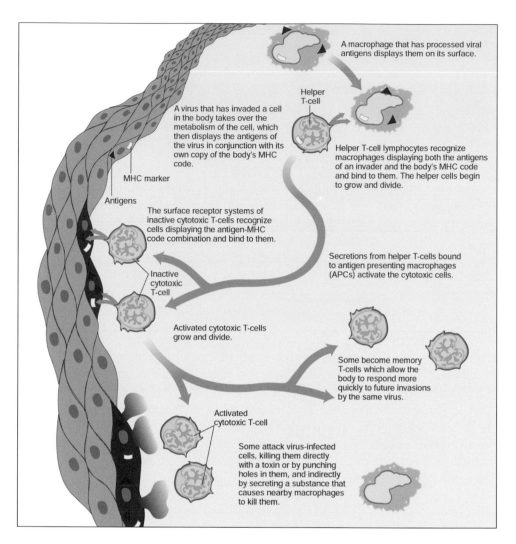

A macrophage that has processed viral antigens displays them on its surface.

A virus that has invaded a cell in the body takes over the metabolism of the cell, which then displays the antigens of the virus in conjunction with its own copy of the body's MHC code.

Helper T-cell

Helper T-cell lymphocytes recognize macrophages displaying both the antigens of an invader and the body's MHC code and bind to them. The helper cells begin to grow and divide.

MHC marker

Antigens

The surface receptor systems of inactive cytotoxic T-cells recognize cells displaying the antigen-MHC code combination and bind to them.

Secretions from helper T-cells bound to antigen presenting macrophages (APCs) activate the cytotoxic cells.

Inactive cytotoxic T-cell

Activated cytotoxic T-cells grow and divide.

Some become memory T-cells which allow the body to respond more quickly to future invasions by the same virus.

Activated cytotoxic T-cell

Some attack virus-infected cells, killing them directly with a toxin or by punching holes in them, and indirectly by secreting a substance that causes nearby macrophages to kill them.

How the human immune system works is really pretty complicated. Many types of cells are used by the body to defend against viruses and other invaders.

other microscopic organisms live in the air, water, and soil that make up our world. They are on the things and people we touch and in the food we eat. Many of them are beneficial: bacteria are needed to make cheese, some bacteria help vegetables like peas and beans grow, and some bacteria clean the environment and enrich the soil by feeding on dead plants and animals. But there are other microscopic organisms that invade the bodies of plants and animals—and people—and cause diseases.

How do the **disease-causing germs invade** my body?

Your skin is a wonderful protective barrier that keeps a lot of the disease-causing germs that you run into each day from entering your body. Only when you have an opening in your skin—like a cut or a scrape—are germs likely to enter there. Most germs enter through your mouth and nose, making their way farther into your

222

body through your respiratory or digestive tracts. But even then, certain chemicals in body tissues and fluids keep many harmful germs from causing problems. When an infection does begin—with the germs multiplying inside your body—your immune, or defense, system goes into action to get rid of the foreign organisms. Your white blood cells produce special substances called antibodies that attack and destroy the invaders, helping you to recover.

What does the **immune system** do?

The immune system protects the human body against germs, which are microorganisms that cause sickness and disease. There are four major types of germs—harmful bacteria (pathogens), viruses, fungi, and protozoa. This defense system begins with the skin, which stops germs from getting into your blood or tissues. If germs get into your body, for example through your nose or mouth, white blood cells called phagocytes and lymphocytes attack them. Phagocytes scout out and destroy invaders, and long-living lymphocytes remember the invaders and release chemicals called antibodies to make the body resistant, or immune, to them. White blood cells live in the bloodstream, lymphatic system, and spleen.

The lymphatic system (or lymph system, for short) is a far-reaching network that extends throughout your entire body. A clear liquid called lymph runs throughout the system, washing the body's cells with nutrients and water and detecting and removing pathogens. Lymph is filtered through the lymph nodes, and then passes into the body's bloodstream.

What is the difference between **bacteria** and **viruses**?

Bacteria are single-celled organisms that have the ability to feed themselves and to reproduce. They are found everywhere, including the air, water, and soil. They divide and multiply very quickly, which means that one cell can become 1 million cells in just a few hours! Viruses are microorganisms that are smaller than bacteria, but they cannot grow or reproduce without the help of a separate living cell. Once the virus gets inside your body, it attaches itself to a healthy cell and uses the cell's nucleus to reproduce itself.

Do our **intestines contain germs**?

Yes. Germs aren't *all* bad—in fact, some are helpful. For example, the common bacterium, *E. coli,* is found in our intestines and helps us digest green vegetables and beans (also making gases). These same bacteria also make vitamin K, which causes blood to clot. If we didn't have this bacteria inside of us, we could bleed to death whenever we got a small cut.

Where are some **other places** that **germs hide**?

Germs are everywhere! Most germs spread through the air, invading our homes, pets, and family, and sometimes they make us sick. Besides your bathroom toilet and the kitchen sink, everyday items like shopping-carts, restaurant menus, computer keyboards, and the shower curtain contain germs. These items contain bacteria, mold, and rhinoviruses (instigators of the common cold) that can lead to sickness. In fact, cold and flu viruses can survive for 18 hours on hard surfaces. Common household items can be swabbed with a disinfectant wipe easily before use in order to prevent germs from spreading. Washing your hands with soap and water, using a hand sanitizer, and avoiding touching your face with your hands after using these items also helps keep germs away from you. To eliminate dust mites—those little critters that live in your bed sheets and feed on dead skin cells—don't make your bed for a while. Studies have found that dust mites need humidity levels above 50 percent to survive and cannot live in the arid conditions of an unmade bed.

What are **allergies**?

An allergic reaction is a reaction to a substance that is normally harmless to most other people. Allergies happen when a person's immune system overreacts to a normally harmless substance that the person has breathed in, touched, or eaten. Allergens—the antigens that bring on an allergic reaction—may be foods, medications, plants or animals, chemicals, dust, or molds. Some common allergic reactions are hay fever, allergic conjunctivitis (an eye reaction); asthma, pet-dander allergies, and skin reactions, such as hives. A common cause for allergies are dust mites, a large part of household dust. If they are breathed in by an allergic person, the body parts of the dead mites can trigger asthma, a lung condition that causes a person to have difficulty breathing. Cat and dog dander, or skin flakes, can cause an allergic reaction, such as sneezing, wheezing, and running eyes and nose. Common food allergy triggers are the proteins in cow's milk, eggs, peanuts, wheat, soy, fish, shellfish, and tree nuts.

What are **antibiotics**?

Antibiotics are medicines that help the human body fight bacteria, either by directly killing the offending germs or by weakening them so that the body's own immune system can fight and kill them more easily. The most widely known antibiotic is penicillin, which is made from mold. Penicillin kills bacteria by interfering with the formation of the cell walls or cell contents of the bacteria.

Was **penicillin** discovered by **accident**?

Yes. In 1928, the Scottish research scientist Alexander Fleming found that mold had accidentally contaminated one of his experiments. The mold created a bacteria-free circle around itself, and Fleming deduced that the mold was an antibacterial agent that could kill many harmful bacteria. He named the active agent penicillin. By the middle of the twentieth century, Fleming's discovery birthed a pharmaceutical industry that made synthetic penicillin to treat many bacterial diseases of the day, including syphilis, gangrene, and tuberculosis. He won the Nobel Prize in 1945 for his discovery.

Who discovered **vaccination**?

Edward Jenner, an army surgeon and country doctor from Gloucestershire, England, tried his first experimental vaccination in 1796. At the time smallpox

Antibiotics like penicillin fight against bacteria. Antibiotics do not kill viruses, however. For viruses, doctors use antiviral drugs. Antiviral drugs do not kill viruses; they only keep them from spreading.

was a fatal disease that mostly affected infants and young children. Jenner recognized that dairymaids infected with cowpox virus (a minor virus that affected cows) were immune to smallpox. He used material from the arm of Sarah Nells, a dairymaid who had contracted cowpox, to infect James Phipps, an eight-year-old boy. He then exposed Phipps to smallpox, which Phipps did not contract. It worked because cowpox and smallpox have common antigens (proteins), which aroused the young boy's immune system. After repeating the experiment on other children, including his own son, Jenner concluded that vaccination provided immunity to smallpox without the risk of the person contracting the disease. Jenner used the word "vaccination" for his treatment, which comes from the Latin word *vacca,* meaning "cow." Jenner's findings were published two years later, in 1798, and today vaccines are used around the world to produce immunity to disease.

Who was **Louis Pasteur**?

The French research chemist Louis Pasteur continued Jenner's work with vaccination. Vaccinations work by presenting a foreign antigen to the body's immune system in order to evoke an immune response. Pasteur reasoned that if a vaccine could be found for smallpox, then a vaccine could be found for all diseases. In the summer of 1880, he accidentally found a vaccine for chicken cholera, a disease that affected many poultry farmers. He also found a vaccine for rabies, a disease that affected animals and that humans contracted after being bitten by infected animals, mainly dogs. Pasteur and his research team discovered that the rabies germ attacked the nervous system only after it had made its way to the brain. The team traced the germ to the brain and spinal cord of infected animals and by

225

Why is laughter called "medicine" for the human body?

Research shows that laughter has many health benefits—in fact, it is so good for you, that doctors sometimes call it "medicine." Why? Laughter can help strengthen the body's immune system by increasing the number of antibody-producing cells and boosting T cells (a white blood cell that protects the body from infection). Humor also relieves the stresses and pressures of everyday living, by reducing the body's stress hormones like cortisol, epinephrine (adrenaline), dopamine, and growth hormone. It also increases the level of good hormones like endorphins, which promote a feeling of happiness. A deep belly laugh exercises the diaphragm and contracts the abdominal muscles, leaving them more relaxed afterward. And it provides a good workout for the heart.

using dried spinal cords, produced a vaccine for rabies. The vaccine was first tried out on animals, and in 1885 it was used successfully on a young boy who was bit by a rabid dog.

Can **chicken soup** help a **cold go away**?

It doesn't cure a cold but it can help lessen the symptoms. For centuries, people around the world have used chicken soup to help cure the common cold. Chicken soup can help people feel better, but scientists learned that chicken fat may help relieve cold and flu symptoms in two ways. First, the chicken broth acts as an anti-inflammatory by slowing down the movement of neutrophils (immune system cells that play a role in the body's inflammatory response). Second, it temporarily speeds up the movement of mucus through the nose. This movement helps relieve congestion and limits the amount of time viruses are in contact with the nose lining.

Why is **exercise important** to **health**?

Exercise—like playing tag on the playground, participating in a team sport, or twirling in dance class—is good for your health. Regular physical activity helps a person have stronger bones and muscles, helps control body fat, helps prevent certain illnesses, and contributes to a good outlook on life. Regular exercise helps promote digestion and a good night's sleep. When children exercise as part of their busy lives, they are better equipped to manage the physical and emotional challenges of a busy day, like walking to school, climbing stairs, catching a school bus, or studying for a test. According to the Department of Health and Human Services (HHS), all children two years and older should get at least 60 minutes of moderate to vigorous exercise on most, if not all, days of the week.

Can my **cat or dog benefit** my health?

As a matter of fact, yes! Researchers believe that regular contact with pets can reduce levels of stress and reduce blood pressure (the force of blood pushing against the walls of the arteries as the heart pumps out blood). Pets offer stability, comfort, security, affection, and intimacy. Owning a dog also provides a great opportunity to get exercise and fresh air, since it will need to go for a walk every day.

Yawning is a reflex action that is your body's way of telling you that you need more oxygen.

What causes a **yawn**?

Some people yawn when they are bored, tired, or in the presence of another yawner. Yawning happens when a person is not getting enough oxygen. Oxygen, the gas needed to run body processes, and carbon dioxide, the waste gas produced by these processes, travel in your bloodstream and enter and exit your body through your lungs. When you don't breathe deeply enough, too much carbon dioxide builds up in your body and your brain gets the message, telling you to breathe more deeply to fix the problem. A yawn is a great big breath that clears carbon dioxide from your lungs and forces you to take in fresh, oxygen-rich air.

Why do I **need sleep**?

Scientists do not know exactly why people need sleep, but studies show that sleep is necessary for survival. Sleep appears to be necessary for the nervous system to work properly. While too little sleep one night may leave us feeling drowsy and unable to concentrate the next day, a long period of too little sleep leads to poor memory and physical performance. Hallucinations (seeing things that aren't really there), vision problems, and mood swings may develop if sleep deprivation continues.

Do **people dream** every night?

Yes. The average person has three or four dreams each night, with each dream lasting 10 minutes or more. Almost all dreams occur during REM sleep, a period of sleep characterized by fast breathing and heart rates. Scientists do not understand why dreaming is important, but one theory is that the brain is either cataloging the information it acquired during the day and discarding the data it does not want, or is creating scenarios to work through situations that may be causing emotional distress. Like sleep, most people who are deprived of dreams become disoriented, are unable to concentrate, and may even have hallucinations. Sometimes it is hard to remember our dreams because they are stored in our short-term memory.

DISABILITIES AND SUBSTANCE ABUSE

What is a **disability**?

The word "disabled" usually refers to a person who has a physical or mental handicap that keeps him or her from doing certain tasks—or makes performing them unusually difficult. Most physical disabilities, like blindness or paralysis, are easily noticed, but many mental disabilities are harder to detect. Mental disabilities can include diseases like schizophrenia, which causes severe disturbances in people's thoughts and emotions. Another type of disability is a learning disability, such as dyslexia, which is a learning disorder that makes reading very difficult because the brain reverses the order of letters and words. Many disabled people prefer the term "differently abled," a description that doesn't divide people into categories like "normal" and "disabled" but addresses the idea that every person has different abilities.

Why do people become **disabled**?

A disability can be the result of a disease, an accident, or of genetics, which means that it is a condition that a person is born with. A lot of times disabled people can learn new ways to do things or use special machines or specially trained animals to help them work around their disability.

Why are some people **blind**?

Blindness is complete loss of sight. It can happen when the optic nerves, which carry visual signals from the eyes to the brain, or the sight centers of the brain are damaged. Such damage can occur as a result of injuries or diseases. A person can also be born with eye or brain abnormalities that cause blindness. In many cases, particularly in very poor countries, infectious diseases and poor diets can also cause blindness. A lack of vitamin A, in fact, is the leading cause of blindness worldwide. With basic medicines and proper nutrition, such cases could be prevented.

For every one person in the United States who is totally blind, there are four others who are visually impaired or "legally blind." These people have some ability to see, but they see so poorly—even with eyeglasses—that they cannot do things that require good vision, like driving a car.

How do **blind people get around** in the community?

Some people use canes or guide dogs to get around. A white cane indicates that the person using it is visually impaired. Blind people use their canes on sidewalks, floors, and streets. They learn to identify the locations of things—like steps, walls, or doors—simply by the different sounds that their cane taps make. Various high-tech devices have been invented, such as laser canes, which use sound or light waves that bounce off objects and send signals to the user about where these objects are located, what they might be made of, and how big they are. Guide dogs are specifically trained to lead blind people around, with the guide dog following commands that help the blind person go about his or her day.

Why **can't** some people **hear**?

The inability to hear, or deafness, can occur for many reasons. Some types of hearing loss result from something blocking sound as it travels from the outer ear to the eardrum and the tiny bones in the middle ear. Other types of loss arise from damage to or a defect of the inner ear or the auditory nerve, which is the nerve that carries sound signals from the inner ear to the brain. Deafness can happen as a result of disease, including severe ear infections, or it can be inherited, with the deafness being apparent at birth or sometimes showing up years later. Injuries and accidents also account for many cases of deafness. Extremely loud noises, like those that come from an explosion, can cause deafness, though that loss of hearing is sometimes temporary. People who work in noisy factories or those who are frequently exposed to very loud music can also develop hearing loss over time. Many people gradually lose some or all of their hearing when they reach old age, but some of those types of hearing loss can be overcome by wearing a hearing aid, which makes noises like speech or music louder.

What is **substance abuse**?

Substance abuse means taking drugs (other than those prescribed by a doctor for a specific illness) in amounts that are dangerous or that prevent a person from doing everyday things, like going to school or work. The substance being abused can be alcohol, marijuana, pills called tranquilizers that make people feel very tired or relaxed, household products that are inhaled, or a number of other drugs. Drug abuse happens all over the world, to all kinds of people, young and old. It frequently causes terrible damage to a person's body, to relationships with family and friends, and to career or education. In some cases, substance abuse leads to death, because the abuser gets involved in an accident or because he or she overdoses, or takes enough of the substance to cause the body to completely shut down.

Why is **alcohol bad** for your **health**?

Alcohol is a type of drug known as a depressant that slows down the body's central nervous system. After a person has had a few drinks, it immediately affects the way he or she thinks and acts. Alcohol can make a person feel sleepy, less coordinated, and slow to react to things. And it can cause your brain to feel foggy, and make you think and see differently. After years of drinking, alcohol use can cause stomach and intestinal problems, liver damage, nerve and muscle damage, heart problems, and brain damage. Alcohol is difficult for the brain to process, and can cause everything from blackouts to permanent loss of brain function and memory. Researchers have also linked long-term drinking to cancer of the throat, mouth, liver, esophagus, and larynx. Drinking alcohol can also lead to emotional and psychological problems like sadness, depression, and even hallucinations (seeing and hearing things that are not

Smoking is legal for Americans who are 18 or over. At any age, though, smoking is really bad for your health and is banned from many public places.

real). If a pregnant woman drinks too much alcohol, it can seriously injure her unborn baby and lead to birth defects.

Why is **smoking cigarettes bad** for your **health**?

In addition to the stimulant nicotine, cigarettes contain many harmful chemicals, like tar and the poisonous gas carbon monoxide. These chemicals present health risks that range from bronchitis to cancer. Doctors believe that cigarette smoking is the cause of 90 percent of all cases of lung cancer. Heart disease, heart attack, and stroke are far more common in smokers. One of the effects of nicotine is constricting the blood vessels, which causes high blood pressure. Another effect is that smoking raises your heart rate, which adds extra stress on your heart. Smoking also affects every part of the body's circulatory system. Your blood becomes thicker and stickier, making it harder for your heart to work well. The lining of the blood vessels is damaged, allowing fat deposits to stick, which most likely causes arteriosclerosis, or hardening of the arteries. Smoking also stains teeth, fingernails, and lung tissue and causes bad breath.

Is **second-hand smoke** bad?

Yes. Secondhand smoke, also know as environmental tobacco smoke (ETS), is a mixture of the smoke given off by the burning end of a cigarette, pipe, or cigar and the smoke exhaled from the lungs of smokers. It is involuntarily inhaled by nonsmokers, lingers in the air hours after cigarettes have been out, and can cause a wide range of illnesses, including cancer, respiratory infections, and asthma.

Why do I see "**No Smoking**" signs in the windows of restaurants?

In the 1990s, when the dangers of second-hand smoke became widely known, may laws were passed in the United States to protect nonsmokers from having to inhale another person's smoke. Some of these laws prevent people from smoking in public or government buildings. Nonsmoking sections in restaurants have grown larger and larger, with many restaurants banning smoking altogether. Smoking is banned in most office buildings. California and New York have also passed statewide laws banning smoking in public places.

DAILY LIFE

HOME LIFE

Why do **people work**?

People usually work to get the things that they need to live. The most basic needs are food, clothing, and shelter. In some places, people grow their own food, make their own clothes, and build their own shelters, living much as their ancestors have for thousands of years. In other places people earn money to buy those things. Work in industrialized, or developed, nations frequently takes place in office buildings or factories, while some people still make their livings as farmers. The economies of such countries are based on advanced technologies and large-scale manufacturing, which create products and services that earn workers more money than people can make in the less industrial, or developing, countries of the world, where farming is the main industry (and most farmers can barely grow enough food for their own families). People who live in industrialized nations—like the United States, Canada, Japan, Australia, and many countries in Europe—are able to buy far more than the basic things they need to live. They are able to make their lives easier and safer by paying for clean water, electricity, good medical care, reliable transportation, and much more. Those who live in developing countries, located mainly in Africa, Asia, and Latin America, still struggle to acquire the most basic necessities. It may be hard to believe, but half of the world's people do not have enough of the right foods to be healthy.

When were **coins first used**?

Coins were first made in the seventh century B.C.E. in Lydia, Asia Minor (present-day Turkey). They were issued by the early Lydian kings—probably Alyattes or Sadyattes—about 600 B.C.E., several decades before the reign of the famous Lydian king Croesus. Lydian coins were made out of electrum, a mixture of gold and silver, and each was weighed and stamped with a lion's head, the king's symbol. About 0.03 pounds (14 grams) of electrum was one stater (meaning "standard"). A stater was about one month's pay for a soldier. Today's coins are not made from precious metals like gold and silver, but from inexpensive alloys such as cupro-nickel, which is a combination of copper and nickel. Unlike early coins, the metal in today's coins is worth far less than its value in the marketplace.

What is an **allowance**?

An allowance is an amount of money usually given each week to a child by his or her parents. Kids can use this money to pay for their personal expenses, for things like special snacks, toys, or activities with their friends. In some families, parents do not give their kids allowances, and children just ask their parents when money is needed. But allowances are useful because they help teach kids how to manage money—including spending, saving, and donating money to charity. Children learn how to control their expenses by staying within their weekly budgets. And children learn to save—if they want to buy something expensive, such as a new bicycle—by holding onto a portion of their allowances each week. In some families, allowances are considered payment for doing household chores, and they increase when children get older and do more work around the house.

Does **everyone** in the world live in a **house or apartment**?

No. Although people need houses for the same reason—to provide shelter—people live in different styles or types of houses. Their homes are determined by their country's climate (wet, dry, cold, or hot), location (in the desert, near a river, in a big city), natural resources (such as wood, stone, or snow), number of people living in the dwelling, and the amount of money they have to spend on a home. In China, for example, families who fish may still live on boats called junks, while city dwellers usually live in apartments. The Mongolians of Inner Mongolia in northern China live in transportable homes called yurts, a dome-shaped tent made of dried grass, animal wool, and leather hides. Herdsmen sleep in them when they are driving their herds, because they can carry them easily and set them up in an hour. In parts of the Philippines, near rivers that often flood, families live in homes on stilts. Some Navajo families today live in traditional eight-sided homes called hogans, but most of them live in ranch-style homes. The Inuits, who live along the northern coast of Canada, live in homes called igloos or snowhouses, which are made from blocks of snow fitted and shaped together in an arc. In some villages in Tanzania people live in mud homes, with roofs made from dried grass and banana and palm leaves.

Do these homes have **fireplaces, stoves, running water,** and **electricity**?

Many homes around the world, like igloos, tepees, and mud huts, do not have running water, stoves, bathrooms, electricity, or many of today's modern appliances.

In the United States, running water and electricity were not introduced until the mid-1800s, when power-driven machinery came into use. Sawmills, using steam power, provided abundant lumber. Nails and other metal products became cheap and plentiful. Steamships, canals, and finally railroads made these materials available in all settled communities. Inventors and manufacturers introduced many household conveniences. By the 1850s, fireplaces were being replaced by coal-burning stoves. Later in the nineteenth century, central heating by furnaces and radiators became available. Many homes today enjoy modern plumbing and use gas or electricity for cooking and lighting.

Where does the **water** from my **toilet go**?

When you flush the toilet or wash your clothes, the used water, called wastewater, goes down the drain. This wastewater travels through a network of underground pipes known as the sewer system. The city system treats the wastewater to keep it clean. Both large objects, such as sticks, cans, rocks, and small debris, such as gravel and sand, are separated from the wastewater. It is treated with oxygen, which allows micro-organisms to grow and eat small bits of organics. The wastewater is then recycled and clarified again. The wastewater is then disinfected with chlorine to kill harmful pathogens before being released into a nearby river, lake, or sea. In towns that do not have a sewer system, each house has its own septic system. Toilet water flows into a big underground tank where bacteria helps break down the waste. Then the water flows out into the soil, where it is absorbed.

Why do I have to do **household chores**?

Running a household is a lot of work. Your parents do most of the chores required to take care of your family's food, clothing, house, and yard, especially when you are young. But as you become older, your strength and skills increase, and you can help out. Household chores are called chores because they aren't fun to do. But these things—like taking out the trash, doing the dishes, and vacuuming—are necessary. When all family members pitch in, household chores get done more quickly, and everyone has more time to do the things they like. So when you do household chores, you are showing that you care about your family. Also, taking on additional responsibilities is a part of growing up, preparing you for the time when you will have to do those jobs by yourself.

Helping around the house with chores not only keeps the home clean but is also an important part of contributing to your family.

233

What is **dust**, exactly, and why might it be **bad for me**?

Dust is made up of particles of all sorts of things. In places where people live, a great deal of dust comes from flakes of dead skin, which are being shed all the time. Dust mites, tiny microscopic creatures that feed on this dead skin, make up dust, too (including their waste and tiny skeletons). Particles of the environment contribute to dust as well: grit from the sidewalk, salt from the sea, dry earth, pollen from plants, pet dander, molds, and smoke from burning materials. And Earth gets 10 tons of dust from outer space every day, from the meteors that burn up as they enter our atmosphere. Sometimes these ingredients cause allergic reactions, such as sneezing and coughing.

What's a **cobweb**?

A cobweb is an old, abandoned spider web that has collected dirt and dust. Sometimes the cobwebs you see in ceiling crevices and along floorboards are several draglines that spiders no longer use. The common house spider—which feeds on many insects daily—often abandons webs that do not yield prey, and then constructs new ones until it finds a productive site. It's best to sweep these old cobwebs away, and let your house spiders spin new webs, preferably outdoors!

How **many spiders** live around the **house**?

Probably too many to count. Spiders live everywhere, and tens of thousands can be found in a 1-acre (0.4 hectare) grassy field. There are more than 3,000 species in North America alone. No matter how clean your home is, most have a spider population that feeds on household insects, mites, and stray flies. They often live in dark, neglected areas, like closets, attics, and basements, and behind and under furniture, bookcases, or curtains. Corners and baseboards are two of their favorite locations. Most house spiders are seldom seen except during housecleaning, but some of the larger species mature and become more active from late August to early October. But spider specialists say this is no cause for alarm—very few spider species have venom that can harm humans, dogs, or cats.

Can **houseplants** help the **quality of air** in my house?

Yes. The air inside your home might be filled with toxins from tobacco smoke, cleaning products, ceiling tiles, and upholstery. Scientists have discovered that many types of houseplants absorb airborne pollutants as part of their normal "breathing" process—they take carbon dioxide in through their leaves, and let oxygen out. The plant transports these toxins to their roots, where microbes feed on and detoxify them. Although scientists disagree about how many—and what types of—houseplants it takes to clean the air, they suggest using a mix of plants. Bill Wolverton, a former NASA scientist and environmental engineer, studies the effects that plants have on air quality and has rated the areca palm, lady palm, bamboo palm, rubber plant, and dracaena as highly effective at clearing pollutants from the air.

Why does the **floor creak** at night?

All matter—gases, liquids, and solids—expands when heated and shrinks when cooled. This principle explains some of the funny and unexpected sounds that your house makes at night. During the day, the Sun's rays warm the materials your house is made of—like the wooden frame that supports its roof and walls—and they expand. Heat from the Sun may also make the interior of your house warmer and even shine on some of its furniture. When night comes, the temperature outside can drop 30 degrees or more as Earth turns away from the Sun. Things like wooden floors, house-building materials, and furniture become cooler, too, shrinking and slipping a little, which can sometimes cause creaking and groaning sounds. These noises are particularly noticeable at night because your home and neighborhood are so much quieter than they are during the day.

Why does the **wind make noise** outside my window?

When the wind (moving air) blows outside your window, you can often hear it. When the air speed increases, the friction over objects, such as leaves, tree branches, bushes, and the glass in your window, increases also. The process of friction can release whistling sounds and swooshing sounds, especially as wind speed becomes very high.

FAMILIES

Why do **people** get **married**?

Throughout the centuries—and in different parts of the world—men and women have married for a variety of reasons. It used to be common for young people to marry the person their parents chose for them, and some cultures continue to practice arranged marriages. Throughout most of the world today, however, a man and a woman usually marry because they love each other and want to be together and care for one another for the rest of their lives. Adults often want to have children together and raise them in a family. While people don't have to be married in order to have children, many people feel more comfortable raising a family as part of a married couple. When a man and a woman marry they make their permanent partnership public. After a marriage ceremony, they are connected by a legal contract— a marriage license—that can be dissolved by another legal decree known as a divorce (though death legally ends a marriage as well). Marriage grants a couple a new legal and social status, changing such things as the way they pay taxes and the amount they pay for health insurance.

Where do **babies** come **from**?

Babies grow in their mother's uterus, a special organ that houses the baby until it is born. At the start of pregnancy, a mother's egg is fertilized, which makes a new cell. The cell divides quickly into many more cells. At about one week, this tiny mass, called an embryo, sticks to the wall of the uterus, and begins to grow. From

235

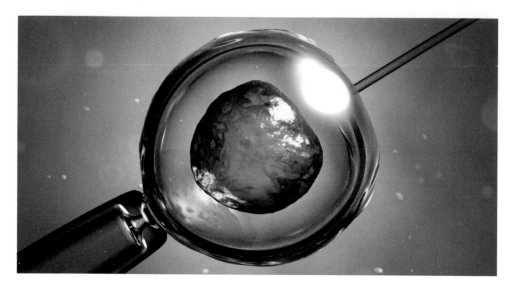

Sometimes parents have a hard time having a baby in the usual way, so the mother has her egg fertilized in a laboratory using the father's sperm. Then the fertilized egg is put back in the mom, where it grows in the womb naturally.

the moment of conception, 46 chromosomes and tens of thousands of genes combine to determine a baby's physical characteristics—the sex, facial features, body type, and color of hair, eyes, and skin. At the eighth week, the embryo is called a fetus. By the end of the twelfth week, the fetus is completely formed and is able to make a fist, can turn his or her head, and can squint and frown. Until the baby is ready to come out, it grows inside its mother's uterus. When the baby is ready to be born, at about 40 weeks, the mother starts to feel labor contractions. The uterus squeezes and pushes the baby out of the uterus and into the world.

What is a **test-tube baby**?

Sometimes, a man and a woman who want to have a baby have trouble conceiving. Many factors can contribute to a fertility problem, and sometimes medical science can help fix it. One solution to infertility is called in vitro fertilization. With this method a woman's eggs are fertilized with a man's sperm outside the woman's body. Fertilization takes place in a laboratory, in a glass dish (not really a test tube). Once fertilization occurs and the fertilized eggs begin to grow, they are placed inside the woman's uterus to develop further. Eventually a baby is born—and sometimes multiple babies are born if more than one of the fertilized eggs attaches to the uterus and develops fully. Children who originate from this method of fertilization are no different from other kids. They are simply children who began their lives outside of their mothers' bodies.

Who decides what is **right and wrong**?

When you are young, it is mainly your parents, but also teachers and other grown-ups close to you, who decide what is right and wrong. They are the ones who make the rules that they believe will keep you safe and help you learn how to become a

How can I get a baby brother instead of a baby sister?

There is no way specific way to place an order for a baby brother or a baby sister. The gender (boy or girl) of a baby is determined by whether the father's fertilizing sperm has an X or a Y chromosome. An X chromosome will lead to a girl, and a Y to a boy. (Mothers always contribute an X chromosome.) Although scientific methods are available to help parents organize their chromosomes and take advantage of the fact that the "boy" sperm has less DNA than "girl" sperm, they can be expensive and unreliable. One method, called the Shettles method, recommends that if parents want a girl, they should plan to make a baby right around the time of ovulation. At this time, the egg is as far away as possible from the incoming sperm so the long-distance runners of the sperm world, the X sperm, have a better chance of making it to the egg. For a boy, the method suggests that parents plan to make a baby about two to four days after ovulation. That way, the short-distance sprinting Y sperm can make it to the egg first. Many doctors say that although this method is based in science, it is no guarantee that a couple will have a baby boy or a baby girl.

good person and get along in the world. Adults make the best teachers because they have experienced a lot of different situations while growing up themselves, and they have learned lessons from those experiences that they can share with you. Grown-ups are wiser than children, who have lived just a short time in the world. But, as you continue to mature, you will have your own experiences and learn your own lessons. You may begin to question certain rules, and your ideas about what is right and wrong may change. This development is a normal part of growing up, the point at which you start to become the independent and unique person you are meant to be.

Why are **"please"** and **"thank you"** magic words?

Saying "please" and "thank you" is a part of etiquette, or good manners. And good manners make both your home and the world a more thoughtful and generous place. The words "please" and "thank you" are special words because they make dealing with other people go more smoothly. People have to ask for help or permission all the time. Saying "please" shows that your request also comes with respect for the person you are asking. People are usually more willing to fulfill the requests of those who treat them with respect. And after someone gives you something or assists you, it is polite to say "thank you" to show your appreciation. Someone whose actions are appreciated will be more likely to help you out or be generous again.

Why do I sometimes need a **time out**?

When troubling situations and conflict occur, our feelings come first before our thinking takes over. When someone does something we don't like, or that upsets us, our first reaction is to act on our feelings, which might include yelling or hitting.

A person can get pretty worked up physically, which doesn't allow him or her to listen to the thinking messages that are going on inside the brain. When an adult makes you take a "time out," it takes you away from the upsetting situation. Your body and feelings can settle down then, and you can start to think. It is normal and natural to react strongly to things that put your body on alert, but as you get older you begin to recognize that most situations can be handled calmly, using your words. You will be able to control your feelings better and use thinking to guide your actions. It is this development of self-control that shows you are growing up!

Why do I sometimes **wet my bed** at night?

Bed-wetting is fairly common and is often just a developmental (age-related) stage. Twenty percent of five-year-olds and 10 percent of six-year-olds wet the bed, according to the American Academy of Pediatrics. And it's twice as common in boys as it is in girls. Although there are many reasons for wetting the bed at night, doctors say it is often because these children have a difficult time waking up from their deep nighttime sleep. Some children have a small bladder that is more easily overfilled. Since bedwetting is physical, the child has no control over it when it is happening. However, there are things that you can do to help limit bed-wetting accidents, such as not drinking liquids after dinnertime and using the bathroom right before you go to bed. The majority of children grow out of bed-wetting naturally.

Why do my **clothes** need to be **washed**?

If you want to look clean and smell nice, your clothes need to be washed frequently. Most clothing is made of tiny threads that are woven together. As you go about your day, dirt and odors get trapped in the weave of your clothes and can only be removed by washing. Clothes must be jiggled and swished around quite a bit in water—as is done in a washing machine—to best remove dirt and odors. Detergent is added to the water to help the process: it can break up oily particles into smaller pieces that can be whisked away, and it can surround other dirt particles and pull them away from fabric.

Your hands can get very dirty with germs and gunk that you might not see, but the dirt is there! That is why it is important to always wash your hands before eating.

Should I **wash my hands** before I eat?

Yes. Washing your hands with soap and water cleans them of pathogens (bacteria and viruses) and chemicals that can cause disease. Hot water is not enough to clean your hands. Using soap adds to the time spent washing and breaks down the grease and dirt that carry most germs. The most important times to wash your hands with soap and water

My older sister says it's a bad idea to stick jellybeans up my nose. Why?

The nasal cavity is made up of two narrow passages that lead from the nostrils to the nasopharynx. In the nasal cavity, air is prepared for its journey into the lower airways and lungs. It is a sensitive space. Jellybeans (as well as other candies, nuts, and peas) are about the size of a child's nostril, and when lodged inside might get stuck there, or travel too far backward to manually remove. It may take a special trip to a doctor to get any foreign objects removed. Your older sister (or brother) is right: don't stick anything up your nose, *ever*.

are after you use the toilet or before handling food. When not washed with soap, hands that have been in contact with human or animal feces, bodily fluids like mucus, and contaminated foods or water can transport bacteria, viruses, and parasites to others. When done thoroughly and at least for 20 seconds, hand washing can prevent all types of illness and disease, skin infections, and eye infections.

Why do we need **table manners**?

It does seem that there are more rules about eating at a table with others than just about anything else. Put your napkin in your lap. Don't take huge bites. Don't talk with your mouth full. Ask for something to be passed to you instead of reaching for it. Don't start eating until everyone is seated and food has been offered all around. How can a person remember so many rules? And why are there so many in the first place?

Meals bring people into very close contact with each other. When you're sitting so near to one another, you can't help but notice everyone's behavior. Table manners were developed to make the dining experience as pleasant as possible, focusing on safety and consideration for others. Believe it or not, when you examine each rule separately, it actually makes sense. You shouldn't take big bites, for instance, because you could choke if you have too much food in your mouth. You shouldn't talk with your mouth full because that too increases the risk of choking, and because other diners will be able to see your half-chewed food, which is unpleasant. Reaching for things far away on the table could lead to knocking something else over along the way, including someone else's drink, for example, creating a real mess. The good reasons for different table manners go on and on. Maybe if you think about the reasons behind the rules, it will be easier to remember and follow them.

Why do **hugs and kisses** make me feel good?

Human beings communicate through language, a complicated system of vocal symbols that our complex brains allow us to learn after we are born. But we also communicate through our bodies and senses. Our organ of touch is our skin, covering the outside of our bodies. (Nerve endings under the surface of skin give us our sense of touch.)

239

Hugging and kissing are ways to share love and caring through touch. When you were born, well before you knew language and could understand caring words, you were learning about love through your sense of touch. As a newborn, when everything was frighteningly new, you immediately experienced the comfort of touch when you were held in your mother's arms, feeling the warmth of her body and the beat of her heart, sensations familiar to you when you were inside her womb. You were held close when you first learned about food and about how good it felt to have milk in your empty stomach. Your parents' caring hands kept you clean and dressed in dry clothes when you could not yet do those things for yourself. So, from your earliest days, you learned that someone's touch usually made you feel comfortable and safe.

Loving and caring about special people in our lives is a feeling inside that is hard to describe in words. But hugs and kisses make it easy to show that love—and their message is clear. Giving hugs and kisses feels as good as getting them. (Because the lips have an extra supply of nerve endings, kissing is an especially intense way to touch.) The human need to share affection through touch is something we all experience throughout our lives.

Why do I **cry** when I'm **unhappy or hurt** myself?

Scientists don't really know why we cry when we're unhappy or hurt (or sometimes, even joyful). But tears help express deeply felt emotions and often release stress and tension from the body. From our earliest days, when we were babies and could not yet communicate through language, crying let the people around us know that we needed something. Frequently, even after we become older, crying still serves as a wordless signal that something—help or comfort—is needed. In places all over the world, no matter what language is spoken, crying expresses emotions that are easily understood by all.

When will I be a **grown-up**?

In the United States you are considered a grown-up when you reach the age of 18. You are no longer legally connected with your parents, and you are entitled to the rights—and expected to fulfill the duties—of an adult American citizen. (You may vote and be called for military service, for instance.) There is a good chance, though, that when you are 18 your body has not yet reached full maturity. Many people continue to grow for a few more years. Most are fully grown—at least in height—by the time they are 20 years old, though boys may keep on growing until they are 23.

PETS

What is the most **common household pet** in the United States?

According to a national survey conducted by the American Pet Products Manufacturers Association in 2008, Americans owned about 75 million dogs and 88 million cats. Approximately 39 percent of U.S. households own at least one dog, and 34 percent own at least one cat. According to the American Kennel Club, Labrador retrievers are the most popular dog breed, followed by Yorkshire terriers, German shepherds, and golden retrievers. Persian cats are the most popular feline breed, followed by the Maine coon and the Siamese. Combined reptiles are the next popular type of pet, followed by birds and horses.

According to surveys, cats are now the number one pet in America, but dogs are still a very strong number two.

What **kinds** of **household pets** are common **around the world**?

Not all people own dogs and cats. While many Europeans, including the British, French, and Italians, own dogs and cats, other people have different relationships to them. In Islamic tradition, dogs are shunned as unclean and dangerous, and thus it has never been common for Arabs to own pets. However, in Saudi Arabia and Egypt it has become fashionable among the upper class to own dogs and cats. (As early as 3500 B.C.E., Egyptians domesticated wildcats from Africa, which became their treasured pets and honored for their skill in hunting snakes, rats, and mice.) In China, cats are thought to bring good luck and are kept in shops and homes; the country also has about 150 million pet dogs—about one for every nine people. The Japanese keep birds and crickets as pets. The Inuit Eskimo of northern Canada adopt bear cubs, foxes, birds, and baby seals. And Australian Aborigines capture dingo (wild dog) puppies and raise them for a time before letting them go.

Why does my **dog wag its tail** when it's happy to see me?

Because a dog cannot use words to communicate, it uses its tail wagging, facial expressions, ear position, posture, and vocalization to communicate. Puppies start wagging their tails when they are about six or seven weeks old, as they begin to interact with their fellow littermates and humans. At this time, puppies begin using their tails as a means of communication and social interaction. You may have noticed that if your dog is happy, content, and confident, he will wag his tail. Animal specialists believe that tail wagging is in the dog's genes: since wolves (the ancestors of today's domesticated dogs,) ran in packs, communication—whether by barking, growling, or wagging tails—was essential to survival. Researchers agree that a dog with a loosely wagging tail is usually "saying" that he is friendly or excited. However, a wagging tail is not always a sign of friendliness: an aggressive dog might hold its tail high and wag only the tip, while a submissive or scared dog is more likely to hold its tail low and wag it stiffly. Look for these clues in your own dog. If you ever approach anyone else's, ask the owner for permission to pet the animal before making contact.

241

Why do **dogs bark**?

Dogs bark to communicate with other dogs and with humans. Dogs are descendants of wolves, which are social animals that live in packs, and they share many of the behaviors that define the complex relationships that exist within such animal groups. Few domestic dogs live together in packs (though they often consider their human family their group), but they still use complicated behaviors that involve smell, sight, and hearing to communicate.

A dog has many scent-producing glands that it uses to communicate. The scent that a dog leaves behind (in its urine, feces, and paw prints) can reveal its sex, age, and even its mood to other dogs that come sniffing by. A dog uses its posture, facial expression, and ear and tail position to communicate with other dogs, too. And it uses its voice to communicate by whining, growling, howling, or barking. A dog usually whines or whimpers when it is in distress: when it is hungry, cold, or in pain. Growls indicate that a dog is angry and ready to fight. Barks usually show excitement.

Why does my **dog** sometimes **howl**?

Like barking, growling, and whining, howling is one of the few forms of verbal communication that dogs have. Its roots go back to dogs' wolf ancestry, when wild wolves used howling to communicate over long distances. The howl swept through different pitches, which helped the sound carry over longer distances. Wolves use howl-

ing to let other pack members know their precise location if they happen to get separated. Other members of the pack howl back in reply—an acknowledgement that the sent message has been received. Wolves also howl to discourage a rival pack from encroaching on their territory. Dogs today still display some of this behavior. If you leave your house or apartment, your dog may howl to try to reestablish contact with you. If the howling persists after you've left, it could be a sign of separation anxiety. And sometimes dogs howl to establish their territory.

Dogs bark and howl for a lot of different reasons. The sounds they make can mean they are excited, mad, happy, afraid, or guarding their territory.

Why don't **dogs get hoarse** when they bark a lot?

It seems like some dogs can bark and bark for hours. Yet they never seem to get hoarse or lose their voice (bark) like people do when they talk, yell, or sing too much. Veterinarians (animal doc-

Can a pet help me when I am having a bad day?

Yes! Research shows that regular contact with pets benefits a person's over-all health by reducing heart rate, blood pressure, and levels of stress. Pets offer stability, comfort, security, affection, and intimacy. They teach children how to care for others, and they help teach children responsibility as they feed them and tend to their daily needs. In addition, studies show that playing with pets helps people feel happy and may contribute to fewer feelings of loneliness and depression. The whole family can bond around an animal as they share the tasks of walking, feeding, grooming, and interacting with a household pet.

tors) think that is because a dog's voice box, or larynx, is not as complicated as the larynx of a human, who needs to make a wide range of different sounds to speak. So the stress that results from excessive barking doesn't do nearly as much damage as overusing a human voice does.

Why does my **cat purr**?

Animal specialists believe that cats purr to show contentment. Cats are born with the ability to purr; kittens make tiny rumbling sounds when they are nursing. Scientists think that purring starts out as a form of communication between a mother cat and her kittens. The purr lets the mother cat know that her babies are happy and feeding well, and she may purr back in response. Later, cats continue to purr when they are in a contented mood or as a friendly greeting. But scientists aren't really sure how cats purr. Many think that it comes from the vibration of blood in a large vein in the cat's chest, caused when surrounding muscles repeatedly squeeze and release the blood vessel. Air in a cat's lungs and windpipe increase the sound of the vibrations that can be heard (although sometimes the purring is silent and can only be felt). Other scientists think that cats purr when membranes called false vocal chords, located in a cat's throat near the real ones, start to vibrate.

Why does my **cat arch its back**?

Like meowing and purring, a cat's arching back is part of its complex body language system, usually associated with feeling threatened. The arch is able to get so high because the cat's spine contains nearly 60 vertebrae, which fit loosely together. Humans have only 34 vertebrae.

How does a **cat's tail** help keep the animal **balanced**?

Almost 10 percent of a cat's bones are in its tail, and the tail is used to maintain the animal's balance. A cat's tail plays a vital part in its "righting reflex" that allows it to land on its feet after falling from a height. Cats often survive a long fall based on their agility and balance, which they develop as kittens. When falling, the fluid in the inner ear shifts and the cat rotates its head until it equalizes and the fluid is

243

> **My pet iguana was tiny and now it's more than 3 feet (0.91 meters) long! What happened?**
>
> If cared for properly, green iguanas can live more than 20 years. But they do indeed grow … grow … and grow along the way. Although iguanas make popular pets, they need lots of time, attention, care, and room to grow. A healthy iguana will grow to be 5 to 6 feet (1.5 to 1.8 meters) in length, and will require a very large cage or an entire room to live in. Iguanas need tall cages because they are tree-dwelling (arboreal) creatures, and prefer to spend the majority of their time as high off the ground as possible. Iguanas also need a special diet, plenty of sun, places to climb, and human interaction and stimulation.

level. The body automatically shifts to follow the head, and the cat lands on its feet. A cat also uses its tail to communicate. A cat's tail held high means that it is happy. A twitching tail is a warning sign that it may be angry or on guard, and a tail tucked in close to the body is a sign of insecurity or fearfulness.

Why do **mice** cry **red tears**?

People who own rats and mice may be shocked when they see their pet rodent has red tears and nasal secretions. Red crusts may also develop around your pet's eyes and nose, and the forepaws may be red from rubbing the face. This redness is not caused by blood, but by the secretion of a red pigment called porphyrin. This pigment is released from a gland behind the eye called the Harderian gland. (The scientific name for the colored tears is *chromodacryorrhea*.) Although the red coloration is not blood, the red tears suggest your pet rodent may be ill because they cry these tears when they are sick or stressed.

Why does my **guinea pig** have **buck teeth**?

Pet rodents—hamsters, rats, mice, gerbils, and guinea pigs—are very popular pets. Common to these pets is large front teeth, called incisors, which grow continuously throughout the pet's life. Overgrown incisors are a common problem and can be prevented by allowing the pet to chew on pieces of wood chewing sticks. Often a veterinary surgeon (a pet doctor) can trim these front teeth. Rodents are herbivorous (plant-eating) animals, and the digestive tract is, in some ways, similar to that of other plant-eaters, such as horses and cattle. They love to use their front teeth to nibble and chew!

Can my **turtle** take **off its shell**?

No. The turtle's outer shell is made of a thin layer of keratin, like your fingernails. But underneath that layer, there is a layer of bony plates that give the shell its shape. The ribs and vertebrae (backbones) are part of the shell, too. So removing

Kissing a reptile like a snake or turtle is not a great idea. Reptiles can carry germs that cause salmonella, which will make you very sick to your stomach.

the shell would remove part of the skeleton of the turtle—which is why it is impossible for a turtle to remove its shell.

Why do I have to **wash my hands** after **handling** my pet **turtle**?

Turtles and other reptiles, such as snakes and lizards, can carry salmonella bacteria. Although this does not affect the animal's health, it can make humans very sick. In order to avoid getting salmonella, a few rules of hygiene should be followed. First, don't put reptiles in your mouth. Wash your hands carefully with soap and hot water after you handle the turtle. Very young children should just look, and not touch, reptiles. Don't let reptiles walk (or slither) around in the house—keep them in their cages and tanks. The most common source of the salmonella bacteria is undercooked food, especially eggs and poultry, so be sure to tell your parents or adult caregiver to thoroughly cook your eggs and chicken. (And don't lick the cake batter if it contains raw eggs!)

Is it okay to bring my **pet snake** to school for **show and tell**?

Because animals are unpredictable and because schools have rules, it is never okay to bring animals out in public without the permission of both a parent and teacher. Even if you have permission, these creatures—such as snakes, rabbits, hamsters, gerbils, lizards, frogs, and other small critters—should be contained in their habitats and handled very carefully. Sometimes in public animals are outside of their natural habitats because they play a role in helping humans. Guide dogs (also called seeing-eye dogs) help the blind or visually impaired move around cities and neighborhoods. These dogs are trained to behave properly on public transportation, in restaurants, in stores, and in any other place their masters go. Other times people carry their dogs and cats in pet carriers to the vet, to the park, or on shopping trips. However, they

245

must have the store's permission to enter, since many businesses (like restaurants and supermarkets) do not allow pets or require them to be contained and/or on leashes.

Why should I **walk my dog** every day?

Walking with your dog strengthens the bond between you and your pet, and it is also the healthy thing to do. Dogs, like people, benefit from exercise to help control weight and to maintain a healthy heart, lungs, and muscles. They love going for a walk, running and jumping, and retrieving a ball or Frisbee. Aging pets must be kept as agile and fit as possible, but may not be motivated to exercise without encouragement. The pleasure of your company is one of your dog's greatest motivations to exercise. In addition to exercise, dogs also need social interaction, positive attention from their owner, and mental stimulation. Many of these needs can be met by simply taking your dog for a walk. Always remember to walk your dog on a secure leash (with identification tags) and pick up after your pet. During warm weather carry water for your pet, and always pause when your dog needs a rest.

What do I do if my **pet dies**?

Like all living things, your pet will die someday. A pet can die from old age, an accident, or an illness. Even when a veterinarian (an animal doctor) helps, there are some illnesses that can't be cured. If your pet is in a lot of pain and will never get better, your parents and the vet may decide that the animal should be allowed to die, or "put to sleep." To make the process pain-free and peaceful, the vet can give the pet a special kind of injection (shot) to help it die. If your pet dies naturally, you may want to bury it in your back yard. But check with your town or city first to make sure burial on your property is legal. Some laws permit homeowners to bury their pets on their property, while others do not. Other options include burying your pet at a pet cemetery or cremating the animal, then scattering the ashes throughout your garden or under a favorite tree.

No matter what you decide to do when your pet dies, many emotions are likely to surface, such as sadness, loneliness, or even anger. Talk to your parents about how you are feeling. You and your family may want to find special ways to remember your pet. You might have a ceremony, tell stories, write a poem, or make a scrapbook. And there are animal organizations, such as the ASPCA (the American Society for the Prevention of Cruelty to Animals) that can help you with the grieving process. A new animal can't replace your old pet, but someday the time might be right for you and your family to adopt a new animal for everyone to love.

GOING TO SCHOOL

Why do I have to **go to school**?

Much of what you need to know to live successfully as an adult does not come naturally—it has to be learned and studied and memorized. Children learn to speak naturally, for example, by listening to those around them, but reading and writing must be specifically taught. The complicated process of learning the alphabet and the sounds it represents, putting letter sounds together to make words, and learning the meaning of words in order to read and write are skills that only come with special effort. Knowing how to figure out problems that involve numbers, and learning how the world is run or how nature works are important things to learn, too.

Although your parents might be able to teach you these things, they would need many hours each day to do it. Most parents work outside the home and wouldn't have the time to give proper instruction (although some kids are "home schooled" by their parents instead of going to school). In the United States, a public school system provides years of free education for all children. Teachers, who are specially trained to know what children should learn, and how, and when, are the people who do the job. To ensure that children learn what they need to, state governments now require that all children go to school for a certain number of years (usually until age 16). Kids who skip school a lot can find themselves in court. (Children who go to private schools or whose parents have received special permission to teach them at home are exceptions.)

What is **home schooling**?

Home schooling (also called home education or home learning) is the education of children at home, typically by parents or professional tutors, rather than in a public or private school. Most parents cite family togetherness, more control over curriculum, and having a say over what their children learn as reasons to home school. Many of the families who home school also do so for religious reasons. Because each state makes its own laws for education and schooling, home schooling is defined differently in each state. According to different surveys, between 1.7 and 2 million children in grades kindergarten through 12 were home schooled in the United States during the 2002-2003 school year (the most recent data available).

Did our **Founding Fathers discuss school** in the country's founding documents?

America's founders did debate a bit as to whether or not to force children to attend schools, and they decided to leave such decisions to individual families and local and state governments. The words "education" and "school" do not appear in any of our founding documents, such as the Declaration of Independence, the Constitution, or the Bill of Rights. Some of our most famous inventors, writers, and politicians were

Many parents teach their children at home rather than sending them to a public or private school because they feel they can give their kids a lot more attention and help them learn more.

How long has home schooling been practiced in the United States?

The concept of home schooling was first introduced by early republic families, before schools were built and made in America. Family, community, religious institutions, and work were all integrated into the daily lives and upbringing of children. Through involvement in daily life, children gathered knowledge of everything from growing food, construction, caring for livestock, and making tools, clothing, and soap. Sometimes families hired or shared professional or informal tutors who instructed children at various times for short periods each year; other families used daily chores, apprenticeships, and internships to educate their children. Many home schoolers incorporate these traditions into their home school curriculum today.

self-taught, learning through mentoring or apprenticeships, conversation, and reading. In 1850, Massachusetts became the first state to institute a compulsory schooling law.

What is **school** like in **other countries**?

Schools are different in every country in the world. A school may have lots of classrooms, books, play equipment, and a playground, or lessons may take place under trees or in an open outdoor space. A temple, a tent, or a building on stilts may serve as a classroom for some children. In poor places that have no money to build schools, children may learn their lessons outdoors. In isolated places—such as the Australian outback or the Alaskan wilderness—where families live hundreds of miles apart and far from cities or towns, children may get their lessons from teachers over two-way radios or the Internet. All around the world, schools are a reflection of the culture in which they are formed. In Japan, as students enter school, they remove their shoes and put on slippers, a Japanese custom. They do not write with pencils; instead, each child has his or her own ink well, brush, and ink for writing the kanji (Japanese characters). Children often clean their classrooms (including dusting cubbies and mopping floors), and at the end of each class the students thank their teacher and bow. In schools in Brazil and other South American countries, children often go to school barefoot. In India, children practice yoga in school. And many children that go to public schools in European countries, such as Germany and France, ride their bikes to school or take public transportation, rather than school buses.

My friend says he's a **genius**. Is that possible?

Some people use the term "genius" to mean a genius I.Q. or extreme intelligence. I.Q. stands for intelligence quotient, and it is supposed to be a measurement of how naturally intelligent a person is. Scientists think that each person is born with a certain amount of intelligence or mental ability. Still, how well a person uses his or her natural intelligence has a lot to do with the person's desire to learn and the learning environment he or she grows up in. I.Q. tests measure things like the ability to use words, the ability to see how things relate to one another, and the ability to store and use information. The term "intelligence quotient" comes from the mathematical equation used to score intelligence tests. A person's mental age—which is determined by how many questions he or she has answered correctly on such a test—is divided by his or her actual age. Then that number is multiplied by 100 to give an I.Q. score. A person whose mental and actual age are the same will have an I.Q. that is 100, which is average. A person with an I.Q. of 170 or greater is considered a genius.

When people think of geniuses, they often think of great men and women from history, including the Italian painter of the *Mona Lisa,* Leonardo da Vinci, the great scientist Albert Einstein, and the child genius Wolfgang Amadeus Mozart, the famous Austrian musical composer. Before he was even five years old, Mozart could master complicated musical compositions in just a half an hour. Even at this early age, before most of today's children start formal schooling, Mozart was composing his own works. He is called "gifted" and a "child prodigy," because he mastered many talents at an early age.

Why are **some kids better** at **schoolwork** than others?

Some children do better in school than others for many reasons. All kids have different talents and abilities, and some of these just show up better in school. Some children may be naturally better at reading and writing, working with numbers, and at storing and using information. Some children are very organized, good with managing their time, and diligent about doing their homework. Most schoolwork requires these skills, so kids who are strong in these areas are likely to be better students. Still, most kids have enough ability to earn the basic skills taught in schools, things that they will need to know to get along well in the world once they graduate. Kids succeed by putting a lot of time and effort into their studies, by getting help when they need it, and by not giving up!

What is a **learning disability**?

Learning disabilities are disorders that keep people from understanding or using spoken or written language in typical ways. Learning disabilities are not due to physical handicaps, like blindness or deafness. Instead, they have to do with problems in the brain and the way it perceives things. About 10 percent of all children in the United States have some type of learning disability. The most common of these are dyslexia—where the brain has trouble understanding words, sometimes reversing the order of letters and words—and attention deficit hyperactivity disorder (ADHD), which is marked by difficulty with concentration. Special teaching methods have been developed to help such children learn successfully despite their disorders. The teaching is done either in the regular classroom, in special classes, or at a specialized school.

American Sign Language is a system of hand gestures used to communicate to people with severe hearing impairments.

Why do I have to do **homework**?

The hours in a school day and the amount of time a teacher can spend individually with students are limited. As a result, teachers need the understanding and help of their students, parents, and families in supporting classroom instruction and learning outside school hours. Homework has been part of school life since the beginning of formal schooling in the United States. It is important because it can improve your thinking and memory. It can help you develop positive study habits and skills that will serve you well throughout your life. Homework also can encourage you to use time well, learn independently, and take responsibility for your work. And if you have an adult supervise you, it benefits them as well. It helps your mom and dad see what you are learning in school and helps your family communicate with you and your teachers.

Where did the **English alphabet** come from?

An alphabet is a system of writing in which symbols or letters represent all the sounds of language. Because ancient Egyptian hieroglyphics sometimes used symbols to represent language sounds, they are considered the root of true alphabets. The English alphabet came from the ancient Romans, who based theirs on the ancient Greeks. Modern English uses a modified form of this Latin alphabet. The written languages of western Europe, Africa, and the Americas, as well as scientific writing, all use the Roman, or Latin, alphabet. It has 26 letters, and is written from left to right.

What is **American Sign Language**, and does it have an alphabet?

American Sign Language (ASL) is a complete, complex language that uses signs made with the hands and other movements, including facial expressions and postures of the body. It is the first language of many deaf North Americans, and one of several communication options available to deaf people. ASL is the fourth most commonly used language in the United States. Even though ASL is used in America, it is a language completely separate from English. It contains all the basic fea-

> ### Which library has the most books?
>
> **A**ccording to the American Library Association, there are an estimated 123,291 libraries of all kinds in the United States today. The Library of Congress, founded in Washington, D.C., in 1800, is both the oldest and largest library in the United States. On August 24, 1814, British troops burned the Capitol building (where the library was housed) and destroyed the library's core collection of 3,000 volumes. The following year, Congress approved the purchase of statesman Thomas Jefferson's personal library of 6,487 books for $23,950. Today, the Library of Congress is the largest library in the world, with more than 138 million items on approximately 650 miles of bookshelves. The collections include more than 32 million books and other print materials, 2.9 million recordings, 12.5 million photographs, 5.3 million maps, 5.5 million pieces of sheet music, and 61 million manuscripts.

tures a language needs to function on its own, including a finger alphabet, and rules for grammar, punctuation, and sentence order.

What does it mean to be **bilingual**?

A bilingual person is able to speak two languages. A person who speaks more than two languages is called "multilingual." A person does not have to speak two languages with equal fluency to be considered bilingual; usually, a person will be stronger in one language than another. It is common for most of the world's societies to be multilingual; in the United States, one in five children enters school speaking a language other than English, according to the 2000 Census. Some children who learn English in school speak their native language at home. Bilingualism often allows children to communicate with their grandparents, which can strengthen family bonds across both generations and countries. Bilingualism teaches an appreciation of the arts and traditions of two cultures. It promotes tolerance and cross-cultural understanding; research indicates that children who are raised with a bicultural identity tend to be more accepting of cultural differences in others.

What is **literacy**?

Literacy is more than just the ability to read and write. According to the Department of Education and other government sites, literacy is defined as an individual's ability to read, write, speak in one's native language, and compute and solve problems at levels of proficiency necessary to function on the job, in the family, and in society. This is a broader view of literacy than just an individual's ability to read. As information and technology have increasingly shaped society, the skills we need to function successfully have gone beyond reading.

What is a **pen pal**?

Pen pals (also called pen friends) are people who regularly write to each other, particularly via postal mail. They are often located in faraway places, such as other states and countries. A pen pal relationship is often used to practice reading and writing in a foreign language, to improve literacy, to learn more about other countries and lifestyles, and to feel connected to people in other parts of the world—which helps the world feel like a much smaller place!

Pen pals come in all ages, nationalities, and cultures. Pals may seek new pals based on their own age group or a shared common interest, such as a specific sport or hobby, or they may select someone totally different to gain knowledge about a foreign culture (such as the Far East, Europe, or South America). With the advent of the Internet, a modern version on the traditional pen pal arrangement has developed, and many pen pals also exchange e-mail addresses as well as, or instead of, paper letters. In order to connect with a pen pal, get your mom or dad's permission first. Often, online sites dedicated to pen pal communication can help you connect with a student your own age.

Why should I **visit the library** often?

Libraries offer books for people of all ages, and much, much more—they are places of learning and discovery for everyone. Besides books, public libraries offer videos, DVDs, free access to computers and the Internet, and many literacy-related programs. For elementary school children, there are variations of the read-alouds and storytelling hours that often include discussions and presentations by the children themselves, as well as summer reading programs. For middle-school kids, there may also be book talks, summer reading programs, creative writing seminars, drama groups, and poetry readings. The more you read, the more you learn! In addition, the library is a place to find information and help with schoolwork. Your school library may offer some of these services as well.

Librarians are not just people who tell you to be quiet at the library. They love to help kids and adults find information and learn new things!

What is the **librarian's job**?

Librarians have many responsibilities. One of the most important ones is to help the public (called patrons) find the books and materials that they are looking for—this is their specialty. For example, if you don't know which books to select, the librarian can help you select books that are both fun and suitable to your age level. They can also show you the other programs and services the library has to offer. Ask a librarian for help when looking for books and materials, so that you become comfortable with the library system and the process for getting the information you need. Keep in mind, however, that a librarian is there to point out different choices, not to decide what you should read. If you are unsure if a book is appropriate for you, ask a parent to help you select books and participate in your reading programs.

What can **parents do** to **help kids** with their **library assignments**?

Very often school-age children will ask their parents for help with library assignments. And very often parents will find themselves gradually taking over and doing a report for their son or daughter. Instead, ask your parents to try the following ideas to motivate you and increase confidence in wading through a book report or library assignment (courtesy of Reading Rockets, a nonprofit educational service of WETA, Washington, D.C.'s leading public broadcasting station):

- Ask your children questions about the assignment and encourage them to ask their teacher questions. This helps children to clarify what they are trying to do. Help them to identify smaller components of the topic they are researching or to see the topic as part of a larger topic. (For example, brontosaurus is a subgroup of dinosaurs, which is a subgroup of extinct animals.) These classifications will help them to identify useful references.

- Suggest that they look up the topic in the library catalog, periodical guides, and reference books. The librarian will direct them and help them get started. Be sure they know how to use a table of contents and index. Suggest they start with something general about the subject and be prepared to consult more than one source.

- Help them to break assignments into logical segments and avoid last-minute panics by setting deadlines for each phase of the work. Allow them plenty of time to gather the materials they need.

- Help them to determine if the community library has the resources they need or if they need to check other information sources.

- Encourage your kids to ask the librarian for help in locating materials and let them do their own talking.

- Give them encouragement, advice, and a ride if they need it, but resist the temptation to take over an assignment. Let your children assume responsibility for researching and writing reports. It is the best way for them to library skills that they will able to use for the rest of their lives.

What's the best way to **make friends** at a **new school**?

Although it might be overwhelming your first few days at a new school, you'll find it's easier to make friends than you might think. Especially if you try to behave in a way that you think would make a good friend. By being inviting, smiling, and making eye contact, people will naturally greet you. If you see someone you recognize from class, the basketball court, or the community, give a smile or say hi. Introduce yourself. Tell them your name and where you're from. Asking questions, such as "What sports do you like to play?" or "Have you been here since kindergarten?", is a good way to begin a friendship.

And it's always good "friend etiquette" to do something nice for someone, such as saving someone a seat, saying hi in the hall, or offering congratulations on a good test score. Even a simple compliment, such as "I like your backpack," can go a long way toward making friendships. Other ways to make new friends is to join a sports team, engage in school activities, such as choir or theater, or form or join a study group. All are great ways to make potential friends, establish common bonds, and get academic support. And guidance counselors can arrange for "buddies" with similar interests and the same classes to introduce new students to the school campus the first few days of school.

And here's a fun tip: Look for other people who are new to the school. You'll discover you're probably not the only new student. At the very least, you'll share the fact that you're both in an unfamiliar environment. And if you are starting at a new school in start-up year, almost everyone is new! Talk about your old school, your new school, your opinions, grades, teachers, and interests with a wide variety of people—you'll soon find you have more than one new friend, but several or many!

What is **stress**?

Stress is your body's way of responding to any kind of demand. It can be caused by both good and bad experiences. When people feel stressed by something going on around them, their bodies react by releasing chemicals into the blood. These chemicals give people more energy and strength, which can be a good thing if their stress is caused by physical danger—such as steering a bike out of a driveway if a car is approaching. But stress can also be a bad thing, if yours is in response to something emotional and there is no outlet for this extra energy and strength. Young people experience stress at a high rate, and females more than males, an extensive Associated Press/MTV survey showed in 2007. People under large amounts of stress can become tired, sick, irritable, and unable to concentrate or sleep, so it's important to identify when you might be "feeling stressed" and take steps to lessen your stress level.

Why do I have to be a **"good sport"** when I **lose a game**?

Sports games, board games, and competitions—such as spelling bees and gymnastics competitions—always have winners and losers. When you agree to play a game you have to prepare yourself for the fact that you may not win. If you can see the game as a way to improve your own skills and to have fun, you may even be able to admire (and learn from) the talent of the person who beats you and congratulate him or her. After all, it's only a game.

So remember that when you play a game, the *object* is not to win, but to participate well. Play fairly, with courtesy and respect for your teammates and oppo-

How can I manage my stress?

Stress usually comes from a combination of your schedule and schoolwork. Notice whether your schedule allows you enough time to get all your schoolwork done or whether you need to budget your time better to accomplish all your assignments. If finding time to get your schoolwork done seems almost impossible, plan to find a quiet place (like a library or study hall) to spend the first hour or two after school to do your homework. If scheduling is not the problem and the schoolwork is too difficult for you, plan to spend the first few hours after school in your teacher's classroom, at study hall, or in a tutoring program to get the help you need. Avoiding budgeting your time or asking for help may be unnecessarily increasing your stress level at school. And, if you have trouble discerning what kind of help you need, ask your parents and teacher to help you decide where your stress is coming from.

Three of the easiest and best ways to deal with stress are to get plenty of exercise, eat a good breakfast every day, and get lots of sleep (7 to 10 hours per night, depending upon your age). It is also important to stay away from caffeine and sugar, because they do not help your body manage stress in the long term. Stress experts say it's also important to have practical expectations about school, make to-do lists when necessary, and take creative study breaks, such as going rollerblading or biking. Do not make grades the most important—or only—thing in your life. It is important to have friends and find hobbies and activities that you like. If you feel overwhelmed, remember to talk to friends, a parent, a teacher, or your guidance counselor about what's going on in your school life. Often, there are several ways to juggle assignments, extend deadlines, or work together as a team to get a project done.

nents, and with your best effort. It is also important to show good behavior following the game, whether you win or lose (which is why many coaches have all teammates shake hands with or "high five" members of the opposite team post-game).

What do I do if I am **being bullied**?

Lots of kids have been picked on by a bully, for many different reasons. Bullying is intentional tormenting in physical, verbal, or psychological ways, and can range from hitting, shoving, name-calling, threats, and mocking to taking lunch money or personal items. If you've been the target of a bully, you know it can be very scary and upsetting to be teased, hit, or threatened. Sometimes it helps to simply ignore what the bully is saying—most bullies tease or threaten other kids to get a reaction from those they tease, and if they get no reaction at all, it's a lot less fun for them. It usually helps to have friends around. A kid walking alone is more vulnerable than a group of kids. And even if you don't *feel* confident, sometimes *acting* confident helps. If you hold your head high and tell a bully to stop calling you

255

Bullying can be a big problem at school or just around the neighborhood. If you are being bullied by someone, you should not keep it a secret. You should tell an adult and ask for help.

names, you may just surprise that bully into silence. One approach to avoid is responding to bullying with fighting or bullying back—aggressive responses will only make matters worse.

Should I **tell my parents** I am being **bullied**?

Yes. Even though it may feel awkward or embarrassing, it helps to tell your parents, a teacher, or a counselor about a bullying experience. A trusted adult can make you feel better by explaining why bullies behave the way they do and by reassuring you that what a bully says about you has nothing to do with who you really are. Adults can help keep you safe if you're being threatened, and come up with solutions to deal with the bullying. Many states have bullying laws and policies, and many schools have programs in place that educate parents and kids about bullying.

What do I do if **witness bullying** on the playground?

If you are on a playground and you see a kid hurting or making fun of another kid, your first impulse might be to turn around and pretend you don't see it. But imagine how that bullied kid is feeling, and you'll know that the right thing to do is to try to put a stop to it. The best thing to do is to find a teacher or another adult and tell that person what is happening. Or, if the situation doesn't feel like it could threaten your personal safety, the best thing you can do is stand up for the kid being bullied. Kids who make fun of others usually expect to get a laugh from their friends, and if you show the bully that his or her teasing isn't funny and that you support the person being teased, it could end the teasing.

What is **head lice**?

The head louse is a tiny, wingless insect that lives in human hairs and feeds on very small amounts of blood drawn from the scalp. Although they may sound kind of disgusting, lice appear often on young children in common settings, such as school. Lice aren't dangerous and they don't spread disease, but they are contagious and can be very annoying. Their bites may cause the scalp to become itchy and inflamed, and scratching may lead to skin irritation. They can be hard to get rid of, and take lots of work to make them go away and *stay away*. Usually, using special medicated shampoos and thoroughly cleaning sheets, carpets, clothing, and personal products, like combs and brushes, gets rid of the pesky insects. Kids should try to avoid head-to-head contact at school (both in classrooms and on the playground) and while playing at home with other children. They also shouldn't share combs, brushes, hats, scarves, bandanas, ribbons, barrettes, towels, helmets, or other personal care items with anyone else, whether they may have lice or not.

SERVING MY COMMUNITY

What **type of people** help make a **community operate well**?

Firefighters, police officers, ambulance drivers, garbage collectors, mail carriers, crossing guards public-school teachers, school-grounds and maintenance workers, public librarians, bus drivers, and parks and recreation workers are just a few of the city-service people that make a town or city run well. Every day, these and hundreds of other workers labor to make communities across the United States safe, clean, and healthy. Many of these workers are paid for their jobs, but many also volunteer (work without pay) to help their neighborhoods be safe. The government estimates that about 60 million people volunteer each year, most often in religious, educational, youth, or community service organizations. Volunteers commonly perform activities such as firefighting, coaching, campaigning, fundraising, delivering goods, and serving on boards or neighborhood associations.

How do **police officers** help the community?

There are about 800,000 police officers in the United States. Police officers protect the lives and property of citizens. They maintain order, catch lawbreakers, and work to prevent crimes. Also called "peace offers," police officers have different responsibilities depending upon the size and structure of the communities in which they serve. Police officers may patrol the streets on foot or in squad cars, control traffic, or work as detectives investigating crimes. At the police station, officers may be assigned to work in the crime laboratory or the records department. All officers file reports of incidents, and many testify at trials and hearings.

Lots of kids dream of being firefighters or police officers when they grow up. A desire to help your community is a great thing, and you should pursue it if you are really interested.

How do **firefighters** help the community?

There are about 355,000 firefighters working in communities across the United States. Firefighters work under extremely dangerous conditions, risking their own lives to save others as they battle fires. Called "first responders," they are usually the first emergency personnel at traffic accidents or explosions and may be called upon to put out fires or treat injuries. Once at a fire, they use axes to break down walls or windows so they can evacuate people trapped by flames and other obstacles. Rescue squads take first-aid equipment to fires and help the injured until ambulances arrive. They also may be called for injuries and accidents not caused by fire, such as heart attacks. Despite the dangers, firefighters take satisfaction from providing an important public service.

What is **philanthropy**?

The word "philanthropy" comes from two Greek words, *philos* (meaning "loving") and *anthropos* (meaning "man"), and is translated as "love for mankind." Today's definition includes the concept of voluntary giving of money by an individual or group to promote the common good and improve people's quality of life. The modern notion of philanthropy began with steel tycoon Andrew Carnegie, who, in an essay titled "The Gospel of Wealth" published in 1889, gave birth to the idea that the rich should, instead of leaving their wealth to their families, "administer it as a public trust during life."

Why is it important to **volunteer**?

In 2007, many Americans—about 60 million people, or about 26 percent of Americans age 16 or older—volunteered, or performed unpaid work for a nonprofit

> ## Why do people wear uniforms?
>
> **S**ome jobs require special clothing or uniforms. Sometimes these special clothes are meant to protect workers or the people they work with. An emergency room doctor, for instance, may wear special clothes to protect herself from blood and infectious agents as well as to protect patients from the germs and impurities that may be present on ordinary clothing. Most often, though, special clothes or uniforms are worn so that workers can be easily recognized by other people. Occupations that require uniforms are frequently service jobs, where workers help or perform services for other people. Workers in stores and restaurants frequently wear uniforms so that customers know whom to ask for help or service. Uniforms help police officers do their jobs better, because people recognize them and go to them for help or give them the cooperation they need to maintain the law. On the battlefield, soldiers wear uniforms to identify which country they are from, signaling whether they are friends or enemies.

organization (or charity), according to the Corporation for National and Community Service. They understood that volunteering is an important part of life. It provides an opportunity for us to see our world from a different perspective, gain exposure to new people, places, and situations, and make a difference in someone's life. Volunteering provides us with a chance to interact with people from different backgrounds, who come together to support a common cause. Whether you serve in the arts, music, parks and recreation, sports, technology, or education, your neighborhood schools and nonprofit organizations always appreciate reliable and dedicated volunteers. Your reward is the feeling you get inside when you give your time and energy to help a person less fortunate.

Why do people **beg for money** and push grocery carts around town?

In the United States, millions or people are hungry or homeless. Many people do not have the necessary amount of money to live each month, some do not live in homes or apartments, and some do not have jobs. A grocery cart may carry all of their belongings. Some people are too ill to work and don't have money to afford a house or apartment. Being homeless means that a person does not have a place to live. It might be for a day or two or for many weeks or months. The person (or family) might live in a shelter with a lot of other people, or in a car, or have no structure surrounding them. Homelessness is not necessarily permanent and often people just need some help to get settled again.

What is a **homeless shelter**?

A homeless shelter is a building that helps homeless people by giving them a place to stay for awhile. It can include beds, bathrooms, showers, clothing, and hot meals.

Homelessness is a problem in the United States and countries all over the world. You can help by collecting food or other items and taking them to a church or local shelter.

They also have activities for children. Some homeless people also move into "transitional housing," which are housing facilities that also have job training and other services to help the homeless eventually get their own homes.

How can **kids help** the **homeless**?

Kids can help the homeless in a number of ways. You can collect canned food or freshly baked items and take them to a shelter. You can ask your parents if you can clean out your closet and give some of your old clothes to homeless children. You can collect toys from your friends, and then donate them to a local shelter. You can open a lemonade stand or have a bake sale and give the money you make to a shelter or an organization that helps the homeless. And, if you are old enough, you can volunteer to help out at a local shelter—you can baby sit, read, help with homework, or play games with the children.

What is a **food bank**?

A food bank is a warehouse or "bank" where contributed food is collected, sorted, and distributed to different agencies, such as shelters and church pantries, who then give or prepare and serve the food to those in need. There are many ways to help out at your local food bank. You can donate money. You can donate food. If your school does not already collect food for your community's food bank, you can speak to your principal about setting up a food drive one day per month to collect food from your student body. (Perhaps each child brings from home one can of nonperishable food the first Tuesday of every month.) You can volunteer. And you can take political action by writing to your congressman, state senator, or representative, and telling them that you will not accept hunger in your town or city.

INTERNET SAFETY

What is **cyberbullying**?

Cyberbullying (also called griefing) is the act of harassing someone online. It is illegal to communicate repeatedly with someone if your communication causes them to fear for their own safety or the safety of others. Always speak to a responsible adult if you are uncomfortable with any conversations occurring online. You can block the person sending the harassing messages using the block

My friend spends all his free time playing games online. Is he addicted?

Kids often use the Internet for many things—doing research for home-work, exploring new cultures, and building relationships with other kids. Kids who are shy in person may feel more comfortable initially connecting with people over the Internet. Excessive computer use, however, might further isolate shy kids from their friends. Or it can take away from other activities such as homework, exercise, sleep, or spending time with others. Parents and teachers are often unaware that a child has an Internet problem until it is serious, because it is easy to hide online activity and because Internet addiction is not yet widely recognized. You may want to talk to your friend and his parents; have an adult accompany you if you feel you need support. It is important to promote healthy Internet use in your home, whether through limiting online time, balancing computer time with physical and social activities, or making sure your Internet-connected computer is in a public space in your home.

options that come in many e-mail and instant messaging programs. And your parents can help you save any harassing e-mail messages and forward them to your e-mail service provider. Most providers have appropriate-use policies that restrict users from harassing others over the Internet. If the harassment consists of comments posted on a Web site, you can contact your Internet service provider (ISP) and ask for help locating the ISP hosting the site. You can then contact the ISP and bring the offensive comments to their attention. You can also contact your local police department.

What are **house rules** and **family contracts** for Internet use?

Often parents and guardians work with their kids to create an online agreement that outlines the rights and obligations of computer use at home. It might be a list of rules that you agree to together, or it might be a more formal contract that both the parent and the child sign. It covers topics like where kids can go online and what they can do there; how much time they can spend on the Internet (and how much of that time is dedicated to school work); and what they should do if anything or anyone makes them feel uncomfortable. You can write down the rules for protecting your personal information and how to use chat rooms, newsgroups, and instant messaging services. Families often print the rules out and keep them by the family computer to remind everyone of the rules.

What should I do if someone **asks for my name** when I am **online**?

The Internet is an amazing place where you can find information on all kinds of things. You can chat with friends, e-mail long-distance pen pals, and read what other people are saying about things you are interested in. But just as you should not talk to strangers when you are in the outside world, you should also use caution when chatting in the cyber world. Unfortunately, there are people surfing the Web who present a threat to kids. They may be adults posing as another kid or somehow lying to you about who they are and what they want. To be safe, never give anyone you don't know personal information about yourself online—including your name, address, phone number, or e-mail password. And never agree to meet a person you've chatted with online, even if that person seems friendly or harmless. Let your parents know if a stranger is sending you e-mail or instant messages.

Computer games are really fun, but playing them all the time is called an addiction. It is not healthy for you or your friends to do nothing but play video games all the time.

Can I **register** at **any Web site** I choose?

No—it's important to ask your parents first before registering at a Web site. Many sites offer special benefits if you register as a member, which involves providing your name, e-mail address, and sometimes home address, phone number, and other information. While some sites protect your privacy and only use that information to send you things you want, others sell your information to advertisers or organizations. As a result of registering at a Web site, your family may end up getting lots of unwanted e-mail, regular mail, and phone calls from companies trying to sell you things. And even if you find a great deal online for something you really want, never give out your parents' credit card information unless they say it's okay.

What is a **computer virus**?

A virus is a malicious software program that infects computer files or hard disk drives and then makes copies of itself. Many activities that kids do online can leave computers vulnerable to viruses. E-mail attachments are a common means of distributing viruses, but viruses can also be downloaded when you share files and open instant message attachments. In order to keep your computer safe, never open an e-mail attachment you haven't requested. Send an e-mail to friends to confirm that they meant to send you an attachment. Also, you can configure your instant messaging program so you can't receive files from other users. Never download any program without checking with a parent first. You can protect your computer by always running up-to-date firewall software, by running antivirus software regularly, and by periodically scanning your computer for spyware or other unwanted software and immediately removing it.

BICYCLE TIPS

How does a **bicycle work**?

A bicycle is a simple device that increases the power that you have in the muscles of your legs, taking you faster and farther than you could ever run. When you push the pedals of your bike around once, the pedal sprocket—the wheel with teeth to which the pedals are attached—goes around once, too. But it pulls a chain along, one that is connected to a much smaller sprocket (with fewer teeth to grip each link of the chain) in the center of your bike's rear wheel. This smaller sprocket moves around a number of times for each single turn of your pedals, moving your bike wheels a lot faster than you're moving your feet!

Some bicycles have several "speeds," which means that they have a number of gears (called derailleurs) that vary the rate at which the wheels turn. These extra sprockets are located at the pedals and rear wheel of a bike, where levers move the driving chain sideways, from one to another. A special spring system keeps the chain tight when it changes from a larger to a smaller sprocket. Although you might think that a rider would always want the wheels of his or her bike to move as fast as possible for each pedal turn, that is not always the case. When going uphill, for instance, a rider can get more force out of a wheel that turns fewer times, making the task easier.

How do I **brake**?

Brakes can quickly stop the rotating wheels of a bicycle. On some bikes you can stop by pedaling backwards, which activates a braking mechanism (coaster brake). On other bikes, you activate the brakes by squeezing levers located on the bike's handlebars. While a person's leg strength is far greater than the strength in his or her hands, a hand brake uses a set of three levers that increase the original squeezing force, making it strong enough to stop a speeding bike. A compressed hand brake pulls a cable connected to two metal arms with rubber pads that grip a bicycle tire rim, causing enough friction to stop it. After a quick stop, feel the brake blocks on your bike—the friction makes them hot.

Why do **bicycle tires lose air** so fast?

Early bicycle tires were made out of solid rubber. (Before that, iron covered the edges of wooden bicycle wheels.) Solid rubber tires made bicycling a bumpy experience because they were unable to provide any cushioning on rough roads. When the air-filled rubber bicycle tire was invented, it made riding a lot more comfortable.

263

Why are men's and women's bicycles built differently?

The crossbars on bicycle frames give them added strength. On a man's or boy's bike the crossbar extends straight across the top of the frame, just below the seat. On a woman's or girl's bike the crossbar is attached to the seat tube at an angle, far below the seat. Because of this structure, women's bikes are not nearly as sturdy as men's bikes.

When bicycles were first built, women didn't wear pants; they always wore skirts or dresses. The low crossbars on their bikes allowed them to get on, ride, and get off with dignity—without showing their underwear! The design of bicycles for women and girls, then, is based on a long-standing tradition and still offers the advantage of easier mounting and dismounting. But today, women and girl bicyclists wear pants or shorts when riding and can easily use bikes designed for men. As a matter of fact, serious female bicyclists who do a lot of riding or travel through tough terrain and need bikes with sturdier frames buy those made for men.

But along with the comfort of air-filled tires came the frequent task of filling them up. The rubber that is used to make bicycle tires is thin and porous, which means that it has tiny microscopic pores, or holes, through which air can escape over time. Air that is pumped into bicycle tires is pressurized, meaning it is compressed into a much smaller space than it would ordinarily occupy. Without pressurized air inside, a bicycle tire would not have its firm shape. Air under high pressure, like all gases, moves or migrates to surrounding areas that have lower pressure, traveling even through fairly solid materials. Air in a bicycle tire naturally tries to escape through the valve stem that is used to fill it and the inner tube that holds it. So even bicycles that don't undergo the wear-and-tear of frequent use eventually end up with flat tires.

Why do little kids ride **tricycles** instead of bikes?

The triangular shape of a tricycle, with its three wheels spread apart, is much more stable than a regular bicycle, which balances on two aligned wheels. (The "tri" [three] and "bi" [two] before "cycle" refers to the number of wheels each vehicle has.) Tricycles suit young children well; with larger heads and undeveloped muscles, little ones lack the coordination and balance needed to ride regular bikes. But as soon as they can learn to pedal, children can ride a tricycle, turning leg power into wheel power.

A tricycle is built for stability and not for speed: its pedals are attached to a sprocket in the center of its large front wheel, which moves around once for each completed pedal turn. So the larger the front wheel of a tricycle, the faster it will go—but it cannot be so large that young legs cannot reach the pedals! This design makes a tricycle unlike a regular bike, which has chain-driven sprockets that move its wheels a lot faster than its rider's feet. Tricycles are also easier for little ones to steer and turn because they are pulled forward by the movement of their front wheels; regular bikes are powered by their rear wheels.

What were **high-wheelers**?

A high-wheeler was an early type of bicycle that had pedals attached to its front wheels, just like tricycles. To give high-wheelers greater speed, bike designers kept enlarging the front wheels, some of which measured up to 64 inches (163 centimeters) across. Known as "high-wheelers," they were quite dangerous to ride—bicyclists couldn't touch the ground with their feet when they stopped, and they often fell forward over their handlebars when they hit bumps. A high-wheeler was also hard to balance because it had only one rear wheel, not two.

It's important to wear a helmet whenever you ride your bike. Accidents leading to head injuries can happen when you least except them. Be prepared!

Can I **ride** my **bike or scooter** anywhere or whenever I want to?

While riding bicycles and scooters are a lot of fun, it is important to remember that these items are not just toys. They are machines that can sometimes be involved in accidents that result in injury. So all bike riders—as well as in-line skaters, skateboarders, and scooter riders—must follow certain rules, for their own safety and the safety of others.

Bicyclists have to follow some of the same traffic laws as people who drive cars do, like stopping at stop signs and obeying traffic lights. But bike riders also have their own special set of safety rules. They have to make sure that their bikes have reflectors in order to ride safely at night. They can't let other people ride with them on their bike—like on bicycle handlebars—because that threatens their balance and could lead to accidents. One of the most important of all bicycling rules is wearing a protective helmet. So, it doesn't matter where you will be riding or for how long—you should always follow traffic laws and safety tips.

Why is it important to always **wear my helmet**?

Each year, about 150,000 children are treated in emergency rooms for head injuries that occurred while riding their bikes. Many bike-related injuries could be avoided

Why don't school buses have seatbelts?

School buses provide students with the safest form of transportation to and from school, according to research by the National Academy of Sciences. School buses have to meet rigid federal construction standards for the sides and top of the bus, fuel tanks, and inside of each bus. The thick padded seats and seatbacks provide a passive form of crash protection known as "compartmentalization." This padding, combined with the placement of the seating area high above the impact zone (with most other vehicles), offers a protection that has resulted in an unmatched record of passenger safety. Especially for small students, seatbelts can be more harmful than helpful, and in most states these are being phased out from school buses. Only since the early 2000s have lap-shoulder seatbelts been available on school buses in some states.

if riders wore their helmets properly. Wearing a bike helmet reduces the risk of brain injury by as much as 88 percent and reduces the risk of injury to the face by 65 percent. That is why many state laws say that bicyclists under the age of 14 are required to wear approved bicycle helmets when they ride their bicycles. If your friends don't wear helmets when you bicycle together, teach them by your wise example. In the United States, bicycle helmets save one life every day and prevent one head injury from happening every four minutes.

What are the **reflectors** on my bike or scooter for?

Reflectors help keep you safe if you are riding in the dark. When a car approaches you the light waves produced by its headlights hit your reflectors and bounce back into the eyes of the driver, making him or her aware of where you are. This helps that person drive past you carefully. Reflectors are usually made of hard colored plastic with a backing of reflective material. The inner surface of the plastic is cut into many tiny angles, kind of like the sides, or facets, of a diamond. These bounce light waves around inside before they are reflected away, which explains why they are so startlingly bright. Reflectors are located at the front and back of your bike, as well as on your pedals. That way you can be seen regardless of the direction in which you are heading.

OTHER SAFETY TIPS

Why do I need to wear a **seatbelt** in the **car**?

Seatbelts rock! Studies have found that wearing a seatbelt can save your life in the event of an automobile accident. In fact, you are 45 percent more likely to survive a crash if you're wearing a belt. According to the National Highway Traffic Safety

Administration (NHTSA), an estimated 5,500 lives could be saved each year by increasing the level of safety belt use in the United States to 90 percent. That is why there are mandatory safety belt laws in 49 states and the District of Columbia. In most states, these laws cover those riding in the front seats, although belt laws in 19 states and the District of Columbia cover all rear seat occupants, too.

How can I **stay safe** when I am **walking**?

Even in the daytime, crossing the street can be dangerous. Be aware of your surroundings, wear bright-colored clothes, and walk with friends and family whenever you can.

Walking is a great way to exercise. Walking burns calories, strengthens back muscles, strengthens bones, reduces stress, helps improve your mood, helps you sleep better, and requires no equipment. Best of all, it is free and can be done almost anywhere! Walking also helps build community. A simple wave as you walk by your neighbors' yard helps strengthen community connections. Walking, instead of driving, also reduces traffic congestion and pollution.

It is important to be careful when you walk. During the day, wear bright, light clothing; at dusk, dawn, or nighttime, wear reflective clothing, with strips of material or tape attached that bounce back light. Be careful. *Always* look both ways before crossing the street, obey traffic signals, and use the crosswalk. Be aware of all traffic, and make sure that drivers see you by making eye contact with them before you cross the street. Walk against the direction of traffic whenever possible. And remember, too, that walking with a friend is always safer than walking on your own. Encourage a friend or family member to join you! Be thoroughly familiar with your route. Know the location of phones, police or fire stations, and businesses, and always bring along some form of identification, like a school ID card.

Should I **talk to a stranger**?

No. Although most of the strangers you encounter treat children with respect, there are dangerous people who do harmful things to children. Sometimes hurtful people can fool kids into thinking they are gentle and helpful. They may have pleasant faces and friendly voices, and they may say nice things. So it's important to follow personal safety rules with all strangers. What can you do to stay safe when you are outside or away from home? Play with at least one other kid in familiar places. Don't go near a car with a stranger in it, even if the person says he or she has a gift for you, or needs your help to find a lost pet, or is asking for directions. Think about it this way: if an adult really needed help, he or she would ask another adult, not a kid. Do not accept a ride home from school or anywhere from someone you don't know, even if that person says your parents asked him or her to pick you up, and even if that person knows your name. Avoid situations where you are alone with an adult you don't know unless it is a person your parents have arranged for you to meet with, like a doctor, teacher, or counselor.

If a stranger approaches you, tell that person to please not speak to you because you don't know him or her. If the stranger continues toward you, start yelling and run away. If you need help, your best bet is to go to a public space like a store, a library, or a police station. Afterward, be sure to tell your parents about your experience with the stranger.

What should I do if I **find a gun**?

Studies have shown that hundreds, perhaps even thousands, of children and teenagers are accidentally killed by guns in the United States each year. Millions of American kids have access to guns in their homes. People use guns all the time in movies and television shows, and the action scenes in these shows make guns look exciting and powerful. What these shows can't really convey is the massive, painful destruction an exploding bullet causes when it hits a person's body.

While many kids understand that, in real life, guns can be very dangerous and can cause great harm, most still find guns fascinating. If an adult is supervising and your parents have given their approval, it's okay to look at and even touch an unloaded gun. But if you are alone or with other kids and you come across a gun, remember that it is not a toy and should not be handled. Guns should never be pointed at another person, even if you intend it as a joke. If you find a gun in your own house, a friend's house, or elsewhere, as tempting as it might be to play with it, remember the damage that guns can cause and leave it alone. If you're away from home, leave right away and tell your parents what happened. Your parents may be upset and worried that you found a gun, but they will be very glad that you told them about it because then they can help you stay safe.

What is a **Neighborhood Watch**?

Neighborhood Watch is a crime-prevention program based on safety education and common sense. It teaches citizens how to help themselves by identifying and reporting suspicious activity in their neighborhoods. It allows you, your family members, and your neighbors the opportunity to participate in your neighborhood, make your neighborhood safer, and improve the quality of life in your area. There are many Neighborhood Watch programs in towns and cities across the United States, and each one is a bit different. The groups typically focus on observation and awareness as a means of preventing crime. People in the neighborhood meet (usually at potlucks or backyard barbeques), get to know one another, agree to look out for the welfare of each other, and sometimes patrol their neighborhood on bikes or by car, much as a police officer would. They report suspicious activity to the local authorities. Most neighborhood groups are organized around a block or a subdivision and are started with help from a local law-enforcement agency, such as the

> ## What are the odds against being struck by lightning?
>
> The National Oceanic and Atmospheric Administration estimates the odds of being struck by lightning are 1 in 700,000. However, the odds drop to 1 in 240,000 based on the number of unreported lightning strikes. The odds of being stuck by lightning in one's lifetime are 1 in 3,000.

police or sheriff's department. Often there is a sign in the area that states that it is a Neighborhood Watch neighborhood.

What **safety rules** should be followed **during a thunderstorm**?

If you find yourself in a thunderstorm, the government's National Weather Service recommends following a few safety rules. First, get away from metal fences at ball fields. Drop metal objects such as golf clubs, and backpacks. Remember: metal is a very good electrical conductor, and you don't want to attract lightning! Lightning may be ready to strike near you if you feel your hair stand on end or your skin tingle. Crouch down or drop to your knees, but do not lie flat on the ground. The safest place in a lightning storm is inside a sturdy structure—such as your home, school, or a local business. Get inside the building, but do not stand by open windows, doors, or patios during a storm. Experts also recommend unplugging unnecessary appliances and staying off the phone.

My **nose** sometimes **bleeds** while I play sports or after practice. Why?

Nosebleeds are fairly common because the nose is located in a vulnerable area (the center of the face!) and filled with blood vessels that can easily bleed. In some cases, nosebleeds can be severe and involve lots of blood; in other situations, bleeding is minor. The sensitive nose can bleed easily when hit or when fractured—even a brush against the nose can cause it to bleed. Often this happens in contact sports, and if practice takes place outdoors, where it is cold and dry, there may be a higher chance of getting a nosebleed. A dry climate or heated indoor air irritates and dries out nasal membranes, causing crusts that may itch and then bleed when picked. The common cold may also irritate the lining of the nose, and bleeding may happen after repeated tissue blowing. When you combine a cold with dry winter air, you have the perfect formula for a nosebleed!

What items should be in a **first-aid kit**?

Whether you go to the store with an adult to buy a first-aid kit or work with an adult to put one together, it should include all the items you may need in case of an emergency. Make sure an adult includes any personal items such as medications and emergency phone numbers or other items your doctor may suggest. Check the kit regularly. Make sure the flashlight batteries work. Check expiration dates and

A well-supplied first-aid kit is a good thing to always keep at your house and in the car.

replace any used or out-of-date contents. If you are compiling your own, the Red Cross and the American Medical Association recommend that all first-aid kits include the following items:

- absorbent compress dressings
- adhesive bandages, in assorted sizes
- adhesive cloth tape
- antibiotic ointment packets
- five antiseptic wipe packets
- aspirin or aspirin substitute
- blanket
- breathing barrier (with one-way valve)
- first-aid manual
- hydrocortisone ointment packets
- instant cold compress
- nonlatex gloves
- oral thermometers
- roller bandages
- scissors
- sterile gauze pads
- triangular bandages
- tweezers

TOUGH QUESTIONS: DIVORCE, DEATH, AND GOD

Why do husbands and wives **divorce**?

Husbands and wives divorce when they can no longer live happily together. It is usually a sad thing, because when people marry they expect to be with their partner for the rest of their lives. But over the course of a marriage things happen, people can change, and the happiness that the couple was so sure of in the beginning sometimes disappears. When couples with children get divorced it is even more unfortunate because more people are affected. Many children feel bad when their parents divorce because their family will not be the same. After a divorce, they generally do not see one of their parents as much as they did before. Still, just because the feelings between a mother and a father change doesn't mean that their love for their children changes in any way. It's important to remember that divorce is something that happens between a husband and wife—it has nothing to do with the kids. Many children feel that if they adjust their behavior somehow their parents will want to stay together, but divorces are not caused by anything children do.

What happens as we age?

As people age, skin may begin to sag and wrinkle, and hair may turn thin or gray. Over time muscles become less strong and flexible, and bones may become more brittle and breakable. Blood may not flow through the body as well as it once did, which slows the activity of the brain and the senses. The immune system becomes weaker and does not fight off sickness as well as before. People experience these changes at different ages, but all will grow old as they near the end of their life cycle. It may seem sad that a person has grown old and cannot do all the things they once did, but try to look at it this way: When people grow old, that means they have been lucky enough to avoid things like accidents and diseases that could have cut their lives short. And better yet, regardless of the physical changes of old age, many people remain healthy and lead full and happy lives.

Who decides **which** of the **divorced parents** their **children** will **live with**?

Because a marriage is a legal partnership, its dissolution, or end, takes place by a judgment of a court. The court, then, awards custody of children after a divorce. The judge that presides over the court makes this decision, ideally keeping the best interests of the children in mind. A judge's involvement is especially important when parents cannot agree about who should be the main caregiver for their children and provide their main home. But in the best cases, both parents and children decide together how they would like custody to be awarded, and they let the court know their preferences. Sometimes joint custody is the solution, which means that the parents share responsibility for the kids and the children divide their time equally between their mother and father and their separate homes. Most of the time, however, one parent becomes the custodial parent and the children live with her or him, while the other parent has visitation rights, which means that he or she can see the children at certain times, like on weekends or during summer vacations.

Why do people have to **grow old**?

Growing old is part of being a living thing. Every plant and animal must go through a cycle of life that involves a beginning, a middle, and an end. Actually, as soon as we are born we begin aging or growing older. But when we talk of growing old we think of the physical changes that occur when bodies cannot grow and repair themselves as they once did. At about age 30 the signs of aging start to appear, though for most people the physical changes are not really obvious until many years later.

Why do **people** have to **die**?

All living things must die. It is a part—the final part—of the biological cycle of life. A flowering plant, for instance, springs from a seed, grows, blossoms, pro-

Dealing with the death of a loved one is never easy, but it is a natural part of life. Don't be afraid to talk to your family about this issue if you have questions.

duces seeds for the next season, fades, and dies. Similarly, an animal is born, grows and matures, reproduces, ages, and dies. Old plants and animals must make way for new plants and animals, through which the cycle of life can continue. If plants and animals did not die, eventually there would not be enough food, water, or space in the world for life to flourish. Even dead plants and animals contribute to the cycle of life, for their remains enrich the soil for the next generation of living things.

New generations of plants and animals are needed to ensure the survival of life on our planet. The world's environment is constantly changing, and new plants and animals—with unique characteristics resulting from the combined genetic contributions of their parents—may be better equipped to survive under the evolving conditions. This process of change and improved survival, which has taken place gradually over millions of years (ever since life began), is called evolution.

Just like all plants and other animals, people also experience this biological cycle of life. A person is born, grows into physical maturity during adolescence, experiences adulthood, ages, and then dies. At death, the cycle of life is completed as that individual makes way for following generations.

What **happens** when **people die**?

When death occurs, blood—which carries oxygen to all the cells of the body—has stopped circulating. This stoppage may be caused by damage to the heart, which is the muscle that pumps blood throughout the body, or by damage to the brain, which gives the signals that direct the heart to do its pumping. (Other circumstances, like severe accidents, also stop blood flow.) But whatever the reason, once blood stops bringing its life-giving oxygen to the body's billions of cells—the building blocks that make up the human body—the death of those cells starts to occur. When the brain, which is the body's command center, goes without oxygen for about 15 minutes, all cells there die. While machines can help our lungs breathe or our hearts pump blood, no machine can assume the complex functions of the brain. Without a brain, we cannot live. Soon after a person dies, an official document called a death certificate is filled out and later filed as a record with the local government. It includes such information as time, place, and cause of death.

Can people who die see and talk with living people after they are gone?

Although for centuries living people have reported seeing and talking to people who have died, there is no scientific proof that this can be done or that visiting with "ghosts" is possible. Although some people claim they have special skills allowing them to contact and receive messages from the deceased (such people are known as spiritualist mediums), their communications—usually conducted during meetings called séances—have generally proven to be fake. Sometimes, though, people who have recently had a loved one die feel that they can sense that person's presence with them; they may even talk to the deceased. It is likely that these sensations arise out of very powerful feelings of loss and vivid memories of the loved one. For many people, believing that a physical connection continues after death lessens their sorrow. It is one of many ways through which people keep alive the memories of those who have died.

Does it **hurt to die**?

Nobody who has died has been able to come back to tell us about it, so it is impossible to know whether dying hurts. But people who have had "near-death" experiences—those whose hearts have stopped, for instance, but were later restarted—have only good things to report. Most tell of a peaceful sensation of floating above their bodies. A number also describe traveling through a tunnel toward a beautiful light or having loving meetings with friends and relatives who have died before them. Scientists know that when a person is in a state of very low oxygen—often a condition that precedes death—he or she experiences feelings of euphoria, or great happiness. So as far as we know, the act of dying is not painful at all.

Many sick people welcome death. The same wonders of medicine that have allowed people to reach old age have also enabled them to live through long, and sometimes painful, illnesses. Often, death is seen as a welcome end to pain, both for the ill person and for the family and friends who have watched their loved one suffer. People with strong religious faith, too, may fear death less because they believe they will journey to a better place.

What do we do **after a person dies**?

Throughout human history and in places around the world, people have done many different things with their dead. The ancient Egyptians, for instance, took great care when preparing the bodies of their dead rulers; it was believed that their leaders were immortal and would need their bodies in another world after death (the afterworld). In a process that took several months, ancient Egyptians carefully preserved dead bodies through a process called embalming. They wrapped the bodies with layers of linen, wax, and spices. Some of these mummies still exist today, some 6,000 years later.

273

In the United States today, most people are buried in coffins. Funeral ceremonies take place so that people can honor the deceased and give comfort and support to his or her family and friends. Music, prayers, and eulogies—speeches remembering and praising the dead person—are often a part of these ceremonies. A funeral usually ends when the deceased is taken to a cemetery, a place where bodies are buried in the ground. A headstone or marker listing the person's name, birth and death date, and other information is placed at the burial spot. Family members and friends may later visit and decorate the grave site with flowers in memory of their loved one.

Many times, too, people choose to be cremated instead of buried. In a cremation, the body is burned until nothing but ashes remain. According to the wishes of the person who died, these ashes might then be buried, or kept in an urn, or sometimes they are scattered over the land of a place that was important to the deceased. One of the most creative things that were done with somebody's ashes happened when Gene Roddenberry (the creator of the *Star Trek* series) had his ashes put aboard the space shuttle *Columbia* after his death in 1991. Later, his wife Majel's ashes were also launched into space, as were the ashes of James Doohan, who played Scotty in the original series.

Why do **people cry** when someone **dies**?

Crying is a way of expressing sadness. It helps people who have lost someone close to them express their grief and sorrow. (Talking about the dead person also helps.) People cry because they will never again see the person who has died and they know they will miss that person. If the death is unexpected, the tears may also be caused by feelings of shock and anger. During the period immediately following a person's death, when the loss of that loved one is felt most sharply, grieving people usually are not comforted by the fact that dying is a natural and necessary process that happens to all living things. As time passes, however, many people begin to accept the loss of their loved one, and the pain of that loss becomes a bit easier to bear. Thinking of the person after some time has passed brings less sadness and maybe even some pleasure as good times with the loved one are remembered.

Where do people go **after they die**?

Because no one has come back to our world after dying, it is not possible to know for sure what happens to people after death. Nearly all the religions of the world believe that some kind of existence continues after life on Earth stops, that a person's soul or spirit continues to exist—in a way we can't really imagine—even after his or her body is dead. In fact, a lot of religions teach the belief that our life on Earth is a stage or time of preparation (or a test by which we're judged) that leads to a final, perfect state of existence that we will share with God in a spiritual realm after we die. Some people who don't subscribe to religious beliefs about an afterlife think that people simply end when they die, that once the physical body has died, all awareness and existence ceases.

What is **heaven**?

According to many religions based on Judaism and Christianity, heaven is a state of existence where a person's spirit is at last united with God forever. In a number of Christian religions, heaven is believed to be the reward for people who have lived good lives according to certain rules of thought and behavior that God has made known through scriptures (sacred writings, like the Bible) and through the teachings of churches and religious leaders. (Those who have not followed these rules, it is believed by many, go to a place of punishment known as hell.) Many Christians believe that at the end of the world their human forms will be resurrected in a perfect state—just as the body of Jesus Christ was, when he arose from the dead on Easter morning—and join their souls or spirits in heaven for eternity. This idea has led to the concept that heaven is an actual place—located above—with physical characteristics. Over the centuries, through pictures and writings, people have tried to create images of heaven, imagining a place of perfect happiness perched atop fluffy white clouds. It has often been portrayed as a place full of things that would bring happiness on Earth, possessing, for instance, pearly gates and streets of gold.

Is there a heaven? Are angels real? Many people believe they are, but only you can decide for yourself whether you believe in these religious issues.

What is **hell**?

In many Christian religions, hell is the place of punishment where people go after death if they have not lived good lives and followed the rules of thought and behavior set forth by God in scriptures (sacred writings, like the Bible) and in the teachings of churches and religious leaders. Hell is believed to be a horrible place because it is the opposite of heaven; hell is a place where a person's spirit will forever be deprived of the presence of God. To never know the joy of God's presence, believers feel, is so painful that it is compared to burning in fire forever, one of the most awful things that can be imagined. Just like with heaven, people have tried over the centuries, through paintings and writings, to create images of hell, a place of enormous suffering. And as heaven is thought to be located above, hell is said to be down below. Satan, or Lucifer—who, according to the Bible, was a favorite angel of God's until he disobeyed God—is the ruler of hell. In many Christian religions, Satan and his wicked angel followers (devils) are thought to be the cause of evil in the world, always tempting people to be bad. Many non-Christian religions also teach of a place like hell where people who have led bad lives on Earth must go after they die. Even the ancient Greeks and Romans (who lived before the development of Christianity) believed in an underworld, a place where people traveled to after death. Good and bad people lived in different places in this ancient underworld.

Are **angels real**?

In many religions, angels are powerful spiritual beings who live with God but who sometimes become involved in the lives of people on Earth, often bringing God's messages to them. According to the Bible, for instance, the angel Gabriel appeared before the Virgin Mary and announced that she would become the mother of Jesus Christ. In the Muslim religion, Gabriel revealed to the Prophet Muhammad the words of Allah (God), which were recorded in the Koran, the sacred book of Islam. Angels are not believed to have physical bodies, but they may look like people when visiting Earth. Over the centuries, artists have portrayed them in many ways: neither men nor women, angels have human forms (appearing as babies, children, or adults) and are winged for travel to their heavenly home. In a few religions, like Roman Catholicism, it is believed that each person on Earth has a special angel who watches over him or her and gives protection from the temptations of the devil; such a being is called one's guardian angel. The answer to the question of whether angels are real, then, is a matter of faith.

Who is **God**?

It is believed by many people that God is the perfect spiritual being who has always existed and who created everything. (Although having no physical form and therefore no gender, God is usually referred to as a male.) Believers feel that God made the universe and all that is in it. God is thought by many to be all-knowing and all-powerful. In many religions, it is thought that the souls of people who have led good lives on Earth join God after they die.

While many of the world's most widely practiced religions—Christianity, Islam, Judaism—teach of the existence of a single supreme being (called God in Judeo-Christian religions and Allah in Islam), some religions teach that there are many gods. Hinduism (practiced by many people in India and elsewhere) teaches that there are many gods, but all are part of one divine being, called Brahman. Some people feel that God is everywhere and part of everything—the universe itself, and all life, and all natural occurrences, are divine. Others, called atheists, do not believe a supreme being exists in any form.

For More Information

BOOKS

Animals: A Children's Encyclopedia. New York: DK Publishing, 2008.

The American Medical Association Family Medical Guide. New York: Random House, 1994.

Arnold, Caroline. *Cats: In from the Wild.* Minneapolis: Carolrhoda Books, 1993.

Baron, Connie. *The Physically Disabled.* New York: Macmillan, 1988.

Black, David, and Anthony Huxley. *Plants.* New York: Facts on File, 1985.

Burnie, David. *The Concise Encyclopedia of the Human Body.* London: DK Publishing, 1995.

Chiarelli, Brunetto, and Anna Lisa Bebi. *The Atlas of World Cultures.* New York: Peter Bedrick Books, 1997.

Cribb, Joe. *Money.* New York: Knopf, 1990.

Dow, Lesley. *Incredible Plants.* New York: Time-Life, 1997.

Farndon, John. *What Happens When …?* New York: Scholastic, 1996.

Feldman, David. *Why Do Clocks Run Clockwise? And Other Imponderables.* New York: HarperCollins, 1988.

Fogle, Bruce. *The New Encyclopedia of the Dog.* London: DK Publishing, 2000.

Ford, Brian J. *The Random House Library of Knowledge First Encyclopedia of Science.* New York: Random House, 1993.

Guinness World Records 2009. New York: Bantam, 2009.

Gundersen, P. Erik. *The Handy Physics Answer Book.* Detroit: Visible Ink Press, 1999.

Halley, Ned. *Farm.* New York: Knopf, 1996.

The Handy Science Answer Book® Centennial Edition. Detroit: Visible Ink Press, 2002.

Haywood, John, et al. *The Illustrated Children's Encyclopedia of the Ancient World.* London: Southwater, 2007.

Hickman, Pamela. *Starting with Nature: Plant Book.* Toronto: Kids Can Press, 1996.

Hile, Kevin. *The Handy Weather Answer Book, 2nd ed.* Detroit: Visible Ink Press, 2009.

James, Elizabeth, and Carol Barkin. *Social Smarts: Manners for Today's Kids.* Boston: Clarion Books, 1996.

Knox, Jean McBee. *Death and Dying*. Broomall, PA: Chelsea House, 2000.

Langone, John. *National Geographic's How Things Work: Everyday Technology Explained*. Washington, D.C.: National Geographic Society, 1999.

Leach, Penelope. *Your Baby and Child: From Birth to Age Five*. New York: Knopf, 1997.

LeShan, Eda. *What Makes Me Feel This Way?: Growing Up with Human Emotions*. New York: Macmillan, 1974.

Macaulay, David. *The New Way Things Work*. Boston: Houghton Mifflin, 1998.

The New York Public Library Amazing Space: A Book of Answers for Kids. New York: John Wiley and Sons, 1997.

Oxlade, Chris. *Houses and Homes*. Danbury, CT: Franklin Watts, 1994.

Parker, Steve, and Giovanni Caselli. *The Body and How It Works*. London: DK Publishing, 1992.

Pascoe, Elaine, Deborah Kops, and Jenifer Morse. *Scholastic Kids Almanac: Facts, Figures, and Stats*. New York: Scholastic Reference, 2004.

Tucci, Paul A. *The Handy Geography Answer Book,* 2nd ed. Detroit: Visible Ink Press, 2009.

Silverstein, Alvin, and Virginia Silverstein. *Dogs: All About Them*. New York: William Morrow, 1986.

Things around Us. New York: Time-Life, 1988.

The Ultimate Book of Knowledge. New York: Oxford University Press, 2008.

The Universe (First Facts series). New York: Kingfisher, 1994.

Visual Encyclopedia of Science. London: DK Publishing, 2000.

Waldbauer, Gilbert. *The Handy Bug Answer Book*. Detroit: Visible Ink Press, 1998.

Wood, Robert W. *The McGraw-Hill Big Book of Science Activities: Fun and Easy Experiments for Kids*. New York: McGraw-Hill, 1999.

The World Book Encyclopedia of People and Places. Chicago: World Book, 2005.

WEB SITES

The American Presidency: http://ap.grolier.com.

ASPCA Animaland: http://www.animaland.org.

Ben's Guide to U.S. Government for Kids: http://bensguide.gpo.gov.

DiscoverySchool.com: http://school.discovery.com.

Enchanted Learning: http://www.enchantedlearning.com.

Flags of the World: http://www.fotw.net/flags/index.html.

50 states.com: http://www.50states.com.

Guinness World Records: http://www.guinnessworldrecords.com.

Infoplease.com: http://www.infoplease.com.

Kidport Reference Library: http://www.kidport.com.

KidsHealth: http://kidshealth.org.

Kids' Stuff—Ref Desk.com: http://www.refdesk.com/kids.html.

Marshall Brain's How Stuff Works: http://www.howstuffworks.com.

The Math Forum: http://mathforum.org/k12/mathtips.

"Science Q&A." The Learning Network: The New York Times on the Web: http://www.nytimes.com/learning/students/scienceqa/index.html.

Yahoo! Kids: Maps, Flags and Country Facts in the World Factbook: http://kids.yahoo.com/reference/world-factbook.

Zoobooks—The Encyclopedia of Animals: http://www.zoobooks.com.

Index

Note: (ill.) indicates photos and illustrations.

working for a living, 231
World Wide Web, 164–65
worms, 50, 77
Wright brothers, 152–53, 153
   (ill.)
wrinkles, 212–13
wristwatch, 195

X

X chromosome, 237
X-ray, 170

Y

Y chromosome, 237
yawn, 227, 227 (ill.)
year, 189

Z

zebras, 61 (ill.), 61–62
zero, 182–83
zipper, 172
zits, 212